Wars Civil and Great

Wars Civil and Great

THE AMERICAN EXPERIENCE IN THE CIVIL WAR AND WORLD WAR I

Edited by
David J. Silbey
and
Kanisorn Wongsrichanalai

 University Press of Kansas

Published by the University Press of Kansas (Lawrence, Kansas 66045), which was
organized by the Kansas Board of Regents and is operated and funded by Emporia
State University, Fort Hays State University, Kansas State University, Pittsburg State
University, the University of Kansas, and Wichita State University.

Library of Congress Cataloging-in-Publication Data

Names: Silbey, David, editor. | Wongsrichanalai, Kanisorn, editor.
Title: Wars civil and great : the American experience in the Civil War and
    World War I / [edited by] David J. Silbey and Kanisorn Wongsrichanalai.
Description: Lawrence, Kansas : University Press of Kansas, 2023. | Series:
    Modern war studies | Includes index and bibliographical references.
Identifiers: LCCN 2022042392 (print) | LCCN 2022042393 (ebook)
    ISBN 9780700635375 (cloth)
    ISBN 9780700634736 (paperback)
    ISBN 9780700634743 (ebook)
Subjects: LCSH: United States—History—Civil War, 1861–1865. | World War,
    1914–1918—United States. | United States—History—Civil War,
    1861–1865—Influence. | World War, 1914–1918—United States—Influence.
Classification: LCC E468 .W37 2023 (print) | LCC E468 (ebook) | DDC
    973.7—dc23/eng/20230103
LC record available at https://lccn.loc.gov/2022042392.
LC ebook record available at https://lccn.loc.gov/2022042393.

British Library Cataloguing-in-Publication Data is available.

Printed in the United States of America

10 9 8 7 6 5 4 3 2 1

David Silbey dedicates this volume to his
daughter, the best person he knows.

Kanisorn Wongsrichanalai dedicates this volume to
Kathryn Ostrofsky and Christine Lamberson,
who let him play in the twentieth century, and to
Brian J. Maxson, who is always welcome in the nineteenth.

CONTENTS

Chronology, the noting of the passage of time by listing events, is the bedrock of history. It generates the history student's greatness lament—"history is nothing but names and dates"—and the history professor's retort that history is about asking questions and answering them with evidence.

In *Wars Civil and Great: The American Experience in the Civil War and World War I*, editors David J. Silbey and Kanisorn Wongsrichanalai frame this conversation somewhat differently. They astutely note that dates can be misleading. When do wars end? One answer might privilege the politicians' decisions, another the memory that burns deeply in the societal psyche. Likewise, the turn of a century implies a differentiation from what came before and directly impacts understanding of the past, present, and future, even to the point of becoming the descriptor—twenty-first-century—of the world in which we live. How, Silbey and Wongsrichanalai ponder, might traditional interpretations of two key conflicts in American history, the Civil War and the Great War, change if historians viewed chronology differently?

The Civil War looms large in American history, and rightly so. The ending of slavery during the "Second American Revolution" did not resolve contestations over the rights of emancipated Black people or eradicate white supremacy. The Great War occupies a much quieter space in American memory. The failures of the July Crisis and Versailles Peace Conference dominate common understandings of the war, offering warnings that failed diplomacy can result in deadly and expansive conflicts. In this framing, neither war has much to do with the other, although the memory of each is linked to present-day anxieties.

The essay authors in *Wars Civil and Great* offer a refreshing challenge to this bifurcation. They pose new questions about these seminal conflicts and offer a range of insightful comparisons and connections between the two wars.

This challenge to chronology is not just an attempt to nitpick around the edges; instead, it goes to the heart of how we conceptualize and remember these wars. This volume's reconfigured chronological framing pairs the Civil War and Great War as key conflicts of the "long nineteenth century," generating a new narrative about how Americans experienced these pivotal conflicts. The Civil War occurred within the lived memory of many families in 1917 and shaped understandings of the current conflict, as the recurring figure of Abraham Lincoln on Great War propaganda posters and in political rhetoric attests. This easily overlooked detail suddenly gains new significance in the narrative reset offered by these essays, and the contributors to this volume force us to broaden our gaze and consider new interpretations at odds with our classic assumptions.

Jennifer D. Keene
Chapman University

ACKNOWLEDGMENTS

First and foremost, the editors wish to thank the National Endowment for the Humanities (NEH) for their support of the lecture series that led to the conception of this volume. Deborah Hurtt at the NEH was a champion of a grant awarded to Angelo State University, which allowed Kanisorn and co-director Christine Lamberson to invite nationally renowned scholars to our campus in rural West Texas as part of a series to commemorate the centennial of the Great War. David Silbey arrived on campus as the first of many speakers and a comment he made during his lecture sparked a conversation about comparing Civil War and Great War leaders. Over drinks at a local establishment, we sketched out plans for *Wars Civil and Great*. The NEH gave us the opportunity to come together and fostered this intellectual experiment. The agency performs a pivotal public service and has led to untold numbers of collaborations and scholarly pursuits in the name of learning more about and acknowledging our shared humanity.

Projects, especially ones like this, incur an enormous number of debts from various sources. The editors would like to thank our authors for their patience and dedication to the project through various challenges and many delays. We thank Steve Trout for being supportive of this endeavor from the start and for agreeing to write the afterword to the volume. The editors are grateful for comments from all the readers of the manuscript who offered critical corrections and helped us sharpen our focus. We thank Dan Waterman for his assistance during an early draft of this project. Thanks especially to Joyce Harrison and the remarkable team at the University Press of Kansas for shepherding this project to the finish line.

David Silbey would like to thank his co-editor, Kanisorn Wongsrichanalai, who, more than anyone, brought this work to fruition. His patience and insight made it a success. His students at Cornell in Washington have always been a source of energy and excitement that fed into his work on the book. Much of this was done during the pandemic, and the intelligence, discipline, and maturity of the entire Cornell community was wonderful to see, even if in the midst of a crisis. Caroline Kleiner helped invaluably with the research. As always, David's wife Mari and his daughter Elia have made him laugh at all the right times. His mom, Rosemary Silbey, showed him every day of what toughness is. Finally, two scholars now gone from us reminded him always of what wisdom is: Walter LaFeber, forever the dean of American foreign policy, and Joel Silbey, David's father, who would have liked to see his son write a book about the Civil War.

Kanisorn Wongsrichanalai thanks his NEH project co-director, Christine Lamberson, for her professionalism, creativity, tirelessness, enormous patience, and, above all, her friendship. He would also like to thank co-editor David Silbey for sparking the idea for this project and for being a mentor and friend since first meeting him in that military history class many years ago. At Angelo State University, Kanisorn owes special thanks to Katie Plum, whose guidance and advice made the grant and subsequent project possible. Kanisorn acknowledges and appreciates the encouragement and support of Arnoldo DeLeón. Thanks also to Meg Hacker and her staff at the National Archives and Records Administration in Fort Worth. This volume followed Kanisorn to a new job and position where he also found a wonderful scholarly community that nurtured this book. He would especially like to thank the following people at the Massachusetts Historical Society and in the greater Boston community: Catherine Allgor, Conrad E. Wright, Peter Drummey, Anne Bentley, Katie Finn, Kathy Griffin, Brenda Lawson, Maureen Marcucci, Kate Melchior, Katy Morris, Elyssa Tardif, and Mary Yacovone. Finally, Wongsrichanalai would like to thank his long-time correspondents who have supported and encouraged him: Brian J. Maxson and Julie Mujic.

October 2022
Washington, DC, and Boston

Introduction

Remembrance of Wars Past—The American Civil War and the Great War at Their Sesquicentennial and Centennial Anniversaries

David J. Silbey and Kanisorn Wongsrichanalai

On Saturday, April 4, 2015, Virginia governor Terry McAuliffe participated in a ceremony on the steps of the Confederacy's former capitol marking the sesquicentennial of the American Civil War. An audience of approximately five thousand observed the ceremonies as Civil War reenactors portraying soldiers of the United States Colored Troops marched in solemn procession. "Today is a reminder to all of us that we still have unfinished business in the goal of real equality for our nation," McAuliffe declared, urging Americans to participate in the electoral process and arguing for greater educational opportunities. The governor made a clear link between the struggles of the past and the ongoing challenges in the present. "Just remember," he continued, "150 years ago right here, the Richmonders who tasted freedom for the first time in 1865 understood the importance of the right to vote and the right to education."[1] The Civil War resulted in the destruction of slavery and opened a new chapter in American history, wherein those who had gained their freedom also sought to become part of a larger American community and demanded both political and educational equality. The federal government, after the Civil War, attempted to provide them with those tools to succeed even as it stitched the fabric of Union back together. One of the other consequences of the Civil War was that Americans developed a stronger national identity. State and regional loyalties had become subsumed by a greater one, bound by

heritage, and forged in fire.[2] What new world would the Civil War generation make of their society reborn?

On May 29, 2016, President Francois Hollande of France and Chancellor Angela Merkel of Germany participated in a wreath-laying ceremony to
mark the centennial of the Battle of Verdun. Remembering the three hundred thousand soldiers who perished in this horrific episode of the Great
War's carnage, the two leaders used the occasion to pledge unity and, like
Governor McAuliffe in Richmond a year earlier, remind people of the challenges that the European Union faced. "We are side by side to tackle the
challenges of today and first of all the future of Europe," President Hollande
explained, "because, as we know disappointment was followed by disen-
chantment, and after doubts came suspicion, and for some even rejection or
break-up."[3] The two leaders observed a world on the edge as nationalist sentiment and political power expanded in their respective countries while the
United Kingdom's voters stood on the verge of deciding whether to remain
in the European Union. A strong proponent of the continental alliance,
Chancellor Merkel reminded the audience of the importance of unity for
tackling "the European debt crisis, our dealing with the many people who are
seeking refuge in Europe, and for all the other great challenges of our time."[4]

Both the Civil War and Great War commemorations have been shaped by
the early twenty-first-century context from which we view the consequences
of these cataclysmic events. Scholars have long been aware of the inescapable
fact that humans examine their past through the lens of the present. The
lessons we glean from history depend on what we are searching for in our
own time. After the passage of important commemoration milestones—the
150th of the Civil War and the 100th of the Great War—and on the precipice
of seismic changes both to the American safety net, itself arguably created
as a result of the Civil War and emancipation—and the European alliances
(arguably created as a result of the end of the Great War), the third decade of
the twenty-first century is also an appropriate time to take stock of what historians have learned from these two conflicts in decades past. Additionally,
it is an opportunity to re-periodize the conflicts as part of the same era—the
long nineteenth century—rather than viewing them as products of separate
times.

Nothing punctuated the end of the nineteenth-century world and her-
alded the dawn of a new twentieth century like the conclusion of the Great
War. On one side lay westward expansion, the conflict between free and

slave labor, the birth of industrialization in the United States, agrarian revolt, and attempts at reforming the most egregious abuses of working conditions and reducing economic inequality. On the other lay greater urbanization, the Jazz Age, the Harlem Renaissance, radio, and the age of the automobile. Those who lived through the period also noticed a key distinction. The period between the Civil War and the end of the Great War led to the passage of seven constitutional amendments aimed at bettering society. After all, the animating idea of the nineteenth century revolved around the notion of continual betterment and change. The disillusion caused by the end of the Great War and the sense that the American public now turned to revelry and self-indulgence certainly suggested that a different attitude toward life now prevailed. Senator Henry Cabot Lodge, the powerful Republican senator from Massachusetts who clashed with Woodrow Wilson over America's role in the League of Nations, lamented to Brooks Adams, "We were all of us in our youth more or less under the spell of the nineteenth-century doctrines that we were in continual evolution, always moving on to something better with perfection as the goal." "Now," however, "it is all over."[5] The end of the Great War had finally shed the United States free of the nineteenth century and its culture and ideas.

Why should students of history consider the Civil and Great Wars together? Traditionally, the Great War has been viewed as a mere prelude to World War II, overshadowed by that much more destructive conflict of the 1940s.[6] Yet, viewing the Civil and Great Wars as part of the same period allows for a greater understanding of both. The Civil War generation was still alive when the Great War erupted in Europe. Several members of the US Congress had served in the Civil War and two justices of the US Supreme Court—Chief Justice Edward White and Associate Justice Oliver Wendell Holmes Jr.—ranked among the veterans in political power in the second decade of the twentieth century.[7] The culture of honor and duty that had motivated Civil War–era Americans still held true of the Great War generation.[8] Americans have long believed in the exceptional nature of their republic and those whose lives bridged the two conflicts drew a straight line connecting the periods and causes. For example, in 1919 Civil War veteran Abraham Gilbert Mills made the case that, had the United States failed to prevent secession in the 1860s, "the savage, bloodthirsty, hun [sic] would now be bestriding the world like a Colossus." He even claimed that when future generations wrote of the Great War, "and the contributing causes of our final triumph are fully appraised, foremost among such contributions will be found the triumph of the armies and navies of the Union in that historic struggle."[9]

The Civil War also served as an inspiration to the next generation of Americans. Young men who had learned about the heroics of the Civil War veterans sought the same romantic adventures on European battlefields.[10] After their ordeal in combat, many doughboys referenced the Civil War when trying to articulate their experiences. Many referred to the quotation by Gen. William Tecumseh Sherman that "war is hell." One marine "learned that Sherman told the truth, the whole truth, and nothing but the truth," while another veteran remarked, "Sherman was right but mild in expression."[11] Certainly those who had grown up in the shadow of the Civil War sought to apply the lessons they learned from it to the global conflict in Europe. As a political scientist and historian, President Woodrow Wilson certainly looked to the example of his predecessor, Abraham Lincoln, for how to lead the nation through a conflict of such scale. When John J. Pershing was a young boy in Missouri, his father almost died in a Confederate raid on his hometown, a fact he remembered well as an adult. After the conflict, he enjoyed the pageantry of postwar celebrations and parades. Later, as a young cadet at West Point, Pershing attended the funeral of Ulysses S. Grant and surely had the Union commander in mind when he led the American Expeditionary Forces over to France in 1917. Both Wilson and Pershing remembered the war of their childhood and sought to apply what they learned from it to their present circumstances.[12]

How did the Great War generation's understanding of the Civil War influence their decisions? What did they view as mistakes that they should not repeat? And what did they think should be replicated to assure victory in their own time? When he planned his own strategy, Pershing may have sought to emulate Ulysses S. Grant's war of maneuver. He later argued that due to their Civil War experience, Americans knew about trench warfare before it became the bane of European generals on the Western Front. Knowing that Grant had detested the static nature of the trenches, Pershing sought a more open and maneuverable strategy (so too did the Allied commanders who doubted Pershing's ability to break the Western Front stalemate).[13] The war ended before American forces crossed into German territory even though Pershing believed that the Allies should have pushed through to Berlin. Here again, perhaps he took a lesson from Grant's capture of Richmond and defeat of the rebel army.[14] Wilson, meanwhile, chose his army commander wisely, knowing full well how much trouble George McClellan had given Lincoln. When Wilson considered his options, Pershing stood out for many reasons, one being his lack of interest in politics.[15] Here then, perhaps, lay one key difference between the two commanders in chief: Lincoln did not care if the war bolstered a political enemy as long as he helped preserve the Union. Wilson, a man with enormous ambition and a substantial ego, did not want anyone who would steal his limelight and obstruct his opportunity to shape the world.[16] But, again in contrast to Lincoln, Wilson also learned how to organize a draft. Together with Secretary of War Newton Baker, he made sure that those eligible for the draft could not purchase a substitute and avoid service, hoping to democratize the process and prevent the disruptive and deadly draft riots of the Civil War era.[17]

In examining the two conflicts, one is struck by the multiple parallels. In both cases, a political system that had been established to balance competing interests began to fracture and fail. In the United States, it was the compromise between slave states and free states embodied in the Constitution; in Europe, it was the agreement between the Great Powers set up by the Treaty of Vienna. The slave/free compromise began to strain as westward expansion raised the of question how a flood of new states would enter the Union. The Treaty of Vienna sundered as Germany, the growing behemoth at the center of Europe, became an expansionist rather than a status quo power. In both cases, expansion and ideological clashes brought forth conflict. The secession of the Lower South sparked the American conflict while the assassination of Austro-Hungary's crown prince lit the fuse for the resulting global war. But neither secession nor Franz Ferdinand's death actually led to the firing of the guns. Pressured to keep the *Star of the West* from replenishing Fort Sumter's dwindling supplies, Confederate president Jefferson Davis ordered Southern troops to fire on federal troops, inaugurating civil war. Convinced by the dictates of the Schlieffen Plan that only a quick strike to incapacitate France would allow them to defeat Russia, German military leaders violated Belgium's neutrality and brought the United Kingdom into the fighting, sparking the world war.

When the United States mobilized for war in both cases, it expanded the scope and authority of its federal government. Lincoln and his officials instigated the draft, raised revenue from income taxes, and issued greenbacks. Woodrow Wilson's government followed suit but also nationalized the railroads and pioneered a government-led propaganda campaign to drum up support for the war. Both wartime governments dealt with the issue of dissenters on the home front and called upon African Americans to join in the fight.

The aftermath of the wars in the United States also mirrored each other in many ways. Both conflicts left scores of casualties but, unlike in the Civil War, the United States did not face the physical destruction that scarred Europe. US leadership in both instances suffered from the sudden loss of its wartime leaders. While an assassin's bullet felled Abraham Lincoln, Woodrow Wilson's fight for the League of Nations exhausted him, leading to physical and mental collapse. Both conflicts led to domestic reforms in the United States. The Civil War's end brought the Thirteenth, Fourteenth, and Fifteenth Amendments, while the Great War made the Eighteenth and Nineteenth Amendments possible. Postwar chaos marked American society in both periods. While President Ulysses Grant attempted to defend African Americans' hard-won civil rights, he found himself hampered by strong guerrilla resistance in the South and a northern populace with no stomach for ongoing violence in the midst of peace. The Panic of 1873 did not help, as Northerners turned to their own financial concerns and fretted that a president swamped with accusations of corruption was too focused on a conflict that had closed in 1865. Similarly, the sudden halt of wartime contracts and a curtailment of workers' gains led to financial turmoil after the Great War. Fear of communism, bombs sent through the mail, and federal raids exacerbated the chaotic nature of the period. Finally, the memories of both conflicts have been "diluted" by other wars. The tradition of Decoration Days, originating after the Civil War to honor the dead from that conflict, became Memorial Day and now stands for commemorating all of America's war dead. Set up for the Great War dead, the Tomb of the Unknown Soldier in Arlington Cemetery later housed the remains of Americans from other twentieth-century wars as well. The memories of both conflicts became blended with the rest of American history.[18]

Given these similarities, a comparison between the two conflicts seems wise. But how? On what topics? By whom? Unlike more explored conjunctions, where models exist, putting the Civil War and the Great War in comparison comes without much precedent.[19] Given such uncertainty, we decided that, rather than seeking chapters on tightly defined topics, we would ask a range of contributors—each with their own area of expertise—to answer a shared set of questions. While the questions would be shared, the lessons and analysis would be distinct to each chapter. In this way, we acknowledge the ambiguity of all historical research, at least at the start. Scholars *start* with questions and investigate from there, but, at the end, usually simply report their conclusions without any sense of the hesitancy and uncertainty of the process itself. Starting with the questions acknowledges that historical process and reflects the studied uncertainty with which we approach this comparison.

The following chapters compare the American experience in the Civil War and Great War by having scholars answer questions, focusing and drawing on their own particular area of understanding. Each chapter author addresses four overarching questions. First, what legacy did the Civil War leave? Second, did the Great War generation interpret the lessons of the Civil War and, if so, how? Third, how did the Great War change the lessons from the Civil War era? And, finally, how did both wars contribute to the modernization of the United States?

When soliciting contributions, we made clear that how each author chose to answer the question was up to them. They might answer all the questions equally. They might focus on one question more than the others. They might bring their own interpretation to the questions and not just the answers. We are, in some ways, deliberately positioning ourselves at the beginning of the process of historical inquiry, rather than the end, but in addressing these topics in this fashion, the chapters aim to help the reader see across both of the studied conflicts and note how the Civil War cast a wide shadow over the American experience of the Great War.

The first section begins with an examination of military and political leadership. David Silbey examines two pivotal American commanding generals—Ulysses S. Grant and John J. Pershing—and looks at the unique positions each occupied in the military history of their conflict. Brian Dirck's chapter focuses on political leadership, by comparing Presidents Abraham Lincoln and Woodrow Wilson. While the two chief executives navigated treacherous times, they also grasped the potential of the times for reform. Dirck sketches how both men made the best of their circumstances and identifies the constant element that all great political leaders need: pragmatism.

Debra Sheffer's chapter also emphasizes the consistent themes in both historical periods: racial bias and the perseverance of African Americans who sought to serve their country and prove themselves worthy of social equality. Unfortunately for those clamoring for rights, superpatriotic elements in society considered any deviation from the cause of winning the war as superfluous at best and treasonous at worst. And a majority of Americans of both the Civil War and Great War generations proved willing to curtail and even suspend civil liberties in order to win the war, as Kanisorn Wongsrichanalai's chapter reveals. The irony, however, is that there was greater opportunity for dissent in Civil War America than there was in the later conflict. Wongsrichanalai suggests that President Wilson's appeal to volunteerism and reluctance to use federal power as Lincoln had done ultimately encouraged anxious Americans to take matters into their own hands in dealing with dissenters, leading to a rise in vigilante action and violence against those suspected of harboring disloyal sentiments.

The next set of chapters deals with the issue of medicine, mental health, and the environment. Shauna Devine and Dale Smith trace the development of physicians, collaboration between military and civilian doctors, disease management, medical technology, and the dissemination of medical knowledge between the Civil War and the Great War. But while Devine and Smith can point to improvements in treating the physical body, Kathleen Logotheis Thompson finds that any understanding of post-traumatic stress disorder—a psychological impairment not officially diagnosed until the Vietnam War—regressed during the Great War as Americans, as they had initially done in the Civil War, resorted to blaming a soldier's moral flaws for their symptoms. The Great War generation, therefore, did not have a better understanding of the inner workings of the human brain than their Civil War fathers. In another chapter that explores the lived experience of war, Brian Allen Drake takes a close look at the development and experience of trench warfare in front of Petersburg, Virginia, and compares that environment with the stalemated muddy lines in France.

The final chapter considers postwar challenges as survivors engaged in a lengthy debate about what the nation owed the returning veterans and how best to commemorate the dead. In his second chapter in the book, Kanisorn Wongsrichanalai examines the challenges that veterans faced after both conflicts. The Civil War generation left a legacy that hindered Great War veterans from obtaining aid. Because of the high cost of pensions and ongoing concern about government waste, American leaders of the Great War era tried to discourage any thought of postwar compensation for the doughboys. At first willing to accept this state of affairs, the doughboys soon turned to veterans' organizations such as the Veterans of Foreign Wars and the American Legion to fight for pensions, and that urgency only increased with the deepening of the Great Depression.

In his afterword, Steven Trout makes a case for comparative studies like this collection and takes on another aspect of the two wars not covered in earlier chapters: memoirs and commemoration. Trout compares Ulysses S. Grant's *Personal Memoirs of U.S. Grant* to John J. Pershing's *My Experiences in the World War*. Picking up where David Silbey's work in this book leaves off, Trout considers the challenges both authors faced as well as the contexts in which their writings reached the public. Using a "memory studies approach," along with some literary criticism, he demonstrates again the usefulness of considering these two military figures and time periods in American history side by side.

While these chapters cover a broad range of topics, they do not cover everything. We do not look at the experiences of women, youth, religious groups, ethnic minorities, political parties, and postwar home-front issues, among other topics. This is not meant to suggest they lack importance, only that this investigation is intended as a beginning comparison, not a comprehensive final word. The point is to start to ask how experiences in the Civil War and the Great War, when compared and analyzed, tell us more about those experiences and those conflicts. We have pointed out how the Civil War and the Great War share specific similarities, but the chapters of this book are shaped by the overarching likeness between the two. For the United States, as well as all the countries involved, these conflicts were on a scale beyond what they had ever experienced and fought in before. The Civil War was the first mass-industrialized war that America had ever fought, while the Great War was the first great commitment of America's might to an overseas war. For the European powers, the Great War was the first modern total war, one that required the mobilization of entire societies. For all those countries, both conflicts were seen at the time and ever since as unprecedented wars, as wars that stood out in their size and cost from all others (with the obvious exception of World War II). These are wars whose consequences are still being felt. Nowhere is that more clear than in the mass remembrances and commemorations that marked the centennial and sesquicentennial of each. Both wars are remembered and commemorated because both still exert deep influence a century or more later. "The past is never dead. It's not even past," wrote William Faulkner. He might have been writing about the Great and Civil Wars.[20]

Editors' Note: The authors have chosen to use the term "Great War" throughout this volume, since that is how contemporaries in the English-speaking world referred to the conflict. "The name 'First World War,'" as Michael Howard has pointed out, "was coined a few years after the event by a sardonic and farsighted journalist."[21]

Notes

1. Katherine Calos, "Civil War 150th: Richmond Commemorates End of War and Visit by Lincoln," *Richmond Times-Dispatch,* April 4, 2015, http://www.richmond .com/news/special-report/the-civil-war/civil-war-th-richmond-commemorates -end-of-war-and-visit/article_f7362d95-9366-5fa7-ba27-5fbdb902ccea.html.

2. James M. McPherson, *Battle Cry of Freedom: The Civil War Era* (New York: Oxford University Press, 1988), 859. See also Susan-Mary Grant, *North Over South: Northern Nationalism and American Identity in the Antebellum Era* (Lawrence: University Press of Kansas, 2000).

3. Reuters, "Hollande and Merkel Remember WWI Dead 100 Years after Verdun Battle," *France 24,* May 29, 2016, http://www.france24.com/en/20160529-hollande -merkel-remember-wwi-dead-100-years-after-verdun-battle.

4. Gregory Viscusi and Arne Delfs, "Merkel Joins Hollande to Defend EU at World War I Commemoration," *Bloomberg,* May 29, 2016, http://www.bloomberg .com/news/articles/2016-05-29/merkel-joins-hollande-to-defend-eu-at-world-war -i-commemoration.

5. Quoted in G. J. Meyer, *The World Remade: America in World War I* (New York: Bantam Books, 2016), 572.

6. Historian Jennifer D. Keene argues that "World War I became the 'forgotten war' because Americans never developed a unifying collective memory about its meaning or the political lessons it offered." Kimberly J. Lamay Licursi agrees with this assessment but also notes that the generation of Americans who would have been most influenced by Great War cultural representations ended up fighting in and having their memories overwhelmed by World War II. Jennifer D. Keene, "Remembering the 'Forgotten War': American Historiography on World War I," *Historian* 78, no. 3 (Fall 2016): 439, 442; Kimberly J. Lamay Licursi, *Remembering World War I in America* (Lincoln: University of Nebraska Press, 2018), xv, xxii–xxiii, 146, 191–192; Meyer, *World Remade,* xvi.

7. Garrett Peck, *The Great War in America: World War I and Its Aftermath* (New York: Pegasus Books, 2018), 18.

8. Edward A. Gutiérrez argues that "honor and duty" compelled many doughboys to fight. This argument taps into the lengthy historiography on Civil War soldiers' motivations. Gutiérrez, *Doughboys on the Great War: How American Soldiers*

Viewed Their Military Experience (Lawrence: University Press of Kansas, 2014), 1–2. For works that discuss the importance of honor and duty in Civil War soldiers, see, among others, Gerald F. Linderman, *Embattled Courage: The Experience of Combat in the American Civil War* (New York: Free Press, 1987); James M. McPherson, *For Cause and Comrades: Why Men Fought in the Civil War* (New York: Oxford University Press, 1997); Peter S. Carmichael, *The Last Generation: Young Virginians in Peace, War, and Reunion* (Chapel Hill: University of North Carolina Press, 2005); Kanisorn Wongsrichanalai, *Northern Character: College-Educated New Englanders, Honor, Nationalism, and Leadership in the Civil War Era* (New York: Fordham University Press, 2016).

9. Quoted in M. Keith Harris, *Across the Bloody Chasm: The Culture of Commemoration among Civil War Veterans* (Baton Rouge: Louisiana State University Press, 2014), 50.

10. Christopher C. Gibbs, *The Great Silent Majority: Missouri's Resistance to World War I* (Columbia: University of Missouri Press, 1988), 93–94.

11. Gutiérrez, *Doughboys on the Great War*, 12.

12. Andrew Carroll, *My Fellow Soldiers: General John Pershing and the Americans Who Helped Win the Great War* (New York: Penguin Books, 2017), 60.

13. Carroll, *My Fellow Soldiers*, 87.

14. Carroll, *My Fellow Soldiers*, xx.

15. Carroll, *My Fellow Soldiers*, 107.

16. G. J. Meyer has a critical view of Wilson's personality and motivations. The president's reasons for involving the United States in the war included having a say in the peace talks in order to "stop the Allies from imposing a kind of peace that could never be more than unstable and short-lived." "This," Meyer insists, "was a quintessentially Wilsonian aspiration, at once noble and egotistical. It accorded perfectly with his sense of his own great destiny." In another example of Wilson's egoism, the president's once-close associate "Colonel" Edward House found himself outside Wilson's inner circle after the war. House represented Wilson at the Supreme Council in France during the hectic time when Wilson split his time between Europe and the United States. Meyer argues that House's greater visibility (he had preferred to operate in the background in the past) with the press led some writes to suggest "that it was he more than Wilson who was making things happen." For Wilson, Meyer suggests, "the colonel's growing celebrity was a maddening new source of distress. The role of great peacemaker was his alone." Meyer, *World Remade*, 209–210, 501–502.

17. Carroll, *My Fellow Soldiers*, 126; Meyer, *World Remade*, 256–257.

18. Keene, "Remembering the 'Forgotten War'," 443.

19. Joseph G. Dawson III, *Commanders in Chief: Presidential Leadership in Modern Wars* (Lawrence: University Press of Kansas, 1993); Gabor S. Boritt, ed., *War Comes Again: Comparative Vistas on the Civil War and World War II* (New York: Oxford University Press, 1995); Alexander Watson, *Enduring the Great War: Combat, Morale and Collapse in the German and British Armies, 1914–1918* (Cambridge, UK: Cambridge University Press, 2008).

20. William Faulkner, *Requiem for a Nun* (1950; New York: Vintage Books, 2011), 73.

21. Howard makes the case that the Seven Years' War (1756–1763) has claim to being the actual first global conflict. He notes that the French referred to the Great War as *la Grande Guerre*, while the Italians called it *la Grande Guerra*. The Germans, meanwhile, referred to it from the start as *das Weltkrieg* (the World War). "Perhaps," Howard notes, "that in itself tells us something about German aspirations in 1914." Michael Howard, "The First World War Reconsidered," in *The Great War and the Twentieth Century*, ed. Jay Winter, Geoffrey Parker, and Mary R. Habeck (New Haven, CT: Yale University Press, 2000), 14.

"On Each Side There Emerged a Supreme Commander"

Ulysses S. Grant and John J. Pershing (and Douglas Haig), 1861–1918

David J. Silbey

The questions Kanisorn Wongsrichanalai and I posed in the introduction speak to the fundamental issue of how the Civil War and Great War interacted as historical events, the lessons of each, and how our understanding of both has shaped their legacy.[1] Those lessons and that legacy are nowhere more important than in a discussion of the military leaders involved and the way in which they occupied unique positions because of the wars they waged. For the purposes of this chapter, I want to take a particular facet of both wars—the unique positions of the most important military commanders—and examine what the effects of those positions had on a range of issues that swirled during and after the wars: casualties, politics, memorialization, and alternatives. Each of those issues addresses one or more of the questions asked in the introduction about lessons and legacy. Because I am largely focused on the perception of the generals and their wars, I am less concerned about their specific military actions and decisions. This chapter is not about evaluating them as generals and combatants but rather about understanding how their position as supreme commander was shaped by and shaped the wars in which they led. It is about how they came to be *icons* rather than simply individuals.

Such an approach is important because the Civil War and the Great War were and are iconic wars, wars which stand as critical parts of modern history. They are not only part of that history but also help define it. Even the very chronology of the modern world is defined by the Civil War and Great War, both of which bookend traditional historical eras. Further, they continue to be relevant to current political issues, remaining freshly urgent into the twenty-first century, whether through arguments over their memorialization or through the lingering fallout of decisions taken during and after the conflicts. As with all such foundational events, the two wars are overwhelming to understand in their entirety: too big, too complicated, too nuanced, and too ambivalent. One of the responses to that complexity is to look for a way to personalize the conflicts, to connect them with a human being. Some look for ancestors who fought, some participate in reenactments, and some focus on those responsible for waging the wars. In this latter category, particularly, are politicians and generals who become the avatars for their wars.

This is a legacy of all such conflicts. The American Revolution gave the United States George Washington. World War II deeded America Franklin Delano Roosevelt, George S. Patton, and Dwight D. Eisenhower. These men have become entry points into the much larger historical moments, personalized representations of the war itself. So, too, in the Civil War for Abraham Lincoln, Ulysses S. Grant, and Robert E. Lee. So, too, in the Great War, for Woodrow Wilson and John J. Pershing. This has been true for other countries as well. The Napoleonic conflicts gave France Napoleon Bonaparte and Britain Arthur Wellesley, the Duke of Wellington. The Great War gave the British Douglas Haig and the French Ferdinand Foch.

Generals, in particular, have become identified with the wars, with their roles often iconically connected in popular memory with one particular conflict. Grant fought in the Mexican-American War, but that is not why or how he is remembered. Pershing fought in the Philippines, but that is not why he is remembered.[2] In contrast, Winfield Scott, when he is remembered, is connected with a number of American wars in the nineteenth century. None that he really participated in, however, rose to the level of iconography of either the Civil War or the Great War.[3] Mostly, frankly, Scott is not remembered at all.

Thus, the generals examined here were closely identified with the military effort itself, the combat and carnage that marked both wars. Grant represented the overwhelming effort of the Union from 1864 to 1865, when the United States had finally mobilized itself both economically and militarily on a scale that would not be seen again until World War II. He was the man who wielded the Union's bloody sword. In a similar way, Pershing symbolized the American effort in the Great War, the embodiment of US commitment to the conflict. He was the general who took American boys to the Western Front and led them through the victorious battles of 1918.

This representation was a particularly military one. None of the politicians who rivaled the generals historically had a military background: Lincoln and Wilson were all civilians without much martial experience. While they all involved themselves closely in the war effort, whether in the form of Lincoln sleeping in the DC telegraph office to get news of Gettysburg or Wilson having his fixer Colonel Edward House handle diplomacy with America's wartime allies, neither of them really came to be identified as closely with the military effort as the generals. (Brian Dirck provides a closer look at these two commanders in chief in his chapter for this book.) This has not always been the case. Franklin Delano Roosevelt in World War II was more closely identified with the military effort because he had substantial experience with the military as assistant secretary of the navy in the Great War.[4] In contrast, Grant and Pershing were seen as the main military faces of the final war effort, and in that they stood pretty much alone in 1865, 1918, and after. Such a status made them symbolize the war effort as a whole. Comparing this *perception* of them (both during and after the war) tells us as much about the war as about each general.

What does that connection teach us about the lessons and legacies of those wars? To figure this out, I'm going to use three generals—from the Civil War and from the Great War—to explore what it meant to be an icon of a certain war. How does being in that position shape both the experience and perception of each general? For the Civil War, I will focus on Ulysses S. Grant, the most important US general of the Civil War.[5] For the Great War, I will look at John J. Pershing, the leading American general of the Great War, if one whose experience echoed Grant's position rather than duplicated it.[6] For the third general, I am going to break away a bit from the book's stated focus and add a non-American one to the comparison. Why? Though this book has a solidly American focus, it is important to remember that the United States exists in a larger world. Engaging with that transnational context will, I hope, illustrate the way in which the themes I examine are not unique to the United States. Thus, into the mix, I will add Douglas Haig, commander of the British Expeditionary Force (BEF) in the Great War. Haig occupied a similar, though not identical, position to both Pershing and Grant and became an icon to the British in parallel ways. Haig was not the only option to choose from for such a comparison—certainly Ferdinand Foch held similar status in the French war effort of the Great War, as did Erich Ludendorff of the German. Nonetheless, the deep and connected history between Britain and the United States and the way in which the British Army had a long "fascination" with the Civil War make Haig particularly useful, and so Haig it is.[7]

What exactly were their positions? Obviously, they all had specific military ranks, but, more importantly, Grant, Pershing, and Haig were the commanding officers of an enormous military effort, responsible for forces locked in unprecedented conflicts. Grant led the main army in the main theater of the most important war in American history against the main weight of the enemy.[8] He was the commander at the war's center of gravity. The forces that Grant led in 1865 were the most powerful American army to that point in US history, not to be surpassed in relative terms until World War II.

Pershing had a somewhat lesser position. He led the primary American army in the main theater of war, fighting the main weight of the enemy, but he was not the overall commander of the war effort, he did not command the largest forces in the theater, and he never carried quite the weight that Grant did. But, unlike Grant, Pershing had to not only command the army but also build it. Where Grant found the Army of the Potomac already largely organized, Pershing had substantial responsibility in the effort to create and build up the American Expeditionary Force. Then, to add to the difficulty, he had to lead that force across thousands of miles of ocean to a foreign country. There, he and his inexperienced doughboys faced a well-emplaced and battle-hardened foe in the Germans and, perhaps equally threatening, a set of well-emplaced and battle-hardened friends in the British and French. If Pershing never quite reached Grant's level, he was in the same league. "Not since Ulysses S. Grant took control of all the Union's armies in March 1864," historian Andrew Carroll noted, "has an American general been saddled with more responsibility."[9] Haig, too, did not carry the same weight as Grant. He commanded his own national army, but not the overall force.[10] That force, the BEF, was, comparatively speaking, the largest and most powerful in modern British history, rivaled perhaps only by the Indian Army under William Slim in 1944–1945, and may at times have been the largest force on the Western Front, but it was not carrying the weight of the conflict alone.

In this, Grant was close to unique in modern American military history and, as well, without real parallels in modern British military history. In almost no other modern conflict of the scale of the Civil War did an American (or British) general successfully command the most important army in the main theater against the main weight of the enemy. George Washington commanded the most important army in the American Revolution, but not terribly *successfully*, at least in battlefield terms. Winfield Scott's forces fighting their way to Mexico City in the Mexican-American War might qualify, but Zachary Taylor, commanding a similar size army in northern Mexico, would dispute such a conclusion vociferously (as he did most things connected with Scott). Grant's predecessors in the Civil War were impressively helpless against the Confederates.[11] In the twentieth century, even Dwight D. Eisenhower, the overall commander of Allied forces in Western Europe in World War II, never faced the main weight of the German Army, which was pouring most of its resources into the desperate struggle against the Soviets on the Eastern Front. No British commander of the twentieth century would truly qualify: Bernard Montgomery of World War II falls prey to the same thing that disqualifies Eisenhower. No one else comes as close, except perhaps for the momentary case of Lord Gort in France, 1940.[12] Perhaps the only parallels are the Soviet generals of World War II, like Marshal Zhukov, who did command his country's largest force against the enemy's main weight.

This fine parsing seems somewhat overwrought, more appropriate for social media or a blog post. Why then is it important? The rareness of their position has important consequences for how we analyze these men. They were generals in extraordinary positions. Winston Churchill once said of Admiral Sir John Jellicoe, the commander of the Home Fleet in Britain in the Great War, that he was "the only man who could lose the war in an afternoon."[13] Churchill was exaggerating, but the kernel of the truth remained. Even more important, it was not so much that Jellicoe could actually lose the war in an afternoon—it was that he was in a command position where the perception was that his decisions had that level of power and effect. So, too, to a greater or lesser degree were Grant, Pershing, and Haig. They—like Jellicoe—occupied command positions that were critical enough to have a substantial effect on the war and were perceived that way. They had responsibilities and carried risks that few other generals in their respective countries' history had. Their effect on the legacies of the wars was immediate and ongoing. That position thrust them into situations that other generals only rarely encountered. They cannot be easily compared to generals who were not the commanders of their countries' main effort; they cannot be easily compared to generals who did not face the main enemy army. They cannot be easily compared to generals who could not "lose the war in an afternoon." They can, however, be compared to each other. Doing so allows us to understand better Grant, Pershing, and Haig, the Civil War and Great War, and even generalship as a whole.

Thus, I will broaden out the original question. What does examining the shared experience of Grant, Pershing, and Haig tell us about them? What does it tell us about their wars? How does looking at their situation begin to help us think about our original questions and the lessons of the Civil War and Great War, about how the Civil War influenced the later conflict, and the legacies of both?

The Legacy of the Civil War and the Great War: Historiography

Let us first look at how historians have treated the three generals, to see one form of the legacy that the wars left behind. The most notable part of this is how subsequent wars and events changed the perception of previous generals. Their legacies were not set in stone but remolded by successive generations. In the immediate aftermath of the wars, each general was lauded for his victories, by the historians as well as the public. But then each became captive of the larger historical perception of the war, for both good and ill. Grant's historical standing, for example, was prisoner of the "Lost Cause" school of Civil War era historiography, one written by ex-Confederates, political rivals, and historians eager to recover and justify the South's behavior before and during the Civil War.[14] The "Lost Cause" historiography cast the South as a noble endeavor overwhelmed by the sheer might of the North, Robert E. Lee as the hero, and Grant a butcher who stumbled his way drunkenly to victory.

Grant's image bounced around in the twentieth century. The world wars started the shift. Here were two more total wars won at great expense and great violence by a new generation of generals. The Great War, as we shall see, disappeared too quickly from American consciousness to help Grant, but World War II had a substantial effect on his reputation. The Civil War was no longer such an outlier in American military history, but seemingly a precursor to later wars. Historians of the post–World War II era, like Bruce Catton, rehabilitated Grant's image, and he enjoyed a moment of resurgence.[15] This did not last. Vietnam shifted things back. Here was a war whose sanguinary futility echoed the most negative perceptions of 1861–1865. Grant cratered again, once more an inept butcher.[16] William McFeely, whose 1981 biography cemented the returning vision, wrote that Grant's 1864 Virginia campaign was "a nightmare of inhumanity and inept military strategy [and] an exercise in carnage," a description that sounds more like the conflict in Vietnam than in Virginia.[17] Only after the trauma of Vietnam faded did Grant recover, as historians of the late twentieth and early twenty-first century have reexamined the Civil War in a much more nuanced way. There has been no recent war that had the overwhelming influence of either World War II or Vietnam, and so historians like Brooks Simpson and Joan Waugh have written about Grant much more as an individual rather than an avatar of a particular conflict, to be counterpointed to other iconic American wars.[18] There has even been the chance, as in Waugh's work, to analyze the evolving history of Grant as an icon, his "shifting legacy."[19] The point here is not to argue which generation of historians was correct,[20] but to point out the way in which Grant (and the Civil War's) legacy was changed by later conflicts, including (though less so) the Great War. For historians, the Civil War existed in a context of military history, and as that context evolved and shifted, so too did the understanding of the Civil War.

John J. Pershing's legacy—and the legacy of the Great War—is much the opposite of the Civil War. Unlike that war, the Great War has largely disappeared from the historical consciousness in the United States. While Grant and the Civil War remained subject of discussion, the Great War did not. The rapid postwar collapse of the alliance that had won and general disillusion with the war as well as a sudden overshadowing by the onrushing World War II, led the Great War to be neglected historically for most of the twentieth century.[21] It was simply one part of the long sequence of American wars, acknowledged but not emphasized. As Edward Coffman put it:

The First World War faded quickly from American memory. The postwar disillusionment was a major contributor. After all, the treaty makers of Versailles neither made the world safe for democracy nor ensured that the war did in fact end all wars. Historians thus studied the why and how of the American intervention and puzzled over the what of Versailles rather than the experience of the war. The advent of World War II, in which Americans played a larger role, served to erase further traces of the earlier conflict. Military historians, led by those who had served in that capacity during World War II, understandably devoted themselves to their war, while others became increasingly fascinated by the Civil War.[22]

The Great War became one of the *other* wars of American history, not in the ranks of the Revolution, the Civil War, or World War II. The historian Russell Weigley, in discussing the "greatest wars of the United States," not only did not judge the Great War to be one of them but also did not even deign to mention it as a competitor.[23] This relegation also pushed Pershing into the background. During the interwar period (1918–1941), Pershing's name was mentioned in books at about the same frequency as that of Ulysses S. Grant. But after World War II, Pershing dropped off, and Grant surged ahead.[24] Pershing had few biographies written about him in the decades after the Great War, with some only starting to appear in the 1960s and 1970s.[25] The lack of emphasis on the Great War is visible even down to the text of those biographies, which were much more balanced than those of Grant and Haig. Their biographies were largely about the Civil War or the Great War, with only stubs for their lives before and after.[26] Pershing's biographies, on the other hand, treated the Great War as only one part of his life.[27] His biographies were about him, not the most important war he fought. The centennial of the Great War in the early decades of the twenty-first century has recovered it historiographically in the United States, but it still remains a lesser war, and Pershing a lesser general.

This is in distinct contrast to Britain. British historians treated the Great War like Americans treated the Civil War: the legacy changing but always critically important. Part of that narrative was the destruction of an entire generation of young men. Their loss and the enforced singleness of a generation of British women made this the story of a "Lost Generation," the death of not just men but the families and children who might have been.[28] Such a destruction required villains, ones beyond the Germans. They were readily available in the older generation of British leaders and so, after an initial period of positivity, the narrative took hold that the Great War was the story of old men sending young men to die. Haig, like Grant had before him, was labeled an inept butcher, excoriated for causing the deaths of hundreds of thousands of his own men for nothing. Even the victory of 1918 was recast as simply German exhaustion, not an achievement of the British army. The historian David French later summarized this process: "Haig has passed into popular historical mythology as the archetypal 'donkey' who created a lost generation of British manhood by his supposedly insensitive and incompetent handling of his forces on the western front."[29] In this narrative, World War II became the counterpoint, a war in which British generalship achieved much more than the "donkeys" of the Great War.[30] Though a revisionist school emerged that cast Haig in more positive light, he has never really escaped his role as villain.[31]

A comparison between Grant, Pershing, and Haig is instructive: in each case, the generals experienced the initial popularity of victory followed by a long slide into criticism or irrelevance, if perhaps punctuated by the occasional recovery. These reputational shifts echo what happened with the American and British efforts in the wars themselves—an initial sense that the war had gone well for the respective countries, followed by much more ambivalent ideas about it.[32] The legacy of each general and each war was not concrete but fluid, shifting as each generation of historians grappled with it. It is only with Pershing that the legacy has simply settled into neglect: stability through inattention, as it were. Historians have never, on the other hand, been able to stop discussing Grant and Haig and their legacies. Like their wars, the image of those generals remains a live one, even to this day. The wars they fought were too great and too important for leave alone; so too the generals who epitomized those conflicts. For American historians, the Civil War remains one they cannot let go, while the Great War is easily put aside. For the British, the Great War remains perhaps the defining moment of modern British history. Those visions are visible in how each historical community treats its generals, with only Pershing spared the inescapable and ironclad identification with his war. That close identification with their conflict is the true legacy for both Grant and Haig, one that they will never escape.

Changing the Lessons of the Civil War: Casualties and Bloody Victories

What were the lessons of the Civil War? And how did the Great War change them? For this section, I will engage with two of our overarching questions, both focused on the lessons of the wars. By way of starting that, it is important to note that an enduring characteristic of the mass industrialized wars of the nineteenth and twentieth century was sustained and heavy casualties. This was true in the Civil War and the Great War, whether at Cold Harbor in 1864, at Passchendaele in 1917, or the Meuse-Argonne in 1918. It was true in World War II on all the fronts and among all the combatants. Total war meant a massive butcher's bill. The casualty rates were a built-in feature of industrialized mass war.

Having said that, the lesson of the Civil War (and the Great War) was that those casualties nonetheless came to be identified strongly with the individual generals, with the implied sense that they *were* actually avoidable. Casualties became an ongoing cultural issue even to this day, whether in the idea of the "Lost Generation" in the 1920s or the discussions in 1990s America about the dropping of the atomic bomb on Japan in 1945, which most focused on how many casualties each side could have expected from an invasion of the Japanese home islands.[33] Because Grant, Pershing, and Haig all commanded the armies at the war's center of gravity, the fixation on casualties attached to them. Both the public and civilian leaders blamed them for the dead and wounded. This was particularly so with Grant and Haig. What was in reality simply a function of total war, impossible for any general to avoid, became personalized to the commanding generals.

Grant's identification with the casualties comes largely from the campaign of 1864–1865. His earlier campaigns, except for the Battle of Shiloh, had not been particularly bloody. That changed when he came east in 1864. The Overland Campaign of 1864, when the Army of the Potomac marched south toward Richmond and Petersburg, was long and sanguinary. It was an inevitable function of the fact that the Confederates had to defend their capital at all costs, and that the Union was determined to end the war. Those were decisions made by Jefferson Davis and Robert E. Lee and Abraham Lincoln, but Grant came to own the casualties. An observer at the time—a newspaper editor—attacked Grant in an editorial by saying that he was "the death's head of a whole people. What is the difference between a *butcher* and a *general*? . . . A Butcher kills animals for food. A general kills men to gratify the ambition or malice of politicians and scoundrels."[34] Secretary of the Navy Gideon Welles echoed that sentiment, lamenting "the slaughtered thousands of my countrymen who have poured out their rich blood for three months on the soil of Virginia, from the Wilderness to Petersburg *under his generalship*" (emphasis added).[35] In both comments, the inextricable lesson was not victory or defeat but the casualties, and Grant was deliberately made responsible for them.

The generals of the Great War did not both get the same treatment. On the one hand, as the war continued and casualties mounted, Haig became strongly identified with the dead and wounded. The BEF was taking staggering casualties, especially starting in 1916 with the Battle of the Somme, and Haig was seen as the man responsible. The first day at the Somme on July 1 was a disaster, with horrific losses and little gain. When Haig continued to press forward, Chief of the Imperial General Staff William Robertson remonstrated with Haig, writing that "at one time audacity and determination to push on regardless of loss were the predominating factors but that was before the days of machine guns and other modern armaments."[36] While Robertson's phrasing suggests how war has changed, it still assigns blame to a general who does not understand and react to the changed circumstances. More, a comparison with Grant is particularly illuminating because what disturbed observers was not simply the fact of the casualties but that the casualties seemed to be coming without *much to show for them*. The attritional warfare that marked both the Civil War and the Great War meant that victory only came after the slow eroding of the enemy war effort, both military and economic, and not in the visible conquest of enemy terrain. Both generals thus seemed stuck, unable to move their forces in any meaningful way. The massive casualties they suffered seemed pointless.

That such lack of movement on the battlefield was in fact a foundational part of the kind of war they were fighting was both true and irrelevant to the lessons taken. Robert E. Lee suffered substantially higher casualties as a percentage of his forces than Grant did, but Lee's reputation for movement and dash—for *achievement*—made those casualties appear as though they were in service of something. With Haig, the interesting comparison is to the 1918 campaigns. The casualty rates in the Entente's winning offensives of the summer of 1918 were similar to those of 1916–1917, the years of stagnation, but because they pushed the German army back those rates have been ignored. Even more fascinating, the ex post facto credit for that success has tended to be given to everyone but Haig. Rather than recognizing that the same commander of the battles of 1916 and 1917 was in command in 1918, the tendency instead has been to focus on other commanders, crediting them with making the difference in the summer of 1918. There is at least an argument for Ferdinand Foch on the French side, but Haig's role is also diminished in favor of generals like John Monash of the Australian Corps, or Walter Rawlinson of the BEF.[37]

Contrast this to the case of Pershing. The Americans came late to the Great War, with substantial US forces only appearing on the battlefield in 1918. Luckily for the United States, this was also the year that the war broke open, away from the stalemated trench warfare of the previous years. It was also the year that the Entente triumphed. The combination of those things— more free-flowing combat and the ensuing victory—meant that while US forces suffered substantial casualties in such battles as Belleau Wood and the Meuse-Argonne, they never experienced the sustained and seemingly useless grinding of 1916–1917. The casualties of Belleau Wood and the Meuse-Argonne seemed in service of a great victory. Unsurprisingly, therefore, the criticism that attended both Grant and Haig never attached itself to Pershing. Rather, during the war and after, he was seen as the triumphal victor, someone deserving the thanks of "a grateful nation," as the *New York Times* headlined on September 8, 1919.[38] Congress promoted him to general of the armies, a rank they had created just for him.[39] There was never the ambivalence about Pershing that marked the other two generals.

Comparing all three shows that the central lesson taken from the wars was that the casualties suffered had to be for something visible. Mere attrition was not enough. Rather there had to be movement, conquest, and gain in return for those casualties. World War II highlights that lesson, as the casualty rates of both the United States and Britain during the reconquest of Europe in 1944–1945 were in the same range as that of the Great War, but the near constant advance of that period made those casualties seem worthwhile. This lesson, notably, is less about what the Civil War deeded to the Great War than about what people took from both those wars and later ones.

Lessons of the Civil War: Hoping for Alternatives

There were, however, lessons that came more directly from the Civil War to the Great War, in particular the continuing sense that there were alternatives to the gainless slaughter. Both the Americans and the British saw in the Civil War ways of fighting that did not imitate Grant's methods. There were other models on both the Union and Confederate side, models that provide more resolution than attrition. In this, the lesson reinforced the notion that the casualties and lack of gain were a choice rather than an inevitable part of total war, and that choosing a new leader would have some useful effect.

This interpretation of the facts on the ground dates prior to 1865. During the Civil War, Abraham Lincoln, seeking alternatives to the way the war was being waged, ran through commanders at a rate of speed that would have made former New York Yankees' owner George Steinbrenner proud. Though this was perhaps justified—Ambrose Burnside was no one's idea of a great captain—the president often failed to recognize that the situation was creating the issues, not the specific commander. George Meade was particularly badly treated when, having won a critical victory at Gettysburg in 1863, he was soon essentially superseded by Ulysses S. Grant. Still, by the time Grant came east, Lincoln had seemingly learned that repeated relief of his overall commanders would not change the war that they faced, and he showed substantial loyalty to Grant through the rest of the war, even under public pressure.

The other form that this search for alternatives took during the Civil War was an ongoing push for a compromise peace. The effort, which became especially strong in 1864, was predicated on the idea that the war was a failure. The "Chicago Platform" of the Democratic Party in 1864 was an explicit attempt to provide an alternate strategy to end the "failure" of the war. The lessons learned "after four years of failure to restore the Union by the experiment of war" were that "immediate efforts [should] be made for a cessation of hostilities, with a view of an ultimate convention of the States, or other peaceable means, to the end that, at the earliest practicable moment, peace may be restored on the basis of the Federal Union of the States."[40] Governor Horatio Seymour of New York, the president of the convention, explicitly connected this belief in the failure of the war to the "sacrifice [of] the blood and treasure of our people." It was time, Seymour argued, to look for some other way. "Never in the world's history have soldiers given up their lives more freely than have those of the armies which have battled for the flag of our Union in the Southern States. The world will hold that they have done all that arms can do."[41] The way to stop the slaughter was to end the war—not by victory, but by peace.

After the Civil War, a new generation of American soldiers was educated in its lessons. The officers of the Civil War went on to become the educators of the postwar era. When John J. Pershing went to West Point, the superintendent was Wesley Merritt, who had risen to the rank of (brevet) major general in the cavalry during the Civil War. Pershing remembered that "among General Merritt's friends were Grant, Sherman, Sheridan, and other great soldiers of the Civil War, several of whom came to visit West Point during my cadet days."[42] The "greatest thrill" of his life came later at West Point, as he was part of the honor guard for the train carrying Grant's body to his funeral in New York.[43]

But Pershing, despite thinking that Grant was "the greatest general our country has produced," did not remain wedded to Grant's approach.[44] What he drew from the Civil War, the "wellspring" of doctrine, was rather an alternative approach.[45] "Trench warfare," Pershing wrote, was "not new to Americans, as both the Union and Confederate armies in the Civil War had used them extensively."[46] But the Great War was doomed to "stalemate" unless the Entente forces fought differently, using methods of "open warfare."[47] Americans, Pershing believed, had a "unique character" that made them well suited to "open warfare" where soldiers moved quickly and aggressively to attack the main body of the enemy army.[48] Coming to France in 1918, Pershing argued publicly that the Americans could break open the stalemated war. "Victory could not be won by the costly process of attrition," he wrote later, "but it must be won by driving the enemy out into the open and engaging him in a war of movement."[49] The British and French, after years of stalemate, thought Pershing to be wildly overconfident.

The events of 1918, though, proved Pershing right—or so he believed. The Entente offensives of the summer and fall of that year broke open the German lines and restored the speed and mobility of 1914, bringing the combatants out of the muck and back into the green fields of France. It was the "American soldier," Pershing thought, who had forced the German enemy out of his trenches and then used their skill to "annihilate him in the open."[50] Woodrow Wilson agreed, writing to Pershing with his congratulations, emphasizing the method as much as the result: "the boys have done what we expected of them and did it in a way that we most admire."[51] Never mind the heavy casualties the United States experienced, the "new spirit of aggressiveness" that Pershing and the Americans had brought with them had broken open the stalemate and returned the war to a state where it could be won.[52]

Douglas Haig, of course, believed quite strongly that the American methods did not work, causing casualties among them that rivaled what the British and French had suffered. What had really worked was the concerted and combined efforts of the British and French offensives in the summer of 1918. But, in some regards, Haig's vision of war was similar to Pershing's. It came from a comparable wellspring of knowledge about the Civil War. When Haig had been at the British Army Staff College in the 1890s, one of his instructors had been G. F. R. Henderson, a British officer who had done extensive studying of the Civil War and thought it offered a great deal of insight for future conflicts involving British forces. Henderson believed that a future British general would command a giant army of draftees, one composed of mass numbers of conscripts, inexperienced at war, "constituted . . . as were the armies of the American Civil War."[53] To use that army effectively, British leaders should look to Grant's behavior in the Battle of the Wilderness in 1864, "a better clue to the fighting of the future than any other which history records."[54] The Wilderness, and indeed the entire Overland campaign, was, Henderson thought, "the first time [that] the enormous armies of the Union were maneuvered in harmonious combination, and the superior force was exerted to its full effect."[55] Henderson also recognized that trenches would play a substantial role in conflicts to come but thought that a general who maneuvered effectively could overcome such defenses. Haig did indeed end up with an army much like Grant's, full of volunteers and draftees, civilian rather than professional. He could not maneuver in the way Henderson pointed to because of the ubiquitous trench system, but it is notable that Haig always aimed his offensives (sometimes in wildly overoptimistic ways) to not just grind the Germans down but also to break through the trench system and get back into open terrain, to get back to even the limited freedom that Grant had had. Like Pershing, he had visions of a war that was open and about victory rather than attrition.

Haig did have other alternatives to think about, presented in the form of threats against his own position. When David Lloyd George became British prime minister in 1916, he emphasized the idea of moving Britain's main effort outside of the Western Front, whether in Italy, Turkey, or the Middle East. Win the war, Lloyd George thought, but do it anywhere other than the Western Front (and the British generals there). Much of Lloyd George's maneuvering was aimed at putting resources into a theater where Haig wasn't present, as if that would change the course of the war. But, while Lloyd George succeeded in building up the British effort in the Middle East, he never quite succeeded in shifting the main effort from the Western Front.

If not a change in theater, then how about a change in commander? Lloyd

George made efforts in that direction as well, especially after the disaster at Passchendaele in 1917 and the near catastrophe of the March 1918 German offensives but found that Haig's identification with the war made him hard to fire. Firing Haig would concede that the war effort was going badly wrong and potentially put Lloyd George himself in political danger. Thus, while Lloyd George could get rid of the chair of the Imperial General Staff, Sir William Robertson, and pack Haig's command with officers he liked, Haig himself proved untouchable. Instead, Lloyd George was reduced to trying to control Haig by limiting the flow of replacement soldiers for the latter's casualties. Through 1917 and into 1918, this policy starved Haig of manpower in order to reduce potential offensive action. "[Haig] wrote of offensives," Lloyd George said in 1918, "and asked for men. He would get neither. He had eaten his cake, in spite of warnings."[56]

The military lessons of the Civil War offered a rich bounty for the two later generals. They might invoke Grant or Sherman or Robert E. Lee or Stonewall Jackson to make their case. For both, Grant remained a notable figure, but what is truly distinctive is the difference between Pershing and Haig. Haig was trapped by the circumstances of the war into an attritional fight with little room for the kind of maneuver that Henderson had highlighted for him. Pershing, by contrast, came in with a vision, one which he then (at least in his own mind) carried out. Whether the vision was correct was less important than that he and the rest of the United States believed it. He had used the lessons of the Civil War effectively and well.

Lessons of the Two Wars, Continued: National Political Fights

The lessons of the two wars were not just military, and not just for the generals. They were also political, in ways that are important for future generations to understand. As with most wars, both the Civil War and the Great War were marked by domestic political fights, which Grant, Pershing, and Haig were drawn into because of their military preeminence. This is not unique to them, as other generals in the histories of both countries have had roles in political infighting. What made things different for Grant, Pershing, and Haig was that, unlike most of the other generals, these three were involved in politics at the highest level. Because they were avatars of the national war effort they were inevitably involved in political discussions around the conflicts.

That level of political involvement is remarkable, given how little-known the three generals were in national political terms before their wars. Grant was essentially unknown on the national political scene until fairly far into the Civil War. It was only when he started succeeding in the western theater and then particularly when he came east in 1864–1865 that he became a political figure, even potentially as a presidential candidate. Abraham Lincoln worried that Grant would try to become a political rival to him and so the president made inquiries before Grant came east as to whether the general was interested in politics. When assured he was not, the president reacted positively, "for when this Presidential grub once gets to gnawing at a man, nobody can tell how far in it has got."[57] But if Grant himself had no ambition, others did for him, anointing him as a possible alternative to Lincoln.[58] When Vicksburg was captured, one of Grant's officers wrote, "Vicksburg is ours. The Mississippi River is opened, and Gen. Grant is to be our next President."[59] While Grant never represented a genuine political threat to Lincoln, the prediction came truer than not, as Grant was in fact the next elected president of the United States.

While Grant was not a direct political rival to Lincoln, he nonetheless represented a political danger. The bloodiness of the Eastern Theater in 1864 seriously threatened Lincoln's political prospects.[60] The weekly casualty reports essentially became political advertisements against Lincoln. As the summer of 1864 progressed with little more news than that Grant continued to sustain tens of thousands of casualties (and that Sherman was moving slowly southward), Lincoln and the Republicans grew increasingly nervous about the upcoming election. The criticism could be fierce, with the *New York Herald* calling Lincoln's administration "a deplorable failure."[61] The arrival of Confederate General Jubal Early and thousands of soldiers in front of the fortifications of Washington, DC, in early July 1864, coupled with Grant's slow response, seemed to symbolize all that was going wrong with the war effort.[62] Lincoln, standing on the ramparts of Fort Stevens in full sight of Confederate snipers, may well have been contemplating the political rather than physical peril of the situation, ignoring as he did repeated admonitions to get down from his perch.[63] By August 1864, Lincoln, his evaluation driven by the military campaign, thought that losing the election was "exceedingly probable."[64] Lincoln's opponent in 1864 was George McClellan, who had been one of Grant's predecessors, illustrating how the person in the senior military position acquired substantial political weight, either personally or indirectly. Former president Millard Fillmore wrote in March 1864 that "as a general rule, I am not in favor of electing military chieftains to the Presidency;" he was, however, willing to make an exception for McClellan, a "truly patriotic and skillful military man of disinterested devotion to his country." "It would," Fillmore continued, "save the United States from 'ruin.'" [65]

Lincoln was saved not by Grant but by Admiral David Farragut and General William Sherman. Farragut's capture of Mobile Bay, Alabama, in August 1864 put the last great Southern port in Union hands and almost completely blocked international trade with the Confederacy. Sherman's capture of Atlanta in early September 1864 added the largest industrial city in the South to the Union haul and seriously undercut the Confederate war effort. Both victories were the good military news that Lincoln desperately needed. As William Seward put it at the time, "Sherman and Farragut knocked the bottom out of [the Democrats]." [66] The pro-Lincoln "Peace Dial" newspaper ran a cartoon after Atlanta and Mobile with a sickly figure in bed labeled "Alarming Illness of Mr. Peace Democracy," while a nurse stands over him holding a bottle of "Mobile Bitters" and an "Atlanta Pill." [67] Philip Sheridan's victories in October 1864 in the Shenandoah Valley continued Lincoln's resurgence and he won reelection in 1864. Nonetheless, Grant—or any person in Grant's position—had a strong effect on domestic politics, whatever their personal ambitions.

Pershing, too, was spoken of presidentially. [68] Woodrow Wilson, the Democratic incumbent in 1920, was coming to the end of his second term, which, to honor George Washington's precedent, had traditionally meant he would not run for reelection. While Wilson wanted to ignore that precedent, he did not have a great deal of support in the Democratic Party. [69] Pershing, because of his exalted status, came to be seen as a potential replacement, even during the war. His maneuverings on the terms of a German armistice in 1918 were seen as a first step toward the presidency. Edward House, who was in Paris in his usual role as Woodrow Wilson's fixer, wrote that "everyone believes" that Pershing's actions are "a clear announcement of his intention to become a candidate for the Presidency in 1920." [70] Pershing did not actually seem to have intended that, but his position meant that he could not escape such interpretations. [71] When he came home, the speculation intensified. As the historian Donald Smythe has noted, every major American war sent one of its generals to the White House.[72] Pershing, the hero of France, seemed a natural part of that progression, and there was even the suggestion that he be nominated by *both* parties.[73] But because of the rapidly growing unpopularity of Wilson's policies in the aftermath of the war, Pershing's identification with those policies, and the general's deep-seated inability and unwillingness to campaign, Pershing's candidacy withered on the vine. As with Grant, the situation had more to do with position than person. Pershing was largely unknown politically before the Great War, and it was his commanding role that elevated him, not anything particular to the man. Again we see the lesson of how the unique role of a particular general can make them inherently a political presence, whatever their background or personal preference.

British Prime Minister Lloyd George, unlike Lincoln, never faced an election during the Great War, but Douglas Haig was still a political threat. Lloyd George knew that, just as he had replaced Asquith as prime minister without going to the polls, so too might he be replaced. He was thus always aware of potential threats. In 1917–1918, Lloyd George's ally Lord Northcliffe, the great—if somewhat deranged—press baron, began to champion Haig against Lloyd George's interventions in military matters. His papers ran editorials criticizing interference with the military and exhorting politicians to keep their "Hands Off the Army!"[74] Lloyd George, snorting that Northcliffe was "the mere kettledrum of Sir Douglas Haig," saw the threat in political terms rather than policy ones.[75]

Haig's political position was not simply a domestic one. Forces under his command included substantial contingents from Canada and Australia, and imperial politics forced the British to keep them unified on the Western Front. The governments of both countries paid careful attention to how those forces were used, even down to the battlefield level, something that made their employment as much a political issue as a military one. Worse, Haig had the habit of refusing to tell anyone what he was doing with the imperial forces, something that annoyed not only Lloyd George but also the Australian and Canadian leaderships. Canadian prime minister Robert Borden resorted to cultivating sources within the Canadian Corps to find out when the force was being used.[76] In the aftermath of the twin disasters of Passchendaele and the German spring offensives of 1918, Borden sidestepped both Lloyd George and Haig by summoning the senior Canadian commander on the Western Front, Sir Arthur Currie, to demand a full briefing. Enraged by what he called the "incompetence and blundering stupidity of the whiskey and soda British H.Q. Staff," Borden went after Lloyd George.[77] Haig might have defended himself on the movement issue by pointing out that such decisions did not rise to the level of a prime minister's office, but that ship had long since sailed; the Western Front and Haig were simply too much identified with the national and imperial war effort by that point for it not to be a political issue. Haig, like Grant and Pershing, held military responsibility at such a level that his decisions and actions inevitably had political implications and ones that affected the entire political scene.

In many ways, this seems an obvious lesson: that in a conflict, the top of the military hierarchy inevitably shades over into the political side, and the generals at that top become national political figures. The key difference is that it is the *position*, not the man, that creates this dynamic. Generals like Grant, Pershing, and Haig, were not particularly politically ambitious before the wars. Instead, their positions inevitably transformed them into political figures.

The Legacies of the Civil War and Great War, Again: Memorialization

One of the greatest legacies of both the Civil War and the Great War was how they remained a central presence in the lives of the Americans (the Civil War) and the British (the Great War). These are two of the most memorialized wars in modern history, their remembrances still omnipresent in cities large and villages small. That memorialization included the generals. Their central role did not end when the conflicts stopped. How Grant, Pershing, and Haig were remembered after the war was shaped by their identification with the war effort itself. Passing judgment on them was passing judgment on the war, and their reputations rose and fell alongside perceptions of their wars. We have already seen the historiographical form this took, but there was a public one as well.

That public ebb and flow affected Grant immensely. In the immediate aftermath of the Civil War, Grant was an immensely popular figure. With Lincoln's assassination, he was the victorious leader of the Union effort, and with Robert E. Lee's passing in 1870, his status as the lone remaining figure of legend grew ever higher. He was elected president in 1868 and reelected in 1872. Grant thus not only fought and won the Civil War in popular imagining but also oversaw America's recovery from that war, helping define not just the war but its aftermath. When he died in 1885, there was a wave of mourning, with a quarter of a million people visiting his body lying in state in New York City. A paper in South Carolina (!) noted that his death "will be honestly felt as a national affliction all over the wide Union, without reference to section or party."[78] Roughly 1.5 million people lined the course of his funeral parade.[79] At his passing, his future reputation seemed assured. "When prejudices pass away and time brings calmness, justice, and reason to pass upon General Grant's life, character, and achievement, he will hold a very high place in the esteem of the citizens of this country," said the *Vicksburg Post*.[80]

The *Post* could not have been more wrong. As the myth of the Lost Cause continued to grow in the late nineteenth century, Grant, much more than Lincoln, became the face of destruction of the Confederacy. Robert E. Lee was the heroic central figure of the mythos, and Grant, the man who beat him, was fit into the narrative as a villain, a slovenly drunk who shoveled men into bloody battles to overwhelm the gallant Confederates. Grant's public legacy became that of a butcher, a renewal of the 1864 image. His close identification with the Union war effort played into that evolution in a way that no other Northern general's (with the exception of William Sherman's) did. So it stayed in the public mind through the twentieth century. Films made about the Civil War disproportionately sympathized with the South, and the most popular documentary about the conflict, Ken Burns's *Civil War*, used a notably Lost Cause narrative, casting Lee as the gallant and outnumbered defender of the South overwhelmed by Grant's resources and sheer numbers.[81] Grant's image has improved in the twenty-first century, as the United States began to reckon with the racial inequities of the Lost Cause view, but his public recovery has not risen as high as it has with historians.

Like Grant, Pershing became the public face of his own great conflict. During the interwar period, both the Great War and Pershing loomed large in the public mind. The image was somewhat ambivalent—the revelations of secret diplomacy and the failure of the peace process in the 1920s had soured Americans on their participation. The war no longer seemed like it had been such a valiant crusade. It took more than a century to create a monument to the Great War in Washington, DC. Fairly or not, this ambivalence affected Pershing. When mandatory retirement caught up with him in 1924, there was no serious attempt to keep him on the active list (as had been done with Admiral George Dewey after the Spanish-American War). The event was marked by a dinner with a number of dignitaries, including Theodore Roosevelt Jr., but no general celebration. President Calvin Coolidge sent a letter of thanks. The *New York Times* ran a front-page article, but not on the top line.[82] The nation had moved on from the conflict and the general who embodied it.

The forgetting of the Great War and Pershing accelerated after World War II. The latter conflict not only dwarfed the American effort in the Great War but also did not have the same ambivalence associated with it. World War II was "the good war."[83] Pershing's funeral in 1948 reflected this overshadowing. It was an impressive ceremony but did not compare to Grant's. The ceremony did not bring the country to a halt, and even President Truman decided not to give a eulogy.[84] Pershing's legacy after his death was to be almost forgotten, much like the war he fought. The plans to build a memorial to him quickly lost steam because neither Congress nor the public was willing to pay for it. Land was set aside in central DC but was so neglected by the early 1960s, squalid with litter and overgrowth, that the *Washington Post* wondered if the memorial would ironically actually resemble the Great War battlefields over which Pershing had led the American Expeditionary Forces. Something looking like the "plains of Verdun," the newspaper intoned, might be an appropriate spot for a statue of the general.[85] Though the monument was eventually built and finished in 1981, the categorical difference in the ways in which Pershing were remembered is clear. Grant was, and remains, among the indispensable men of American public memory, whether that image was positive or negative. Pershing does not.

Haig's legacy and its evolution more resembles Grant's than Pershing's. He did not have the postwar political career that Grant did. Instead, he spent his remaining years still deeply connected to issues of that war, working for the better treatment of ex-servicemen and founding the British Legion. When he died in 1928, like Grant, he was publicly mourned by hundreds of thousands, who saw his death as a final sacrifice to the conflict. As his body lay in state in St. Giles Church in Edinburgh, the line to view it stretched more than a mile on each of the three days it remained there.[86] The crowds were larger than for any other Great War general and seem to have been greater than for Bernard Montgomery's funeral in 1976. Cities and villages held local ceremonies to mark his death, and the funeral was broadcast by the BBC.[87] Many of the attendees were ex-servicemen, who felt linked to Haig through war, and to the war through Haig. As one observer put it, "One felt that the overpowering impulse which brought thousands of ex-servicemen . . . was the desire that members of a family feel to press close to a beloved relative before a train carries him from sight, and to assure him till the very last of their affection."[88] This linkage was continued by his gravestone in Scotland. Haig had chosen the standardized one that the Commonwealth War Graves Commission used for all the British fatalities of the war. It was a conscious marking of the war and the soldiers that fought it.

Haig's gravestone paralleled another monument to the war, the Cenotaph in London. Originally built only as a temporary structure to honor the war dead for the 1919 Victory Parade and Peace Day, the Cenotaph's focus and simplicity was so compelling to the British that public and elite pressure mounted to make it a permanent memorial. An editorial in the *Times* of London commented that "no feature of the Victory March in London made a deeper impression than the Cenotaph erected in Whitehall to the memory of 'The Glorious Dead.' Simple, grave, and beautiful in design, it has been universally recognized as a just and fitting memorial of those who have made the greatest sacrifice; and the flowers which have laid upon it since the march show the strength of its appeal to the imagination."[89] The Cenotaph memorialized the sacrifice that made victory possible, a complicated and ambivalent legacy. After Haig's death, the government moved to build a statue of him near the Cenotaph, connecting it to the man most publicly associated with that victory and that sacrifice. There was a massive controversy over the statue, but not because of Haig himself. Rather, the problem lay in the form of the statue.[90] The first proposal was a grandiose one of a towering Haig atop a rampant horse, the very symbol of victory and conquest. That was not the legacy people wanted expressed and the public outcry was fierce. One veteran wrote, "It seems to many of us who fought under him that it would be little less than a tragedy if the essential Haig were to be travestied by a rampant figure on horseback facing the shrine of our million dead."[91] Here was a strong public sense of what legacy to take from the Great War, and one that demanded that Haig's memorialization fit into that legacy. The statute ultimately put up—though still of Haig on a horse—was much less bombastic, a "realist memorial" suitable for the commander of "British armies in a realist's war."[92]

But if Haig's legacy could still be positive in the interwar period, public memory of him would sour after World War II. The failure of wartime demobilization and Lloyd George's promise to make Britain "a fit country for heroes to live in,"[93] coupled with the Great Depression and another world war that started in 1939, darkened and soured the British on the Great War. A growing sense that the conflict had been useless affected visions of Haig and, similar to Grant, the wartime perception of Haig's incompetence revived and spread through the public. Rather than the general who won the war, Haig came increasingly to be seen as one of the reasons why the war had been such a failure. He was not the only general so blamed, but his near complete identification with the British effort on the Western Front meant that he was the largest culprit. Haig alone came to stand for the bloody battles at Somme and Passchendaele and received no credit for the triumphs of 1918. The popular encapsulation of this was Alan Clark's best-seller *The Donkeys*, published in 1961, which excoriated the British generals for stupidity. The book itself was about a number of different generals, but Haig was the one remembered. "A millennium of Churchills," the *Guardian* wrote in its review, fascinatingly invoking another historical figure with an evolving public reputation, "could not undo the disaster of a single Haig."[94] The partial rehabilitation of Haig by historians has never really penetrated to the public, and his legacy remains one of mud and blood.[95]

Comparison and Conclusion

What, then, does engaging with the lessons and legacies of the Civil War and Great War tell us about generals like Grant, Pershing, and Haig? Though we have looked at different aspects of their experiences, the binding thread is the way in which Grant, Pershing, and Haig came to be inextricably identified with the wars they fought, in a fashion that happened with few other generals and few other wars in modern American or British history. The result of that identification, both during the war and after, was that, to a greater or lesser extent, all three generals became identified with the heavy casualties of the industrialized mass wars they were fighting, had to deal with the search for alternatives to the fighting they were doing, were inevitably sucked into the larger political fights of those wars, and were remembered in ways that were inextricably linked to the image of the wars themselves.

There were obvious differences in how these played out, of course. Grant's relationship with Lincoln was much more congenial than Pershing's with Wilson or (especially) Haig's with Lloyd George. Grant's war was one that

America fought alone, while American and British forces in the Great War were part of a much larger coalition. Pershing and Haig not only had to react to their own political and military issues but also had to deal with the French and other coalition partners. Grant and Haig were involved in the entirety of their wars; Pershing did not come to the Great War until several years in.

All three generals themselves felt some ownership for their respective conflicts and acted accordingly; it was not entirely imposed on them from the outside. Grant, for example, was motivated to run for president in 1868 largely because of his feeling that the administration of President Andrew Johnson was throwing away the results of the Civil War. If he did not run, Grant wrote to Sherman in 1868, no matter who was elected, it "would lose to us, largely, the result of the costly war we have gone through."[96] Pershing wrote a two-volume account of his experience in the Great War, published in 1931, perhaps partly to stop the gradual fading of that war from the American mind.[97] Haig did not write memoirs but, more subtly, spent much of his postwar years carefully rewriting the course of the war to portray himself as always being the dominant figure. Haig edited his own diary, lobbied the official historian, and wrote copious letters to others to make sure his version of history triumphed, with himself as the hero of the story. The war, and its course, was Haig's, he believed, and he made sure that that is what "the history will show."[98]

A major legacy for both wars that this has left us is the anthropomorphizing of the conflicts. We have been considering the effect of identifying the war so closely with a single person on Grant, Pershing, and Haig, but perhaps most important is the effect of such identification on the wars themselves. There is a danger in seeing a single man as the representative of a larger war. Doing so obscures much of the complexity of that war, subsuming it into the simplicity of the man. In the Civil War, a fixation on the eastern theater and on the fight between Grant and Lee (important as it was) has skewed Civil War studies, leaving somewhat neglected the great expanse of that war in the middle and west of the country. The Union capture of the Mississippi River was, arguably, more important than anything that happened in the East, but it remains comparatively ignored. British understanding of the Great War has been held back by the obsession with Haig; "subjective assessments of his character" have stood in for "more complex studies of the performance of the British military machine."[99] Pershing's case is a bit more ambiguous, as the understanding of the United States in the Great War was mostly just neglected, but even here the danger of focusing on Pershing's experience is that it elides the way that the United States joined the conflict in the middle of the war rather than at the start. This danger is obviously not one limited to war leaders. Both British and American cultures tend to try and use individuals as stand-ins for larger social, political, and economic movements and evolutions: Martin Luther King as the avatar of the American civil rights movement of the 1960s or Margaret Thatcher for the conservative retrenchment of 1980s Britain. The effects are similarly distorting. Historians, too: the Great Man approach to history has long been problematic, as it shifts everyone on the historical stage to the role of supporting actor to the leading man.

That larger issue is beyond the scope of this chapter, however, and what we have seen in this examination and comparison is that Grant, Pershing, and Haig have to be understood not only for what they did themselves but also for what they came to represent. They cannot be analyzed apart from the conflicts they waged. For their respective societies, they *were* the conflicts they waged. The Civil War remains the iconic war of American history, and Grant one of its most critical characters. Such is the case also with the Great War, Haig, and the British. If Pershing is not the symbol that the other two are, it is because his war has faded in a way that Grant and Haig's never have, their wars remaining as much a presence now as when they happened.

Notes

1. The quote in the title is from George S. Duncan, *Douglas Haig as I Knew Him* (London: Pen and Sword, 1954), 136.

2. In fact, one recent biographer summarized Pershing's entire life up to the Great War as his "formative years," that is, the years that prepared him for the important stuff. Tim McNeese, *Time in the Wilderness: The Formative Years of John "Black Jack" Pershing in the American West* (Lincoln, NE: Potomac Books, 2021).

3. It is notable that biographies of Scott tend to give equal space to all the wars he participated, a great contrast to biographies of Grant and Pershing. See, for example, Timothy D. Johnson, *Winfield Scott: The Quest for Military Glory* (Lawrence: University Press of Kansas, 1998). Scott's most important conflict, the Mexican-American War, has never been seen as one of the truly iconic wars in American history, unlike the Revolution, the Civil War, or World War II.

4. His closer connection gave him solid control over grand strategy and also a tendency toward a fair bit of micromanagement over the US Navy, as his naval subordinates would have been happy to testify (anonymously).

5. Robert E. Lee was not, of course, a United States general during the Civil War, having committed treason by taking up arms against it.

6. Pershing was something of an accidental general. President Wilson preferred General Frederick Funston to command the American Expeditionary Force, but Funston died of a sudden heart attack in January 1917.

7. Nimrod Tal, "The American Civil War in British Military Thought from the 1880s to the 1930s," *Civil War History* 60, no. 4 (December 2014): 409–435, at 410. One of Haig's biographers specifically invoked Grant as a comparison. G. D. Sheffield, *The Chief: Douglas Haig and the British Army* (London: Aurum Press, 2011), 370.

8. Technically, General George Meade commanded the Army of the Potomac, but Grant traveled with that army rather than remaining in Washington. Certainly, Meade did not really feel that he led the army.

9. Andrew Carroll, *My Fellow Soldiers: General John Pershing and the Americans Who Helped Win the Great War* (New York: Penguin, 2017), 108.

10. In fact, when Pershing first arrived, there was no overall commander of the Entente and Allied forces on the Western Front. It was only in March 1918, during the panic of the German Spring Offensives, that General Ferdinand Foch of France was put in supreme command.

11. Though even they have their defenders, even McClellan. Ethan S. Rafuse, *McClellan's War: The Failure of Moderation in the Struggle for the Union* (Bloomington: Indiana University Press, 2005) is a solidly argued example.

12. Gort is a criminally underrated general, who gave the appearance of being an aristocratic dilettante but made perhaps the single most courageous command decision of World War II when, against orders, he turned the British Expeditionary Force toward Dunkirk and the coast and, by doing so, saved the British war effort. For a work that explains the decision in nice detail, albeit one that buys into the dilettante image, see Hugh Sebag-Montefiore, *Dunkirk: Fight to the Last Man* (London: Viking, 2006).

13. Quoted in Arthur Jacob Marder, *From the Dreadnought to Scapa Flow: The War Years—To the Eve of Jutland, 1914–1916* (London: Pen and Sword, 1965), 77.

14. Brooks Simpson, "Continuous Hammering and Mere Attrition: Lost Cause Critics and the Military Reputation of Ulysses S. Grant," in *The Myth of the Lost Cause and Civil War History*, ed. Gary W. Gallagher and Alan T. Nolan (Bloomington: Indiana University Press, 2000). I'm including the historians of the Dunning School of Reconstruction in this larger group. See John David Smith and J. Vincent Lowery, eds. *The Dunning School: Historians, Race, and the Meaning of Reconstruction* (Lexington: University Press of Kentucky, 2013).

15. Bruce Catton, *A Stillness at Appomattox* (Garden City, NY: Doubleday, 1953) is a good example.

16. Ethan Sepp Rafuse, "Still a Mystery? General Grant and the Historians, 1981–2006," *Journal of Military History* 71, no. 3 (July 2007): 849–874. Rafuse's essay is essential reading on modern interpretations of Grant.

17. Quoted in Rafuse, "Grant and the Historians," 853. McFeely could only barely put at the end of his evaluation that the only redeeming feature of the campaign was that "it worked." McFeely's work was criticized by some, including James McPherson and Brooks Simpson. It is interesting to note, however, that Grant was not subject to another major biography for a fair while, with historians preferring to focus on William Sherman, who seemed to have less of a bloody hand. It should also be noted that McFeely disliked Haig, if anything, more than he did Grant. "Nor was there in Grant the icy disdain of a Douglas Haig, the British Commander in World War I who, safely behind the lines and deafened to reality, could send his men out of the trenches into the roar of almost certain death." William S. McFeely, *Grant: A Biography* (New York: Easton, 1987), 80.

18. Joan Waugh, *U.S. Grant: American Hero, American Myth* (University of North Carolina Press, 2009); Brooks D. Simpson, *Ulysses S. Grant: Triumph over Adversity, 1822–1865* (Boston: Houghton Mifflin, 2000). See also Jean Edward Smith, *Grant* (New York: Simon and Schuster, 2001), especially for the useful historiographical discussion in the preface; Ronald C. White, *American Ulysses: A Life of Ulysses S. Grant* (New York: Random House, 2016) is thoughtfully written.

19. Waugh, *U.S. Grant*, 1.

20. The answer as to who is correct is the revisionists, but that's an argument for another day.

21. Steven Trout, *On the Battlefield of Memory: The First World War and American Remembrance, 1919–1941* (Tuscaloosa: University of Alabama Press, 2010), 118–141.

22. Edward M. Coffman, "The Emergence of Military Managers: Pershing and Marshall," *Reviews in American History* 6, no. 2 (June 1978): 243–248.

23. Russell Weigley, "The Necessity of Force: The Civil War, World War II, and the American View of War," in *War Comes Again: Comparative Vistas on the Civil War and World War II*, ed. G. S. Boritt and Stephen E. Ambrose (New York: Oxford University Press, 1995): 225–244, at 225.

24. Google Ngram of "John J. Pershing, Ulysses S. Grant," accessed November 10, 2020, https://books.google.com/ngrams/graph?content=John+J.+Pershing%2C+Ulysses+S.+Grant&year_start=1800&year_end=2019&corpus=28&smoothing=3&. Google Ngram has its flaws but this is highly indicative.

25. Coffman, "Emergence," 244.

26. Sheffield, *The Chief*, for example, spends about 280 pages on Haig's experience in the Great War and about 80 pages on the entire rest of his life. Chernow's biography of Grant spends more than 650 pages on his war experience and slightly over 400 pages on his two-term presidency. This is not to say that this is *wrong*, just to point out the emphasis. Ron Chernow, *Grant* (New York: Penguin, 2017).

27. Frank Vandiver's biography of Pershing, for example, spends two-thirds of its pages on Pershing's life outside of the Great War. Frank E. Vandiver, *Black Jack: The Life and Times of John J. Pershing* (College Station: Texas A&M University Press, 1977). Donald Smythe's two-volume biography of Pershing spends less than 50 percent of its time on the war. Donald Smythe, *Guerrilla Warrior: The Early Life of John*

J. *Pershing* (New York: Scribner, 1973) and Donald Smythe, *Pershing, General of the Armies* (Bloomington: Indiana University Press, 1986).

28. Unlike the Lost Cause, the Lost Generation narrative has the virtue of being reasonably accurate, albeit focused on the middle and upper class. See Jay M. Winter, "Britain's 'Lost Generation' of the First World War," *Population Studies* 31, no. 3 (November 1977) and idem., *The Great War and the British People* (Cambridge, MA: Harvard University Press, 1986), 65–102.

29. David French, "Sir Douglas Haig's Reputation, 1918–1928: A Note," *Historical Journal* 28, no. 4 (December 1985): 953–960.

30. Notably, Alan Clark, *The Donkeys* (New York: Morrow, 1962), from which the label "donkeys" came, emerged after World War II.

31. Haig's historiography rivals Grant's. Examples are J. P. Harris, *Douglas Haig and the First World War* (Cambridge, UK: Cambridge University Press, 2008), something of a neutral arbiter between the bad general/great captain schools; Sheffield, *The Chief* is of the revisionist school; Gerard J. De Groot, *Douglas Haig, 1861–1928* (London: Unwin Hyman, 1988) is a bit old, but decidedly *not* revisionist.

32. For the evolution of the image of the Great War, see Dan Todman, *The First World War: Myth and Memory* (London: Continuum, 2006).

33. D. M. Giangreco, "Casualty Projections for the U.S. Invasions of Japan, 1945–1946: Planning and Policy Implications," *Journal of Military History* 61, no. 3 (July 1997): 521.

34. To be fair, the editor was a Peace Democrat. Quoted in Waugh, *U.S. Grant,* 94.

35. Quoted in Anna Maclay Green, "Civil War Public Opinion of General Grant," *Journal of the Illinois State Historical Society (1908–1984)* (1929): 1–64.

36. Paul Harris and Sanders Marble, "The 'Step-By-Step' Approach: British Military Thought and Operational Method on the Western Front, 1915–1917," *War in History* 15, no. 1 (January 2008): 17–42, at 37.

37. Tim Travers makes the argument for Rawlinson in Tim Travers, "The Evolution of British Strategy and Tactics on the Western Front in 1918: GHQ, Manpower, and Technology," *Journal of Military History* 54, no. 2 (April 1990): 173–200, at 197, 199.

38. *New York Times,* September 8, 1919.

39. Smythe, *General of the Armies,* 260.

40. "1864 Democratic Party Platform," accessed August 29, 2017, http://www.presidency.ucsb.edu/ws/?pid=29578.

41. *Official Proceedings of the Democratic National Convention, Held in 1864 at Chicago* (Chicago: Times Steam Book and Job Printing House, 1864), 23.

42. John J. Pershing and John T. Greenwood, *My Life before the World War, 1860–1917: A Memoir* (Lexington: University Press of Kentucky, 2013), 45.

43. Quoted in Smythe, *Guerrilla Warrior,* 7.

44. Pershing, *Life before the World War,* 33.

45. Gene Fax, "Pershing's 'Open Warfare' Doctrine in the Light of American Military History," *Army History* 113 (Fall 2019): 32, 34.

46. John J. Pershing, *My Experiences in the World War* (New York: Frederick A. Stokes, 1931), 11.

47. Pershing, *My Experiences*, 11.

48. Fax, "Pershing's 'Open Warfare' Doctrine," 32, 34.

49. Quoted in Fax, "Pershing's 'Open Warfare,'" 32.

50. Fax, "Pershing's Open Warfare," 36. "Annihilate," of course, invokes the classic argument made in Russell Weigley, *The American Way of War: A History of United States Military Strategy and Policy* (Bloomington: Indiana University Press, 1977).

51. Mitchell Yockelson, "General John J. Pershing and His Quest to Form the American First Army," *On Point* 23, no. 1 (Summer 2017): 36–43, at 42.

52. John J. Pershing, "Addresses Made By General John J. Pershing, U. S. A., and Secretary of War Newton D. Baker: To Officers and Soldiers of the 33rd Division in the Field, Luxembourg, April 22, 1919," *Journal of the Illinois State Historical Society (1908–1984)* 15, no. 1/2 (1922): 519–523, at 519.

53. Quoted in Jay Luvaas, "G. F. R. Henderson and the American Civil War," *Military Affairs* 20, no. 3 (Autumn 1956): 139–153, at 146.

54. Quoted in Luvaas, "G. F. R. Henderson and the American," 148.

55. Quoted in Luvaas, "G. F. R. Henderson and the American," 148.

56. Quoted in David R. Woodward, "Did Lloyd George Starve the British Army of Men Prior to the German Offensive of 21 March 1918?" *Historical Journal* 27, no. 1 (March 1984): 241–252, at 248; Elizabeth Greenhalgh, "David Lloyd George, Georges Clemenceau, and the 1918 Manpower Crisis," *Historical Journal* 50, no. 2 (June 2007): 397–421.

57. Quoted in John Y. Simon, "From Galena to Appomattox: Grant and Washburne," *Journal of the Illinois State Historical Society (1908–1984)* 58, no. 2 (Summer 1965): 165–189.

58. David Lindsey, "The Presidential Campaign of 1864 as Viewed by a Federal Army Colonel," *Georgia Historical Quarterly* 39, no. 2 (June 1955): 187–192.

59. Quoted in Waugh, *U.S. Grant*, 64.

60. Witness, for example, the extreme overreaction to a false proclamation about raising troops that was published in a few New York newspapers during May 1864. Lincoln, tense about the political-military situation, imprisoned not only the editors of the papers but even took control of the telegraph network he thought responsible. Menahem Blondheim, "'Public Sentiment Is Everything': The Union's Public Communications Strategy and the Bogus Proclamation of 1864," *Journal of American History* 89, no. 3 (December 2002): 869–899.

61. Blondheim, "Public Sentiment."

62. B. Franklin Cooling, "Civil War Deterrent: Defenses of Washington," *Military Affairs* (Winter 1965): 164–178.

63. William V. Cox, "The Defenses of Washington: General Early's Advance on the Capital and the Battle of Fort Stevens, July 11 and 12, 1864," *Records of the Columbia Historical Society, Washington, DC* 4 (1901): 135–165.

64. Quoted in George C. Osborn, "The Atlanta Campaign, 1864," *Georgia*

Historical Quarterly 34, no. 4 (December 1950): 271–287; see also William Frank Zornow, "The Unwanted Mr. Lincoln," *Journal of the Illinois State Historical Society* 45, no. 2 (Summer 1952): 146–163.

65. Quoted in Harold Dudley, "The Election of 1864," *Mississippi Valley Historical Review* 18, no. 4 (1932): 500–518.

66. Quoted in Dudley, "Election of 1864."

67. Gary L. Bunker, "The 'Campaign Dial': A Premier Lincoln Campaign Paper, 1864," *Journal of the Abraham Lincoln Association* 25, no. 1 (Winter 2004): 38–75.

68. Smythe, *Pershing, General of the Armies*, 269.

69. Though Wilson did not give up on the idea, his support slipped away after his stroke in 1919 and subsequent physical incapacitation. Wesley M. Bagby, "Woodrow Wilson, a Third Term, and the Solemn Referendum," *American Historical Review* 60, no. 3 (April 1955): 567–576.

70. Quoted in Bullitt Lowry, "Pershing and the Armistice," *Journal of American History* 55, no. 2 (September 1968): 281–291, at 287.

71. Lowry, *Pershing and the Armistice*, 288–289.

72. Smythe, *Pershing, General of the Armies*, 269. For the record: Washington from the Revolution, Jackson and Harrison from the War of 1812, Taylor from the Mexican-American War, Grant from the Civil War, and Roosevelt from the Spanish-American War.

73. Smythe, *Pershing, General of the Armies*, 270.

74. *Daily Mail*, October 13, 1916, quoted in John M. McEwen, "Northcliffe and Lloyd George at War, 1914–1918," *Historical Journal* 24, no. 3 (September 1981): 651–672.

75. Lloyd George was never at a loss for a telling phrase. Quoted in McEwen, "Northcliffe and Lloyd George," 651–672.

76. George L. Cook, "Sir Robert Borden, Lloyd George and British Military Policy, 1917–1918," *Historical Journal* 14, no. 2 (June 1971): 371–395, at 389.

77. Cook, "Sir Robert Borden," 385.

78. John Y. Simon, "Ulysses S. Grant One Hundred Years Later," *Illinois Historical Journal* 79, no. 4 (Winter 1986): 245.

79. Simon, "Grant," 245.

80. Simon, "Grant," 245.

81. For movies, see John B. Kuiper, "Civil War Films: A Quantitative Description of a Genre," *Journal of the Society of Cinematologists* 4 (1964): 87. For Burns's *The Civil War*, see Gary W. Gallagher, "How Familiarity Bred Success: Military Campaigns and Leaders in Ken Burns's *The Civil War*," in *Ken Burns's The Civil War: Historians Respond*, ed. Robert Toplin (New York: Oxford University Press, 1996), 37–60.

82. *New York Times*, September 14, 1924.

83. The phrase is, of course, Studs Terkel's. Studs Terkel, *The Good War: An Oral History of World War I* (New York: New Press, 1997).

84. William C. Mossman and M. Warner Stark, *The Last Salute: Civil and Military Funerals, 1921–1969* (Washington, DC: Department of the Army, 1972), 33.

85. Andrew S. Walgren, "The 'Forgotten Man' of Washington: The Pershing Memorial and the Battle over Military Memorialization," (Master's thesis., University of South Carolina, 2016), 41.

86. Daniel Todman, "'Sans Peur et Sans Reproche': The Retirement, Death, and Mourning of Sir Douglas Haig, 1918–1928," *Journal of Military History* 67, no. 4 (October 2003): 1086.

87. Todman, "Sans Peur," 1086.

88. Quoted in Todman, "Sans Peur," 1089.

89. *Times* (London), July 26, 1919, quoted in Allan Greenberg, "Lutyens's Cenotaph," *Journal of the Society of Architectural Historians* 48, no. 1 (March 1989): 5–23, at 6.

90. This account is drawn from Stephen Heathorn, "A 'Matter for Artists, and Not for Soldiers'? The Cultural Politics of the Earl Haig National Memorial, 1928–1937," *Journal of British Studies* 44, no. 3 (2005): 536–561.

91. Quoted in Heathorn, "A 'Matter for Artists,'" 558.

92. *Glasgow Herald*, 1931, quoted in Heathorn, "A 'Matter for Artists,'" 559.

93. Philip Abrams, "The Failure of Social Reform: 1918–1920," *Past and Present* 24, no. 1 (April 1963).

94. David Rees, "Death of a Generation: Alan Clark's *The Donkeys* review," *Guardian*, July 28, 1961.

95. Dan Todman's work on the evolution of the Great War's image over the twentieth century is wonderfully insightful on this evolution. Todman, *First World War*, esp. 70–121.

96. Quoted in White, *American Ulysses*, 463.

97. Pershing, *My Experiences in the World War*.

98. Elizabeth Greenhalgh's article on this process is remarkably thorough and impressive. See "Myth and Memory: Sir Douglas Haig and the Imposition of Allied Unified Command in March 1918," *Journal of Military History* 68, no. 3 (July 2004): 771–820. Haig quote from fn. 136, p. 818.

99. Todman, "Sans Peur," 1084. Also see Stephen Badsey, "Douglas Haig and the First World War," *War in History* 17, no. 3 (2010).

2

Abraham Lincoln, Woodrow Wilson, and Dying for One's Country

Brian Dirck

"Why has God put me in this place?" an anguished Abraham Lincoln asked when he was informed of the Union's lopsided defeat at the Battle of Fredericksburg in December 1862. Eighteen thousand soldiers on both sides were either killed or wounded; thirteen thousand were Union men. Worse still, the North was no closer to victory. "If there is a place worse than hell, I am in it," he ruefully remarked. At about the same time, he jotted down a few private thoughts regarding the relationship between God's will and the war's seemingly endless suffering. "God wills this contest, and wills that it shall not end yet," he wrote. "By his mere quiet power, on the minds of the now contestants, He could have either *saved* or *destroyed* the Union without a human contest. Yet the contest began. And having begun He could give the final victory to either side any day. Yet the contest proceeds." To Lincoln, immersed as he was in the unique "hell" of a president leading the nation through a major war, God's will in allowing the deaths of so many people must function somewhere above and beyond the mortal ken of humanity.[1]

Woodrow Wilson experienced a similar moment in May 1915, when both he and the American people were reeling from the news that the British ocean liner *Lusitania* had been torpedoed by a German U-boat, sending 1,200 passengers and crew to their deaths, including 128 Americans. The United States was not yet at war with Germany, and public opinion was sharply divided on the matter of whether America should involve itself in the Great War. But the sinking of the *Lusitania* stunned the nation, and President Wilson was furiously inundated with calls for a declaration of war against

Germany. Wilson hesitated, knowing full well that such a move would end the lives of many American soldiers, adding further to the Great War's grisly toll. "In the name of God and humanity, declare war on Germany," read one angry telegram sent to the White House. Wilson's patience broke. "War isn't declared in the name of God," he snapped. "It is a human affair entirely."[2]

As wartime presidents, Abraham Lincoln and Woodrow Wilson carried uniquely onerous burdens. Their times and their wars were quite different, and in many respects those differences do not lend themselves to easy comparison. The Civil War absolutely engulfed the Lincoln presidency from practically the moment it began until his assassination four years later, whereas Wilson enjoyed a comparatively peaceful first term until he was reluctantly compelled to involve America in a global conflict by Germany's pursuit of unrestricted submarine warfare soon after Wilson's reelection to a second term in 1916. The two wars did share a grim reality of terrible bloodletting, but Lincoln's war was truly without peer: seven hundred thousand dead Americans in four years. Wilson's war killed fewer American soldiers: approximately 116,000. Set in the context of the Great War's total casualty numbers—a staggering thirty-eight million people—America's casualties were relatively minor.

Lincoln also prosecuted the war within a different political and constitutional environment than Wilson. He faced questions regarding civil-military relations and wartime civil liberties that were unprecedented in his day. When Lincoln took the oath of office in March 1861, there was no significant congressional legislation regarding suspension of the writ of habeas corpus during wartime, for example; nor had the US Supreme Court weighed in on this important matter. Lincoln was largely left to his own devices regarding when, how, and by whom the writ could be suspended. By contrast, fifty years later, President Wilson would enter the Great War with at least some guidance on these matters from Congress and the Supreme Court. The Habeas Corpus Suspension Act of 1863 established guidelines for presidential and congressional action that Lincoln did not possess during the fraught first two years of the war; it was further refined by the habeas corpus provisions contained in the Civil Rights Act of 1871 and several relevant Supreme Court cases. In this and many other aspects of war-making, Lincoln was often forced to improvise in ways Wilson was not. (For a lengthier discussion of civil liberties in these two eras, please see Kanisorn Wongsrichanalai's first chapter in this volume.)

Wilson was of course keenly aware of Lincoln's dominating presidential legacy; at various times during his academic career as a political scientist and then later as president, he offered what might be characterized as a mixed bag of praise and criticism for his illustrious predecessor. In a tribute delivered in 1909 (the centennial of Lincoln's birth), Wilson offered the usual praise for Lincoln as a man of "great nature" who was "absolutely direct and fearless" and possessed a cool head under duress, which is required of presidential leadership in critical times. "The most valuable thing about Mr. Lincoln was that in the midst of the strain of war, in the midst of the crash of arms, he could sit quietly in his room and enjoy a book that led his thoughts from everything American, could wander in a field of dreams, while every other man was hot with the immediate contest," Wilson wrote, perhaps thinking of himself and his own ideals as he did so. Wilson was certainly not the first American to project his sense of himself upon Lincoln and see in him the traits he wished himself to emulate.[3]

At the same time, however, Wilson the Southerner pointedly omitted both any mention of Lincoln's role as the Great Emancipator and (perhaps deliberately) the natural-rights abstractions regarding human equality that lay at the very core of Lincoln's thought. One might therefore argue that Wilson's commentary on Lincoln must be taken with a large grain of salt, further complicating any direct comparisons between the two men.[4]

Yet there is value in a careful comparison: the backgrounds Lincoln and Wilson brought to their presidencies, and the parameters of their wartime leadership, highlight interesting differences and similarities between them as men and also lays bare some of the consistent and ongoing challenges experienced by any president faced with the challenge of waging war within the context of America's political system. Perhaps most of all, a comparative analysis of their respective approaches to battlefield deaths suggests an understanding of their respective wars' legacy that were markedly different in their expansive, or restricted, visions of the nation's postwar future.

Beginning with a look at their upbringing, notice the traits of strength and weakness that would mark the two in time of war: Lincoln's adaptability and connection to the people served him well, while Wilson's knowledge of past examples—the challenges Lincoln faced—gave him a strong start. Then, consider their communication skills and, finally, their attempts to justify the war's devastation by envisioning and outlining a postwar world. To start with, note that both Lincoln and Wilson were born in the South but experienced the region in different ways. Lincoln's parents attended churches led by antislavery ministers; and while this tells us little regarding Thomas Lincoln's actual views on slavery or race, his son later claimed that Thomas moved the family from Kentucky to Indiana at least "partly on account of slavery."[5] Lincoln left his Kentucky birthplace as a small child, so his Southern roots were a distant memory at best. Still, he occasionally identified himself as a Southerner and was known to exhibit a slight southern dialect in his speech: pronouncing "chair" as "cheer," for example, or occasionally lapsing into an "I reckon." But on the whole, he was not inclined toward seeing himself as a Southerner, nor did he generally adhere to a regional identity, even as others viewed him through the lens of region: a Chicago newspaperman, for example, who confessed that he could not fully trust Lincoln because he "is Southern by birth, [and] Southern in his associations."[6]

Wilson's southernness was more prolonged and intense and played a more prominent role in shaping his personality. Wilson was born in Virginia; his father, Joseph, was one of the leading figures of the Southern Presbyterian Church after it split from its Northern counterpart. Joseph Wilson supported the Confederacy, nursed wounded Confederate soldiers in his home, and was an unapologetic slaveholder. The future president grew up in Virginia and South and North Carolina, imbibing southern culture and customs in ways Lincoln never would. "The only place in the country, the only place in the world, where nothing has to be explained to me is the South," he later claimed.[7]

Although they both served as the nation's father figure in time of crisis, Lincoln and Wilson had different relationships and levels of respect for their own fathers. Thomas Lincoln endured a strained relationship with his son Abraham, who for his part was nonplussed by Thomas's lack of ambition and semiliteracy. Thomas "never did more in the way of writing than bunglingly sign his own name," Abraham disparagingly wrote. But Wilson stood in awe of his strict Presbyterian minister father; he was "one of the most inspiring fathers that ever a lad was blessed with," Woodrow later recalled. He inherited his father's sober-minded seriousness, his intense work ethic, and his preoccupation with issues of morality.[8]

Lincoln and Wilson both came of age in deeply religious households but developed different ideas about religion. Thomas Lincoln was a "Hard Shell Baptist" who took his piety seriously, as did (of course) Joseph Wilson the minister. But Abraham and Woodrow reacted to their respective religious backgrounds in different ways. Throughout his life, Lincoln kept organized religion at arm's length, and as a boy he drew rebukes from his father for lampooning the local minister. "I Dont Think he held any [religious] Views Very Strong," remembered one relative. But Woodrow thoroughly imbibed the Reverend Joseph's pious intensity; he saw faith and the moral code it embodied as the bedrock of his character. "Every thoughtful man born with a conscience must know a code of right and of pity to which he ought to conform; but without the motive of Christianity, without love, he may be the purest altruist and yet be as sad and as unsatisfied as Marcus Aurelius," Wilson observed. "Christianity gave us, in the fullness of time, the perfect image of right living, the secret of social and of individual well-being."[9] Wilson's unyielding positions may have stemmed from his certainty in his faith.

Wilson and Lincoln also came from different educational backgrounds, even if both were to a large degree self-taught, at least early on. Wilson studied at home as a boy and taught himself a shorthand system to overcome what was probably dyslexia; Lincoln famously only attended school "by littles" in rural Kentucky and Indiana, while Wilson graduated from college and later pursued a successful academic career at Princeton. Lincoln never attended any university and was embarrassed by his lack of formal learning: "education: defective," he would record in a brief autobiography in 1858.[10] When he became commander in chief in a time of war, Lincoln sought to bolster his knowledge on the subject by checking books out of the Library of Congress. Wilson, meanwhile, had the benefit of studying Lincoln's actions from the Civil War.

Lincoln and Wilson were both lawyers. But Wilson found more that was appealing in the abstract subjects of political science, history, and ethics than the law when he studied at Princeton. He performed well in debates but found only tedium in the dry pages of law books. "Law served with some of the lighter and spicier sauces of literature would no doubt be at all times to us of the profession an exceedingly palatable dish," he confessed to a friend. "This excellent thing, the Law, gets as monotonous as that other immortal article of food, Hash, when served with such endless frequency." When he practiced law in earnest after he graduated, Wilson was, if anything, even more bored than before; he whittled away his time writing articles on politics, stayed out of actual courtrooms as much as possible, and hankered for a posting in academe—which he eventually received.[11] Ideas, theory, and structure rather than engaging with people and practicing law appealed to him.

The courtroom was Lincoln's bread and butter—it was a place in which he excelled. He never complained about the law's tedium, and he rode Illinois's Eighth Circuit, trying cases with alacrity. He used those courtrooms to make connections—a vast web of friends, acquaintances, and colleagues who proved instrumental in paving his way to the presidency. Wilson, on the other hand, was not much given to these sorts of relationships. By the time he was an adult, words like "stuffy" and "aloof" were applied to him; or, more charitably, "reserved" and "reticent." Wilson seemed sometimes to be the beau ideal of an academic; no one would ever have mistaken Abraham Lincoln for a professor. For Abraham Lincoln, the law was about people. For Woodrow Wilson, it was academic.

Lincoln had his cold, calculating side; but he could at least *seem* to be warm and friendly when it suited his purposes. His stock in trade here was a nearly endless supply of jokes and stories, some bawdy in nature, of the sort Wilson would rarely (if ever) tell. Wilson was far more given to introspection than sociability. "What do I wish to become?" Wilson wrote a college friend (and probably at least in part to himself) as a young man, after which he launched into an extended defense of his decision to abandon the law and enter politics. Lincoln was certainly ambitious enough, but he does not seem to have often questioned his own decisions to practice law or enter politics.[12]

With his strong religious background, Wilson thought more often than Lincoln in terms of moral abstractions; but Lincoln possessed his own high idealism, rooted more in the law, the Constitution, and the Declaration of Independence than the Bible. He exuded an almost mystic reverence for America's Founding Fathers and the constitutional system they created, arguing that the Constitution was the "frame of silver" to the Declaration of Independence's "apple of gold." "The Constitution and the Union . . . are not the primary cause of our great prosperity," he wrote on the eve of the Civil War. "There is something back of these, entwining itself more closely about the human heart. That something, is the principle of 'Liberty to all'—the principle that clears the *path* for all—gives *hope* to all—and, by consequence, *enterprize*, [sic] and *industry* to all. . . . The *expression* of that principle [is] in our Declaration of Independence."[13]

Wilson brought to those same subjects a cold academic's unsparing eye, arguing that the American constitutional system was in some respects outdated for the modern age, particularly its separation of powers, which he believed impeded efficient problem solving by impartial bureaucratic experts.

He was also not much inclined to revere Lincoln's "apple of gold" and its language of equality. "If you want to understand the Declaration of Independence, do not repeat the preface," he argued in his history of early America, *Division and Reunion*. He cared far more about the Declaration's statement of grievances against the British Crown than he did about the document's abstract statement of universal equality among all Americans.[14] He did not openly question the declaration's ideas regarding equality, per se, writing only in a rather opaque fashion that the declaration's abstract language of equality had unfortunately allowed "French doctrines of the 'Rights of Man'" to sneak their way into the American constitutional tradition.

Wilson practiced Jim Crow–era inequity when he entered the White House. He systematically removed African Americans from various government posts in favor of white replacements and allowed members of his cabinet to enforce rigid racial segregation in their departments. He was an enthusiastic participant in the ongoing process of whitewashing slavery and African Americans from the memory of the Civil War—his handling of Lincoln's legacy in *Division and Reunion* devoted a great deal more attention to Lincoln's character as "Honest Abe" and his wartime management skills than his status as the Great Emancipator—and he allegedly remarked after viewing the racist, pro–Ku Klux Klan movie *Birth of a Nation* in 1915 that it was "like writing history with lightning, and my only regret is that it was all so terribly true."[15]

Lincoln was not perfect when it came to the topic of race either. He was (like Wilson) a product of an overwhelmingly white supremacist time, and he was not free from the influence of the racism endemic to the American society around him. He could indulge the occasional racist joke, both he and Mary were fond of blackface minstrel shows, and more than once before the war he publicly declared that, despite his consistent opposition to slavery, he had no interest in racial equality. "I have no purpose to introduce political and social equality between the white and the black races," he declared in 1858. "There is a physical difference between the two, which in my judgment will probably forever forbid their living together upon the footing of perfect equality."[16]

Unlike Wilson, however, Lincoln began to rise above this background as the war progressed, particularly as he became ever more firmly committed to immediate emancipation as his official war policy. His long-held support for voluntary colonization of freed slaves out of the country gradually faded away, and he began to envision that which was almost unthinkable before the war—a peaceful, multiracial American society. Lincoln's change of tone may have been due to the fact that Black soldiers ultimately comprised 10 percent of the federal armies and helped win the war. He also developed a firm friendship with Frederick Douglass, the foremost Black leader of his day. "He treated me as a man," Douglass would later say of one of his visits to the president. "He did not let me feel for a moment that there was any difference in the colour of our skins."[17]

Lincoln and Douglass's relationship had no analog in the Wilson presidency. Indeed, when civil rights activist William Monroe Trotter led a group of fellow activists to the White House in 1914 to protest the president's segregationist policies, Wilson tersely told Trotter, "Your tone, sir, offends me," and showed Trotter and his allies the door. He later expressed regret at both this incident and his fulsome praise of *Birth of a Nation*. But a sense of betrayal among African American leaders was palpable, given that at least some of them had been cautiously optimistic about Wilson's Progressive politics.[18]

The most generous reading of Wilson's position on race is that it did not occupy a prominent position in his view of the world. Perhaps due to his own belief in the radicalism of Reconstruction and conviction that segregation benefitted both races, he often evinced an incomprehension of Black life in early twentieth-century America. This included his own perspective on Abraham Lincoln, who, by the time Wilson entered the national political stage in the early twentieth century, was fully ensconced within the pantheon of American heroes. This was true even among many in the South; but for this to be so, white Southerners downplayed Lincoln's emancipation policies. Wilson was no exception; he never spoke of Lincoln the Great Emancipator, dwelling instead on those facets of Lincoln's character of more immediate concern to him: Lincoln's rise from a humble background, his intellect and ability to reason, and his status as a "man of the people." Lincoln was "sufficiently detached to be lifted to a place of leadership and to be used by the whole country," Wilson declared.[19] "Detached" was the heart of the matter. Wilson could admire Lincoln—the author of the Civil War that Wilson and other white Southerners found so traumatic—only by focusing upon those traits in Lincoln that reminded Wilson of himself: the professor-turned-politician, capable of coolly analyzing and solving problems. Additionally, when he became a wartime president, Wilson did not need to rely on Black troops as much as Lincoln had and neither his views of African Americans nor his policies toward them changed. (For more on the challenges faced by Black soldiers in the Civil War and the Great War, see Debra Sheffer's chapter in this book.)

Once he was elected president, Wilson developed a well-deserved reputation for relentless reform, as he aggressively pursued Progressive overhauls of the nation's banking system, tariffs, and antitrust mechanisms. He brought to these tasks a high-minded sense of purpose that some critics characterized as a snobbish judgmentalism and that—combined with his strict Presbyterian upbringing—could leave an impression of stuffy condescension toward those Wilson deemed not to share his high-minded motives. This was not entirely fair. Still, as one critic observed, that reputation for unbending righteousness "wearies his audience, and many a voter has turned from Wilson in the spirit that led the Athenian to vote for the ostracism of Aristides, because he was tired of hearing him called 'the Just.'"[20]

Lincoln detested the brand of high moralism that gave Wilson his reputation of professorial coldness, of pursuing reform without a heart and with an overly high opinion of the reformer's own rectitude. He often found the reformers of his own day to be lacking in humility and empathy. "Too much denunciation against dram sellers and dram-drinkers was indulged in," he rather bluntly told a meeting of the Springfield Temperance Society in 1842, and "this, I think, was both impolitic and unjust. It was *impolitic*, because, it is not much in the nature of man to be driven to any thing; still less to be driven about that which is exclusively his own business; and least of all, where such driving is to be submitted to, at the expense of pecuniary interest, or burning appetite. . . . In my judgment, such of us as have never fallen victims, have been spared more from the absence of appetite, than from any mental or moral superiority over those who have. Indeed, I believe, if we take habitual drunkards as a class, their heads and their hearts will bear an advantageous comparison with those of any other class."[21]

Both Lincoln and Wilson, as leaders of the world's largest democracy, faced the difficult task of, in essence, justifying all that death to the American people. They were commanders in chief, and this gave both men immense power to raise and deploy the nation's armed forces. But the title of commander in chief alone did not automatically convey plenary powers on either man. Americans would follow Wilson and Lincoln into war—but only to a point. Their support among other political leaders and the American people generally was, during both the Civil War and the Great War, fungible and prone to the waxing and waning common in any democracy.

Their task highlights a larger, more abstract problem: how does a democracy engage the bloody consequences of a major war? Given that the American people possess choices and freedom of will often muted or entirely unavailable by other forms of government, how could Lincoln and Wilson persuade their countrymen to court death in battle, and then to accept the dying when it occurred? It was indeed their central, fundamental challenge, arguably more important than any other issue they faced; for if and when public tolerance for the dying ended, so too would American involvement in that respective war.

Wilson and Lincoln were both compelled to lead war efforts mounted primarily in the name of abstract ideals, on battlefields far from their homes, and with no plausible argument available for self-defense. Germany was not going to invade the United States, and the Confederacy's forays into the Union states were more raids than serious invasion efforts. Abraham Lincoln and Woodrow Wilson each had to explain the dying to a sometimes-skeptical America, and sometimes even to themselves.

War was relatively new for Lincoln and the Americans of his generation. Few living Americans in 1861 had directly experienced war's travails. Lincoln himself knew nearly nothing about war. His only military experience, such as it was, occurred in the Black Hawk War of 1832, when he served in the Illinois state militia during a brief incursion of Sauk and other Native Americans led by Black Hawk to reclaim tribal lands in northwest Illinois. "I had a good many bloody struggles with the musquetoes [sic]," he later joked, "and, although I never fainted from loss of blood, I can truly say I was often very hungry."[22]

Lincoln was never enamored of war or military culture. He was strikingly unmilitary in his bearing, a commander in chief who often misunderstood or ignored military protocol, failed to return salutes and other martial courtesies, and who looked out of place among spit-and-polish soldiers. Ordinary soldiers could find this endearing, being in many cases rustic farm boys themselves, but others were simply embarrassed. "There is no need of your being so infernally awkward," groused one man to the president. "For God's sake consult somebody, some military man, as to what you ought to do on these occasions in military presence."[23]

Lincoln stumbled in other ways as well. As the casualty lists mounted from the war's first battles, Lincoln did little to prepare the nation for the grisly battlefield news or the ever-lengthening casualty lists. His early speeches were usually either carefully reasoned political documents or anodyne calls for prayer and fasting in the face of "faction and civil war." Privately he agonized over the war dead, and he did what he could to lower the body count—routinely commuting soldiers sentenced to execution for desertion or dereliction of duty, for example, and greatly reducing the numbers of Sioux slated for hanging due to their part in a bloody uprising on the Minnesota frontier in August 1862. When told that his constituents demanded the executions by way of retribution, Lincoln retorted that he would not "hang men for votes."

But these efforts to hold back the tide of suffering were quiet and behind the scenes. Publicly Lincoln said little—at least early in the war—regarding the reasons so many soldiers were dying, and what exactly they were dying for. He also resisted anything that smacked of a call for visiting bloody retribution on the Confederacy, of killing and dying to revenge the deaths that had already occurred, even as many others in the North so indulged in such rhetoric. All around him Northern men and women were thinking increasingly about revenge. "Three of my most intimate friends were shot down by my side," one Union soldier wrote after the First Battle of Bull Run in August 1861. "I felt so badly I almost fainted, but I rallied immediately, and clenching my teeth, went in, and every shot I fired I made it tell, as I can assure you that I saw five of the rebels fall dead, and I thought the death of my friends avenged."[24]

It would have been natural for Lincoln to have harnessed such bloody sentiments for political gain. He might have told his people to redouble their efforts and their resolve by fueling their patriotism with righteous anger over the graves of the fallen. His counterpart, Confederate president Jefferson Davis, did not hesitate to do so. "We have taught [Northerners] a lesson in their invasion of the sacred soil of Virginia," Davis declared in a victory speech following the Confederate triumph at First Bull Run. As a reporter on the scene described it, Davis "pronounced the victory great, glorious and complete. . . . he eulogized the courage, the endurance and the patriotism of our victorious troops and to the memory of our honored dead, who shed their life's blood on the battlefield in the glorious cause of their country, he paid a glowing tribute, which could not fail to dim with tears the eyes of the least feeling among his hearers."[25]

Lincoln was fully capable of painting vivid and memorable images of the battlefield dead by way of motivating the living. But during the first two years of the war, he did not do so. Why? There was the newness of the thing, this great and awful war that had already by its first year claimed many thousands of lives. And there was the relative newness of the presidency, an office that had not yet truly been tried by a major war, and which lacked many of the tools modern presidents take for granted in trying to mold public opinion. Presidents in Lincoln's day did not have access to any of the bureaucratic machinery a president like Wilson could later manipulate to suit his purposes. Aside from the annual State of the Union address, mandated by the Constitution, they did not give regular speeches—and even then, the annual "address" was a statement read aloud to Congress by someone other than the president, it being thought unseemly that a president should directly address the halls of the legislative branch. Even had it occurred to Lincoln to make active efforts in shaping the public's perception of battle deaths, he did not have at his immediate disposal the means to do so.

He was also distracted by personal encounters with death early in the war that left him shaken. In one of the first combat deaths of the war, a close friend and former law student from Springfield, Elmer Ellsworth, was killed while trying to remove a secessionist flag from the roof of a building in Alexandria, Virginia. Not long afterward, another close friend, Edward Baker, was killed during the Battle of Ball's Bluff. Then in February 1862, Lincoln was subjected to the most grievous blow of all when his eleven-year-old son, Willie, succumbed to what was probably typhoid, lingering for weeks before dying in his White House bedroom.

Outwardly, Lincoln maintained a public façade of stoic acceptance in the wake of Ellsworth's, Baker's, and Willie's deaths. But numerous eyewitness accounts suggest his (and Mary's) great inner anguish behind closed doors. "I never saw a man so bowed down with grief," remembered one observer of Lincoln's despair over his son's passing. "Well, Nicolay, my boy is gone," Lincoln said to his private secretary, John Nicolay. "He is actually gone." The president suddenly broke down into tears and fled Nicolay's office.[26]

This was the entirely human and understandable reaction of a severely stricken father, but it meant that Lincoln still perceived death in largely private terms. He was slow to grasp that during war, death is as much public as private. The Civil War battlefield was a grisly polis, a blood-soaked public square wherein soldiers' deaths carried unavoidable public consequences. It was a central truth of the war that Abraham Lincoln did not immediately comprehend.

For Wilson, the dynamic was much different. He had even less familiarity with war than Lincoln in terms of military experience; he never served a day in uniform, in any capacity. But he did experience war's ravages in ways Lincoln did not. "My earliest recollection is of standing at my father's gateway in Augusta, Georgia, when I was four years old, and hearing someone pass and say that Mr. Lincoln was elected and there would be war," he recalled; and even as a young boy, he was struck by "the intense tones of his excited voice."

Wilson was nine years old when the Civil War ended. He later recalled seeing Jefferson Davis being led in chains by his Union guards as he was marched through Augusta on his way to a federal prison. He also saw Robert E. Lee pass through town, en route to retirement and enshrinement in the southern pantheon as a war hero. "The civil war is something which we cannot even yet uncover in memory without stirring embers which may yet stir into a blaze," Wilson later observed. "There was deep ardor and color of blood in that contest. The field is lurid with the light of passion."[27]

Perhaps surprisingly for a man who prided himself on his sober ability to separate emotion from reason, Wilson allowed the sights and sounds of the Civil War that lay at the heart of his childhood to assume a highly emotional centerpiece in his thoughts about war. "Wilson grasped the tragedy that overcame the South after the Civil War," noted biographer A. Scott Berg, "in which the aftermath, at times, proved worse than the defeat."[28]

It was this sense of the pathos and suffering that a war could visit upon a society that lay at the heart of his reluctance to embrace any military solution to a diplomatic problem. This became evident in his reluctance to authorize an invasion of Mexico in the summer of 1916. He was urged by many Americans to punish Mexico with force in the wake of complications stemming from Pancho Villa's raids and the US Army's "Punitive Expedition" into Mexico to find and punish him. During a brief battle with Mexican forces, twenty-five American soldiers were captured and held by the Mexican government, which insisted they would not be released until the Americans withdrew all soldiers from Mexican soil. Wilson stoutly resisted the subsequent calls for a declaration of war. "I came from the South, and I know what war is," he declared, "for I have seen its wreckage and terrible ruin. . . . I will not resort to war against Mexico until I have exhausted every means to keep out of this mess. I know they will call me a coward and a quitter, but that will not disturb me."[29]

More to the point, his early experiences gave Wilson a keen sense of war's public dimensions. He spoke more often and frequently regarding the war he hoped to avoid than Lincoln, who hardly addressed the possibility at all even as the South prepared to leave the Union in 1860. In contrast to the relatively sudden, crashing crisis of the Civil War, Wilson spent much of his first term contemplating the increased possibly of a war, like a slow-burning fuse. Even as he deprecated the idea of entering the European conflict, Wilson labored quietly behind the scenes with his secretary of war Lindley Garrison in 1915 and 1916 to modernize and increase the size and funding of the army and navy. He also began to massage the public mind for the possibility that American entry into the war might prove unavoidable, and he repeatedly disparaged American isolationism as an affront to American honor. "There is a price which is too great to pay for peace," he told a crowd of Iowans in February 1916. "One cannot pay the price of self-respect. One cannot pay the price of duties abdicated, of glorious opportunities neglected, [and] of character, national character, left without vindication and exemplification in action."[30]

The dynamic here was far different in many ways from that which Lincoln faced. But there were certain underlying (and revealing) points of comparison. The fact that Lincoln was embroiled in a civil war with his countrymen meant that he faced both a more and less difficult task than Wilson. It was more difficult in the sense that he was required to motivate Americans loyal to the federal government to kill Americans who sided with the Confederacy. But his task was less difficult in that, unlike Wilson, Lincoln did not need to explain at length just why Americans must involve themselves in a war the origins of which had very little to do with the United States and which had indeed been in progress for years prior to US participation. Secession for Northerners was immediate and profound: the dissolution of the nation was a spectacle that lay nearly at their doorsteps. The killing fields of France lay an ocean and thousands of miles away from American shores.

To be sure, there were those people in the North who were willing to simply let the South go and the nation dissolve; but just as many (probably more) Northerners understood the stakes with an immediacy unavailable to Wilson as he tried to relate the average American to what was occurring on the Somme or in Gallipoli. Wilson well understood his limitations and challenges in this regard. "The Americans who went to Europe to die are a unique breed," he would observe after the war, in that they "crossed the seas

to a foreign land to fight for a cause which they did not pretend was pecu-
liarly their own."[31]

Like Lincoln, Wilson confronted the possibility of a war-torn America
while simultaneously facing illness and death within his own family. His wife
Ellen died in the White House from Bright's disease in August 1914, during
Wilson's second year in office. He would not remain a lonely widower for
long, marrying Edith Bolling at her Washington, DC, home in December of
the following year. Edith Bolling Wilson would prove to be a devoted wife
and first lady; but in many ways Wilson had been as close to his first wife,
Ellen, as Lincoln was to Willie. Moreover, Ellen had been a valued advisor.
She had helped Wilson draft speeches and frequently offered political advice.
"When I carefully prepared an address and read it to Ellen, she would usually
suggest some change—an idea," he recalled, and as often as not "it was just
that passage which made the strongest impression in the whole speech." As
Ellen languished, the war erupted in Europe; Germany declared war on Russia the very week Ellen died. "It seems fateful that she should go just as the
world seems crashing to ruin," he mused. "She could hardly have stood all
that. It would have broken her heart."[32]

Wilson harbored no illusions about the war and what it meant. He called
it the "incredible European catastrophe," and in doing so directly referred
to his Civil War predecessor, writing in August that "just now I am held in
Washington by the most serious duties any President has had to perform
since Lincoln" and observing that the new European war "has wrought effects upon the business, and the public affairs, of this country which, for the
time being at least, are of the most disturbing kind."[33] The European war
was to be avoided, Wilson argued, because of those awful scenes of carnage
at the Somme and elsewhere—scenes that hearkened back to the stories he
had heard about the Civil War and its gravesites in his younger days. While
his speeches explaining the decision to stay out of the war carried typical
high-minded idealism—arguing that Americans must be carefully neutral
in thought as well as deed—Wilson was also willing to reference the horrors
of war.

He ran his reelection campaign in 1916, as the European war produced
ever more ghastly numbers of deaths, on a similar note. "We have been neutral . . . because it was manifestly our duty to prevent, if it were possible,
the indefinite extension of the fires of hate and desolation kindled by that
terrible conflict and seek to serve mankind by reserving our strength and our

resources for the anxious and difficult days of restoration and healing which must follow, when will have to build its house anew," Wilson declared in his acceptance speech for the Democratic Party nomination. But the ground was shifting underneath his feet even as he soundly defeated Republican Charles Evans Hughes on a staunchly antiwar platform, "He Kept Us Out of War," which vied with partisan domestic arguments about the scope of federal domestic authority to produce an overwhelming Wilson victory. Yet the president himself seemed to realize, even as he celebrated his second term, that the nation was quite likely to be drawn into the war.[34]

He had warned in his acceptance speech that belligerent nations risked American retaliation should they tread upon American rights. Much of what Wilson had to say in this regard pointed to the troubles in Mexico, but he was speaking to war-torn Europe as well. "Loss of life is irreparable," he pointed out—perhaps an oblique reference to the deaths of 128 Americans aboard the British vessel *Lusitania*, torpedoed by a German U-boat in May 1915— and while damages to American property from the war's travails could be settled via peaceful negotiation and reparations, American graves could not. "The nation that violates these essential rights must expect to be checked and called into account by direct challenge and resistance," Wilson declared.

Death, and dead Americans: this was the breaking point for Wilson in his antiwar stance. And while he did not clarify what "direct challenge and resistance" might mean, most Americans must have understood the message that was buried beneath the diplomatic language: any further loss of American life in the war risked direct military intervention by the United States. "The effects of the war can no longer be confined to the areas of battle," he pointed out, and "no nation stands wholly apart in interest when the life and interests of all nations are thrown into confusion and peril."[35]

By early 1917 Wilson was becoming increasingly convinced that America's entry into the conflict was necessary, and well-nigh inevitable. Germany's declaration of unrestricted submarine warfare in January proved to be a major tipping point, as did the discovery one month later of rather clumsy German attempts to draw Mexico—that other thorn in the president's side— into war against the United States. Further loss of American life appeared inevitable, just the line in the sand Wilson had drawn. "I cannot bring myself to believe that [the Germans] will indeed pay no regard to the ancient friendship between their people and our own or to the solemn obligations which have been exchanged between them, and destroy American ships, and take

the lives of American citizens in the prosecution of the ruthless naval program they have announced their intention to adopt," Wilson incredulously
opined in a February message to Congress, but "if this inveterate confidence
on my part . . . should unhappily prove unfounded: if American ships and
lives should in fact be sacrificed . . . I shall again come before the Congress
to ask for that authority be given me to use any means that may be necessary
for the protection of our seamen and our people."[36]

Ongoing German attacks—and subsequent losses of American lives—led
Wilson to do just that. On April 2, 1917, he requested from Congress a declaration of war. A distinction between what we might call legitimate and illegitimate death was an important component of Wilson's justification for
entering the war. In his message to Congress asking for a war declaration,
he repeatedly utilized this motif—the Germans inflicted death upon the innocent. This was a key component in his indictment of Germany's policy of
unrestricted submarine warfare. "Vessels of every kind, whatever their flag,
their character, their cargo, their destination, their errand, have been ruth-
lessly sent to the bottom without warning and without thought of help or
mercy for those on board, the vessels of friendly neutrals along with those
of belligerents," he told Congress. The Germans were immoral dealers of
indiscriminate slaughter. "Even hospital ships and ships carrying relief to the
sorely bereaved and stricken people of Belgium . . . have been sunk with the
same reckless lack of compassion or of principle," he said.

Wilson also sounded the familiar tone of a sober, serious academic. "We
must put excited feeling away," he declared. But from the time he asked for
that declaration of war, Wilson pursued both military victory and what he
perceived as victory's necessary corollary—total national unity behind the
war effort—with a fairly ferocious single-mindedness. This minister's son
found within himself a crusading mindset that superseded his earlier doubts
regarding the war. He articulated a purpose for America's involvement that
at least met if not exceeded Lincoln's efforts to tie the Civil War to high ideals
of democracy and equality. "What we demand," Wilson thundered, "is that
the world be made fit and safe to live in; and particularly that it be made safe
for every peace-loving nation which, like our own, wishes to live its own life,
determine its own institutions, be assured of justice and fair dealing by the
other peoples of the world as against force and selfish aggression."[37]

Prior to this point, the references to the war dead abounded to justify Wilson's refusal to enter the war, as he cited the war's human cost as one reason

Americans should refuse to actively participate. Now he needed to pivot and ask Americans to fight and sometimes die as active participants in that same war he had strenuously avoided; and (perhaps surprisingly) he proved rather adept at the task.

Wilson's wartime speeches often referenced the higher moral meaning of the dead, and the necessity of sacrifice for not only the national good but also the betterment of the world—something akin to the connections Lincoln made, late in the Civil War, between that war's human cost and the principle of self government, as soldiers both "gave their lives that the nation might live" and died to vindicate the American experiment in democracy as the world's "last, best hope." "We know what the war must cost," he admitted; it required "our utmost sacrifice, the lives of our fittest men and, if need be, all that we possess." But the sacrifices were worthwhile, for "the man who knows least can now see plainly how the cause of Justice stands and what an imperishable thing he is asked to invest in. Men in America may be more sure than they ever were before that the cause is their own, and that, if it should be lost, their own great Nation's place and mission in the world would be lost with it."[38]

Like Lincoln, Wilson was an innovator where presidential communications were concerned; but he went further than his nineteenth-century predecessor, predictably so, given that Wilson had at his disposal a more sophisticated media and White House communications apparatus than Lincoln might ever have hoped to possess. Wilson was the first American president to hold regular press conferences, and he carefully cultivated a relationship with the nation's press corps, which he could do in a more focused and comprehensive way than Lincoln, given the somewhat ad hoc and preprofessional nature of journalism in Civil War days. Lincoln was able to forge excellent working (and sometimes personal) relationships with newspapermen like Noah Brooks, a California journalist who was a regular White House visitor, but Wilson was able to forge relationships with large numbers of correspondents at once by inviting them to the White House en masse, shaking each one's hand as he entered, and—presaging the modern White House press secretary—referring them to his personal secretary Joseph Tumulty, who might be able to answer detailed questions that Wilson could not. "Wilson, in Friendly Chat, Says He Likes Reporters," ran the headline for his first such gathering.[39]

Wilson therefore systematized presidential press communications in ways unheard of during Lincoln's day. This was occurring well before 1917, but once the United States became involved in the war, Wilson's media campaigns took on added urgency, sophistication, and arguably alarming dimensions. In April 1917, he authorized by executive order the establishment of the Committee on Public Information, also known as the Creel Commission for its chairman, George Creel, a journalist and political operative who had worked on Wilson's reelection campaign. Creel was nothing if not exuberant in his support for Wilson and the war—exuberant, and combative. Before the war he had written fiery pro-Wilson, pro-Progressive editorials for newspapers in Missouri and Colorado, once publicly calling for the lynching of several senators in a dispute regarding public ownership of Denver's water company. He had a superb organizational mind and a keen appreciation for the power of the written word and the well-designed image to move public opinion.[40]

The Creel Commission acted as a clearinghouse for the federal government's efforts to both justify the war and arouse the popular "ardor and enthusiasm" necessary for victory. Creel always denied that his committee's work was "censorship" still less "propaganda," arguing rather that its purpose was "educational and informative."[41] If so, there were definite limits to that mission, as the commission banned the publication of photographs of dead American soldiers for fear of adversely affecting public morale. On the other hand, the commission showed fewer scruples where the German war dead were concerned, circulating grisly rumors of German wartime atrocities, along with lurid stories of German soldiers murdering (and even eating) dead babies and the like.

Wilson apparently supported Creel's work wholeheartedly, though it is difficult to assess just how much direct input the president exercised on the Creel Commission and its activities. But he at the very least did not stop the more exuberant expressions of wartime patriotism, or the demonization of Germans and their allies by way of motivating Americans to enlist. In the meantime, his own speeches shaded into denunciation of Germans as a menace to civilized society; and the war dead, with Germany's responsibility thereof, was a key theme. Germany was a "sinister power," he declared, "that has at last stretched its ugly talons out and drawn blood from us." Lambasting German U-boats that torpedoed American seagoing vessels, resulting in American dead, Wilson very early in the war went where Lincoln did not go: portrayal of the enemy as a dire and direct threat to American lives, and the necessity for heroic sacrifice and the laying down of some American lives by way of protecting the nation and making the world a better place. "For there is but one choice," he believed, "and we have made it. Woe be to the man or group of men that seeks to stand in our way in this day of high resolution when every principle we hold dearest is to be vindicated."[42]

Lincoln possessed nothing remotely comparable to the Creel Commission—such an institution was beyond the imaginations of most Civil War–era Americans. His White House staff consisted primarily of two young secretaries, John Hay and John Nicolay, who daily sorted the mountains of mail Lincoln received and screened visitors as best they could (though Lincoln was notorious for allowing pretty much anyone to come see him, regardless of the reason). But this is not to suggest that President Lincoln was indifferent to public opinion—far from it. One reason he allowed so many unsolicited visitors was his appreciation of their revelations regarding the mood of the country, what he called his "public opinion baths." "Many of the matters brought to my attention are utterly frivolous," Lincoln admitted, and yet they "all serve to renew in me a clearer and more vivid image of that great popular assemblage from which I sprung."[43]

It was an informal and hazy method of gauging such matters, but the best Lincoln could manage in an era prior to scientific polling. Like Wilson, he well understood the power of public opinion in a democracy. But given the circumstances of his times and his office, Lincoln was compelled to grope his way toward management of that opinion. Occasionally he invited visitors to call upon him and, during their visit, spoke in carefully prepared, formal terms, making certain that his words were recorded and made their way into print.

On other occasions he wrote what amounted to public press releases that took the form of ostensibly private letters that he knew would end up in the newspapers. Such was the case with his famous letter to *New York Tribune* editor Horace Greeley, written in August 1862, whereby Lincoln assured Greeley that his "paramount object in this struggle *is* to save the Union and is *not* either to save or destroy slavery." It was a message Lincoln felt was vital to communicate, even as he moved toward emancipation; he needed to shore up support among the more conservative elements in American society by reassuring them that he had not embarked upon a revolutionary course of action regarding slavery. Possessing no White House public information apparatus to speak of, no Wilsonian-era press secretaries, "educational" commissions, or the like, he used a subtle but powerful alternative: a communiqué to an individual that he knew would find its way into print throughout the country.[44]

References to the highest price paid by the war's honored dead began to steadily creep into these communications after the fall of 1862, as Lincoln grew particularly cognizant of the connections he must make between the battlefield slain and the war's higher aims after he had issued his Emancipation Proclamation on New Year's Day, 1863. His first proclamation of a national day of thanksgiving and prayer, for example, issued in August 1861, said nothing about the thousands of young men on both sides who were already slain by the point. But in March 1863 he dwelt at some length on the connections between the battlefield dead and America's sin of slavery, and perhaps national arrogance and excessive pride. "May we not justly fear that the awful calamity of civil war, which now desolates the land, may be but a punishment, inflicted upon us, for our presumptuous sins," he mused, "to the needful end of our national reformation as a people?"[45]

Perhaps Lincoln's highest and most eloquent invocation of the war's greater meaning occurred in that brief but majestic address he delivered in November 1863, at the dedication of the cemetery in Gettysburg to honor the fallen soldiers from that titanic battle. The Gettysburg Address is justly famous for many reasons: as an expression of the value of American democracy, as a clarion call for Americans to bring a new "birth of freedom" from the wrack of war, and as a penultimate example of presidential rhetoric at its very finest. He "cast a spell" with a "transcendental declaration," notes historian Garry Wills.[46]

Lincoln's address was all these things: but it was, at its most fundamental level, a speech providing a direct, powerful link between the battlefield dead and American national ideals, a link such that Lincoln himself had not prior to that point forged in any significant way, and that more generally had never been forged so effectively or with such searing intensity by any president in American history. "The brave men, living and dead, who struggled here, have consecrated it, far above our poor power to add or detract," Lincoln intoned, tying the dead to religious imagery of the sacred. "The world will little note, nor long remember what we say here, but it can never forget what they did here. It is for us the living, rather, to be dedicated here to the unfinished work which they who fought here have thus far so nobly advanced. It is rather for us to be here dedicated to the great task remaining before us—that from these honored dead we take increased devotion to that cause for which they gave the last full measure of devotion."[47]

Wilson would give his own version of a Gettysburg Address fifty years later, at the anniversary of the battle, standing not far from where Lincoln had spoken. In his own speech commemorating the battle, Wilson did not directly mention Lincoln or the Gettysburg Address; but its echoes were palpable in Wilson's own language and imagery. "I need not tell you what the Battle of Gettysburg meant," he told an assembled crowd that included Union and Confederate veterans of the battle. "These gallant men in blue and gray sit all about us here. Many of them met upon this ground in grim and deadly struggle. Upon these famous fields and hillsides their comrades died about them. . . . These venerable men crowding here to this famous field have set us a great example of devotion and utter sacrifice. They were willing to die that the people might live."[48]

At the time Wilson spoke those words, the United States was not at war. But four years later, in a Memorial Day speech in May 1917, Wilson spoke before the graves of Arlington cemetery, and he referenced the fallen soldiers as those whose sacrifice was "for liberty accomplished," while with himself and the soldiers of American Expeditionary Forces, "we are in the midst of a work unfinished."[49] What was this great work, according to Wilson? He sounded rather a lot like Lincoln, extolling the experiment not just of American democracy, but the general cause of global freedom. "In one sense the great struggle into which we have now entered is an American struggle, because it is defense of American honor and rights," Wilson declared, "but it is something greater than that—it is a world struggle. It is a struggle of men who love liberty everywhere, and in this cause America will show herself greater than ever because she will rise to a greater thing."

Wilson spoke these words at a segregated ceremony, in Jim Crow America, urging white Union and Confederate veterans to embrace the ongoing process of national reconciliation by effectively reading the African American Civil War perspective and experience out of the national memory. "How wholesome and healing the peace has been!" he exclaimed at Gettysburg. "We have found one another again as brothers and comrades in arms, enemies no longer, generous friends rather, our battles long past, the quarrel forgotten? Except that we shall not forget the splendid valor, the manly devotion of the men then arrayed against one another, now grasping hands and smiling into each other's eyes. How complete the union has become and how dear to all of us." It was an "us" that by and large did not include African Americans, whom Wilson had systematically segregated and marginalized throughout his presidency.[50]

Lincoln employed imagery of national reconciliation and forgiveness himself, in his Second Inaugural Address, a speech rivaling (or perhaps even surpassing) the Gettysburg Address in its majesty and rhetoric. But Lincoln was quite clear that the war was about a grievous American sin that Wilson chose not to mention, either at Gettysburg or elsewhere, as a cause worth dying for. "One eighth of the whole population were colored slaves, not distributed generally over the Union, but localized in the Southern part of it," Lincoln pointed out, and "these slaves constituted a peculiar and powerful interest. All knew that this interest was, somehow, the cause of the war. To strengthen, perpetuate, and extend this interest was the object for which the insurgents would rend the Union, even by war; while the government claimed no right to do more than to restrict the territorial enlargement of it." Like Wilson, Lincoln wished or reconciliation, "malice toward none and charity for all," as he famously said. But unlike Wilson, he did not want Americans to forget the fundamental reason why so many men had died.[51]

Herein lay the final, most important difference in Abraham Lincoln and Woodrow Wilson. Both men would, to a greater or lesser extent, ask their countrymen to remember and venerate the war dead in the successful prosecution of their own particular wars. Both would reference the slain to motivate the living. But in Lincoln's case, his "new birth of freedom," built upon the graves of countless dead Americans, included African Americans. For Woodrow Wilson? Not so much.

Notes

1. September 2, 1862. In Roy P. Basler, ed., *The Collected Works of Abraham Lincoln*, 9 vols. (New Brunswick, NJ: Rutgers University Press, 1953; hereinafter referred to as *CW*) 5:404.

2. Arthur S. Link, ed., *The Papers of Woodrow Wilson*, 69 vols. (Princeton, NJ: Princeton University Press, 1994; hereinafter referred to as *PWW*), 33:138.

3. Mario R. DiNunzio, ed., *Woodrow Wilson: Essential Writings and Speeches of the Scholar-President* (New York: New York University Press, 2006), 99–103.

4. Ronald J. Pestritto, *Woodrow Wilson and the Roots of Modern Liberalism* (Lanham, MD: Rowan and Littlefield, 2005), 57–58, makes this point particularly well.

5. *CW*, 4:60.

6. Charles Ray to Elihu Washburn, quoted in Michael Burlingame, *Lincoln: A Life*, 2 vols. (Baltimore: Johns Hopkins University Press, 2009), 1:88–89.

7. *PWW*, 18:631.

8. "Bunglingly," quote at *PWW*, 4:61; "One of the most inspiring fathers," quote in Leonard Bacon, et al., ed., *Independent* 82 (April–June 1915), 189.

9. Dennis Hanks to William H. Herndon, in *Herndon's Informants: Letters, Interviews and Statements about Abraham Lincoln*, ed. Douglas L. Wilson and Rodney O. Davis (Urbana: University of Illinois Press, 1997), 45; Woodrow Wilson, *When a Man Comes to Himself* (New York: Harper Brothers, 1901), 4.

10. *CW*, 2:459.

11. A. Scott Berg, *Wilson* (New York: Putnam, 2013), 80.

12. Wilson quoted in Iris Dorreboom, *The Challenge of Our Time: Woodrow Wilson, Herbert Croly, Randolph Bourne and the Making of Modern America* (Amsterdam: Rodopi, 1991), 24.

13. *CW*, 4:168–169 (emphases in original).

14. Wilson quoted in Pestritto, *Wilson and the Roots of Liberalism*, 55–56; Woodrow Wilson, *Division and Reunion* (New York: Longmans, Green, 1906), 56.

15. Pestritto, *Wilson and the Roots of Liberalism*, 56–57; see also David Blight's excellent treatment of Wilson and the early twentieth-century narrative of Civil War memory in his *Race and Reunion: The Civil War in American Memory* (Cambridge, MA: Harvard University Press, 2001); "lightning quote," along with a careful treatment of the subject, is from Robert A. Armour, "History Written with Jagged Lightning: Realistic South vs. Romantic South in Birth of a Nation," in *The South and Film*, ed. Warren G. French (Oxford: University Press of Mississippi, 1981), 14.

16. *CW*, 3:16.

17. Douglass quoted in Godfrey Rathbone Benson Baron Charnwood, *Lincoln: A Biography* (New York: H. Holt, 1916), 332.

18. On the Trotter incident, see Dick Lehr, "The Racist Legacy of Woodrow Wilson," *Atlantic*, November 27, 2015.

19. Woodrow Wilson, "Abraham Lincoln: A Man of the People," in *Abraham Lincoln, the Tribute of a Century, 1809–1909*, ed. Nathan William MacChesney (Chicago: A. C. McClure, 1910), 25.

20. Charles Seymour, *Woodrow Wilson and the World War: A Chronicle of Our Own Times* (New Haven: Yale University Press, 1921), 25.

21. *CW*, 1:275, 278.

22. *CW*, 1: 510.

23. Harold Holzer, ed., *Dear Mr. Lincoln: Letters to the President* (New York: DaCapo, 1993), 148.

24. *Massachusetts Spy* (Worcester, MA), August 7, 1861; *CW*, 4:482.

25. Lynda L. Christ et al., eds., *The Papers of Jefferson Davis*, 14 vols. (Baton Rouge: Louisiana State University Press, 1991–2015), 7:262.

26. Elizabeth Keckley, *Behind the Scenes: Or, Thirty Years a Slave, and Four Years in*

the White House (New York: Martino, 2017; originally published in 1868), 43; Nicolay, journal entry, February 20, 1862, found in Michael Burlingame, ed., *Inside Lincoln's White House: The Complete Civil War Diary of John Hay* (Carbondale: Southern Illinois University Press, 1999), 71.

27. *PWW*, 18:634; also Berg, *Wilson*, 38.

28. Berg, *Wilson*, 11.

29. Joseph P. Tumulty, *Woodrow Wilson as I Know Him* (New York: Doubleday, 1921), 158.

30. *Addresses of President Woodrow Wilson*, January 27–February 3, 1916 (Washington, DC: Government Printing Office, 1916), 44.

31. Albert Bushnell Hart, ed., *Selected Addresses and Public Papers of Woodrow Wilson* (New York: Modern Library, 1919), 267.

32. Ray Stannard Baker, ed., *Life and Letters of Woodrow Wilson* (New York: Charles Scribner, 1946), 469, 477fn.

33. *PWW*, 30:328.

34. Lewis L. Gould, *The First Modern Clash over Federal Power: Wilson versus Hughes in the Presidential Election of 1916* (Lawrence: University Press of Kansas, 2016).

35. Wilson speech quoted in Royal Jenkins Davis, *America's View of the Sequel* (Philadelphia: Headley Brothers, 1916), 59.

36. George McClean Harper, ed., *President Wilson's Addresses* (New York: Palaya, 2016), 196.

37. Harper, *President Wilson's Addresses*, 467.

38. Oliver Marble Gale, ed., *Americanism, Woodrow Wilson's Speeches on the War* (Chicago: Baldwin Syndicate, 1918), 112.

39. James D. Startt, *Woodrow Wilson, the Great War, and the Fourth Estate* (College Station, Texas: Texas A&M University Press, 2017).

40. John Maxwell Hamilton, *Manipulating the Masses: Woodrow Wilson and the Birth of American Propaganda* (Baton Rouge: Louisiana State University Press, 2020).

41. Creel quoted in Philip M. Seib, *War and Conflict Communication* (New York: Routledge, 2010), 292; see also George Creel, *How We Advertised America* (New York: Harper and Bros., 1920).

42. Committee of Public Information, *Woodrow Wilson's Flag Day Address, with Evidence of Germany's Plans* (Washington, DC: Government Printing Office, 1917).

43. Frances B. Carpenter, *Six Months at the Lincoln White House* (New York: Hurd and Houghton, 1866), 281.

44. *CW*, 5:388 (emphases in original).

45. *CW*, 4:482; 6: 155–156.

46. Garry Wills, *Lincoln at Gettysburg: The Words That Remade America* (New York: Simon and Schuster, 1992), 20.

47. *CW*, 7:18.

48. Albert Shaw, ed., *The Messages and Papers of Woodrow Wilson*, 2 vols. (New York: Review of Reviews, 1924), 1:15.

49. Hart, *Selected Addresses and Public Papers of Woodrow Wilson,* 209.
50. Hart, *Selected Addresses and Public Papers of Woodrow Wilson,* 10.
51. *CW,* 8:332–333.

3

African American Soldiers

The Struggle for Equality through Service in the Civil War and Great War

Debra Sheffer

The ancient historian Thucydides identified three motives for men in war: fear, interest, and honor. Some men go to war to protect their families and their homes. Others do so to protect their beliefs and to gain recognition as men. Historically, Black Americans sought military service for all these reasons. Trapped in a racist system that denied them full or even limited equality, they also fought to attain freedom, full citizenship, and equal rights. Their success varied in kind and degree. They encountered the same challenges as every soldier: enemy forces, difficult terrain, fatigue, hunger, fear, and boredom. Their greatest challenge, however, was the racist sentiment of white society, which hindered both their potential and postconflict rewards. Despite consistent disappointments, they persisted and sacrificed, many continuing to hold out hope that they would receive justice in the end. Black soldiers in both the Civil War and the Great War had to complete every task and requirement of soldiering on top of fighting for the dominant white society's acceptance and respect. Thus, while the enemy, terrain, and their own legal standing may have changed, Black soldiers in the early twentieth century still faced a racist mindset that shadowed them throughout their military service in the US armed forces. As the historian Ira Berlin wrote, African American soldiers always had "to face enemies on two fronts, battling the foe within and the foe without to achieve freedom and equality. Indeed, again and again, black people have employed the metaphor of 'Fighting on Two Fronts' to describe the unique character of the black military experience."[1] The Civil War era did not resolve that challenge and neither would the Great War. While other chapters in this book examine changes in American society between the two periods, this one highlights the constancy of racism and prejudice aimed at Black soldiers. Because of this constancy, this chapter, while focusing primarily on the Civil War and the Great War, will draw lessons from the entirety of African American military service from the Revolution to the end of the segregated military. In the end, the Civil War produced more change for African Americans than did the Great War and offered a glimpse of what a truly equal American society might become.

Despite the constant injustice and denial of equality over the course of American military history, the period between the Civil War and the Great War did represent an important time for Black soldiers. The greatest leaps forward—emancipation, citizenship, and suffrage—occurred as a direct result of their service during the Civil War. And yet this period also represents bitter disappointment as state laws chipped away at the legal gains that Blacks had made. Still, for Black soldiers, the Civil War left a legacy of great hopes, for they now saw what they might achieve in terms of societal changes through their service. This legacy resonated with Black soldiers fighting in the Great War, who felt themselves fighting again both for a national cause and for personal improvement. Perhaps the rights that they had seen rolled back might yet be regained through Black men answering the national call once more. However, the enemies of Blacks' civil rights also understood what Black soldiers might gain on the battlefield. Maintaining the same doubts as antebellum America about the martial ability of Black men and determined to maintain the segregated status quo, many white commanders sought to limit and play down the contributions of Black men in the Great War.

Yet, as African Americans had in the Civil War, they proved themselves on the battlefields of Europe. When they returned home, however, a new generation of Black soldiers who had tested their mettle in battle saw that their sacrifices had failed to bring change akin to what their fathers had secured after the Civil War, and this only increased their determination to obtain the rights guaranteed to them by the Constitution but denied by Jim Crow laws. A sense of militancy that inspired this new generation of civil rights campaigners would maintain them and strengthen their organizations a few decades before yet another devastating global war ushered in the modern struggle for Black civil rights. One way that Blacks made great strides during this period, despite the imperfect nature of the successes, was by becoming agents of the federal government. That government, while it did not always treat Blacks fairly, did ultimately serve as the engine of greatest advancement for Blacks seeking to demonstrate their loyalty on the national and international stage.[2]

Service in the US military has traditionally been a pathway to citizenship and equal rights. Conversely, military service has also been a duty of citizens of the republic. For most of the history of the United States, white Americans performed their duty and received these cherished rights, but Black Americans did not, even when they provided exemplary service in wartime. Indeed, white Americans sought to deny service and its rewards to Black Americans by blocking African American troops from combat service. From the late eighteenth through the mid-nineteenth centuries, citizenship remained unattainable and equal rights remained elusive for most African Americans. Understanding that faithful service in war might lead to their freedom and gaining citizenship rights, they sought opportunities to prove themselves. The end of the Civil War brought freedom, citizenship, and equal rights, but only briefly, as if these gains were cruel tastes of a forbidden reality. By the time of American entry into the Great War, Black Americans still struggled to fully realize the equal rights other Americans enjoyed and took for granted. The fear that Blacks might attain rights in return for service was perhaps the main reason many white Americans, from the Colonial Era through the Great War, were adamant in their refusal to accept Black service, even if manpower shortages meant defeat.

Indeed, freedom and military service have been intertwined in American history since the Revolutionary War. In 1775 Lord Dunmore, governor of Virginia, offered freedom to any enslaved laborer who would leave his master and fight for the British. Perhaps as many as twenty thousand enslaved laborers ran away to join the British forces. American armies, meanwhile, struggled with manpower shortages and were reluctant to offer freedom for service.[3]

The American colonists for their part viewed military service against the British as the exclusive right of whites and entered the Revolution believing that white soldiers would be sufficient to win the war and determined that they should be the ones to fight. Most colonies banned Black enlistment from the beginning of the war or not long after the war began. The Continental

Army formally excluded Blacks from service as early as October 8, 1775. Army commander George Washington initially issued orders to bar Blacks from combat service. Because of critical manpower shortages, not all recruiters strictly followed the policy, but some colonies steadfastly refused to arm Blacks, even if it meant losing the war. Eventually, British gains in manpower as a result of runaway enslaved laborers encouraged American leaders to reconsider the policy. Colonies increasingly relied on Black enlistment to meet enlistment quotas, and the Continental Army came to appreciate new enlistments, regardless of color. A formal change in policy would bolster American manpower and deny that manpower to the British. Still, some southern colonies, such as South Carolina and Georgia, maintained their policy of Black exclusion to the end of the war. Despite this reluctance to accept Black Americans into military ranks, as many as five thousand enlisted to fight on the side of the colonists, in exchange for promises of freedom.[4]

Although both the British and the Americans promised freedom in exchange for military service, neither side abided by that agreement. Most Black soldiers were returned to slavery at the end of the war. American practices regarding Black military service during the Revolutionary War set a precedent and provided a pattern that would repeat itself in future conflicts. During wartime, Black Americans contributed to critical manpower needs but were quickly excluded from the armed forces once those needs diminished, and they were forbidden to serve in peacetime. With their contributions constantly forgotten or devalued, freedom and citizenship remained an elusive goal for Black Americans.[5]

Post–Revolutionary War white Americans, with rare exception, remained adamant about excluding Black Americans from service. Recruiters had explicit instructions not to enlist Blacks, mulattoes, or Indians. Congress also passed the Militia Act of 1792, which authorized military service for white Americans only. Still, while Black Americans were essentially barred from military service of any kind, including the militia, instances of Black service did occur during the years between the Revolutionary War and the Civil War. Black Americans served in noncombat roles in the navy in the War of 1812, as well as with the British in Virginia, in May 1814. That same year, New York and Pennsylvania raised Black regiments. Louisiana enlisted free Blacks from the beginning of the War of 1812. General Andrew Jackson, desperate for manpower in his effort to defeat the British at New Orleans, recruited free Black Americans with the promise of money and land in exchange for service. They served admirably, earning Jackson's praise. At the conclusion of the war, however, Jackson did not keep his promises. Generally, despite these few incidents of notable service, the United States maintained its practice of excluding African Americans from the military.[6]

The Militia Act of 1792 remained in effect until 1862, well into the Civil War. Yet, despite being prohibited from doing so, Black Americans still sought service opportunities, sparking controversy and debate. When Northern soldiers volunteered to fight to restore the Union, they generally had no desire to have Black Americans among their ranks, and very few of them actually fought to free slaves or end slavery. Even if they were willing to tolerate Black service, white Americans believed that Black Americans would not make effective soldiers, fearing that Blacks could not be trained and that they would display cowardice on the battlefield. Most importantly perhaps, they opposed granting any Black Americans full citizenship or equal rights in exchange for service, which would put them on equal footing with white Americans. Understanding military service as a pathway to rights, they denied that option to Blacks altogether.[7]

When the Civil War began in 1861, Black Americans volunteered for military service. Like the generations before them, they hoped that fighting for the Union would translate into freedom, citizenship, and equal rights, believing that this war would finally make those long-denied hopes a reality. Frederick Douglass, the nation's most prominent Black abolitionist, argued, "Once let the black man get upon his person the brass letters, U.S.; let him get an eagle on his button, and a musket on his shoulder, and bullets in his pocket, and there is no power on earth or under the earth which can deny that he has earned the right of citizenship in the United States."[8] There were obstacles, however. As in previous military conflicts, most white Americans believed this war would be brief, that it was a white man's fight, and that whites were more than sufficient and capable of winning it. At the beginning of the conflict, Union Secretary of War Simon Cameron stated, "The Department has no intention at present to call into service of the Government any colored soldiers."[9]

Despite the administration's early actions and statements, some Union commanders attempted to enlist Blacks for noncombat service. As early as perhaps May 1861, Union General Benjamin Butler employed escaped slaves, referring to them as "contrabands," to perform labor at his military camp in Fortress Monroe in Virginia. Other Northern commanders made similar arrangements. In August of that year, Congress passed the First Confiscation Act, which made the actions of these commanders legal. Blacks filled a crucial manpower gap. The navy, the military branch that few wanted to join because of the harsh conditions of service, authorized the enlistment of Black Americans as paid servants and laborers. All these efforts, however, incorporated Blacks for labor only, not for combat. Some Union commanders in South Carolina, Louisiana, and Kansas took things further. General James H. Lane enlisted Black soldiers—the First Kansas Colored Volunteer Infantry—to fight in "Bleeding Kansas." Despite ongoing resistance to employing Black troops, it became clear early in the war that the North would have to make some decisions regarding African Americans, as by mid-1862 it was evident that the Confederacy was using slave labor in the war effort. Lincoln needed to deny the South a valuable resource and was convinced that Black manpower would help the North win the war. He faced, however, the great challenge of convincing other white Americans to accept the idea of Black emancipation, military enlistment, and combat service.[10]

Even when early manpower shortages required more enlistments, military officials still excluded Black Americans from service. Eventually, the situation became desperate with states unable to meet their enlistment quotas and Lincoln fearing that he would lose the war without more men. Black soldiers might prove the deciding factor. Continuing manpower shortages combined with dwindling white enlistments led the Union government to conscript citizens for the first time in its history. White Americans protested conscription, in some cases with violence. Even as whites were increasingly reluctant to enlist, however, many still adamantly opposed the use of Black Americans in the war effort.[11]

Unable to win the war without the added numbers that Black volunteers would bring, but also unable to fill the ranks with unwilling whites, Lincoln acted decisively after the Battle of Antietam in September 1862. He used his presidential war powers to issue the Emancipation Proclamation, effective January 1, 1863, freeing enslaved people in the states still in rebellion, while leaving those in the Border States untouched and authorizing Black enlistment for combat in the Union effort. Lincoln realized this would create controversy in the North and might well cost him his reelection but understood the necessity of winning the war. He was not changing war aims to include abolition but responding to military necessity. The proclamation would deny the South a valuable war resource, would make it less likely for the South to gain European support for the war, and would pave the way for Black military service to bolster manpower for the United States.

Reaction to the Emancipation Proclamation was mixed. Confederates expressed outrage. Enslaved laborers who learned about the new policy left their homes to head to Union lines. Both the United Kingdom and France had abolished slavery decades earlier and were unlikely to side with the Confederacy now that the United States had also embraced emancipation as its policy. Northern reaction ranged from anger to support. Chilton A. White, a congressman from Ohio, declared, summing up the opposition's position, "This is a government of white men, made by white men for white men, to be administered, protected, defended, and maintained by white men."[12] Black soldiers had fought earlier in the war, but new regiments formed quickly, mustered into service, and joined the war effort, with support from Republican financial elites and the media. The appearance of Black soldiers on the battlefield changed the nature of battle and the nature of the war for both sides.[13]

Although white Southerners staunchly opposed the use of Blacks as soldiers, the Confederacy did employ enslaved laborers in various ways. In order to free white Southerners for the battlefield, enslaved laborers were employed to dig trenches, build fortifications, cook, and tend the sick and wounded. The Emancipation Proclamation and its endorsement of Black military service escalated Southern outrage at the United States government and resulted in the loss of enslaved laborers who ran away to seek freedom. The Confederacy faced the possibility of those same enslaved laborers wearing Union blue and bearing arms against them in battle. When encountering Black units on the battlefield, Confederate troops targeted both the enlisted men and their white officers with a vengeance. As Confederate prospects for victory waned, a few lone voices, such as Confederate General Patrick R. Cleburne, called for permission to enlist slaves to fight, but all requests fell on deaf ears. Confederate General Clement H. Stevens summed up the majority view: "I do not want independence if it is to be won by the help of the Negro. . . . The justification of slavery in the South is the inferiority of the Negro. If we make him a soldier we concede the whole question."[14]

If the Confederacy would not employ Blacks in combat, the United States would. The example of the Louisiana Native Guard is instructive in this regard. The Confederacy allowed this unit of free Black men who volunteered for service early in the war to organize but not to bear arms. Thus, they watched helplessly as New Orleans fell to the US forces in May 1862. In August, Union General Benjamin F. Butler, commander of the Department of the Gulf after the capture of New Orleans, issued General Order no. 63, inviting the men of the Louisiana Native Guard to join the United States Army as part of the Free Colored Brigade. Unit members found the offer attractive for a number of reasons: the Confederacy had not supported them with weapons when they faced battle, and fighting for the Union could lead to freedom for some of their family members still held in bondage. Many of the men of the Native Guard mustered into the United States Army, including Andre Cailloux, a former enslaved laborer who had gained his freedom, married, learned a trade, and acquired property. Unlike most Black regiments that had white officers, the three regiments of the Native Guard were commanded by Black officers. Cailloux became captain of First Regiment's Company E. While mostly assigned to guard duty and labor, they also experienced combat and performed admirably.[15]

Despite their service, these Black Louisianans still encountered doubts from white Americans about their overall ability on a daily basis. The men did not receive pay for the first few months of their service, and their families, dependent on that salary to obtain food, suffered as a result. In addition, they encountered racism from local civilians, policemen, and white Union soldiers. Despite the mistreatment, they remained at their posts, eager to prove themselves in battle. The chance arrived when the United States forces, under the inept command of General Nathaniel P. Banks, marched on Port Hudson in 1863. The Black troops received little preparation for the coming assault on the town and had to cross difficult terrain on the approach to Port Hudson under heavy fire. Cailloux led his men in repeated attempts under withering fire until he fell dead from multiple wounds. His men did not give up until nightfall. In a truce the next day, Union details recovered only the bodies of whites who had been killed or wounded in the battle. They left the Black dead and wounded, including Cailloux, on the field. Port Hudson did not fall to Union hands until early July. Union forces only retrieved the bodies of the Louisiana Guardsmen after the surrender. Having been left out where he fell for nearly forty days, Cailloux could only be identified by the ring on his finger. Despite their heroic sacrifices, General Banks failed to mention the First Regiment on the list of battle participants in his report and thus they could not inscribe the battle on their regimental flag. And yet, despite these indignities, it should be noted that Cailloux and his men had earned the respect of some Union troops who had fought along-side them. Thousands attended Cailloux's funeral on July 29. The all-white Forty-Second Massachusetts also attended and played a funeral dirge for him.[16] More broadly, Black soldiers across Union forces earned respect from their battlefield performance. Real-world examples like these changed the minds of many US troops. Their encounters with enslaved peoples in the South helped them to view Blacks as useful to the war effort in various capacities. This, along with seeing Black troops in action, convinced many to support not just the destruction of slavery but also the granting of rights to freed people.[17]

Before Black troops could reap societal rewards, however, they had to face many challenges in the field. Confederate Secretary of War James A. Seddon explained the rebel policy on the issue of Black soldiers fighting for the Union: "Slaves in flagrant rebellion are subject to death by the laws of every slave-holding state. . . . They cannot be recognized in anyway as soldiers subject to the rules of war and to trial by military courts. . . . Summary execution must therefore be inflicted on those take." All Confederate commanders had to abide by this policy, with some providing additional instructions. Gen. John H. Forney, for example, told his men to hang Black Union soldiers rather than shoot them. The South later expanded the policy to apply to Union officers in command of Black troops.[18]

White Southerners considered the North's use of Black infantrymen to be a violation of the laws of war and believed that Confederate troops were justified in showing no mercy to African American soldiers they met on the battlefield. Since murder was not good for their reputations, commanders preferred that their officers not take prisoners. Many instances of no quarter exist, but perhaps the best-known is the incident at Fort Pillow, Tennessee, which fell to Confederate General Nathan Bedford Forrest's forces in April 1864. Unlike other instances, witnesses, including war correspondents, soldiers, civilians, and Confederate officers, provided ample evidence about the murder of more than two hundred Black prisoners. Victims included not just soldiers but women and children.

The US government did its best to protect Black troops who fell into the hands of the enemy and faced enslavement or execution. In July 1863 Lincoln issued General Orders no. 252, declaring retaliation for Confederate atrocity and mistreatment of Black soldiers and their officers. The action resulted in the Confederacy treating freeborn Black soldiers as legitimate combatants.

However, while General Orders no. 252 forced Confederate military leadership to alter its position, it did not significantly change Confederate battlefield behavior.[19] Confederate battlefield atrocities against Black soldiers in battle, Black soldiers who attempted surrender, Black prisoners of war, and wounded Black soldiers continued from 1863 to the end of the war.

Regardless, Black Americans contributed significantly to the Union war effort. Some regiments became well known for their fighting ability. On July 18, 1863, the Fifty-Fourth Massachusetts Infantry volunteered to assault heavy Confederate fortifications at Fort Wagner in South Carolina. Their commander, Colonel Robert Gould Shaw, led his men over nearly a mile of open, difficult terrain, under heavy fire. Shaw, 3 officers, and 135 men died in the attempt. The First South Carolina Volunteer Infantry Regiment, commanded by Colonel Thomas Wentworth Higginson, meanwhile, conducted a number of highly successful raids in Georgia and Florida. Many other regiments fought as bravely. Approximately 180,000 Black Americans served in 144 regiments. More than thirty-eight thousand died. At least twenty-one received the newly created Congressional Medal of Honor.[20] The United States Army paid respects to the service of Black troops by interring them in the newly established military cemeteries. Thus, the new military cemeteries became "among the first publicly funded integrated cemeteries in American history." Still, despite the fact that they were laid to rest in the same cemeteries as white troops, they were sometimes buried in separate sections. Even in death, there was still segregation.[21]

Although they faced difficult battle assignments, no quarter from Confederates, and the failure of the Union government to consistently protect them, the service record of Black Union soldiers is impressive. They volunteered for impossible missions and fought bravely. They performed their duty even as they confronted a racist hierarchy that paid them less than white troops and sometimes neglected to pay them at all. These men served in the hope that they would receive freedom, full citizenship, and equal rights. It did not take many years after Lee's surrender to Grant for them to realize that most of those hopes would not materialize.

The Confederate surrender in spring 1865 and the ratification of the Thirteenth Amendment that December signaled the end of the war and assurance of freedom for enslaved Blacks. But full citizenship and equal rights still seemed elusive. Black veterans organized and held rallies to gain such rights as male suffrage. Violence frequently erupted when whites disrupted gatherings. Black soldiers who continued to serve out enlistments found themselves stationed as occupation troops in the South among angry and racist white Southerners who resented losing the war and disapproved of Black Americans in any role other than enslaved laborers. The fact that they wore the blue uniform of Union occupation troops exacerbated the situation. Southerners and white occupation forces attacked Black soldiers, their families, and their white officers. Meanwhile, Black troops often received punishment for defending themselves against attack.[22]

One key legacy the Civil War left was the introduction of Black soldiers in the army on a more long-term basis. The conflict marked the first time in American history that the army did not muster out all Black soldiers after the end of the military conflict. Immediately after the war, they received assignments for peacetime service. While some were sent as occupation forces in the defeated Confederate states, several regiments received assignment to join other troops in Texas where the federal government sought to curtail French involvement in Mexico. As they boarded transports to Texas, some Black soldiers learned the government would no longer provide for their families, expecting that the soldier's pay would be sufficient for that purpose. But many of the soldiers had not received pay for months. This was only the beginning of their misery. Many became ill, as a result of poor conditions: their new post had no fresh water, was infested with insects and snakes, and had no suitable housing. Local white civilians targeted the men with violence and falsely accused them of crimes.

Even in such conditions, Reconstruction promised great advances such as equal rights, full citizenship, and equal education. And, indeed, the passage of the Thirteenth, Fourteenth, and Fifteenth Amendments proved revolutionary for African Americans in particular and American society in general. By the end of the century, however, local and state laws, sustained by the United States Supreme Court, had chipped away many of these gains, erecting Jim Crow laws and segregation, which reduced Black social standing, especially in the American South. But no matter how bad the Black citizens suffered from discrimination in the postwar world, however, Black veterans sometimes had access to a model society where their service entitled them to equal treatment: veterans halls. As historian Barbara A. Gannon has demonstrated, integrated units existed all around the nation, and even though many white veterans did not support Black equality in civilian society, they maintained that Black veterans had earned equal treatment in their eyes. In such a world dominated by racist beliefs, service in the armed forces offered some welcome, if imperfect, respite.[23]

Lacking employment prospects in the postwar world, many Black soldiers wished to continue their military service. Congress authorized two all-Black cavalry units—the Ninth and Tenth Regiments—and four all-Black infantry units—the Thirty-Eighth, Thirty-Ninth, Fortieth, and Forty-First Infantry Regiments in the summer of 1866. Army reorganization in 1869 kept the two cavalry regiments intact and reduced the four infantry regiments to two, the Twenty-Fourth and Twenty-Fifth Infantry Regiments. Thus, Black Civil War soldiers accomplished what Black Americans had strived for since the American Revolution: combat and peacetime service. The men of these four regiments became known as the Buffalo Soldiers, who, through decades of service, reflected the motto of the Twenty-Fifth Infantry: "Honest and Faithful Service." These regiments immediately faced significant challenges. Many of the men found military service physically demanding, most were illiterate, and they faced racism at every turn. As was the practice since the American Revolution, white officers commanded Black units. Continued service, however, also allowed illiterate soldiers to gain an education, something denied them under the institution of slavery. Regimental chaplains served as teachers, and many of the men took advantage of the services, demonstrating their eagerness to learn.[24]

As soon as the regiments had full rosters, they headed west. They built roads, telegraph lines, and their own posts; explored; mapped; and provided escorts. They guarded railroad workers, subjugated Indians, and protected settlers. They provided aid during natural disasters, quelled civic disturbances, and patrolled the border with Mexico. Given the nature of their service, they experienced isolation and boredom and also continued to battle discrimination. Unlike white regiments that were rotated to less-harsh climates and less-isolated posts, once the Black soldiers went west, they stayed there. Except in times of national emergency, that is: in such cases, the army recalled Black soldiers from their western posts for service elsewhere. They headed east to board ships to fight in the Spanish-American War in 1898 and in the Philippines after that. On the whole, the white military leadership seemed determined to keep Black troops isolated and far away.[25]

Black soldiers' performance in the Spanish-American War, the Philippine Insurrection, and the Punitive Expedition into Mexico echoed the ambivalence they had experienced in service out west. In the Spanish-American

War, Teddy Roosevelt would both laud the performance of the Black regulars fighting on Kettle Hill and San Juan Hill and then shortly after label those same soldiers as shirkers who needed to be led by white officers.[26] In the Philippines, Black soldiers found themselves fighting against Filipinos to uphold what Rudyard Kipling famously labeled the "White Man's Burden." The tension in that mission led at least one Black soldier, David Fagan, to desert to the Filipino Army, but most fought as required.[27]

Despite their solid record of service in the Civil War, in the West, and abroad, the Buffalo Soldiers had to overcome lingering racist sentiments and doubts about their effectiveness both before and during the Great War. Several incidents marred these men's reputations and led to controversial outcomes. One of the most infamous, the Brownsville Affair, took place in August 1906. In Brownsville, Texas, local white civilians accused the Buffalo Soldiers of protesting against Jim Crow laws with violence, resulting in civilians wounded and killed. Despite lack of incriminating evidence, the federal government discharged over 160 veteran soldiers from the service.[28] Benjamin J. Davis, a Black newspaper editor, called that decision "lynch-law, bold and heartless."[29]

As Americans looked toward possible US entry into the Great War, the Buffalo Soldiers, and some Black Americans more broadly, sought the opportunity for combat service in Europe with the hope that such actions would get them closer to full citizenship and equal rights. W. E. B. DuBois, one of the most prominent African American leaders of the early twentieth century, argued that saving democratic governments abroad might also help combat racism in the United States.[30] DuBois supported the war and viewed it as an opportunity for Blacks to earn their equality in American society and gain skills that could help them economically and politically in the future.[31] Historian Michael S. Neiberg notes that African Americans "were willing to trade their military service to the nation in a time of crisis for promises of greater equality, although many doubted that white America would in the end live up to its share of the bargain."[32]

African Americans initially did not feel the urge to intervene in the Great War and did not share the white community's concern over the conflict. For Blacks, the ongoing violence against African Americans and the oppression of Jim Crow merited greater attention than a military conflict in Europe. Lynchings continued to claim the lives of dozens of African Americans every year and the federal government refused requests to form the National Race

Committee that the NAACP proposed to study the crisis. The Black community also noticed white Americans express sympathy for Belgium, all the while knowing that Belgians had perpetrated horrific crimes against the Congolese in Africa. As one writer put it, "It is not consistent to advocate government with the consent of the governed, and democracy for other lands without applying the principle everywhere in our own land." The *Afro-American* declared, "Let us have a real democracy for the United States and then we can advise a house cleaning over on the other side of the water."[33] One article in the *Cleveland Advocate*, an African American newspaper, pointed out the attention that federal authorities paid to German atrocities while ignoring the crimes against Blacks in the South. "The national administration at Washington has taken pains to see that reports of the alleged atrocities of the Germans generally, and effectively, circulated throughout the length and breadth of this country," the author noted, continuing, "But we challenge a denial of the state that no member of the present national administration has even so much as publicly commented upon the fiendish atrocities common in the Southland upon members of our race."[34]

Many African Americans approved of the neutral stance that the United States took and agreed in the general sympathy for the Allied cause. France, they noticed, had employed Senegalese troops and welcomed African American hero Jack Johnson, the famous boxer, in 1914. The Germans, meanwhile, had waged a brutal war against the Herero in southwestern Africa a decade before the war broke out in Europe.[35] After the sinking of the *Lusitania*, however, several Black newspapers expressed support for a more aggressive intervention if that is what the government chose to do. The *New York News*, for example, argued that Blacks should support their country despite how white society treated Africans.[36]

As the country headed toward the Great War, white Americans, concerned about the behavior and treatment of Black troops, sought to keep them away from the front lines of the conflict. Regardless of what whites feared or believed, Black soldiers were determined to serve in Europe. They considered service as "the most sacred obligation of citizenship."[37] The Buffalo Soldiers, however, were disappointed when the War Department did not assign them to the European front. The Ninth Cavalry spent the entire war stationed in the Philippines. Most of the men of the Tenth Cavalry were stationed at Fort Huachuca, Arizona, and were given border patrol duties. The Twenty-Fifth Infantry was stationed at Schofield Barracks in Hawaii until late 1918, when they joined the Tenth in Arizona in order to free a white regiment for service in Europe. The Twenty-Fourth Infantry were in Houston guarding construction workers at Camp Logan. Stationing Black soldiers in the South led to several confrontations, the most infamous of which took place in Houston in 1917. In that incident, local law enforcement assaulted and wrongfully jailed a Buffalo Soldier, resulting in a mutiny and riot that came to be known as the Houston Riot of 1917 (or the Camp Logan Mutiny). Angry soldiers marched on downtown, killing multiple people including police officers. In the aftermath, officials hanged nineteen and imprisoned sixty-three for life. Forty served lesser prison sentences.[38] After the incident in that city, those not executed or imprisoned were transferred to the Philippines for the rest of the war.[39]

The war, however, required mobilization of vast resources, and, unable to spare anyone already in uniform, the military had no choice but to call upon its pool of Black manpower. White Americans, while wanting to contain Black service to noncombat roles, still felt Black Americans should shoulder some of America's responsibility in the war. Racist ideas entered into debates about whether to include Black men in the draft. On the one hand, Senator James Vardaman of Mississippi, a draft opponent, worried that providing military training to Black men would threaten white supremacy. Others worried that Blacks would feel emboldened to challenge the segregation laws when they returned from military service, endangering cotton production in the South. On the other hand, those who supported the draft argued that, without the federal mandate, Blacks would not register for service. They reasoned that whites would then not register themselves out of fear that their women and children would remain on the home front without protection from Black men (a similar case that planters made in order to press for the "20 Negro Law" in the Confederacy). "As in so many political issues in the early twentieth-century United States," historian Jeanette Keith notes, "racism figured not only as political given but as an arguing point for both sides, each of which justified its position as a means of bolstering white supremacy."[40]

When the draft began, southern Blacks registered but many did not then report for service. Southern governors reasoned that Blacks moved around in search of work. Thus, even if they registered for the draft in 1917, they may have moved on to seek better employment opportunities either in northern states or in southern cities. Southern governors seemed to distinguish between the motions of Black and white deserters. Although they pointed to the politics of white deserters, they portrayed Blacks "as feckless and ignorant but basically good-hearted and loyal." Once again, this response demonstrates the contradictory nature of whites' arguments about Blacks. White Southerners, after all, "had been inundating federal surveillance agencies with rumors of black insurrection for at least a year."[41] Regardless of their beliefs about Blacks' motivations, southern governments sought to enforce federal laws and this too led to violent and sometimes deadly confrontations. In Texas, for example, whites killed a Black draft resister named George Cabiness. Fearing that the victim's family members would seek revenge, these same men attacked their home, killing his brothers and mother.[42] In other regions, southern governors called in federal forces to track down and subdue white draft resisters. "It seems that states' rights had even more to do with race than historians have typically thought," Keith poignantly observes, recommending, "We should rewrite the textbooks and make it clear that after 1877 the federal government did, on occasion, send troops into the South to enforce federal laws: just not the Fourteenth and Fifteenth Amendments."[43]

As in past conflicts, the War Department planned to use African American soldiers as laborers only. Military authorities contained, housed, trained, and equipped Black soldiers in separate and segregated regiments and divisions. Approximately four hundred thousand Black Americans served in the war. Of that number, 170,000 provided labor at stateside training camps, and 160,000 provided labor overseas under the offices of Services of Supply (SOS) and the Pioneer Infantry. Approximately 370,000 were draftees, and 5,000 were members of eight National Guard units.[44] Some officers from each of the four Buffalo Soldier regiments were selected for officer training to serve with the Black draftees. The military even established a Black officer training school, Camp Des Moines, in Iowa. This development bolstered the hopes of African Americans who wished to see a Black officer receive a field command. The country's highest-ranking Black officer, Lieutenant Colonel Charles Young, a graduate of West Point, seemed a logical choice as other officer candidates underwent training. Young, however, was sent to serve out the war in Liberia. While there, he contracted a fever and died.[45] The only other eligible Black officer, Ben Davis Sr., was sent to the Philippines with the Ninth. These arrangements provided needed manpower, moved the Buffalo Soldiers out of sight, and granted Black Americans military service, though not the combat service they desired. Senior command of the Black regiments, as was tradition, went to white officers. One of these, General Charles Ballou, was a known racist and an inept commander. The military was not overly concerned because these troops would serve as laborers, cooks, and stevedores only. They were issued denim overalls instead of uniforms. Historian Barbara A. Gannon has noted that the duration of American involvement in the war may have affected the service opportunities open to Black troops. Had the war continued and the demand for combat troops increased as in the Civil War, American military leadership may have had to employ Black soldiers for combat. In this area then, the Great War differed from the Civil War.[46]

African American soldiers found themselves tasked with some of the worst jobs available. Many, for example, worked for the Graves Registration Service (GRS), the unit of the Quartermaster Corps responsible for removing bodies for burial and transport to final locations. These Black soldiers, however, did not necessarily receive recognition in the official records. "The GRS official history," Lisa Budreau observes, "makes only passing reference to the burial work of African American soldiers, referring to them more often only as cemetery workers or 'men of the GRS.'"[47] Budreau notes the irony "that African American soldiers were members of a Jim Crow army, denied the right to fight in combat with their white compatriots and used primarily as work gangs" but their labor for the GRS "ensured a democratic process for the dead."[48]

The military created two all-Black divisions. The Ninety-Second Infantry Division (Colored), established in October 1917, was an all-draftee division commanded by Ballou. They dubbed themselves the Buffalo Division and adopted a black buffalo as their insignia. They arrived in France in June and July 1918, attached to the US Second Army. Due to lack of training and equipment, poor leadership, and racism, this division performed very poorly. The 368th Regiment did see combat, when they were thrown in to plug a critical gap in General John J. Pershing's Meuse–Argonne offensive in September 1918, but they were placed in a difficult situation without the equipment, training, or experience required to do the job. Though Ballou was directly responsible for their poor performance, he shifted the blame to the Black officers under his command. Five were convicted and sentenced to death, though their sentences were later reduced to lengthy prison terms. The Ninety-Second never recovered from these events and carried a tarnished reputation with them throughout and long after the war.

The story of the Ninety-Third Infantry Division (Colored) is much brighter. The division consisted mostly of volunteers rather than draftees. Many of the volunteers were members of National Guard Units that existed before the war. Men of the Eighth Illinois National Guard in Chicago, known as the "Torch Bearers," had fought against the Spanish and in the Punitive Expedition. The Fifteenth Regiment, New York National Guard—known as the "Harlem Rattlers"—was the first Black National Guard unit in New York history. Their Black junior officers from the Buffalo Soldier regiments brought useful experience with them. The Rattlers also boasted noted jazz musician James Reese Europe and an outstanding regimental band. The unit arrived in France in December 1917. Upon disembarking, they learned each regiment had a new designation. They were disappointed when most of them were quickly assigned to build roads and a dam. An exception was that James Reese Europe and the regimental band spent the war touring and performing across Europe. Shortly after their arrival, the Ninety-Third received a tremendous advantage when, in order to bolster depleted French manpower, General Pershing, who had commanded the Tenth Cavalry during the 1916 Punitive Expedition into Mexico, loaned the Ninety-Third to the French Fourth Army, where they remained for the duration of the war.[49]

As part of the French army, they saw extensive combat on the Western Front. The story of the 369th is one that clearly demonstrates Black fighting ability and willingness to serve. The unit remained in combat for 191 days, longer than any other American regiment. They suffered some of the highest casualty rates of any American regiment of the war and were the first American combat troops to reach the Rhine River. The War Department advised the French against recognizing these soldiers for battlefield valor. In fact, in August 1918, Colonel J. L. A. Linard, the American Expeditionary Forces' liaison to the French Military Mission, issued a memo entitled "Secret Information Concerning Black American Troops." The intent of the memo was to persuade the French that any equal treatment of Black American soldiers would offend the United States.[50] Despite these efforts, the 369th received 170 individual Croix de Guerre and a unit citation.[51] The division's 371st and 372nd Regiments also received unit citations.[52]

Despite American government warnings, the French were grateful for and recognized the great sacrifice and service of these African American soldiers. One member of the Harlem Rattlers, Private William Henry Johnson, received the Croix de Guerre, with palm leaf, for his actions on the night of

May 13–14, 1918. Johnson demonstrated why the Germans started referring to his unit as the "Harlem Hellfighters," by repulsing a German attack on Allied lines and saving a number of fellow soldiers. Johnson and fellow soldier Needham Roberts were sent to man a listening post between the lines. The post itself was no more than a crude and muddy hole in the ground with a wood board floor and walls of tall grass and barbed wire. The two men had their French Lebel rifles, a box of grenades, and Johnson's bolo knife. A number of German soldiers approached and then swarmed the post, wounding and incapacitating Roberts early in the attack. Johnson used the entire box of grenades, emptied his rifle, used his empty rifle as a club, and, finally, used his bolo knife to repel the enemy. The Germans retreated, scrambling to take their dead and wounded with them. Both Americans were seriously wounded. Johnson bled heavily from wounds in the right arm and both legs. The morning after the battle, military officials walked the ground and viewed the incredible carnage inflicted on the retreating Germans. They estimated that Johnson and Roberts had fought off as many as two dozen Germans. Irving S. Cobb, a war correspondent for the *Saturday Evening Post*, called the incident the "Battle of Henry Johnson." Johnson was not the only Black American soldier to accomplish such feats on the battlefield, but his actions received unusual attention, which placed him into the limelight and instantly made him an American hero. The report also brought to light the actions of the Ninety-Third Division, the Harlem Rattlers, and the Black fighting man. For all that, despite their reputation, the unit received the worst labor assignments, loading ships, searching for mines, and reburying the dead. After the war, they returned home and received a parade in their honor but did not receive their most cherished desire: equality. Henry Johnson publicly shared his experiences but found his speaking tour cancelled as soon as he mentioned racism and abuse at the hands of white soldiers and officers. He would not be the only one disappointed after the war. Johnson died alone and penniless in 1929. In 2015 he was posthumously awarded the Congressional Medal of Honor.[53]

After the Great War ended, the US government gave the loved ones of deceased servicemembers several options for burial. The government could return the earthly remains of their departed back for burial in the United States or the dead could be interred in overseas American cemeteries. Almost twenty-five thousand families decided to have their loved ones buried in Europe in the newly established American cemeteries. When the cemeteries were completed in the late 1920s, the government also offered to cover the cost and arrange all accommodations for mothers and widows to travel to see the final resting places of their loved ones.[54] For the purposes of this chapter, however, it is necessary to note that Black mothers and widows were completely segregated on their pilgrimages across the Atlantic. The NAACP protested this unequal treatment and urged Black mothers to refuse the government's offer. W. E. B. DuBois, meanwhile, criticized the whole situation, writing, "Black hands buried the putrid bodies of white American soldiers in France" and, despite this, "Black mothers cannot go with white mothers to look at their graves."[55] Even though Black soldiers had fought, bled, and died in the American Expeditionary Force, their mothers and widows still faced discrimination in traveling to see their gravesites in European fields.

Black Americans served with distinction in the Great War. They fought for their country, with the hope that all Black Americans would realize full citizenship and equality as a result of their honest and faithful service. Once again, these hopes remained unfulfilled. Their service convinced few white Americans that they deserved equality. If returning white doughboys found it difficult to find gainful employment after the war, Black veterans faced even greater challenges. Drawn by job opportunities and hoping to escape discrimination and disenfranchisement in the South, many African American families headed to northern industrial areas during the war. Black veterans joined these waves of migrants who sought new lives for themselves in the North. A lack of jobs coupled with the economic downturn, however, led to rising racial tensions culminating in the horrific violence in Chicago during the summer of 1919. Some people started to encourage newly arrived Blacks to return to the South for employment.[56]

The summer of 1919 was known as Red Summer. Violence and racism against Black Americans escalated as American soldiers returned home from Europe. In 1919, seventy-eight Black veterans were lynched (eleven had been lynched the year before). Some were even murdered while still wearing their uniforms.[57] Not only did their service fail to help them reach their goals but they also suffered increased violence at home because of that service. The federal government not only refused to provide equal rights but also could not or did not protect Black soldiers when they returned home. Twenty-eight cities saw race riots that summer. More broadly, returning to the habitual stance that service by Black Americans should be limited, the War Department determined to immediately dismiss Black Americans from the military or to limit the few allowed to remain to labor battalions. The four Buffalo Soldier regiments, denied service in Europe in the war, barely escaped dismissal. Injustices against the families of those who served and paid the ultimate sacrifice for their nation's cause signaled that Jim Crow remained as powerful as ever in the postwar years. At two funeral ceremonies at Arlington National Cemetery in 1921, officials asked African American family members of the deceased to move when they realized that the soldiers had been mistakenly buried in the section reserved for white soldiers. Yet again, African American wartime service had failed to gain them equality and acceptance in a white-dominated society.[58]

Even organizations that catered to veterans such as the American Legion did not stand up for Black soldiers when they returned to the United States. When African American veterans attempted to form their own posts of the American Legion, unable to join white-dominated ones, the national organization refused to override state-level rejections of proposed charters. Granting charters, the national leadership maintained, rested with state-level officers. The NAACP ultimately championed the cause of Black veterans but was unable to move the national American Legion organization to alter its policy. White members who opposed allowing Blacks to join the organization simply wielded too much influence.[59] Because they lacked the legion's influence, many Black veterans also did not have access to medical care, training, or monetary compensation.[60]

Wounded and suffering Black veterans also faced discrimination at hospitals in both the South and the North. Denied entrance to these facilities, some called for a veterans' hospital just for Blacks in Tuskegee, Alabama. The hospital went through, but the issue of staffing of the facility with Black physicians ran into additional opposition before finally coming to fruition.[61] When the Depression struck and veterans requested the "bonuses" that Congress had authorized for them early, opponents of the payout used racist beliefs about Blacks' laziness to argue against advanced payment. The US Chamber of Commerce, for example, suggested that "the half million Negroes in the South, who probably would receive five hundred or six hundred dollars each, would immediately quit work until the money was spent."[62] In the end, Congress eventually capitulated, and veterans, both Black and white, obtained their bonuses in 1936. In the end, the federal government did not fully commit to helping Black veterans but its minor efforts marked an important moment and made a difference. As Jennifer Keene has noted,

"By forcing the federal government to offer limited protection of black veterans' economic and medical rights, the struggle over veterans' benefits instead served as the opening gambit for a civil rights strategy that would gain momentum throughout the twentieth century as the movement focused on enlisting the federal government as an ally, rather than a foe, in dismantling Jim Crow."[63]

As their nation prepared to wage World War II, Americans realized that, once again, the United States would need its Black citizens to help in the war effort in Europe and Asia. Some Black Americans, once again, contemplated the idea of equal rights in exchange for military service. Others had given up hope after the Great War and Red Summer. Those who did participate in the war effort fought for what they called the Double V—victory in Europe and victory at home. As in past wars, under the initial War Department plans, Black soldiers would supply labor only and would not serve in combat roles. When it became clear that white manpower alone could not win the war, the United States called upon Black soldiers once again. As in the past wars, regiments remained segregated, and Blacks served under the command of white officers. Even with the deck stacked against them, Black Americans found ways to distinguish themselves in combat. Many of the drivers of the Red Ball Express, an emergency transport system designed to get supplies to American forces at the front, were Black Americans. The assignment was hazardous, dangerous, and also critical to American success in late 1944. Multiple Black units distinguished themselves in the war. Among them were the 761st Tank Battalion, known as Patton's "Black Panthers," which played a key role in American success against German Panzers in November 1944. The most well-known Black effort of the war was the 332nd Fighter Group, the Tuskegee Airmen, who flew from June 1943 to October 1945, with one of the best records of the entire war.[64]

Examining the service of Black Americans in the Civil War and the Great War leaves out much of the story. If not for men like Andre Cailloux, the Buffalo Soldiers, and units such as the Ninety-Second and Ninety-Third Divisions in the Great War, the men of the Red Ball Express, the Patton's Black Panthers, and the Tuskegee Airmen might not have had the opportunity to serve at all. Their hope of Double V did not come to fruition. Like the men who served in the Great War, they returned to discrimination, segregation, Jim Crow, violence, and continued lynching. Like the period after the Great War, the fact that a Black man had worn a military uniform did not exempt him from facing racial hostility and violence. Their service, however, along with that of all those who served before them, moved them closer to their goals of full citizenship and equality. On July 26, 1948, President Truman ended segregation in the armed forces with Executive Order no. 9981. The order met stiff opposition and many refused to comply. President Truman then created the Committee on Equality and Opportunity to work with all military branches to bring them into compliance with the order. The end of the Korean War brought desegregation, both legally and in practice. However, it did not end the racism that Black Americans faced serving in the military in peace or in wartime.[65]

As historian John Whiteclay Chambers II has written, "The issues of how to raise an army and what kind of army to raise have always proven particularly troublesome to Americans."[66] Inclusion of Black Americans in the military has been especially controversial and difficult. From the Colonial Era through the Revolutionary War, the Civil War, the Great War, and beyond, each generation of Black soldiers made progress toward the cherished goals of full citizenship and equal rights. Each generation paved the way for the next to go further than they did. Though their goals were elusive, they persisted with honest and faithful service. Black American service in the Civil War led to the first peacetime military service for Black Americans. The infantry and cavalry units after the Civil War continued the impressive service tradition of those who had served before, earning the name of Buffalo Soldiers, a title that signified their fighting abilities and gained them lasting respect. Many Americans had learned the value of Black service. With the Great War looming, they stood ready to faithfully serve in Europe, but Americans forgot their impressive legacy and attempted to deny them service in Europe. They reluctantly relented but relegated Black service to labor and fatigue duty, denying them the battlefield participation they had earned through service since the Colonial Era. Black servicemen had to remind America of their value all over again. The Americans not only forgot their valiant service but also welcomed them home from war with violence once again.

Despite the fact that this chapter has pointed to the consistently poor and unjust treatment of Blacks after their sacrifices and service in America's conflicts, there were key differences between experiences in and after the Civil War and the Great War. The greatest difference concerns the remarkable expansion of African Americans' civil rights, at least in written law, after the Civil War. The passage of three constitutional amendments that struck down slavery and elevated Black men to voting members of the republic was certainly without precedent. Blacks eagerly embraced their new role and participated in political and community leadership in those days when white southern backlash and white northern apathy led to the suppression of those rights. White leaders of the Great War generation tried hard to keep Blacks away from combat situations so that they would not have a postwar claim to call upon as they had after the Civil War. One other major difference in the two periods is the lack of strong Black allies in the federal government in the early twentieth century. The tools of segregation, oppression, and violent suppression remained intact during the Great War period, so Black gains were limited even if the return from Europe inspired some of them to become more militant and vocal to reclaim their lost civil rights. In this sense, then, the Civil War proved much more transformative and radical than the Great War.

Notes

1. Ira Berlin, "Fighting on Two Fronts: War and the Struggle for Racial Equality in Two Centuries" in *War Comes Again: Comparative Vistas on the Civil War and World War II*, ed. Gabor S. Boritt (New York: Oxford University Press, 1995), 127–128.

2. Ira Berlin has written, "The Civil War and World War II transformed the federal government into the strongest friend of black people and their most dependable ally in the struggle for equality." "That is not to say that that ally was always reliable," he cautions, "but, in its executive, judicial, and even legislative guises, the federal government—more powerful than ever in the wake of its great military victories—became the court of first resort to the friends of racial equality. In appealing for federal assistance, black people and their allies continued to play their strong card: black men had served the nation in its moment of need." Berlin's goal was to compare the Civil War and World War II. Indeed, compared to those two conflicts, the Great War seemed to yield relatively little in terms of advances for African American soldiers. More recently, Adriane Lentz-Smith has argued that "change, not stasis, marked the African-American experience in the Jim Crow years" and that the Great War helped change the "struggle for civil rights . . . in contours, strategies, and actors." She identifies the Great War as "one of those transformative moments" in African American history. When white soldiers took Jim Crow to the European war with them, the "resulting senses of entitlement and disillusion that developed would shape how African Americans approached the freedom struggle in ensuing decades and would inform critically their mobilization for the next world war twenty years after the first." See Berlin, "Fighting on Two Fronts," 140; Adriane Lentz-Smith,

Freedom Struggles: African Americans and World War I (Cambridge, MA: Harvard University Press, 2009), 2, 4.

3. Patrick Rael, *Eighty-Eight Years: The Long Death of Slavery in the United States, 1777–1865* (Athens: The University of Georgia Press, 2015), 53, 55; James Oliver Horton and Lois E. Horton, *Slavery and the Making of America* (New York: Oxford University Press, 2005), 59–61, 65.

4. Rael, *Eighty-Eight Years*, 51, 56–57; Horton and Horton, *Slavery and the Making of America*, 57–64; James Kirby Martin and Mark Edward Lender, *A Respectable Army: The Military Origins of the Republic, 1763–1789* (Wheeling, IL: Harlan Davidson, 1982), 91, 95.

5. Horton and Horton, *Slavery and the Making of America*, 65. According to Patrick Rael, "black Loyalists' gamble paid limited dividends. It created freedom, sometimes only temporarily, for the tens of thousands who had fled plantations in Virginia, the Carolinas, and Georgia, and it had badly weakened slavery everywhere in the new states. While distressing numbers of slaves had perished in war, or had been denied the liberty they were promised, several thousand eventually found a qualified freedom—in the Canadian Maritime Provinces, Britain, or the newly established west African colony of freed slaves, Sierra Leone." Rael, *Eighty-Eight Years*, 55. Recommended sources for Black service in the American Revolution include Benjamin Quarles, *The Negro in the American Revolution* (Chapel Hill: University of North Carolina Press, 1996); Gail Lumet Buckley, *American Patriots: The Story of Blacks in the Military from the Revolution to Desert Storm* (New York: Random House, 2002), and Alan Gilbert, *Black Patriots and Loyalists: Fighting for Emancipation in the War for Independence* (Chicago: University of Chicago Press, 2013).

6. Horton and Horton, *Slavery and the Making of America*, 80–82; Bernard C. Nalty, *Strength for the Fight: A History of Black Americans in the Military* (New York: Free Press, 1986), 19; "Militia Act of 1792," transcript, George Washington's Mount Vernon, Education Primary Sources, accessed December 19, 2021, www.mountvernon.org/education/primary-sources-2/article/militia-act-of-1792/.

7. James M. McPherson, *For Cause and Comrades: Why Men Fought in the Civil War* (New York: Oxford University Press, 1997), 120–121; Joseph T. Glatthaar, *Forged in Battle: The Civil War Alliance of Black Soldiers and White Officers* (New York: Free Press, 1990), 28, 80, 81–87, 90–93, 143–144, 227–230.

8. Quoted in James M. McPherson, *Ordeal by Fire: The Civil War and Reconstruction* (1982; New York: McGraw-Hill, 1992), 347.

9. US War Department, *The War of the Rebellion: A Compilation of the Official Records of the Union and Confederate Armies*, 1 Ser., 8 (Washington, DC: Government Printing Office, 2006), 369.

10. Horton and Horton, *Slavery and the Making of America*, 175; Jack D. Foner, *Blacks and the Military in American History: A New Perspective* (New York: Praeger, 1974), 32–35; Glatthaar, *Forged in Battle*, 4, 9; James M. McPherson, *Crossroads of Freedom: Antietam* (New York: Oxford University Press, 2002), 62.

11. Douglass quoted in Elizabeth D. Leonard, *Men of Color to Arms!: Black Soldiers,*

Indian Wars, and the Quest for Equality (New York: W. W. Norton), 2010), 1–2; John David Smith, "Let Us All Be Grateful That We Have Colored Troops That Will Fight," in *Black Soldiers in Blue: African American Troops in the Civil War Era*, ed. John David Smith (Chapel Hill: University of North Carolina Press, 2002), 9–10, 18; Jennifer L. Weber, *Copperheads: The Rise and Fall of Lincoln's Opponents in the North* (2006; New York: Oxford University Press, 2008), 101–112.

12. Reid Mitchell, *Civil War Soldiers* (1988; New York: Penguin, 1997), 11–14; Foner, *Blacks and the Military in American History*, 33; Smith, "Let Us All Be Grateful," 9; White quoted in Forrest G. Wood, *Black Scare: The Racist Response to Emancipation and Reconstruction* (Berkeley: University of California Press, 1970), 43.

13. Smith, "Let Us All Be Grateful," 13–14; McPherson, *Crossroads of Freedom*, 65–71, 139–143; Glatthaar, *Forged in Battle*, 7, 9–10; Horton and Horton, *Slavery and the Making of America*, 184, 186–189.

14. Glatthaar, *Forged in Battle*, 4; Smith, "Let Us All Be Grateful," 43–49; Stevens quoted in Charles Rosenberg, "African Americans, Confederate Army," in *American Civil War: Essential Reference Guide*, ed. James A. Arnold and Robert Weiner (Santa Barbara, CA: ABC-CLIO, 2011), 4–5.

15. James G. Hollandsworth Jr., *Louisiana Native Guards: The Black Military Experience during the Civil War* (Baton Rouge: Louisiana State University Press, 1998).

16. Debra J. Sheffer, *The Buffalo Soldiers: Their Epic Story and Major Campaigns* (New York: Praeger, 2015), 15–19. See also Lawrence Lee Hewitt, "An Ironic Route to Glory: Louisiana's Native Guards at Port Hudson," in Smith, *Black Soldiers in Blue*, 78–100.

17. Chandra Manning, *What This Cruel War Was Over: Soldiers, Slavery, and the Civil War* (New York: Alfred A. Knopf, 2007), 3–18, 213–222.

18. Sheffer, *Buffalo Soldiers*, 28.

19. Sheffer, *Buffalo Soldiers*, 28–29; Smith, "Let Us All Be Grateful," 45–47; Aaron Sheehan-Dean, *The Calculus of Violence: How Americans Fought the Civil War* (Cambridge, MA: Harvard University Press, 2018), chap. 7; Lorien Foote, "A Confederate Concession," *Civil War Monitor* 11, no. 4) (Winter 2021): 34–45, 68–69. See also John Cimprich, "The Fort Pillow Massacre: Assessing the Evidence," in Smith, *Black Soldiers in Blue*, 150–165.

20. Sheffer, *Buffalo Soldiers*, 27, 60. See Keith Wilson, "In the Shadow of John Brown: The Military Service of Colonels Thomas Higginson, James Montgomery, and Robert Shaw in the Department of the South," in Smith, *Black Soldiers in Blue*, 306–327.

21. John R. Neff, *Honoring the Civil War Dead: Commemoration and the Problem of Reconciliation* (Lawrence: University Press of Kansas, 2005), 133, 190; Drew Gilpin Faust, *This Republic of Suffering: Death and the American Civil War* (New York: Alfred A. Knopf, 2008), 236.

22. Donald R. Shaffer, *After the Glory: The Struggles of Black Civil War Veterans* (Lawrence: University Press of Kansas, 2004), 23–38.

23. Shaffer, *After the Glory*, 27; Sheffer, *Buffalo Soldiers*, 34–35, 40–42; Barbara A.

Gannon, *The Won Cause: Black and White Comradeship in the Grand Army of the Republic* (Chapel Hill: University of North Carolina Press, 2011), 5–7, 85–86, 106–107, 169.

24. Foner, *Blacks and the Military in American History*, chap. 4; Sheffer, *Buffalo Soldiers*, 41–42.

25. Foner, *Blacks and the Military in American History*, chaps. 4–5; Sheffer, *Buffalo Soldiers*, chaps. 3, 8.

26. Jerome Tuccille, *The Roughest Riders: The Untold Story of the Black Soldiers in the Spanish-American War* (Chicago: Chicago Review Press, 2015), 181.

27. David Silbey, *A War of Frontier and Empire: The Philippine-American War, 1899–1902* (New York: Hill and Wang, 2007), 108–109, 131.

28. Foner, *Blacks and the Military in American History*, 95–98; Nina Mjagkij, *Loyalty in Time of Trial: The African American Experience during World War I* (Lanham, MD: Rowman and Littlefield, 2011), 66–70.

29. Lewis N. Wynne, "Brownsville: The Reaction of the Negro Press," *Phylon* 33, no. 2 (1972): 155.

30. Mjagkij, *Loyalty in Time of Trial*, xix, 51.

31. Michael S. Neiberg, *The Path to War: How the First World War Created Modern America* (New York: Oxford University Press, 2016), 202.

32. Neiberg, *Path to War*, 204.

33. Neiberg, *Path to War*, 200.

34. Lisa M. Budreau, *Bodies of War: World War I and the Politics of Commemoration in America, 1919–1933* (New York: New York University Press, 2010), 56.

35. Neiberg, *Path to War*, 201.

36. Neiberg, *Path to War*, 68.

37. Chad Williams, *Torchbearers of Democracy: African American Soldiers in the World War I Era* (Chapel Hill: University of North Carolina, 2010), 52.

38. Foner, *Blacks and the Military in American History*, 113–116; Mjagkij, *Loyalty in Time of Trial*, 66–70. For more on the Houston mutiny and riot, see Lentz-Smith, *Freedom Struggles*, chap. 2.

39. Arthur E. Barbeau and Florette Henri, *The Unknown Soldiers: African-American Troops in World War I* (Philadelphia: Da Capo, 1996), 27; Sheffer, *Buffalo Soldiers*, 175.

40. When the draft began, Blacks had no choice but to comply. As Keith notes, "In the context of early twentieth-century America, to do anything else would have been suicidal." Her research also suggests a difference in how Blacks and whites resisted the draft. Black dissenters, she notes, "manifested itself in foot-dragging or evasion, methods befitting the politically and socially oppressed. On the other hand, most white dissenters opposed the draft with tactics taken directly from the vocabulary of nineteenth-century American reform: protest letters, petitions proposing legislation modifying the Selective Draft Act, and lawsuits designed to test its constitutional validity." Jeanette Keith, *Rich Man's War, Poor Man's Fight: Race, Class, and Power in the Rural South during the First World War* (Chapel Hill: University of North Carolina Press, 2004), 52, 84.

41. Keith, *Rich Man's War, Poor Man's Fight*, 180–181.

42. Keith, *Rich Man's War, Poor Man's Fight*, 184.

43. Keith, *Rich Man's War, Poor Man's Fight*, 192.

44. Barbeau and Henri, *Unknown Soldiers*, 70–72.

45. Jeffrey T. Sammons and John H. Morrow Jr., *Harlem's Rattlers and the Great War: The Undaunted 369th Regiment and the African American Quest for Equality* (Lawrence: University Press of Kansas, 2014), 113.

46. Sheffer, *Buffalo Soldiers*, 175–176, 184; Gannon, *Won Cause*, 193–194.

47. Budreau, *Bodies of War*, 55.

48. Budreau, *Bodies of War*, 56.

49. Sheffer, *Buffalo Soldiers*, 173–183.

50. Jennifer D. Keene, *World War I: The American Soldier Experience* (Lincoln: University of Nebraska Press, 2006), 104.

51. Peter N. Nelson, *A More Unbending Battle: The Harlem Hellfighters' Struggle for Freedom in WWI and Equality at Home* (New York: Basic Civitas, 2009), 205.

52. Sheffer, *Buffalo Soldiers*, 182–183.

53. Sheffer, *Buffalo Soldiers*, 173–174, 183; Mark A. Snell, "'The Price Was Made and the Price Was Paid': Grandpa's Scar and Other Memories of the AEF," in *Unknown Soldiers: The American Expeditionary Forces in Memory and Remembrance*, ed. Mark A. Snell (Kent, OH: The Kent State University Press, 2008), 7–8; Steven Trout, *On the Battlefield of Memory: The First World War and American Remembrance, 1919–1941* (Tuscaloosa: University of Alabama Press, 2010), 180–181.

54. Lisa M. Budreau, "The Politics of Remembrance: The Gold Star Mothers' Pilgrimage and America's Fading Memory of the Great War," *Journal of Military History* 72 (April 2008): 372, 377–378; Lotter Larsen Meyers, "Mourning in a Distant Land: Gold Star Pilgrimages to American Military Cemeteries in Europe, 1930–33," *Markers* 29 (2003): 31.

55. Budreau, "The Politics of Remembrance," 400–403; Rebecca Jo Plant and Frances M. Clarke, "'The Crowning Insult': Federal Segregation and the Gold Star Mother and Widow Pilgrimages of the Early 1930s," *Journal of American History* 102, no. 2 (September 2015): 406–432.

56. Nancy Gentile Ford, "'Put Fighting Blood in Your Business': The U.S. War Department and the Reemployment of World War I Soldiers," in *Veterans' Policies, Veterans' Politics: New Perspectives on Veterans in the Modern United States*, ed. Stephen R. Ortiz (Gainesville: University Press of Florida, 2012), 138–139.

57. Sammons and Morrow, *Harlem's Rattlers and the Great War*, 3.

58. Sheffer, *Buffalo Soldiers*, 184–185.

59. Budreau, *Bodies of War*, 145–146.

60. Jennifer D. Keene, "The Long Journey Home," in Ortiz, *Veterans' Policies, Veterans' Politics*, 151–152.

61. Keene, "The Long Journey Home," 160–163.

62. Jerome Tuccille, *The War against the Vets: The World War I Bonus Army during the Great Depression* (Lincoln, NE: Potomac Books, 2018), 6–7, 17.

63. Keene, "The Long Journey Home," 165.

64. Sheffer, *Buffalo Soldiers*, 187–195; Jennifer D. Keene, "The Memory of the Great War in the African American Community," in Snell, *Unknown Soldiers*, 76.

65. Sheffer, *Buffalo Soldiers*, 187–188, 195–196.

66. John Whiteclay Chambers II, *To Raise an Army: The Draft Comes to Modern America* (New York: Free, 1987), 2.

"By Word or Act Oppose the Cause of the United States"

Loyalty in Civil War–Era and Great War–Era America

Kanisorn Wongsrichanalai

On the morning of July 22, 1918, a man named Edgar Held walked into the railroad ticket offices at El Paso, Texas, and allegedly remarked to the agent, "Well, Mr. Monroe, I see we sunk the *Cleveland*; you cannot blame us; they took the boats from us and we have a right to sink them if we get a chance." Monroe reported the encounter to the authorities, who then arrested the German-born Held for violating the Sedition Act. The indictment claimed that by "we," Held had meant Imperial Germany and explained that the *Cleveland* was a steamship that the US government had confiscated for its own use in the Great War. During the trial, the prosecution called witnesses who testified to Held's other antiwar actions. One claimed that, during a liberty loan drive, Held declared, "Germany had a right to sink the *Lusitania* and that he would not give any of his money to kill his own people over there." Held, when he took the stand, denied having made any antiwar statements and presented himself as a loyal American who had purchased liberty bonds. Unconvinced by Held's testimony, the jury found him guilty and the court sentenced him to sixty days in the county jail and fined him $500.[1] If he had made similar comments during the American Civil War, Held, an ordinary citizen, would probably not have been arrested or tried. Greater civil liberties existed for everyday citizens in a nation racked by a sectional and fratricidal rebellion than in the one that entered a global contest in the name of making the world safe for democracy.

In its nearly two and a half centuries of existence, because of the nature of its societal structure, the United States has, especially during wartime, confronted the issue of determining its citizens' loyalty. Government leaders during wartime have been responsible for ensuring both battlefield victory and home front safety. To accomplish these goals, they have turned their gazes to their own citizens, often suspiciously. That suspicion has led to the suppression of dissenting voices, the limiting of civil liberties, and the incarceration as well as expulsion of the alleged disloyal and dangerous. Immigrants and people with cultural ties to a foreign homeland often faced the greatest scrutiny.

Examining what contemporaries in the Civil War and Great War eras considered the limits of acceptable and unacceptable activities in times of crises highlights the fissures, suspicions, and animosities in American society. It reveals the importance of the government's physical presence in communities, national leaders' tone and example, political parties' role in channeling discontent, and officials' sanction of vigilante actions. Ultimately, the manner in which officials in both conflicts levied charges of disloyalty and sowed suspicion hindered rather than strengthened the goals of unifying the community in wartime.

For the Great War generation, the American Civil War represented an example of a chaotic home front. Draft riots and Copperheads spreading dissent marred the image of a united North, while bread riots and state-level opposition hindered the Confederate war effort. In contrast, during the Great War, Woodrow Wilson's government could not and would not tolerate such actions and took measures to bend the American people to its will. Wilson's government, of course, had several advantages in accomplishing its goal. First, it ruled over a populace much more used to having an active federal government than the Americans of Lincoln's and Davis's day. In addition, the government diverted and diffused public criticism by letting local authorities manage the most controversial home front act of the war, drafting citizens. Wilson also benefited from having a civilian department and federal agency, overwhelmed as it was, in charge of internal policing, thus allowing the military to focus on winning the war. Second, the people it targeted—potential German saboteurs and spies—more clearly stood out than people who simply harbored differing political opinions during the

Civil War. And, finally, it could capitalize on the idea of a reunited nation in the throes of a reconciliationist wave that had swept the nation following the fiftieth anniversary of the Civil War. War with the Central Powers allowed for an expansive American national identity to embrace Northerners and Southerners as they put aside their sectional differences and stood shoulder to shoulder to face a common foreign threat. Wilson and the Congress, with the passage of the Espionage and Sedition Acts, embraced more fully the federal authority and power to control the population—a power previously employed by the Union military in the Border States as well as parts of the conquered Confederacy and by Confederate authorities in areas like East Tennessee and the Hill Country of Texas during the Civil War.

The Great War demonstrated what a determined and robust federal government could do to suppress dissent and police its people in wartime. During World War II, Japanese Americans would bear the brunt of these lessons. In the end, both conflicts saw the expansion of the federal government's power to suppress dissent and, for some Americans, made the case that civil liberties had limitations in wartime. But, for others, the wars helped demonstrate the importance of dissent and speaking out. The American Civil Liberties Union (ACLU), for example, emerged from the oppressiveness of the Great War home front. Both conflicts helped the modernization of the United States by demonstrating the growing reach of federal authority and also establishing a firm tradition of opposition to restrictive measures. That push and pull, that ongoing dialogue between the necessities of wartime and the rights of the people, is perhaps the most lasting legacy of the loyalty debates in these two eras.

The Civil War: In the Union States

The outbreak of civil war heightened preexisting suspicions of various groups in American society. Where ethnic or religious minorities might have occasioned a passing remark in peacetime, the allegiance of outsiders and nonconformists became a matter of life and death in time of war. For example, antebellum Americans viewed members of the Church of Jesus Christ of Latter-Day Saints with distrust. While the nation split on the issue of slavery, most Americans considered the Mormon practice of polygamy immoral. That feeling remained even in the midst of the secession crisis. In the spring of 1861, one major newspaper proclaimed that South Carolina, which had seceded, "was more loyal . . . than Utah."[2] Overall, however, the allegiance of the Union's immigrant population represented a matter of greater urgency in the conflict than what the Mormons would do in the West.

Over four million immigrants from Europe had entered the United States by the time of the Civil War, and nearly a quarter of the white population of the northern states had immediate European roots. (Correspondingly, European-born individuals made up a quarter of the United States Army during the war.) Indeed, the Union army's diversity reflected its own population with men from Ireland, Scandinavia, the United Kingdom, Russia, and the German territories. In the prewar years, native-born Protestant Americans viewed immigrants with wariness because of their growing numbers, their membership in ethnic organizations, and, in some instances, their Catholic beliefs. Additionally, many immigrants, especially the Irish, identified with the Democratic Party, setting them up as opponents to the Republican administration. When war came, however, immigrants rushed to the defense of the Union. Many European-born soldiers had fought in their countries' respective revolutions and, failing in them, came to the United States where they viewed the Union cause as an extension of their own goal of political liberty. Many believed the United States represented the best hope for democratic reform worldwide and fought to preserve it. By serving in the war, these men also hoped to demonstrate their own as well as the loyalty of their immigrant communities.[3] One soldier in the predominantly Irish Sixty-Ninth New York argued that the war allowed immigrants to show "their devotion to the Union," while another explained that he had volunteered "because of my love for my whole adopted country, not the North, or the South, but the Union, one and inseparable."[4] Native-born Americans, however, often questioned the commitment along with the fighting effectiveness of immigrant soldiers.[5]

Civil War Americans' concerns about foreign-born residents stemmed from larger fears about the trustworthiness of all members of northern society. When the nation split apart, many citizens underwent an agonizing process to determine where their true loyalties rested. In the end, some Northerners cast their lot with the Confederacy. One scholar has noted that Pennsylvanians who sided with the rebels sometimes did so for a variety of reasons, including ideological agreement, economic and familial ties, and the simple fact that they happened to live in the new Confederacy at the time of its creation.[6] Whatever the reasons, the shifting loyalties of many groups created a popular anxiety about the very idea of loyalty itself.

The federal government moved quickly to deal with issues of loyalty. In the early weeks of the conflict, Lincoln's administration attempted to stem the loss of states and prepare for the grueling contest ahead. Of these preparations, one of the most important was safeguarding the home front. The president delegated enormous power to Secretary of State William H. Seward who had the authority to arrest any person suspected of disloyal intentions. "I can touch a bell on my right hand and order the arrest of a citizen in Ohio," Seward boasted to a British official, continuing, "I can touch the bell again and order the imprisonment of a citizen of New York, and no power on earth but that of the President can release them. Can the Queen of England, in her dominions, say as much?" Many such arrests, however, came from lower-level officials who interpreted disloyalty on their own terms. Lincoln deferred to his agents closest to local incidents, allowing them to exercise their discretion. While he did urge, in 1863, that unless "manifestly and urgent" threats became known, general arrests of people spouting partisan rhetoric "should cease," Lincoln did not actually put an end to the arrests of political dissenters. Military officials, therefore, exercised considerable agency in bringing cases of alleged disloyal behavior to their superiors in the federal government. Union authorities detained between thirteen and thirty-eight thousand individuals during the Civil War. Most took the oath of allegiance and walked free within a few weeks. Still, the arrests both sent a powerful message to would-be dissenters and galvanized the political opposition. Northern Democrats criticized the administration for the suppression of civil liberties and made the issue a centerpiece of their campaigns.[7]

While some Civil War–era Americans had indeed violated the law by evading the draft, trading with the rebels, or sabotaging the Union's war-waging capabilities, others found themselves imprisoned for acts that would get Great War–era Americans in trouble as well. Provost marshals picked up individuals who criticized the draft, opposed the emancipation policy, professed support for or sympathy with the Confederacy, or who refused to take the oath of allegiance. Sometimes Union civilians took matters into their own hands, threatening Democratic editors with violence. Despite such actions by official and unofficial actors, most of the Democratic presses continued to churn out harsh criticisms of the Lincoln administration throughout the war. During his tenure, political enemies called the president everything from a "despot" and "tyrant" to a "perjurer," "ignoramus," and "fiend."[8] Woodrow Wilson's officers would not have put up with such criticisms.

Although weakened by the loss of its dominant Southern wing, the Civil War–era Democratic Party, which had dominated national politics for a decade, remained an imposing force. The American tradition of guarding against tyrannical governments inspired a peace faction of the Democratic Party (known as Copperheads). The administration's actions provided them with plenty of fodder as the president suspended habeas corpus and declared martial law. Most of the Copperheads sincerely believed that Lincoln's actions threatened the republic. Indeed, one scholar has maintained that the antiwar movement in the Union states, given voice by the Peace Democrats, represented a real threat to the war effort. By encouraging men to avoid the draft or desert, the Peace Democrats forced the army "to divide its attention and at times send troops home to keep order there." Ongoing criticisms of the administration, stirring discontent especially in the Midwest, fretted the president who feared, what he called, "the fire in the rear."[9]

The Lincoln administration's pursuance of an emancipation policy, justified by military necessity, sparked the greatest outrage among his Democratic opponents. Copperheads crowed that they had long seen the hand of abolitionists behind Lincoln's actions. Additionally, the suspension of habeas corpus throughout the Union after the announcement of the preliminary Emancipation Proclamation added fuel to the Democrats' criticisms. The emancipation policy, because it targeted slavery but also opened the door to African American troops, built on Democrats' long-standing racist attitudes toward Blacks.[10]

For Irish Americans, a key Democratic constituency, the fall of 1862 represented a turning point. The president not only announced his emancipation policy but also removed Gen. George B. McClellan, a Democrat and revered military leader, from command. Additionally, the War Department finalized plans to draft citizens as the number of volunteers dwindled. Irishmen who harbored long-standing animosities toward African Americans for fear of economic competition condemned the new emancipation policy. One influential editor declared that "not one volunteer in a hundred" had enlisted in the name of abolition. Other papers expressed similar sentiment, unable or unwilling to see the military benefits of emancipation.[11] Opposed to volunteering in a war that would liberate the enslaved, they even more vigorously protested people being *drafted* to fight in one.

Indeed, many Americans considered the draft—the result of a stalled war effort—as the ultimate threat to their civil liberties by a tyrannical government. Race, ethnicity, fears of economic competition, conspiratorial beliefs, distrust, and paranoia all culminated in resistance to the northern draft. In the mountains of Pennsylvania, a stronghold of antigovernment resistance, residents threatened, harassed, and even murdered draft agents.[12]

Irish immigrants on the home front violently resisted the draft, feeling especially aggrieved that wealthier Americans could pay $300 for a substitute. By the summer of 1863 when the New York City draft riots broke out, Irish anger over the course of the war, the casualties sustained, and people's lack of trust in the administration and the new emancipation policy, combined with their lingering fear of economic competition and racist sentiments toward African Americans, boiled over into violence. On July 13, an angry crowd of native-born Americans, along with Irish and German immigrants, protested the draft. The demonstration quickly spun out of control, and as the first group of skilled workers returned home, a large Irish-Catholic crowd made up of mostly unskilled workers entered the fray, attacking symbols of authority and the Republican Party. The mob also targeted African Americans. When the smoke had cleared after five days of rioting, over one thousand lay dead or injured, and the government had been forced to bring troops straight from the Gettysburg battlefield to restore order. Even though the mob contained people from many backgrounds, critics seized on incidents like the draft riots to question the commitment of the Irish. Unionists painted the Irish and other Democrats as nothing more than dangerous Copperheads of dubious loyalty whose actions jeopardized the nation's war-waging ability. Immigrant groups, therefore, walked a fine line in wartime. Even though they had ample opportunities to demonstrate their loyalty to their adopted homes, any actions considered "disloyal" swiftly played into lingering stereotypes.[13] Even when Irish immigrants filled the ranks of Union regiments headed to war, old animosities did not disappear. At a ceremony to send off Irish troops on Boston Common, one newspaper reporter heard a bystander declare, "There goes a load of Irish rubbish out of the city."[14]

Even some native-born Protestant Americans resisted fighting for the Union. In the rural mountain areas of Pennsylvania, farmers feared for their families, farms, fields, and harvests. Many newspapers even urged farmers to stay at their plows and grow more food as a demonstration of their devotion to the cause. Additionally, attacks by the Democratic press, conflating abolitionists with Republicans, may have given some men pause before enlisting. Perhaps men who opposed Lincoln's leadership kept others from serving their country in this time of crisis.[15] During the Great War, Woodrow Wilson used harsh methods to prevent such phenomena from repeating themselves.

The Civil War: Along the Border

Perhaps nowhere in Civil War America was the issue of loyalty among the civilian population more complicated than in the Border States. In Missouri, for example, Union generals waged a harsh campaign against marauding guerrillas and insurgents whose lack of uniforms made them difficult to identify. Their strategies forced Missourians to reveal their allegiances. Gen. Henry W. Halleck, for instance, demanded that St. Louis residents support the growing number of refugees in the area. He sought to raise funds from rebels, those who provided "pecuniary or other aid" to the rebel cause, and those who voiced their support for the Confederacy. The general maintained that "there can be no middle course of individual neutrality" in this contest, explaining, "All citizens who are not rebels must loyally support the Government. If they aid rebels, they are traitors; if they refuse aid to the cause of the Union, they are disloyal." Gen. John M. Schofield, meanwhile, established the Enrolled Missouri Militia, made up of all able-bodied residents. His orders, in the words of one scholar, "left no real middle ground. Men were either committed to the Union and willing to take up arms to protect it from guerrillas, or they refused to enlist and prove their utter disloyalty."[16]

As usual, immigrants in contested regions found their loyalties questioned. Torn between competing political and sectional factions, most immigrants favored the United States. In war-torn Missouri, pro-Confederate governor Claiborne Jackson pushed anti-immigrant policies with his attacks on ethnic sites of congregation such as saloons. His actions led Missouri's Germans to help organize a pro-Union militia, which also attracted members of other ethnic groups along with native-born Americans. Having picked a side, immigrants had no choice but to stand by their decision, especially when faced with raids by anti-immigrant rebel guerrillas in the contested Kansas-Missouri region.[17]

In addition to Border State residents, those who lived in areas that

switched back and forth between Union and Confederate control faced difficult decisions when it came to expressing their loyalties. Most individuals
did their best to adapt to their shifting fortunes. When Union forces occupied Huntsville, Alabama, for example, resident James Hickman traded cotton with them, took the oath of loyalty, and helped track down guerrillas. He
further antagonized loyal Confederates when he opened a dry-goods store
and began profiting from the war. When Union forces withdrew, Confederate officials, eager to make an example of the collaborator, arrested Hickman and put him on trial. Luckily for the accused, the jury understood the
circumstances of living under occupation and knew how useful an "elastic
definition of loyalty" could be.[18] Hickman walked free, but the trial revealed
the awkward situation that many residents of contested regions faced.

The Civil War: In the Confederacy

Embarking on a war of survival in the midst of its secessionist birth, the Confederate States of America sought to present a united front. As with all revolutions, of course, pockets of opposition to the societal change remained.
The Confederate government sought to stifle dissent but, as its needs for
more manpower grew and its centralized power expanded to meet the demands of the conflict, opposition to the Richmond authorities intensified.
When the war went poorly, many more rebels—from state governors to everyday citizens—reassessed their full commitment to the Davis government
and openly challenged the notion of a united Confederate nation.

From the very beginning of the war, and building on antebellum suspicions of immigrant communities in the South, many Confederates questioned the commitment of foreign-born soldiers. In New Orleans, for example, some immigrants and native-born residents objected to slavery, while
others opposed secession and the Confederate government's policies. Officials had to declare martial law in March 1862, a testament to the unruly
nature of the residents and the need for the rebel government to compel allegiance. Those who openly opposed the Confederacy faced harsh sentences
as well as threats from pro-Confederate mobs that terrorized their less-than-
loyal neighbors. During the siege of New Orleans, dissatisfied soldiers (both
native and foreign-born) went on strike. When the Confederacy's largest city
fell in the spring of 1862, the rebel commander blamed the "mostly foreign

enlistments," meaning those from Irish or German backgrounds, "without any great interests at stake in the ultimate success of the revolution." In fact, however, many New Orleans residents beyond the immigrant community had expressed their ambivalence about the Confederate cause.[19] Those promoting the idea of a unified Confederate populace, however, did not wish to highlight disloyalty by native-born Southerners.

Proponents of the Confederacy preferred to blame immigrants and ethnic minorities for their deficiencies in supporting the cause. Many native-born Southerners questioned the allegiance of the Irish, since some refused to fight for their adopted home. In the capital of the Confederacy, the press blamed Irish women for burdening local resources. Editors charged the women with "speculation and extortion" and selling out to "the enemy on the very first sight of danger." After the "bread riot" of 1863, locals blamed "prostitutes, professional thieves, [and] Irish and Yankee hags, gallows birds from all lands but our own" even though native-born Southerners had a large role to play in the violence.[20] Despite accusations about their lack of loyalty and service, around twenty thousand Irishmen served in the rebel ranks.[21] Meanwhile, despite Confederate officials' best efforts to unify people within their borders and pacify opponents, areas of resistance to Confederate authority still remained from Appalachia to Georgia to Alabama and Mississippi. Even in areas where armed resistance to the Confederacy did not exist, depravations and starvation led to food riots in large cities and small ones across the young nation.[22]

Because the Richmond government kept its attention on the war effort, it deferred issues of internal security in vast regions of its internal territory to local home guards. Such groups, however, tended toward vigilantism and cruelty. From the start of the secessionist movement, those who supported the Union faced the threat of violence and death from rebels determined to enforce loyalty to their new cause. Men who opposed the Confederacy found themselves arrested and punished for voicing their sentiments. One Henry H. Blalock in North Carolina threatened Confederate leadership and predicted that emancipation would result from the crisis. Authorities arrested and charged him with "insurrectional, conspiratorial words against the Confederacy." With the same logic that superpatriotic Americans would voice during the Great War, pro-Confederate forces argued in one instance that "no respectable woman would engage in disloyal behavior and that no disloyal woman therefore deserved the respect of a Confederate soldier." As the war went on, even religious figures faced the wrath of rebel enforcers who lynched and murdered those who did not demonstrate sufficient fealty to the Confederate cause. Meanwhile, jails overflowed with Southerners who refused to swear loyalty to the Confederacy.[23] Perhaps one of the worst wartime atrocities took place in Cooke County, Texas, where Confederate loyalists led by the provost marshal, James G. Bourland, rounded up dozens of suspected Unionists. The "citizens court" then sent forty-four of them to the gallows in what became known as the "Great Hanging at Gainesville."[24]

From the very start of its existence, resisting communities throughout the region contradicted the Confederacy's claim that it represented a united front across its territory. Never as invested in the institution of chattel slavery as others, the mountainous regions of Appalachia opposed secession and, when their votes failed to prevent the sundering of the Union, refused to accept the authority of the Confederate government. West Virginia even seceded from Virginia after the commonwealth left the United States. East Tennessee remained a bastion of unionist sentiment during the war. Meanwhile, pockets of armed resistance in Mississippi, Eastern Texas, and the Piedmont Region of North Carolina held their own against Confederate attempts to silence opposition. Confederate authorities attempted to quash these resisters while retaliation between anti- and pro-Confederate forces led to even more suffering in this war within the war. Whether because they did not wish to leave the Union, fight for slavery, serve in the rebel army, or answer to the central authority in Richmond, these communities bore the brunt of violent retaliation. In the end, Jefferson Davis's government had too much to do in fighting for the survival of their new nation that it simply could not put down resistance to its authority everywhere. Despite home front resistance, however, the Confederacy had an excellent chance to win the war on the battlefield with the armies that it could muster, and previous assertions that the Confederacy lacked a sufficiently strong central government or that its citizens were too wedded to democratic ideals to fully support the war effort simply do not account for the closeness of the military contest. Additionally, as several scholars have convincingly argued, just because citizens of the Confederacy criticized their government officials, it did not mean that they did not support the cause of independence.[25]

The Great War: Federal Sanction

"Patriotism is a value in America," one scholar observed, "and during World War I, it took on a religious quality." The Wilson administration itself stoked patriotic passions in order to mobilize its citizens during the war. As Secretary of the Treasury William G. McAdoo recalled, "We capitalized the profound impulse called patriotism" by enlisting print and performance artists to sell liberty bonds. The secretary's refusal to pay for the war through taxes or borrowing prompted him, in the words of historian David M. Kennedy, "to mobilize emotions . . . to substitute patriotic fervor for the real economic price he would not ask the country to pay." "Every person who refuses to subscribe or who takes the attitude of let the other fellow do it," the secretary explained at the time, "is a friend of Germany and I would like nothing better than to tell it to him to his face. A man who can't lend his government $1.25 per week at the rate of 4% interest is not entitled to be an American citizen."[26] And thus the Wilson Administration proclaimed that one's patriotism could be calculated by accounting for how much one had financially supported the war effort. The government defined loyalty for all, with no room for dissent.

President Wilson viewed unity in American society as a necessity in wartime. He could not afford the draft riots of the Civil War North or the regions of outright resistance to the government of the Civil War South. But although the Civil War offered Wilson a cautionary tale, he also understood the necessity to quickly fill the ranks. Despite his impassioned war message, the president's words did not galvanize young men to rush to arms. Indeed, fewer than forty-five hundred men came forward to serve in the first ten days after Congress declared war against Germany. Volunteering rates lagged behind both the Civil War and Spanish-American War. Government officials resorted to a national draft but also sought to suppress those who opposed or questioned the war because of the belief that such voices spread misinformation and kept men from enlisting or staying in the ranks. The governor of North Carolina, Thomas W. Bickett, explained that troops deserted because "they have not been told the truth about this war. . . . Ignorance and misinformation are at the bottom of all this trouble and all this shame." The federal government went to great lengths to stifle opposition to the draft law, arresting and prosecuting critics like Emma Goldman and Jane Addams.[27]

The vigilante froth and hyperpatriotic sentiments that characterized Great War–era America arose from a federal government that, despite having a

tremendous amount of power and overseeing a massively increasing bureaucracy, was inadequate to the task of monitoring a continent-wide nation.
Wilson and his officials relied on volunteers to galvanize support for the war
and inadvertently opened the floodgates for citizens, eager to prove their
own loyalty, to enforce lockstep patriotism in their own manner. Wilson's
administration emerged from decades of growing governmental power and,
armed with the lessons of the Civil War era, readily unleashed its authority
to shore up support on the home front. Focused on enlisting troops and supplying military needs for the war effort in Europe, the administration coordi-
nated bond drives and recruitment programs with local groups and appealed
to volunteerism through its propaganda arm, thus prompting an anxious
citizenry to become the enforcers of a strict nationalism. Local officials did
not need much urging in order to demonstrate their commitment to the
war effort. In New York City, officers used the broad charge of "disorderly
conduct" to detain public speakers and limit free expression. In some places,
police officers demanded proof of loyalty in the form of draft cards or war
bond receipts. The government, press, and local leaders all contributed to a
climate of suppression and suspicion among the populace. One scholar has
argued that such heavy-handed actions grew out of the fear that a majority
of citizens did not actually support the war. Additionally, the curtailment of
free speech also "altered the definition of democracy" due to the silencing of
"argument, debate, and . . . majority rule."[28]

During the Great War, one's ethnic identity became much more important than it had been during the Civil War. In 1917 the United States went to
war against several foreign nations that had sent millions of their citizens to
American shores in the late nineteenth and the first decade of the twentieth century. Could immigrants from the Central Power nations be trusted
to support American interests? By its own legislation, Wilson's government
appeared to sanction the civilian harassment of alleged dissenters, antiwar
individuals, and those with uncertain loyalties.

Even before 1917 the issue of loyalty had already entered the public conversation in the United States. After he expelled German officials from the
country for their role in attempting to delay American delivery of war materials to the Allies, President Wilson launched an attack on "hyphenated
Americans." "There are," the president proclaimed in his third annual message, "citizens of the United States, I blush to admit, born under other flags
but welcomed under our generous naturalization laws to the full freedom

and opportunity of America, who have poured the poison of disloyalty into the very arteries of our national life. . . . Such creatures of passion, disloyalty, and anarchy must be crushed out." Earlier that year, the president told a group of newly naturalized citizens, "America does not consist of groups. A man who thinks of himself as belonging to a particular national group in America has not yet become an American."[29]

After the United States joined the war against the Central Powers, both government and nongovernment actors sought to solidify public support for the nation's new course. Local authorities, seeking to demonstrate loyalty, mirrored federal actions. In South Carolina, for example, officials limited free speech in order to demonstrate lockstep support for the war. Governor Richard Manning and his allies "promoted patriotism and built support for President Wilson through aggressive education programs and the suppression of what they perceived as dissent" and, in so doing, "conflated national and political loyalty, fearing that any opposition to his program for statewide defense might derail his efforts to align South Carolina with the demands of the American war effort."[30]

At the national level, government leaders called for loyalty but also raised fears about enemies in society. The Committee on Public Information (CPI) led by George Creel functioned as the standard-bearer for government propaganda and drummed up support for the war. In Missouri, officials established the Patriotic Speakers Bureau and even enlisted preachers to the pro-war cause by sending "packets of information stressing God's approval of the war." The nation's entrance into the global conflict also signaled an intensification in Wilson's tone toward anyone who did not fully commit to the national interest. Politics, Wilson had told Congress, "is adjourned" for the duration of the war. The council of defense in Missouri considered this reasonable, proclaiming that "politics are Ousted" in the state and banned any of its members from seeking public office. Wilson had no patience for those who did not fully commit to the war and warned, "Woe be to the man or group of men that seeks to stand in our way." The president continued to heap suspicion on ethnic Germans in American society when he warned during his Flag Day speech on June 14, "The military masters of Germany [have] filled our unsuspecting communities with vicious spies and conspirators and [have] sought to corrupt the opinion of the people."[31] The president truly believed that German spies had infiltrated American society and feared that their plots might hinder the war effort through sabotage or by sowing dissent. Wilson set the tone and example for his officials and other native-born Americans to follow.

And follow they did. Although some Americans volunteered for service, even more answered the call by registering for and responding to the military draft. Reviving the process that both the Confederate and Union governments had resorted to during the Civil War, Wilson's officials set about explaining how the draft would work to the nation. Newspapers also helped explain the process and, at the same time, praised the compliant while condemning those who refused to participate. In the South, writers promised a patriotic response from the region. One newspaper from Georgia declared, "This section, as it has always done in the past, will furnish its quota of men and money to the cause." Some took the opportunity to demonstrate the South's return to the loyal fold yet again. The timing could not have worked out better for those who wished to make the connection between the past and present. Confederate veterans had coincidentally assembled in Washington, DC, for a reunion on Jefferson Davis's birthday on the day before draft registration began. Those who had fought against the US government a generation earlier now celebrated their loyalty by championing the service of their descendants in the name of a nation reunited. "Papers across the South highlighted the historical serendipity," one historian notes.[32] President Wilson, in speaking to Confederate veterans, celebrated registration day as "a day of reunion, a day of noble memories, a day of dedication, a day of renewal of the spirit which has made American great among the peoples of the world."[33]

Despite the focus on foreign-born individuals and the portrayal of a united front, not all Americans supported the war. Indeed, the speaker of the US House of Representatives, Rep. Claude Kitchin of North Carolina, opposed the American entrance into the conflict, reasoning before Congress voted to declare war, "nothing in that cause, nothing in that quarrel, has or does involve a moral or equitable or material interest in, or obligation of, our Government or our people." Religious pacifists remained steadfast, while others continued to doubt that European matters concerned Americans. Others believed that corporations and big businesses rather than national interest drove the administration's actions. Some opponents simply refused to leave their families uncared for and others objected to the draft itself or how their local authorities operated it. Not even all the members of the president's political party supported his administration's actions. Agrarian Democrats and former populists who had joined the Democratic Party opposed the conflict, declaring it a "rich man's war, poor man's fight." One historian has calculated that Southerners deserted at a higher rate than Northerners. Indeed, the deep divides and disagreements about the war "exposed the myth of the politically Solid South and illuminated the class divisions usually sublimated into loyalty to the Democratic Party and white supremacy."[34]

To suppress dissent and wartime opposition, Congress passed the Espionage (1917) and Sedition (1918) Acts. These laws criminalized actions deemed detrimental to the war effort and stifled opposition to the conflict. As a result of these laws, during the war, the federal government prosecuted over two thousand people for "allegedly disloyal, seditious, or incendiary speech." The laws also led to the harassment of antiwar groups and suspect communities. The Socialist Party, for example, represented the largest group of Americans opposed to the conflict. They boasted a membership of almost seventy thousand and had garnered over a half a million votes in the 1916 presidential election. An emergency meeting of the group in St. Louis proclaimed the declaration of war "a crime against the people of the United States" and called for Americans to resist censorship, conscription, and curtailment of rights. By opposing the war, the Socialist Party, in the words of historian Arthur M. Schlesinger Sr., "tarred itself without justification with copperheadism," referencing the Democratic Party's opposition to the wartime policies of Lincoln.[35] The postmaster general, Albert S. Burleson, banned socialist tracts from the mail and suspended mailing privileges for the group, a tactic employed widely during the war. In the South, the post office effectively shut down printing presses that criticized or challenged the government by denying them mailing privileges. This action prevented like-minded individuals and groups that opposed the government's actions from coalescing. Only pro-war government-sanctioned propaganda came through.[36]

The Sedition Act itself emerged out of what some considered the inadequacies of the Espionage Act. Attorney General Thomas Watt Gregory wanted the power to quash "disloyal utterances." He claimed that such statements "naturally irritated and angered the communities in which they occurred." Gregory used the example of a German American who had been lynched by his neighbors as a sign that patriotic Americans found the existing laws inadequate and were *forced* to resort to vigilante justice. Instead of going after the vigilante mobs, the attorney general argued that his agency required additional powers to protect would-be victims of mob violence by arresting them. The resulting Sedition Act prohibited "any disloyal, profane, scurrilous, or abusive language" about the American government. The federal government also reorganized branches of the Justice Department, the military intelligence units, and the post office to monitor groups considered susceptible to foreign manipulation, and antiwar organizations. The state of war and the new internal security laws bred a hyperpatriotic environment that silenced traditional political speech. In the eyes of some Americans, the president himself transcended his mortal being and became a symbol of the nation, thus immune from criticism.[37]

The Great War: Vigilantism

Prompted by government messaging, a majority of Americans eyed dissenters with suspicion and embraced superpatriotic positions. President Wilson himself encouraged this paranoia by warning that Germany had "filled our unsuspecting communities . . . with spies and set criminal intrigues everywhere." In answering the call to exercise vigilance, however, many Americans crossed the line into vigilantism. National leaders attempted to straddle this fine line, praising vigilance as "a valuable work of service and voluntarism that embodied American democracy" while condemning vigilantism as posing a threat to law and order. Those who pursued extralegal activities in the name of the government, however, viewed themselves as performing the duties of patriotic citizens.[38]

Between the Civil War and Great War eras, Americans had gotten used to certain segments in their society monitoring the activities of other groups. Although they did not like the use of the military to enforce laws during peacetime (as President Grant discovered when he tried to quell Reconstruction-era violence in the South), many Americans seemed content to delegate the power of enforcing law and order to certain groups of individuals. The Pinkertons, for example, assumed many peacekeeping and law enforcement duties after the Civil War. Answering to any interest that could pay their fee, some Pinkertons became strike breakers and thus earned the scorn of labor unions and workers. Others, however, tracked down embezzlers and white-collar criminals who fled across international borders. The federal government even supported some of these ventures, since it lacked a law enforcement arm itself. Some countries came to consider the Pinkertons the national police force for the United States. On the domestic front, moral reformers and white Southerners shadowed and recorded the activities of prostitutes and politically active African Americans. But a growing awareness of the uses of federal power also came about during the Progressive Era as temperance campaigners, among others, realized that they needed federal power to achieve their reformist goals. As reformers seized authority at various levels of government, they helped Americans accept the idea of a more powerful federal government. When war came, the American populace had accustomed themselves to monitoring certain groups of people as the price of modernity and reform.

When the war began, the federal government turned to civilians for help in policing their fellow citizens. Unlike the Civil War era when the military arrested and quashed the most egregious critics, the Great War era civilians, with the blessing of federal officials, took on the task themselves with the result that the superpatriotic mob considered even the slightest infractions or flimsiest suspicions grounds for punishment. To demonstrate their own loyalty, these individuals took the task of policing their neighbors very seriously. An editorial in the *Albany Journal* urged both men and women to apprehend any "soft-shell pacifist or hard-boiled but poorly camouflaged pro-German" who made "seditious or unpatriotic remarks about your Uncle Sam" and hand them over to the authorities. Many Americans, following the lead of the president, wanted to purge "disloyal" opinions from the public sphere. In some instances, what local authorities considered a threat could be rather absurd. Kansas City police arrested a Canadian war veteran who regaled audiences with his personal stories with the intent of encouraging enlistments. Officials, however, feared that such vivid descriptions of the horrors of trench life would, in fact, hinder recruitment.[39]

Once the war began, hundreds of thousands of Americans joined vigilance groups with names like the American Defense Society, the Sedition Slammers, and the Boy Spies of America. The American Protective League became the largest such group with a quarter of a million members. Fully committed to maintaining order, these individuals ignored the fact that their many actions, which targeted socialists, ethnic minorities, and other wartime dissenters, actually violated the law. League members "bugged, burglarized, slandered, and illegally arrested other Americans. They opened mail, intercepted telegrams, served as *agents provocateurs*, and were the chief commandoes in a series of extralegal and often violent 'slacker raids' against supposed draft evaders in 1918." Yet such actions, a violation of the authority of the state to maintain order, actually served the interests of the government by suppressing dissent. Understaffed, underfunded, and overwhelmed by the war, the Justice Department made use of these badge-wearing volunteers. Attorney General Gregory, unintentionally echoing Secretary of State Seward's boast from the Civil War, declared, "I have today several hundred thousand private citizens—some as individuals, most of them as members of patriotic bodies, engaged in . . . assisting the heavily overworked Federal authorities in keeping an eye on disloyal individuals and making reports of disloyal utterances." This heightened state of alert and enthusiasm by the vigilantes led to thousands of reports of alleged disloyalty flowing into the Department of Justice. Bands of vigilantes confronted antiwar groups and those suspected of sympathizing with the enemy. They equated a person's antiwar sentiments with being pro-German. While violence flared up on occasion, most activities involved spying on fellow citizens to see if they had registered for the draft or purchased war bonds. The head of the Iowa Council of Defense urged people to "find out what his neighbor thinks." Like most modern wars, as Christopher Capozzola observes, this "blurred the line between state and society" and "tied private coercions to state interests."[40] These "volunteers" mirrored the actions of the Pinkertons in that they operated with government sanction but, not actually holding any official office or representing any agency (despite the fact that some of them carried cards that read "Secret Service Division"), they did not need to conform to any legal restraints or restrictions that bound actual federal officers.[41]

Some sections of the nation seemed more radical than others in advancing superpatriotic activities aimed at curbing potential dissent. A large number of attacks against German culture and the German language took place in the Midwest. In May 1918 the governor of Iowa banned the use of all languages other than English. The American Defense Society, meanwhile, proclaimed German "not a fit language to teach clean and pure American boys and girls." Eager to prove their loyalty, some German organizations supported the Iowa governor's ban on non-English languages. Rev. John C. Orth, head of the German-American Patriotic Association, approved of the order, explaining, "It is impossible to have complete loyalty in this state as long as there is a great faction fighting to preserve the German language."[42] Other German Americans in Iowa refused to suppress their cultural heritage. Instead, they reacted to attacks on their culture by supporting socialist candidates, thus further raising suspicions of their loyalty. In Texas, "the line between perceived disloyalty and ethnic cultural expression dissolved." Large numbers of citizens reported those deemed to have shown insufficient support for the war or suspected of being saboteurs to the authorities. Texas also passed the "Texas Loyalty Bill," which prohibited any criticism of the war effort, the federal government, the armed forces, or the American flag. Additionally, the law banned residents from having in their possession the flag of a nation at war with the United States. The governor then established an unpaid force of "Loyalty Rangers" to identify disloyal elements in the state, arrest violators, and monitor both German-speaking regions along with the Texas-Mexico border region where many feared a German-inspired uprising of disgruntled Blacks and Hispanics.[43]

In many instances, social policing of patriotism went beyond officially sanctioned actions. In Iowa, war supporters set up "slacker" or "loyalty courts" to judge how many war bonds one could afford and, thus, should have purchased. Those who did not contribute their due faced accusations of being un-American. But harassment over bond purchases did not compare to those who faced lynch mobs. The most infamous wartime case involved a German-born man named Robert Prager who had actually tried to enlist in the United States Navy but could not do so because of blindness in one eye. Rumors spread that the coal miner spied for the Germans and, as a result, Prager died at the hands of a mob that lynched him after binding him to an American flag. A jury acquitted the eleven men arrested and tried for his murder. A local editor declared "the city does not miss him" and "his death has had a wholesome effect on the Germanists of Collinsville and the rest of the nation." German Americans in other communities also encountered violence. Citizens in small, rural towns beat up ethnic Germans, not exempting even men of the cloth. In Fayette County, two German Texans, eager to demonstrate their own commitment to the United States, murdered a man who had told his mother not to purchase Liberty Bonds. Despite this violence—"excesses such as lynching," in the words of the *Washington Post*—some praised what they deemed "a healthful and wholesome awakening in the interior of the country."[44]

The war and anti-German hysteria led to the suppression of German cultural heritage. Especially in rural regions, white, native-born Americans worried about a lack of social cohesion. When the war began, German "cultural loyalty . . . conflicted with political loyalty to the United States" as immigrant papers criticized the Allies. The situation became even more critical after the United States became a belligerent. At that point, German ethnicity became associated with disloyalty, and "Americanizers" tried to purge the German language from schools and religious services. Furthermore, they purged even the most innocuous German influences from public spaces. The residents of Berlin, Iowa, for example, changed their town's name to Lincoln while Brandenburg, Texas, became Old Glory. In Houston, Texas, German Street became Canal Street. The city of Pittsburgh banned Beethoven's music. In an attempt to demonstrate their loyalty, German immigrants in Westphalia, Texas, burned German-language books.[45] So eager to purge any German name from society, some Americans went so far as to refer to dachshunds as "liberty dogs" and German measles as "liberty measles."[46]

Voicing opposition to or criticism of the war came with enormous risks. The actions of superpatriotic groups received legal sanction, thanks to Congress. Judges broadly interpreted the censorship laws, and one court in New Hampshire sentenced a man to three years in prison for questioning the constitutional basis for conscription when he claimed that "this was a Morgan war"—referring to the argument that financiers like J. P. Morgan pushed the nation to war—"and not a war of the people." Alleged conspiracies and headline-making arrests fanned the flames of hysteria. In May 1917, for example, authorities arrested over fifty people belonging to the Farmers' and Laborers' Protective Association. The group raised suspicions because its members included those of German descent along with members of the Socialist Party and the despised international labor union, the Industrial Workers of the World (IWW). The group allegedly developed a rather improbable scheme. If the draft became law, they allegedly planned to burn the city of Abilene, Texas; murder conscription officers; destroy railroad tracks and telephone and telegraph wires; and assassinate President Wilson.[47]

Wartime legislation helped the government suppress organizations that they had long suspected. The IWW, for example, found itself targeted across the country. In the coalfield towns of Macoupin and Montgomery counties in Illinois, increasing suspicion of the antiwar IWW, combined with growing concern for soldiers from the community, led to two weeks of violence in 1918. Locals considered the group "a traitorous and subversive fifth column," a view in line with that of government officials. In Montana, a mob dragged one IWW organizer through the streets "until his kneecaps were scraped off" before hanging him.[48] Almost half of the federal cases brought under the

Espionage and Sedition Acts took place in states with active IWW groups. The Wilson administration's prosecutions and mass incarceration of the IWW's leadership ultimately broke the group's influence. The government also acted harshly against pacifist religious groups, forcing drafted members of churches opposed to violence—Quakers and Jehovah's Witnesses—to accept training and wear a military uniform. Conscientious objectors faced harassment, arrests, and imprisonment.[49]

Wartime vigilante activities simply intensified the efforts of groups in some regions of the country. Whites in the South considered their ongoing policing of African Americans an essential wartime service. Already accustomed to the use of force in suppressing African Americans' civil rights during and after Reconstruction, white Southerners continued their reign of terror.[50] Unlike in prior conflicts, the federal government supported white Southerners in their monitoring of Black communities as well. Anxious whites supplied numerous baseless tips that all stemmed from the fear "that German or other enemy agents were actively subverting the loyalties of African Americans, who were believed to be uniquely susceptible to those who would manipulate them for sinister purposes." Black sharecroppers in Arkansas formed peacekeeping groups, only to be attacked by whites who executed and jailed dozens of victims. In East St. Louis in July 1917, a conflict between white workers and Black strikebreakers led to a race riot that left dozens dead. The president of the Vicksburg NAACP branch, meanwhile, became the victim of a mob that included police officers. They tarred and featured him using the excuse that he had not purchased a sufficient number of war savings stamps and had thus not demonstrated sufficient loyalty to the war effort. In fact, of course, the war merely provided a cover for whites to run this civil rights campaigner out of town. The bloody summer of 1919, after the conflict, saw racial violence from Texas up to Nebraska. The dozens of lynching victims included ten Black soldiers who, still in their uniforms, had recently returned from France.[51] The war heightened fears already prevalent in southern society and presented an opportunity to tighten social control over Black communities.

While whites sought to socially control Blacks on the home front, they also discriminated against them in the armed forces. Most African Americans actually expressed indifference when the United States entered the Great War. The draft forced their hand as the armed forces inducted nearly 370,000 African Americans into service. But even here, many saw the unfairness of the system. The draft brought in 72 percent of enlistees but 96 percent of African Americans. Draft boards, meanwhile, placed 52 percent of Blacks in Class I, the most likely to be drafted, but only 33 percent of whites. In the armed forces, Blacks received the most menial tasks in the service. As Debra Sheffer explores in chapter 3 of this book, African Americans fought against racism and discrimination to prove themselves in combat. Many earned honors for bravery from Allied nations. Despite Black soldiers' bravery on the front lines, many white Americans continued to treat Blacks on the home front with suspicion. Whites continued to question the loyalty of African Americans and also expressed fears that German agents would seek to exploit racial tensions in the United States.[52]

The Great War's end did not bring peace to those accused of undermining the American war effort. Nor did the restrictions on foreign languages disappear. Organizations like the American Legion, meanwhile, opposed the use of foreign languages in public places, including schools and churches. The Legion, established as a veterans' organization, sought to enforce the patriotic sentiments of the war years through legal and extralegal methods. The Ku Klux Klan, which had seen a popular resurgence in the 1910s as a result of an anti-immigrant backlash, capitalized on the pro-American sentiment of the war to boost its membership and emerged as one of the most powerful postwar organizations. Like its Reconstruction Era predecessor, the Klan of the early twentieth century also resorted to extralegal means to achieve its terroristic goals. But the violence against dissenting and suspicious groups that Americans had tolerated during the war years seemed out of place in peacetime. Such realizations led to public calls for the government to restrain previously free-ranging vigilance groups.[53] The political violence of the Great War years and after led to a corresponding "invigoration of political arguments that questioned all extralegal authority and laid the groundwork for the legal and political dismantling of vigilantism in the twentieth century." By 1921 membership in the American Legion started to decline. Where wartime Americans believed that citizens could aid the government by keeping tabs on the loyalty of people in their neighborhood, peacetime seemingly reestablished a clearer line between vigilant observation and illegitimate acts.[54]

The virulent anti-German sentiment of the Great War era faded but left lasting effects. In Texas, the war forced the accelerated pace of assimilation as Germans anglicized their names, shut down many newspapers printed in German, ended German-language religious services, and spoke primarily, if not exclusively, English at home. Traditional celebrations, including the popular Texas State *Saengerfest*, did not return in the postwar era. One historian concluded that "German-Americans who lived through the war years would never again feel quite the same about their heritage, or perhaps, about America—for loyalty to the one required severing all ties with the other." Meanwhile, the anti-immigrant environment survived into the postwar period with Congress passing the 1921 immigration bill that "rankly discriminated against people from southern and eastern Europe" and inaugurated the new decade "with an official salute to the 100 percent spirit the war had made ascendant."[55]

Born by revolution against its mother country, the United States has, from its beginning, struggled with the question of loyalty. Its own war for independence, after all, forced those within its borders to proclaim allegiance to either the loyalist or rebel position. Conscious of the agonizing choices forced on people in such times and breaking from British precedent of easily charging and harshly punishing disloyalty, the framers specified and established a high bar for prosecuting treason in the Constitution. But because treason to the nation had a high legal burden to surmount, the government rarely prosecuted such cases. The consequence of this, in all periods of American life, however, has been that everyday citizens took it upon themselves to hurl the accusation of treason upon suspicious individuals or nonconformists.[56] As history has demonstrated, societal accusations of and reactions against disloyalty can be even harsher and deadlier than government prosecution.

Political culture permeated nineteenth-century American life. The fact that members of the nation's oldest party participated in the act of sundering the Union complicated the matter of policing political speech in the Civil War North. Indeed, since the Democrats remained a potent force in the northern states, Unionists found it more difficult to banish or marginalize a party so firmly rooted in the fabric of society. Half a century later, however, a different generation of Americans did not have to worry about the relatively weak antiwar forces, whether they were German Americans, the IWW, or socialists. War supporters found that they could exert pressure on their foes in ways that their fathers could not deploy against political opponents in the Civil War–era North.

The Northern Democrats during the Civil War lent credibility to those who disagreed with the conflict whatever their class or ethnic origins. Antiwar and anti-administration critics during the Civil War would have found Woodrow Wilson's America more oppressive. Political violence did break out in the Civil War years but was consistent with the usually raucous political culture of the era.[57] During the Great War, with the opposition party backing American participation in the conflict, dissenters—whose identification with a foreign power at war with the United States did not help—found no refuge from superpatriots belonging to members of both major political parties who believed they had sanction to root out disloyal elements in their communities.

Americans of the Civil War and Great War eras would have both recognized and been surprised by some elements of their respective societies at war. In both instances, the federal government, under two different stewards and political parties, exercised its power in censoring certain types of speech, fearing the effect of negative sentiments on military effectiveness. In both eras, native-born Americans questioned the loyalty and commitment of ethnic and racial minorities, falling back on crude stereotypes even though members of the suspected communities demonstrated their fealty to the nation during the crises. Additionally, in both instances, the American people let loose their passions on those members of society thought to be aiding the enemy in some manner. In both the Civil War and Great War eras, civilians felt the need to take the law into their own hands most frequently in areas they considered to be either beyond the reach of authorities or where enforcement was lax.[58] The brutal guerrilla war in Kansas and Missouri during Lincoln's time and the sometimes-deadly harassment of German Americans in Wilson's era took place, ironically, where civilians did not feel the forceful presence of the law. In essence, mobs reacted out of fear of their own security when they felt *too free* of government control. On the other hand, urban areas with a concentration of aggrieved residents could chafe under what they perceived too heavy of an official presence, as the New York City draft riots demonstrate. Situational circumstances, therefore, mattered in both periods. President Wilson's Secretary of War Newton Baker knew how the public perceived military conscription during the Civil War. The administration came up with the term "Selective Service" and placed the power to draft in the hands of state and local officials.[59]

Furthermore, the manner in which the government portrayed its antagonists mattered. Lincoln's insistence that the rebels represented wayward countrymen under the sway of bad leaders contrasted with Wilson's portrayal of the Central Powers as brutal and barbaric enemies. This latter representation alongside the president's support for the "anti-hyphen" campaign affected how native-born Americans reacted to German immigrants. Of course, during the Civil War, Americans fought against their fellow countrymen while they identified the enemy in the Great War as coming from outside the nation's borders. Finally, the federal government's level of engagement and sanction of vigilante actions affected wartime experiences as well. Lincoln's officials arrested suspected rebels but did not prosecute them, releasing the detainees after they had sworn an oath of loyalty to the Union. Wilson and his congressional allies, meanwhile, passed the Espionage and Sedition Acts, which signaled a serious government commitment to combating lurking enemies on the home front and suggested to eager patriots that the nation faced imminent threats from within its own borders. Because the federal bureaucracy remained relatively small in both eras, authorities relied on civilian groups for help. Where Lincoln did not fully mobilize the Union public to weed out rebels—he sought to reunite the nation, after all—Wilson's government had no qualms about calling upon the aid of vigilante groups to police their neighbors.

Paradoxically, Lincoln's moderate tone when referencing the Confederates, coupled with his use of military officials to arrest the most high-profile critics, allowed for a more open public sphere. Such actions allowed most people to remain free and demonstrated to would-be vigilantes that the authorities would manage affairs. Wilson's harsh condemnation of the Central Powers, his questioning of "hyphen-Americans," and his willingness to allow civilian groups to monitor and report on the actions of their own neighbors unleashed darker passions during the Great War.

Different circumstances pertaining to the two wars also reveal how the definition and treatment of those accused of disloyalty varied. First, the nature of the war matters. Secession stemmed from a political conflict and the debate about its legality continued on through the war years. Debates on the Union home front revolved around political issues as parties helped channel critical and oppositional voices. And because the war took place in a vibrant and politically aware society, curtailment of speech, although it did occur, did not result in a total suspension of criticism. The level of dissent that the government allowed and the message top officials wished to send also mattered in noting the different experiences that the two generations of Americans faced. The Lincoln administration contented itself with incarcerating its most vocal dissenters for a few weeks without charging them. The Wilson administration arrested and tried its most well-known critics, like Eugene Debs, even as it sought to control the behavior of everyday citizens. Wilson's primary political rivals, the Republicans, meanwhile, did not wish to appear antiwar and found other issues such as economic inequality and sectional animosities with which to challenge the administration.[60] With all major political parties clamoring to demonstrate support for the war, the nature of the Great War–era arrests naturally focused on political and ethnic minorities occupying the lower rungs of the sociopolitical power structure.

Despite the temporary shuttering of some opposition papers, the Lincoln administration did not ban political speech and, indeed, Civil War–era Americans had greater freedom of speech than those of the Great War generation. The anti-administration *Democrat* of La Crosse, Wisconsin, for example, argued that Lincoln's goal was to climb to the top of a "monument of skulls . . . his heap of national ruins." When the editor of the paper received threats against his press, he responded with his own. "When this office is destroyed," he warned, "a hundred buildings in this city will keep it company. Matches are cheap and retaliation sweet. . . . When they ignite the match, let us apply the torch." "If the Administration supposes that it can go much further in its course of lawless violence upon personal rights," the editor continued, "it and its leading supporters may rue the day when these deeds of despotism began. Such blows were never given without producing and justifying blows in return."[61] Such harsh and threatening language would not have been allowed in Woodrow Wilson's wartime society, as the unfortunate Edgar Held discovered.

Notes

1. "Defendant's Bill of Exception," undated [mostly], unpaginated, Criminal Case Files: El Paso, Box 85, File: "CR 2435 US vs. Edgar Held," National Archives and Records Administration, Fort Worth, TX. The title of this chapter comes from a section of the Sedition Act of 1918. Jennifer D. Keene, *The United States and the First World War* (Essex, UK: Pearson Education, 2000), 100.

2. The Union victory during the Civil War did not lessen suspicion of the Mormons even though they had not used the chaos of the conflict to break away from the nation. In fact, for a short period during the war, the Mormons took over protection of overland travelers through their territory when military units moved east to fight

the war. The Civil War led to slavery's demise and crushed Southern domination of the national government but it did not end suspicion toward groups outside the mainstream. Americans still suspected Mormon loyalty and continued to question their practice of polygamy. Kenneth L. Alford, "Utah and the Civil War Press," *Utah Historical Quarterly* 80, no. 1 (Winter 2012): 75–78, 81–82, 88, 91.

3. Opposition to slavery, either as an institution or as an economic system that they did not wish to compete with, also motivated some immigrant soldiers to enlist. Martin W. Öfele, *True Sons of the Republic: European Immigrants in the Union Army* (Westport, CT: Praeger, 2008), xi–xii, 19, 34, 74–75.

4. I have chosen to correct the spelling from the original quotation. Öfele, *True Sons of the Republic,* 70–71.

5. William L. Burton, *Melting Pot Soldiers: The Union's Ethnic Regiments* (Ames: Iowa State University Press, 1988), 220–221; Öfele, *True Sons of the Republic,* 141–142, 145.

6. Christian B. Keller, "Keystone Confederates: Pennsylvanians Who Fought for Dixie," in *Making and Remaking Pennsylvania's Civil War,* ed. William Blair and William Pencak (University Park: Pennsylvania State University Press, 2001), 10, 22. See also David Zimring, "For Their Adopted Home: Native Northerners in the South during the Secession Crisis" in *So Conceived and So Dedicated: Intellectual Life in the Civil War Era North,* ed. Lorien Foote and Kanisorn Wongsrichanalai (New York: Fordham University Press, 2015), 174–192, and idem., *To Live and Die in Dixie: Native Northerners Who Fought for the Confederacy* (Knoxville: University of Tennessee Press, 2014), 469.

7. Quoted in Geoffrey R. Stone, *War and Liberty: An American Dilemma: 1790 to the Present* (New York: W. W. Norton, 2007), 29, 31–32; William A. Blair, *With Malice toward Some: Treason and Loyalty in the Civil War* (Chapel Hill: University of North Carolina Press, 2014), 42–43, 45, 160, 221; Thomas H. O'Connor, *Civil War Boston: Home Front and Battlefield* (Boston: Northeastern University Press, 1997), 80. See also Mark E. Neely Jr., *The Fate of Liberty: Abraham Lincoln and Civil Liberties* (New York: Oxford University Press, 1991).

8. Jennifer L. Weber, *Copperheads: The Rise and Fall of Lincoln's Opponents in the North* (2006; New York: Oxford University Press, 2008), 53, 146; Stone, *War and Liberty,* 129.

9. Jennifer L. Weber notes that the Democrats incurred the wrath of Union soldiers with their antiwar policies. Veterans became "lifelong Republicans," viewing the Democratic Party as treasonous. The Copperheads' vision of the Union was the antebellum nation based on strict constructionism of the Constitution. They opposed many of President Lincoln's actions as unsanctioned by the nation's laws. Weber, *Copperheads,* 1–2, 4–9, 12, 18, 81, 216.

10. Weber, *Copperheads,* 6, 8, 22–23, 43, 59–60, 64–65, 86–87.

11. Öfele, *True Sons of the Republic,* 129–130. See also William Kurtz, "'This Most Unholy and Destructive War': Catholic Intellectuals and the Limits of Catholic Patriotism," in Foote and Wongsrichanalai, *So Conceived and So Dedicated,* 217–235,

and idem., *Excommunicated from the Union: How the Civil War Created a Separate Catholic America* (New York: Fordham University Press, 2015).

12. Over the course of the war, thirty-eight enrollment officers lost their lives and sixty others sustained injuries Robert M. Sandow, *Deserter Country: Civil War Opposition in the Pennsylvania Appalachians* (New York: Fordham University Press, 2011), 100, 109–111; Weber, *Copperheads*, 104–105.

13. Öfele, *True Sons of the Republic*, 134–135, 143; Weber, *Copperheads*, 107–109; David T. Gleeson, *The Green and the Gray: The Irish in the Confederate States of America* (Chapel Hill: University of North Carolina Press, 2013), 148.

14. O'Connor, *Civil War Boston*, 76.

15. Most histories of dissent, Sandow observes, "generally draw on a number of categories of analysis stressing socioeconomic, political, racial, or what might be termed human factors." He cautions, however, that human beings have complicated motivations and "none of these factors can be mutually exclusive." "Choices of service," he notes, "not only reflected a soldier's view toward the cause but also about its leadership and administration." Sandow, *Deserter Country*, 2, 4, 45–46, 51, 55.

16. In the context of the American Civil War, a "Border State" refers to a slaveholding state that remained in the Union (Missouri, Kentucky, Maryland, and Delaware). Halleck maintained that "We must know who are friends and who are enemies; the line will be distinctly drawn." D. H. Dilbeck, *A More Civil War: How the Union Waged a Just War* (Chapel Hill: University of North Carolina Press, 2016), 28–29, 35.

17. Öfele, *True Sons of the Republic*, 39, 41.

18. "Hickman's behavior," writes Christine Dee, "reminded townspeople of the uncertain allegiance of their neighbors—a troubling prospect as loyalists tried to maintain support for the Confederacy during occupation." Dee notes the different understandings of loyalty among "nationalists, who equated a narrow conception of loyalty with political unity" and "conservatives [who] conceived of loyalty as elastic, allowing for dissent and criticism of the government." Christine Dee, "Trying James Hickman: The Politics of Loyalty in a Civil War Community," *Alabama Review* 58 (April 2005): 87–93, 96, 99, 109–112; Victoria E. Bynum, *The Long Shadow of the Civil War: Southern Dissent and Its Legacies* (Chapel Hill: University of North Carolina Press, 2010), 2.

19. Only 10 percent of the immigrants who arrived in the United States lived in the southern states because of the lack of demand for white labor there. During the prewar years, many immigrants in the South kept quiet about their opposition to slavery, while others expressed their opposition. In 1854 one group of San Antonio–based Germans, responsible for an antislavery pamphlet, received criticism from other immigrants, presumably because most nonnative whites hoped to not attract undue attention to their outsider status. See Gleeson, *Green and the Gray*, 80–81; Burton, *Melting Pot Soldiers*, 16; Michael D. Pierson, *Mutiny at Fort Jackson: The Untold Story of the Fall of New Orleans* (Chapel Hill: University of North Carolina Press, 2008), 50–55, 60, 88–89, 191; Öfele, *True Sons of the Republic*, 22–23.

20. David Gleeson has referred to Irishmen as "ambiguous Confederates, supporting the cause in the early days, excited by the sight of their fellow countrymen in gray, but as the fight for survival grew tougher, ready to drop their support when the opportunity arose." Gleeson, *Green and the Gray*, 72, 142–146.

21. Because the British government refused to recognize foreign naturalization, some Irishmen in the South could claim an exemption from service. Such excuses did not endear them to local rebels struggling for independence. Gleeson, *Green and the Gray*, 8–9, 41, 60, 66–67, 141.

22. David Williams, *Bitterly Divided: The South's Inner Civil War* (New York: New Press, 2008), 1–5.

23. Williams, *Bitterly Divided*, 45, 113–117.

24. Bynum, *Long Shadow of the Civil War*, 16–17, 39. Williams, *Bitterly Divided*, 137–138; Richard B. McCaslin, *Tainted Breeze: The Great Hanging at Gainesville, Texas, 1862* (Baton Rouge: Louisiana State University Press, 1997).

25. Bynum, *Long Shadow of the Civil War*, 5–8, 28. In 1925, Frank Owsley published *State Rights in the Confederacy* and argued that state leaders retained too much power, withholding supplies and arms for the national war effort. In 1970, Emory Thomas's *The Confederacy as a Revolutionary Experience* challenged such ideas, pointing to the massive increase in central government power under the Davis government with its adoption of the first military draft in American history as well as its attempts to exert control over the railroads and production. For works that point to the commitment of Confederates to their cause despite complaints about their government leaders, see William Blair, *Virginia's Private War: Feeding Body and Soul in the Confederacy, 1861–1865* (New York: Oxford University Press, 1998) and Anne Sarah Rubin, *A Shattered Nation: The Rise and Fall of the Confederacy, 1861–1868* (Chapel Hill: University of North Carolina Press, 2005).

26. Justine Greve, "Language and Loyalty: The First World War and German Instruction at Two Kansas Schools," *Kansas History* 37, no. 3 (Autumn 2014): 141; David M. Kennedy, *Over Here: The First World War and American Society* (Oxford: Oxford University Press, 2004), 105–106.

27. James Hall, "Manhood, Duty, and Service: Conscription in North Carolina during the First World War," in *The American South and the Great War, 1914–1924,* ed. Matthew L. Downs and M. Ryan Floyd (Baton Rouge: Louisiana State University, 2018), 43, 52; Fritz Hamer, "World War I and South Carolina's Council of Defense: Its Campaign to Root Out Disloyalty, 1917–1918," in Downs and Floyd, *The American South and the Great War*, 61, 70–71.

28. "The prowar position could not bear debate, by the admission of is advocates," writes Christopher C. Gibbs, "so in place of a mere majority they required total support, 100 percent compliance, or total silence." Kennedy, *Over Here*, 143; Christopher C. Gibbs, *The Great Silent Majority: Missouri's Resistance to World War I* (Columbia: University of Missouri Press, 1988), 33–34, 49–50; Frances H. Early, *A World without War: How U.S. Feminists and Pacifists Resisted World War I* (Syracuse, NY: Syracuse University Press, 1997), 34.

29. Former president Theodore Roosevelt also supported the "Swat-the-Hyphen" movement. Matthew D. Tippens, *Turning Germans into Texans: World War I and the Assimilation and Survival of German Culture in Texas, 1900–1930* (Austin, TX: Kleingarten Press, 2010), 76–77; Kennedy, *Over Here*, 12, 24.

30. Hamer, "World War I and South Carolina's Council of Defense," 63, 72–73.

31. Gibbs, *The Great Silent Majority*, 59, 64; Seward W. Livermore, "The Sectional Issue in the 1918 Congressional Elections," *Mississippi Valley Historical Review* 35, no. 1 (June 1948): 29; Kennedy, *Over Here*, 46, 87; Wilson on Flag Day quoted in Early, *A World without War*, 78.

32. Jeanette Keith, *Rich Man's War, Poor Man's Fight: Race, Class, and Power in the Rural South during the First World War* (Chapel Hill: University of North Carolina Press, 2004), 59.

33. G. J. Meyer, *The World Remade: American in World War I* (New York: Bantam Books, 2016), 257.

34. In her analysis of pro- and antiwar letters, Jeanette Keith notes, "Handwritten letters, in pencil or ink, with spelling or grammatical errors, were most often antiwar, as were all the letters surveyed in which writers identified themselves as workers or farmers. On the other hand, small-town merchants and traders with ties to the rural community often shared their neighbors' political sentiments, which they expressed more eloquently in typed letters, often on business or personal stationary." She concludes that "support for the United States' entry into the war seemed to increase in direct proportion to the amount of education achieved by the writer. The poorly schooled scrawled out with great difficulty their prayer that war be averted. Conversely, university faculty and students often registered prowar views." Keith, *Rich Man's War, Poor Man's Fight*, 40–41, 85, 179, 197–198; Hall, "Manhood, Duty, and Service," 43.

35. War opponents, meanwhile, thought they had evidence of a conspiracy in the fact that legislation allowing for censorship had been introduced even before Congress had formally approved of the declaration of war. Stone, *War and Liberty*, 54; Kennedy, *Over Here*, 22, 26–27, 40; Leola Allen, "Anti-German Sentiment in Iowa during World War I," *Annals of Iowa* 42, no. 6 (Fall 1974): 426–427.

36. Keith, *Rich Man's War, Poor Man's Fight*, 109–110; Hamer, "World War I and South Carolina's Council of Defense," 73–74.

37. "What seems most remarkable about this argument," Geoffrey Stone observes, "is that instead of seeking federal authority to *protect* dissenters from mob violence, Gregory sought to expand the prohibition of dissent." Stone, *War and Liberty*, 56–57; Kennedy, *Over Here*, 79–81, 88; Theodore Kornweibel Jr., *"Investigate Everything": Federal Efforts to Compel Black Loyalty during World War I* (Bloomington: Indiana University Press, 2002), 24, 28–29, 33; Gibbs, *Great Silent Majority*, 45.

38. Quoted in Hamer, "World War I and South Carolina's Council of Defense," 61; Christopher Capozzola, "The Only Badge Needed Is Your Patriotic Fervor: Vigilance, Coercion, and the Law in World War I America," *Journal of American History* 88, no. 4 (March 2002): 1356.

39. Capozzola, "The Only Badge Needed Is Your Patriotic Fervor," 1358–1360; Christopher Nehls, "'Treason Is Treason': The Iowa American Legion and the Meaning of Disloyalty after World War I," *Annals of Iowa* 66 (Spring 2007): 132; Gibbs, *Great Silent Majority*, 34.

40. Nehls, "Treason Is Treason," 132; Gibbs, *Great Silent Majority*, 58; Kennedy, *Over Here*, 68, 81–82; Capozzola, "The Only Badge Needed Is Your Patriotic Fervor," 1360–1361; Stone, *War and Liberty*, 49–50.

41. Keith, *Rich Man's War, Poor Man's Fight*, 151–152.

42. Christopher C. Gibbs has questioned the effectiveness of laws banning the use of German, pointing to the ongoing use of the language in regions of Missouri. Tippens, *Turning Germans into Texans*, 93–94; Allen, "Anti-German Sentiment in Iowa"; Peter L. Petersen, "Language and Loyalty: Governor Harding and Iowa's Danish-Americans during World War I," *Annals of Iowa* 42, no. 6 (Fall 1974): 405–407; Gibbs, *Great Silent Majority*, 65; Quayle quoted in Greve, "Language and Loyalty," 139.

43. Nehls, "Treason Is Treason," 149; Tippens, *Turning Germans into Texans*, 89–90, 116–118; Kornweibel, *"Investigate Everything"*, 45.

44. The lynch mob that murdered Prager either did not know or did not care that their victim had attempted to join the US Navy but had been rejected for medical reasons. Tippens argues that "the most distinctive quality of the anti-German hysteria in Texas consisted of the fact that the frenzy did not take place evenly" in that larger metropolitan areas reported few instances of vigilante activity. Those in small rural towns, however, might have feared "the inadequacies of federal and state statutes to deal quickly and harshly with disloyalty." Many rural residents also considered the laws inadequate to combating the threat they thought they faced. Allen, "Anti-German Sentiment in Iowa," 422–423; Kennedy, *Over Here*, 68, 88; Andrew Carroll, *My Fellow Soldiers: General John Pershing and the Americans Who Helped Win the Great War* (New York: Penguin Books, 2017), 125–126; Tippens, *Turning Germans into Texans*, 110–111, 197.

45. Tippens, *Turning Germans into Texans*, 3, 9–11, 94, 103, 110.

46. Carroll, *My Fellow Soldiers*, 125–126.

47. Kennedy, *Over Here*, 79; Tippens, *Turning Germans into Texans*, 96–98.

48. In the case of these two counties, local unions split on the issue of wartime support. Initially supportive of the socialist position that only industrialists benefitted from the conflict, support for the war increased as local boys in the army faced the perils of the Atlantic crossing and frontline dangers. David Dechenne, "Recipe for Violence: War Attitudes, the Black Hundred Riot, and Superpatriotism in an Illinois Coalfield, 1917–1918," *Illinois Historical Journal* 85, no. 4 (Winter 1992): 221–229, 237–238; Nehls, "Treason Is Treason," 132; Early, *A World without War*, 79.

49. "Although nearly 90 percent of the [conscientious] objectors were native born," Frances Early writes, "in the 'crowd-mind' they were dangerous foreigners or at least pro-German." Meanwhile, the military court-martialed and harshly sentenced "absolutists," conscientious objectors who refused to obey any military

orders. Kennedy, *Over Here*, 83, 88; Kornweibel, *"Investigate Everything"*, 161–162, 168–169; Early, *A World without War*, 97, 99, 102, 118–120.

50. So committed to maintaining their racial hierarchy, southern states had a difficult time recruiting men for the Spanish-American War due to the fact that they did not allow African Americans to serve, and many whites feared that, with white men gone, Blacks would take the opportunity to rebel. Great War–era white Southerners shared these same concerns. David C. Turpie, "A Voluntary War: The Spanish-American War, White Southern Manhood, and the Struggle to Recruit Volunteers in the South," *Journal of Southern History* 80, no. 4 (November 2014): 861–863, 876; Kornweibel, *"Investigate Everything"*, 48–49.

51. Kornweibel, *"Investigate Everything"*, 2–3, 28–29, 44–47, 62–63, 72; Capozzola, "The Only Badge Needed Is Your Patriotic Fervor," 1375–1377; Early, *A World without War*, 149; Janet G. Hudson, "The Great War and Expanded Equality?: Black Carolinians Test Boundaries" in Downs and Floyd, *American South and the Great War*, 142–144; Lee Sartain, "'The Race's Greatest Opportunity since Emancipation': The National Association for the Advancement of Colored People, the Great War, and the South" in Downs and Floyd, *American South and the Great War*, 172.

52. Nina Mjagkij, *Loyalty in Time of Trial: The African American Experience during World War I* (Lanham, MD: Rowman and Littlefield, 2011), xx–xxi, 51, 54, 74–76, 99–113, 121–124; Kornweibel, *"Investigate Everything"*, 79–81, 84–85, 247.

53. The legion targeted its victims not because they feared revolution "but because radicals violated the class-free conception of citizenship at the heart of their organization's notion of the nation's democratic identity." Having convinced themselves that the American democratic system represented equal opportunity already, they "rejected the principle of class consciousness as a legitimate motivation for political activity." "Legionnaires," Nehls explains, "tried to permanently extend wartime standards of what was acceptable to coerce conformity in American political life." Allen, "Anti-German Sentiment in Iowa," 428–429; Capozzola, "The Only Badge Needed Is Your Patriotic Fervor," 1379–1380; Nehls, "Treason Is Treason," 136.

54. Capozzola concludes that the critics of mob violence made "the workings of American political coercion invisible" by obscuring "the central role played by organized groups and local elites in the narrow category of events called 'mob violence'" and "by focusing on violent passion and ignoring the ways that vigilance groups had exercised their powers with the consent of the government." Capozzola, "The Only Badge Needed Is Your Patriotic Fervor," 1355, 1381; Nehls, "Treason Is Treason," 153–155.

55. In Texas, Matthew Tippens notes, "German-language newspapers remained in print, German-language religious services continued, and many German Texans resumed following their German cultural organizations, albeit to a lesser degree than before the war." Indeed, Texans "increasingly accepted" Germans "as 'Anglos' to differentiate them from African and Mexican Americans" and "attacks on the German language were replaced by attacks on the Spanish language." Tippens, *Turning*

Germans into Texans, 7, 11–12, 90, 191–192; Allen, "Anti-German Sentiment in Iowa," 429; Kennedy, *Over Here,* 68–69.

56. Blair, *With Malice toward Some,* 2, 214–216.

57. Blair, *With Malice toward Some,* 306–307; Nehls, "Treason Is Treason," 133–136, 148.

58. Blair, *With Malice toward Some,* 114–115; Kornweibel, *"Investigate Everything",* 62–63.

59. Meyer, *World Remade,* 256–257.

60. Blair, *With Malice toward Some,* 46–47; Livermore, "Sectional Issue in the 1918 Congressional Elections," 29–60.

61. Quoted in Weber, *Copperheads,* 142, 146.

5

War and the Shaping of American Medicine

The American Civil War and the Great War

Dale Smith and Shauna Devine

In 1861 William Williams Keen, a medical student at Jefferson Medical College in Philadelphia, entered active service in the United States Army as what would later be named a medical cadet. He completed his medical education in 1862 and became an Army doctor, spending the war years as an agent for the Army Medical Museum. A prominent contributor to the research program at Turner's Lane Hospital, he treated wounded men and published papers on diseases. After the war, he visited Europe, ran an anatomy school in Philadelphia, and became a professor of surgery at his alma mater and an innovative American surgical pioneer. He advanced both the practice of surgery and the issue of patient safety in his campaign to allow surgeons to place private patients in hospitals founded as charitable institutions. In 1918 Major William Williams Keen, United States Army Reserve, was on active service as a part-time consultant to the surgeon general and an ambassador of military medicine during the Great War. Keen's experience of medicine in the Civil and Great Wars meant that he probably saw the best of both and was actively involved in the changes in American medicine that occurred between them. While social, military, and medical historians have examined how medicine and disease influenced practice during the two conflicts, less attention has been paid to the legacy of medical practice during the Civil War—particularly how ideas about medicine changing conceptions of disease and wound trauma during those years laid a foundation for medical practice and advances in the interwar period and established standards that shaped practice in the Great War.

In 1889 Keen published an article outlining recent progress in surgery in the wake of germ theory research. Keen was an ardent germ theorist and his objective was not only to illustrate the broader differences—or rather to contrast the "old or septic" against the "new or antiseptic" surgeries in the wake of the Civil War—but also to court public legitimacy and demonstrate his authority.[1] Keen's article described in detail an amputation that was performed by one he termed "the best surgeon" during the Civil War; he compared it to a similar surgery that took place in 1888. During the Civil War, even with the best understanding of contagion and causation at the time, amputation was a rough procedure. The wound was cleaned, but little else was done by way of preparation. The instruments were not disinfected and may have even come into contact with dirt during the operation; if the sponge happened to fall on the floor, it was "picked up, dipped into water, and used with innocent equanimity."[2] After the operation, it was common practice to tie the arteries with silk threads, check for hemorrhaging, and sew flaps together with sutures. A piece of lint and bandage with grease or perhaps a disinfectant was placed on the wound. Surgeons monitored their patients closely and hoped to avoid the onset of "surgical fever," a worrisome development that signaled infection. Common complications included abscesses, erysipelas, gangrene, and secondary hemorrhage, which would be treated locally while trying to strengthen the patient with stimulants. For a serious amputation, recovery took at least a month. As Keen pointed out, many complications in the Civil War hospitals stemmed from an imperfect understanding of nascent germ theory and lack of technique.[3]

Just twenty years later, Keen described the exact same operation, incorporating some of the lessons learned from the Civil War and using new tools of medical modernization, especially the expansion of anatomical knowledge and the efficacy of disinfectants in the hospital setting. This time, there were well-developed antiseptic surgical protocols derived from a broader understanding of the germ theory. First, the wound was carefully prepared before the operation. The skin around the wound was "scrubbed by a nail brush with soap and water, then with ether, then with some antiseptic solution. . . . and then covered with an antiseptic dressing until the operation" had begun. The surgical instruments were boiled, disinfected with carbolic acid, and placed on a tray with an antiseptic solution. The towels, sheets, and bedding were all disinfected prior to the operation, and sponges were thrown away afterward. The actual operation had not changed drastically, but antiseptic played a much more prominent role. The blood vessels were tied with silk thread and were disinfected with both ends of the thread cut short to avoid discomfort. Thus, blood vessels were "not disturbed upon the healing process" and, as Keen observed, "secondary hemorrhage is now one of the rarest complications following the operation."[4] The wound was drained with a disinfected rubber tube; the flaps were united by disinfected wire, silk, or catgut sutures; and dry cheesecloth was applied by a bandage, followed by a dressing "thoroughly impregnated with corrosive sublimate or some other antiseptic solution." As Keen pointed out, "the finest linen or lint, clean as the driven snow to the ordinary eye, is dirty to the eye of an antiseptic surgeon, since it is not cleansed from the microspial germs that will surely cause infection."[5]

The substantial difference between the two described operations highlights perhaps the major difficulty of Civil War medicine. Despite the best efforts of physicians, and the dramatic transformation in ideas and practice, Civil War physicians were just beginning to debate, manage, investigate, and understand the role of "cells," "animalcules," and "germs" as causes, not beneficiaries, of disease. Consequently, more than two-thirds of all deaths during the conflict were the result of disease. Thus, for Keen and many other ardent germ theorists, his comparison of the two surgeries—one on the eve of Louis Pasteur's and Joseph Lister's seminal publications, the other after these ideas were being disseminated into practice—was a way not only to answer the anti-germ theorists who posited some very effective arguments but also to demonstrate his experience.[6] The Civil War raised questions for physicians that science was slowly beginning to answer. Why did bromine or carbolic acid seem to arrest the spread of disease in the Civil War wards?[7] Why did some surgeons have better results than others? Many physicians returned from the war having seen evidence that at least some diseases might be contagious. The war experience set higher standards for the profession and paved the way for the broader acceptance of scientific research on germ theory and science-based practice.

There were no easy answers to these debates. Germ theory researchers would spend the next few decades perfecting experimental methods that would provide unassailable laboratory evidence. As Keen's description well illustrates, ideas about infectious disease and contagion within the profession were radically transformed in the half century between the Civil War and the Great War. By the time of the latter, bacteriological models and the germ theory were firmly entrenched in surgical practice and these superior understandings had a remarkable effect on surgical outcomes. This was the first large-scale war for which it is generally accepted that more deaths were caused by weapons than disease. Furthermore, other broader changes in medicine had taken shape between the two wars. While many Civil War physicians clamored for an opportunity to doctor in the war for access to bodies and hospital opportunity, by the time of the Great War, the best American medical schools and hospitals had been reformed and operated along more scientific guidelines.[8] Medical technology such as microscopes, stethoscopes, and laboratory equipment was new to many Civil War–era physicians; for many physicians who doctored in the Great War, it was a regular part of daily medical practice.[9] During the Civil War, specialist associations and more professional standards were just taking shape, in large part owing to the war itself; by the time of the Great War, the medical profession and specialization in medical practice were far more established.[10] And finally, the Great War did not come suddenly, and many Americans, including a substantial number of physicians, began to prepare for its eventuality two years before the United States entered the conflict.

Social, military, and medical historians have examined how medicine and disease influenced practice during Civil War and the Great War. Key to this transformation were new forms of institutional support in the new Army Medical Museum, a new social and physical repository for scientific research that helped to set American military medicine on a new course. This resource for American physicians helped transform the scientific culture of the Army Medical Department. The museum, which fostered the collection of "interesting specimens," case histories, experimental researches, and investigation, started to lay the foundation for science-based practice, which in turn paved the way for such further developments in the Great War as research into the physiology of shock, experiments in blood transfusions, and trials of vaccines.[11] During the Great War, physicians saw more value in laboratory-based practice, as well as working together in a referral, group setting, thereby further establishing the military medical experience as a center of professional and scientific expertise.

The war years—Great and Civil, we suggest—do not represent cases of

American medical exceptionalism; rather, physicians brought with them and built upon a deep foundation of medical knowledge that would inform the practical experience. We thus take a longitudinal approach in the relationship between war, society, and medicine and ask: In what ways did the state mobilize to support the medical profession and their soldier-patients? To what extent did the state invest in the development of American medicine during the wars? We suggest that although the context and challenges of the two wars were different, both proved a stimulus for the development of more scientific and epistemological standards in American medicine that transcended any specific theater of war. By examining the medicine of both wars, we can begin to understand not only how physicians affected medical practice during the war but also how they would establish the Army Medical Department as a growing center of scientific expertise in both war and peace and, finally, how the wartime medical experience and knowledge would in turn impact medical practice in America after the wars.

American Medicine and the Civil War

As volunteers responded to Lincoln's call for "three months men," military companies were formed across the North and mustered into service. But the United States Army, particularly its medical department, which had been set up to manage the medical needs of an army of just sixteen thousand men, was woefully unprepared for a large-scale industrial war. The extent of the medical department's lack of preparedness was revealed after the First Battle of Bull Run. Much-needed medical supplies did not get to the front, hospitals were lost, medical personnel were captured by the rebels, and without a proper ambulance system, no plan for evacuation, and a virtually nonexistent military hospital system, it took days to clear the wounded and sick from the battlefield.[12] Nor was Bull Run an outlier. As soldiers fought in such early battles as Winchester, Hampton Roads, Fair Oaks, and Shiloh; thousands of wounded men languished on the battlefields before being transported to makeshift hospitals and examined by a physician.

A number of civilian organizations of various sizes and durations mobilized to assist in the care of the troops, including the Christian Sanitary Commission and the Western Sanitary Commission. Clara Barton headed an often-one-person campaign to nurse and assist the troops, but the primary force for reform and civilian assistance was the United States Sanitary Commission (USSC). The USSC was begun as the Central Relief Association in New York City by concerned middle-class women; it was then taken over by their husbands and friends and led and administered by the men with heavy professional influence. The initial focus was the provision of relief (supplying soldiers and hospital patients with blankets, socks, vegetables, and domestic caregiving in the hospitals), but it later expanded to include disease prevention and administrative reform.[13]

At the local level, the commission was funded and operated by women's committees, which raised the money, rolled bandages, and prepared care packages for the troops. Men provided political influence and mobilized the leaders of the medical profession to prepare educational materials for the volunteer physicians who would serve as the medical officers to the state regiments. The commission was generously funded by interested donors and philanthropists (before such philanthropies as the Rockefeller Foundation were formed and targeted medical research). It was thus a crucially important body and provided much-needed financial support for military medicine. In a letter to the secretary of war, Acting Surgeon General R. C. Wood noted that "the pressure on the medical bureau has been very great and urgent. . . . The medical bureau would, in my judgement, derive important and useful aid from the counsels and well directed efforts of an intelligent and scientific commission, to be styled 'A Commission of Inquiry and Advice.'"[14] The commission sought not legal power but recognition from the government. The object was not to "interfere with but to strengthen the present organization, introducing and elaborating such improvements as the advanced stage of medical science might suggest." Because physicians and sanitary reformers had read of the experiences of Florence Nightingale and the British Army in the Crimea just four years earlier, there was a sense of urgency. The commission members first secured the passage by Congress of the Wilson Bill, providing for the restructure and reorganization of the Army Medical Department.[15] With that legislative battle won, the commission, along with prominent friends of William Hammond, including Silas Weir Mitchell, Henry Hartshorne, and John Le Conte among others, worked tirelessly behind the scenes to replace Surgeon General Finley. On April 25, 1862, the scientifically and reform-minded Hammond was officially appointed as surgeon general of the army.[16]

Hammond had served for a decade as a military physician before he left the service to become a medical professor at the University of Maryland. He returned to the army at the outbreak of the war. The secretary of war, Edwin Stanton, opposed Hammond's appointment, favoring other candidates and resisting political influence in his department. President Lincoln nevertheless appointed Hammond. Stanton worked against Hammond for the entirety of his nearly three-year service before engineering a court-martial to relieve him of office. During his years of service, Hammond transformed the medical department. He had a vision, which was supported by the USSC and many elite, scientifically minded physicians in the country, of how medical practice during the war might accelerate the development of scientific practice, both in civilian and military medicine, and reorient the scientific culture of the Army Medical Department. The *American Medical Times* noted that "no man could be selected who so happily combines in his professional relations the confidence and esteem of both the medical staff of the Army, and the profession of the country as Hammond."[17]

Appointing Hammond and providing for the reorganization of the medical department presumed that the shaping of scientific knowledge would be freed from the limitations imposed on the department by the older operational model under Finley and Lawson.[18] Hammond began with introducing a national military hospital system: chemical laboratories, improved record keeping, and female nurses, storekeepers, and washwomen. He also created the position of medical cadets and hospital stewards and later introduced specialty hospitals. He supported his subordinates in the field armies as they tried various innovations. But as he worked to reform the structure and efficiency of the medical department, throughout his entire tenure he had to deal with competitive rivalries between volunteer and regular physicians in the field and incompetent medical officers in both categories.

Hammond inherited a medical force of more than twelve thousand regular and volunteer physicians, reflecting the diversity of the American medical profession. The majority were so-called allopaths—including some of the best-trained in the country, educated in traditional doctrines in which physicians used physiologically derived medications and procedures to combat diseases. Others were part of minority medical sects—for example, homeopaths, botanists, and eclectics—who were popular with different segments of the patient community. Hammond was a scientifically oriented teacher of physiology and pathophysiology and a strong member of the traditional community of practice. His view that the purveyor should only provide one medical supply table with therapeutics familiar to regular physicians shaped his plan to exclude sectarian practitioners from military service. Official examinations had limited sectarian participation in the regular Army Medical Department before the war, and while state volunteers did not have to pass the federal examination, Hammond worked to provide increased federal positions and used promotion exams to further limit sectarians.[19] Most of the medical cadets (one of Hammond's most innovative programs) were from traditional schools and their military medical exposure was to regular practitioners of the traditional community.

Hammond recognized that the regular profession had a wide array of practitioners. The most elite in American medicine had graduate education in European centers, primarily Paris.[20] The medicine of the Paris Clinical school, which emphasized pathological anatomy and localized pathology to specific disease conditions, was reshaping, albeit slowly, traditional ideas about disease and the body and the practice of medicine before the war. However, although these physicians published widely and made a strong case for the reform of American medicine, by 1860 the use of pathological anatomy remained remote from most areas of practical medicine. Other war physicians had little more than a pill-rolling apprenticeship; some had heard medical lectures in schools of diverse quality, and some had gone to strong schools with extramural opportunities in America's emerging cities, including postgraduate or undergraduate hospital experience. The war years would change this orientation. Rank-and-file physicians were exposed to ideas learned overseas as the elite of American medicine moved from the ivory tower to the center of wartime medicine. Although the elite relished the opportunity to reshape medical practice to their standards, Hammond's most urgent challenge was to create a corps of military physicians who would serve as an effective therapeutic and prophylactic force able to care for hundreds of thousands of troops, keeping the soldier healthy and when injured returned to duty as rapidly as practical. Above all, the medical profession had to assure citizens that those who joined the army for the republic were receiving the best available care.

Hammond acquired a small staff to help administer the department, freeing him to improve medical practice and construct scientific projects. He employed his staff and encouraged friends to write peer-reviewed scientifically inspired books and tracts throughout the war to guide medical officers in their duties.[21] Many of these publications were revised during the war to provide data from service experiences and lessons learned on campaign. These publications reveal a profession not only using all the resources and tools available and providing the best care possible within existing knowledge but also employing the significant strides made.[22] One of the most famous and lasting reforms during the Civil War was the development of the Letterman system of field or operational medical care, named after the medical director of the Army of the Potomac, Jonathan Letterman, who oversaw its creation. When medical support during the 1862 Peninsula Campaign bogged down, the press, the USSC, and the commanding general, George McClellan, all complained; in response, Hammond sent a new medical director, Letterman, to serve the Army of the Potomac.[23] Hammond gave Letterman permission to find alternatives to the regulations that had caused the previous medical director difficulty.

General McClellan had been a member of the Delafield Commission that the army had sent to the Crimea seven years earlier, and recognized the importance of the medical issues physicians faced. With McClellan's support, Letterman instituted ideas that had been circulating in military circles for decades, particularly a medically controlled, military-staffed evacuation system. After the Battle of Antietam, Letterman recognized the need for much more control of the medical support system than just an ambulance corps and thus, over the next year, added control of subsequent removal from battlefields, the placement of field hospitals, the selection of operating teams, control of medical supplies and records, and a medical inspectorate to assure the health of the troops.[24] This system was put into law by Congress in 1864 and taken up by European medical services in the later years of the nineteenth century.[25] It is still the basis of battlefield evacuation and care. But Hammond's appointment and consistent support of Letterman's campaign for a new field medical system, though a triumph, was not his only concern.

Hammond's vision was that every physician should be part scientist and that the serving medical officers would contribute to the advance of military medical practice by sharing experiences with one another. To facilitate and assure this vision, he reorganized the staff, and since anatomical knowledge, both normal and pathologic, was in his view the cornerstone of medical education, he established a medical museum for the collection of specimens from the field.[26] The Army Medical Museum promoted the allopathic physicians' status and authority. Hammond opened an Adams Express Company account (an independent mail and parcel delivery business) and provided glass jars, boxes, and kegs for specimens to be sent to Washington from every post, camp, and station. And, because this was the military, he required medical officers to return those containers full of specimens. The carrot to his regulatory stick was promising that contributions would be acknowledged in the *Medical and Surgical History of the War of the Rebellion,* the official medical history of the conflict, which the medical department would publish from the museum collection.[27] Yet neither orders nor incentive would be effective with many practitioners who had no dissection experience and only limited practical anatomical training. Recognizing these limits, Hammond and his colleagues developed detailed instructions that were circulated among members of the medical department. He also commissioned staff from his office, the USSC, and others on an ad hoc basis to visit the posts and camps to provide practical instruction and guidance. Literally thousands of American physicians had their first, desperately needed, practical anatomical training in such a setting.

Cadet Keen recalled one example of anatomical challenges in surgery based on a lecture-learned anatomy:

One of the wounded required an amputation at the shoulder joint, and the operator asked the brigade surgeon to compress the subclavian artery. This he proceeded to do by vigorous pressure below the clavicle. . . . With a good deal of hesitation I at last timidly suggested to him that possibly compression above the clavicle would be more efficacious, when, with withering scorn, he informed me that he was pressing in the right place, as was proved by the name of the artery, which was subclavian. . . . I had my rather grim revenge, happily, not to the serious disadvantage of the patient. When the operator made the internal flap the axillary artery gave one enormous jet of blood, for the subclavian persisted in running where it could be compressed above the clavicle in spite of its name. I caught the artery in the flap.[28]

Despite the limitations, by the end of the war, the Army Medical Museum had received more than ten thousand specimens from over twelve thousand individual practitioners in the Union service (over seventy-six thousand specimens were curated). It was perhaps the most massive medical educational effort the world had ever seen. Initially specimens from gunshot wounds predominated, but over time medical cases and illustrative pathological specimens increased in number. Of course, even as surgeons learned to do dissection and were officially encouraged to do so by the medical department, the crucial secondary component was the supply of bodies. It is likely that the over 110,000 killed on the field were exempt from autopsy, but approximately 40,000 who died in hospitals were subject to the directive to collect specimens, as were the over quarter of a million who died of disease. This was a substantial change from before the war. The unsavory yet necessary practice of grave robbing had been a significant social impediment to practical anatomy as instruction before the war. Five states had made some provision for anatomical instruction but only two had effective programs.[29] Most Americans were uncomfortable with dissecting deceased relatives and so the supply of bodies was never sufficient even for the small percentage of physicians who felt strongly about the value of dissection. Under the common-law component of the *Laws of War* (adopted to regulate armies in peace and war), the soldier's body was under the control of the army until released to the family, that is, discharged from the service. Family members might still be uncomfortable with dissection but they did not know about it in time to intervene. Even if they did, they had no standing to stop it.

The thousands of case and specimen histories submitted to the medical museum reveal a profession grappling with the magnitude of disease and wound trauma during the war but also finding a new confidence as practitioners. The museum proved important in shaping new research questions and projects. The Army Medical Museum, along with the rapidly growing Surgeon General's Library (they were consolidated into the Museum and Library Division of the Surgeon General's Office in 1883 under the guidance of its new curator John Shaw Billings), continued to be a resource for American physicians long after the Civil War. The museum collected specimens, photographs, microscopical preparations, and photomicrographs; through exchanges and donations, the library grew to be the largest in the United States. As the population and the profession grew, and debates about medical practice and disease causation crystallized, along with the rise of new professional associations and the formal development of specialty practice,[30] both the museum and library continued to shape the scientific culture of not only the medical department but also civilian medicine. Medicine and military priorities were changing, but civilians and regular physicians were still encouraged to send specimens to the museum and to use the collections as a resource. As one example, young Henry Welch could not find enough resources for his essay on goiter in the libraries of New York City during his second year of medical school; so during his Christmas vacation of the third year, in 1875, he traveled to the Surgeon General's Library to "look up some references he could not find in New York."[31]

When in 1917 the United States entered the Great War, none other than Charles Mayo appealed to members of the American Medical Association for their support of the museum. (He even suggested that the museum serve the nation as a basic science resource for transforming medical education.) The medical records of the Great War, Mayo noted, "will be of the greatest value not only to the glory of medical accomplishment, but also a means of interesting and educating the public in scientific matters pertaining to health and disease."[32] As in the Civil War, medical officers overseas were encouraged to submit "interesting" anatomical and pathological specimens, along with case histories and even the carriers of disease (mosquitoes), to the Army Medical Museum for instruction and education. Photographers and anatomical artists were sent to Europe, and physicians were trained in pathology. Sending specimens from Europe was extremely difficult, and the project was not without its challenges, but more than six thousand pathological specimens were nevertheless shipped home.[33] Louis Wilson of the Mayo Clinic was sent to Europe as a Reserve Officer to assist with the development pathological resources in the Army Medical Department hospitals there. In a powerful example of the importance of institutions, General William Gorgas, the Surgeon General of the United States Army, followed Hammond's Civil War example and ordered an office established to produce a medical and surgical history of the war, to encourage and reward participation in the museum projects.[34]

In addition to the museum, the general hospital system was another important medical innovation of the Civil War. Earlier wars had had general hospitals, classic features of military medicine behind regimental hospitals when armies moved, which took those unlikely to return to service when the army was in garrison. In the Civil War North, they were built to last for the duration of the war, in major cities with access to interested civilian consultants. Over a million sick and injured were on their wards in the war and almost 20 percent died there. Hammond and his successor were careful about the assignment of physicians to general hospitals, wanting careful and inquisitive practitioners. Hammond and many of his consultants in the USSC were fully aware of the progress in pathological histology in the hospitals of Europe, especially Paris, and they hoped these research-oriented physicians could use the same technique of correlating postmortem findings with the signs and symptoms of the disease to provide new definitions of many diseases and define some new diseases from ancient composite diagnoses.

For example, in hospitals of cities on the East Coast, Assistant Surgeon Roberts Bartholow used the techniques of physical diagnosis devised in Europe to examine soldiers. He developed such considerable skill and discrimination that Hammond asked him to prepare an official guide to the examination of recruits in 1863. He was then assigned to the West Coast, where he did pioneering work with the new hypodermic syringe to administer medications, and he studied disinfectants (applied to things) and antiseptics (applied to patients) in the management of disease and wounds.[35]

Equally impressive were the chemical healing efforts of Middleton Goldsmith and Benjamin Woodward in Ohio River Valley hospitals. As Keen correctly pointed out, "Our method of treating hospital gangrene, which was empirical, we now know to have been based on sound pathological grounds. Isolation and fresh air, and locally pure nitric acid, the acid nitrate of mercury, the actual cautery, or bromine, as was introduced into practice by Middleton Goldsmith, were our only, but efficient, weapons."[36] Goldsmith began using bromine in 1862 and continued to experiment with it in wards for the entire war. Woodward and many other war physicians were taught to clean and debride wounds with bromine or nitric acid and saw some success: it slowed or stopped the septic changes in wounds and allowed healing in more cases than natural processes. Physicians had seen that disinfectants controlled the spread of infection and epidemics, which translated into the development of public health practice and superior standards in hospitals.[37]

Among the most impressive of the hospital surgeons studying diseases were the 1863–1864 team of Silas Weir Mitchell, George Morehouse, and Keen at the Turner's Lane Hospital in Philadelphia. As the war progressed, hospitals and wards were set aside for similar patients to facilitate both care and study. The team's work for the Army Medical Department marked an important development in the history of medical specialization. With government funding, physicians were able to convince the public and medical department that their skills might usefully be employed in war-related research and experimental medicine.[38] Jacob M. DaCosta, also working at Turner's Lane, introduced the new term "functional diagnosis" to describe a change in function for which he could not identify an organic cause; "soldier's heart" was a forerunner of neuropsychiatric casualties in the Great

War.[39] (Kathleen Logothetis Thompson discusses "soldier's heart" at greater length in her chapter in this book.)

The opportunity of the system of general hospitals, staffed at least in part for research, produced an American medical literature that before the war had been generally pedestrian but which now excited the profession both at home and abroad over the possibilities of American medical science. But the primary purpose of the hospitals, general and field, was the care of the sick and wounded; here too American medicine was transformed. In the almost endless reminiscences and recollections of military service that appeared in the generation following the war, American physicians almost always recount their unprecedented experience in operations during wartime, especially amputation and fracture management; almost as many comment on the need for improved anatomical teaching, especially surgical anatomy. The experience of the First Minnesota Hospital is typical. Its first surgeon, Dr. Jacob Stewart, was captured while caring for patients after First Bull Run and was later exchanged; its second surgeon, Dr. Daniel Hand, finished the war commanding a hospital. They returned to St. Paul, with a new appreciation of a science-based practice, and collaborated in establishing a private anatomical school in 1868. It had two purposes: to teach young physicians and students the anatomy the faculty had learned the hard way on campaign and, secondly, to allow the faculty to continue improving their knowledge of surgical anatomy by teaching.[40] Such schools, based on prewar models in Europe and some East Coast cities, existed in almost every American city in the last third of the century.[41] Keen was the proprietor of one in Philadelphia. Civil War physicians went home with a new appreciation of the complexities and possibilities for medicine; they recognized the importance of collaboration and the dissemination of knowledge, and they brought these ideas to another generation of American physicians.

Finally, the surgery of the Civil War also had other sequelae beyond the realization of the importance of practical anatomy. That surgery occurred in hospitals, some under canvas, some in fixed facilities, but all the hospitals shared some important characteristics. The hospital had staff, frequently with some training: those experienced with anesthetics, those who could change bandages, and those who prepared the food doctors prescribed for healing. Furthermore, the hospital was a place where victims of trauma could be brought for care; there was no rushing about trying to find the doctor. As postwar Union states developed industry, there was an increase in trauma, since there were no safety standards for factories, trains, and mines. Doctors returning home to northern towns and cities began to ask about opening, or in some cases expanding, a local dispensary or hospital; and ladies who led fundraising for the USSC often responded by raising money. Their husbands sat on the board, but the ladies understood domestic management and hired and supervised the matron and staff.[42] This is not to say that the clientele of the hospital changed; it still catered to the worthy poor, but those now worked the industries of the community. Trained nurses were in the future in the United States, and there was no civilian equivalent of the hospital steward who knew drugs and anesthesia. Local arrangements varied but the institution was a useful addition to growing communities and helped those injured by industry.

To sum up, the most significant effects of the Civil War, like Letterman's system of evacuation and triage, the application of sanitary measures in the camps and hospitals, research projects and the dissemination of knowledge through the new Army Medical Museum and Surgeon General's Library, the evolution of anatomically informed surgical practice, and the development of general and specialty hospitals shaped the scientific culture of American medicine. But in a federated republic, not everything happened at once or even in a rational order. For example, in Illinois, Silas Trowbridge led a campaign in the state medical society for licensure and anatomy acts. After service in the Eighth Illinois Volunteers, he noted (with probably some poetic license) to his medical society colleagues:

The day begins to demand that medical men shall know of what the human frame is made, and all that may be known by a minute and diligent study of the all the long array of organizations of the human system. No man, during the late war, could obtain, in this State, a position as surgeon or assistant surgeon, unless his personal qualifications showed him to be in possession of all the essential outlines and minutiae of the anatomical man.[43]

Illinois would not get a viable anatomy act until the mid-1880s, but with the support of the state medical society, John Rauch, following service in the Union Army of Virginia and in New Orleans as an occupation health officer, led the state public health department effort to credential physicians after 1877.[44]

American Medicine and the Great War

During the last quarter of the nineteenth century and the first fifteen years of the twentieth, both the American military and medical profession were transformed. Much of the impetus for that transformation came from the Civil War but other influences became steadily more prominent.[45] These included the rise of public health in the cities and states, the passage of anatomical laws and medical practice acts, and the creation of the urban general hospital as the cornerstone of the health-care system and its impact on the establishment of other health-care professions. In addition to new personnel, the nature of the medical profession was being changed by the new sciences that underpinned a rise in specialized practice. Few practitioners limited their practices to a specialty, but many were, like Dr. Keen in surgery, gaining a consultation and referral reputation in their locality.[46] Military medical services were generally ambivalent about the civilian specialization efforts, as all military medical officers needed to be able to practice in isolation and so to be fully competent in all aspects of practice. So, while the military medical services were scientifically oriented and had begun to play an important staff role in the military organizations of the twentieth century, the Army Medical Department was still dependent upon the civilian community in the case of any significant mobilization.

The 1898 war with Spain was fought under the same Militia Act of 1792 and small-cadre regular army mentality as the Civil War, and while the scientifically sophisticated surgeon general George Sternberg warned of medical problems, the mobilization went forward as planned by political and military leaders. Medical disaster was the result.[47] After the war, President McKinley appointed a commission headed by retired general Granville Dodge to investigate the poor management of the conflict; the "Dodge Commission" made a number of recommendations. Of considerable significance was the commission's recognition that the regular medical officers knew public health and medical science related to prevention, but too few volunteer medical officers were as well informed; equally important, almost no line officers, regular or volunteer, were aware of the new science of prevention. Efforts were made in the military school system to remedy the defects.[48] The Militia Act was revisited in 1903, and a Medical Reserve Corps was established in 1908 to facilitate mobilizations in the future.[49] Recognizing the value of trained nurses in the civilian hospitals and foreseeing the need for them in general hospitals of the future, Congress created the Army Nurse Corps (Female) in 1901.[50] And the medical department personnel played a vital role on the emergence of twentieth-century America with the work of Walter Reed in Cuba and William Gorgas in controlling disease during the building of the Panama Canal.

As the army prepared for potential US entry into the Great War, the Army Medical Department had to find a solution to assure that they had the highest level of medical skill in the coming time of need. While the surgeon general, William Gorgas, knew the academic preventive medicine community, he had less personal knowledge of the expertise in American surgery. Luckily, he knew those who did; however, he was constrained by the Wilson administration's interpretation of neutrality in what he could legally do to prepare for war.

Many American leaders believed the Mexican mobilization of 1911 had shown significant deficiencies in the mobilization plans of the army. When war broke out in Europe, they became increasingly vocal on the need for preparedness. In 1915 the unrestricted U-boat war and especially the sinking of the *Lusitania* encouraged the preparedness community to do more. Some Americans volunteered in Allied forces, while others attended preparedness camps at Plattsburgh, New York, and other places in 1915 and 1916.[51]

One advocate of preparedness was Dr. George Crile, a Cleveland, Ohio, surgeon of international reputation who had served in the Spanish-American War; he volunteered to staff a charity American hospital in Paris as a favor to the former Ohio governor and American ambassador to France, Myron Herrick. In August 1915, after Dr. Crile returned from a charitable three months of surgery in Europe, General Gorgas asked him how he would structure the American preparation for war hospitals. Crile wrote back with the idea of basing the surgical units around the chiefs of surgery in America's medical schools.[52] The army was forbidden to develop new plans for war by the neutrality policy of President Wilson, so General Gorgas assigned Col. J. R. Kean to the Red Cross and asked that the volunteer organization begin working on the reserve hospital program with Dr. Crile and others.[53]

Leaders in American medicine created a Physicians' Committee on Preparedness in 1916 to mobilize the medical profession for the possibility of war. William J. Mayo was the chair. The committee encouraged physicians to enroll in the Reserve Corps and polled county medical societies to build lists of physicians with specialized skills. After the Military Bill or Hays Act permitted some expansion of the National Guard and the Reserves, more medical personnel joined the effort.[54] General Gorgas asked Dr. Mayo to come onto active duty and report to the Office of the Surgeon General (OTSG) as his advisor on surgical personnel. Both Dr. Mayo and his brother, Dr. Charles Mayo (who also joined the OTSG), in conjunction with other leaders in American surgery, worked out a system of assigning surgeons from the Reserves to deployed hospitals, while preserving surgical skill to support the civilian population and wartime industries in the United States. The concern for medical care at home reflected a new issue in American military medicine and mobilization, indicative of the growing value of modern medicine in American culture, especially the "new Surgery."[55]

President Wilson ran on a peace platform in November 1916, but by spring 1917, international relations forced his hand: the Zimmerman Telegram and the resumption of unrestricted submarine warfare pushed most Americans into support for war with Germany. The 1916 reforms had not fully taken effect, but the army Officers' Reserve Corps supplied about ninety thousand officers for the new National Army. Most went to duty in training camps and served as cadre for units destined for the AEF, but about a third were medical officers; many attached to the Red Cross–prepared base hospitals. General Pershing would barely beat the doctors to Europe as base hospital units from Cleveland, New York, Boston, Philadelphia, St. Louis, and Chicago deployed to support the Allies in May. But in addition to the academic–based hospitals, the army would need physicians as regimental surgeons, division surgeons, and staff for a host of other medical posts.[56]

As in the Civil War, the mobilization for the Great War required the army to make sure the physicians were prepared to meet their duties in both prevention and therapy, so schools were established to augment what the practitioner brought to the force. On examination, about two-thirds of the new recruits were found to be safe and competent in the practice of internal medicine, while only a little less than a third were similar skilled in surgical care.[57] New recruits were introduced to army administration and then underwent an intensive review of soldier care with a focus on wounds, orthopedics, respiratory illness, and war psychosis. The largest, and the only camp to continue through the war, was Camp Greenleaf in Georgia, which held over five thousand new Army Medical Department personnel most of the time and occasionally grew to seven thousand. Charles Mayo described it as the "largest medical school in the world." Like newly reformed four-year university-based medical schools, it focused on recitation and active learn-ing; however, like pre-reformed schools, it was brief in duration.[58] There was a deliberate attempt to instill academic medicine values and expose the stu-dents to teaching in the camp hospital, but there was also much criticism that the school tried to do too much and so achieved less than it might have done.

At the same time, while much progress had been made in American med-icine, it remained evolutionary rather than revolutionary. Many states had recognized homeopathy as a legitimate form of therapy so long as the prac-titioner was grounded in the same basic sciences as others, so the creation of academic hospital-based reserve units led to an expansion of homeopathic providers in the Great War.[59] Other nontraditional providers remained ex-cluded. The student officers, regardless of prior education, were assigned fa-tigue duty in sanitation squads to assure they knew the details of camp san-itation. As the war progressed and the academic hospitals moved to France, the need for specialty-qualified practitioners grew. The greatest needs were in radiology, orthopedics, and neurology, and specialty schools were estab-lished in all branches. The army also contracted with civilian institutions to provide special courses of instruction. Even though the schools were abbre-viated, the demand for medical officers was growing faster than the supply, and many students were sent to postings before completing the course of instruction (with the hope they would complete it informally in France).[60] The army had much to learn from the Allies about support of modern mil-itary operations; surprisingly the basics had been developed by the United States Army in the Civil War but forgotten in the small unit deployments of the late nineteenth century. Americans discovered anew the Letterman plan, used by armies on both sides of the Great War to manage casualty flow and triage.[61] The physicians with the forces had to learn about the new occupational specialty of aviation medicine.[62] There were also new weapons, including gas warfare, to learn about treating and preventing.[63] And to be effective, the senior physicians needed more rank than the Reserve forces were allowed to award, so General Gorgas and the Reserve officers mobilized their congressional friends to open more positions at the rank of colonel and above for reservists.[64]

In Europe, medical officers worked with both enlisted personnel and nurses in an intense operational environment. Members of all three groups as well as the dental officers would die on the Continent. Nurses were deployed forward to mobile hospitals despite their ambivalent status as civilians recruited by the Red Cross and attached to the army. Following a French example, first the US Marines, and later the US Army, deployed enlisted personnel from the ambulance units forward to temporary duty with the combatant units to reduce the time before point of wounding care was initiated. Since there were many more enlisted medical personnel than medical officers, and they could be trained in first aid to do almost as much as a physician in the field, the future use of forward medics became a policy norm. The war also witnessed the temporary creation of a new class of medical department officers, the Administrative and Sanitary Corps, nonphysicians with needed skills to contribute in areas that did not absolutely require physician participation—for example, administration, epidemiology, logistics—but which were critical to the industrial-based medical mission of the twentieth century.[65]

Like the Civil War, the Great War pushed ideas that were circulating among a small part of the profession(s) into the wider stream of public and professional awareness. In nursing, the administration of anesthetics had been common in a limited number of practice settings prior to the war, most famously the Mayo Clinic and the Western Reserve Hospital in Cleveland. The army set up training centers at both institutions and used nurse providers of anesthetics routinely both in the United States and in France.[66] Harder to document but probably real as well was a growing utilization of laboratory data in the practice of medicine; every military hospital had an on-site lab and "pathologist" to assist in clinical chemistry and bacteriological work. The larger hospitals had physicians trained in surgical and anatomic pathology.[67]

One of the duties the laboratory performed for the staff was to categorize or type blood into four immunological groups described by Karl Landsteiner in 1901, before blood transfusion was a serious matter of therapy. In the years before the war, patient-to-patient blood transfusion to combat the physiological collapse called shock, pioneered by George Crile, had been used in various teaching hospitals. Hematology and surgical research units across Europe and North America explored ways to collect and preserve blood for transfusion, and on the battlefields of France, the effort went forward with vigor. The value of transfusion in managing shock was clearly demonstrated, but the challenges of having usable blood at the time of need were much harder to overcome. Toward the end of the war, Oswald Robertson developed a technique of storing blood on ice in citrate solution containing bottles that allowed it to be preserved for use at a later date, but it was logistically difficult. Both the British and the French had developed programs of immediately collecting blood from rear area personnel at the time of need, which could be whipped or stored in paraffin-coated tubes to reduce clotting for a brief period.[68]

There was a second area of profound physiological change where the appellation "shock" was applied; the neuropsychiatric reaction to the horrors of war was labeled "shell shock" by some providers and the public. There had been patients with symptoms for which organic lesions could not be found for generations, the best-known being hysterics and victims of railway spine, stiffness, and pain following railroading accidents. Shell shock was employed to provide explanation of the behavioral symptoms of soldiers with no observable lesion by postulating microscopic brain lesions from artillery over pressure.[69] While some neuropathologists thought they saw the lesions, no one was sure.[70] Functional symptoms became an important aspect of the Freudian psychiatry of the interwar era, but little was achieved in screening, prophylaxis, or prevention, since there were inherent difficulties in studying the brain and significant social stigma to psychiatric disease.[71] Most of the work on shell shock was done before America entered the war, but American physicians, led by Thomas Salmon, collected and systematized the experience, and the American psychological and psychiatric communities picked up the experiences in their post–Great War thinking.[72] The American Expeditionary Force was not heavily engaged in the crippling trench warfare of 1915–1917 that generated the masses of shell shock victims: only a little over five thousand of the almost a third of a million American casualties were neuropsychiatric.[73]

Like the treatment of shock, surgery received impetus from the war experience as skilled surgeons, usually academic, put on the cloth of the nation for the duration and applied their skill to traumatized doughboys. At war's beginning in April 1917, America's surgeons were still not ready, still lacking the skills needed for the war. Major Keen made a significant contribution using his lifetime of skills as an educator and surgical author to prepare introductory texts for war surgery.[74] Younger men both operated and taught by example in the United States and Europe. Hugh Young, a Johns Hopkins urologist, served as consultant in Europe and especially improved diagnosis and patient education relative to sexually transmitted diseases.[75] Vilray Blair of Washington University and John Staige Davis of Johns Hopkins Hospital led a group of Americans interested in facial surgery before the war and, inspired by the work of Harold Gilles, brought his innovative techniques back to the United States where they formed the basis for cosmetic and reconstructive surgery in the decade that followed. Literally hundreds of physicians and thousands of patients would move through General Hospital no. 2 at Fort McHenry in Baltimore in 1918 and the years after the war and learn about reconstructive surgery as well as other surgical skills.[76] Harvey Cushing of the Harvard Medical School had developed great skill with surgery of the brain and demonstrated the value of both an academic orientation to diagnosis and the importance of experience to outcomes in managing wounds of the head. All hoped that technology would continue to improve patient care, when Cushing demonstrated a new magnet for withdrawing foreign objects from the brain in Philadelphia; a week after the war began, he used it to encourage innovation and training in wound management because, he noted, "wounds now kill more than disease." Major Keen commented on the paper before the American Philosophical Society, of which he was president, that the challenges of preparedness remained real but the work begun by the army was bringing America's best to bear.[77]

Among the most profound therapeutic impacts of the war was the change associated with fractures of the long bones of the extremities. Little was understood about fracture management when the war began in 1914, but under the influence of the British consultant Robert Jones, significant progress was made in this area by the time America entered the war. The great fear in open fractures was infection, just as it had been in the Civil War, since it was impossible to create an aseptic environment in trauma surgery. While weight-bearing splints were occasionally advocated by individual surgeons, they were rare and often of poor design. Jones had modified the "Thomas splint" to support femoral fractures, dramatically reducing mortality (80 percent to 10 percent) and gained great credibility with other practitioners in the process.[78] He strongly advocated medically supervised postamputation management, and the American Army adopted a new program of amputee management and prosthetic design at Walter Reed Hospital before the war opened. Reconstruction aides were recruited from industry and others trained (the beginning of the physical and occupational therapy communities) and new "scientific" prostheses were pioneered. The success of the prostheses was marginal at best but the new postamputation care was a lasting impact.[79] But saving the extremity was the goal, and, for that, detailed antiseptic treatment was needed, as the bacterial load of the French agricultural lands was significant. To combat infection, antiseptic agents were used. Most effective was the Carrel-Dakin treatment, a continuous irrigation with Dakin solution, but its application required that the fracture be managed by traction rather than casting so the caregivers could assure the ongoing antiseptic treatment. [80] The dominant feature of fracture management therefore came to be the so-called Balkan Frame, inexpensive over-bed framing to support limbs under traction.[81] The name supposed an origin in the Balkan Wars just prior to the Great War, but direct links are ambiguous at best.[82] Americans had much to learn from the Allies as they entered the war in 1917; for example, on examination of the patients in one hospital in November 1918, army consultant Hiram Orr found that half had been splinted but with windows in the casts to manage infection. Of those, 60 percent were improperly managed and needed to be reoperated.[83]

Reconstruction, cranial surgery, and fracture management—all aspect of surgery and medicine broadly considered—revealed a microcosm of issues that had been developing in American medicine for a decade. In this new era of scientific and increasingly specialized medicine, how would physicians work together and with others in the care of the patient? Practitioners had diverse skills. Some did well with abdominal surgery but had no experience with endocrine surgery; others were comfortable with gynecologic patients but not acute abdomens. There was almost no agreement on what constituted a specialty, and few practitioners limited their practices in any systematic way. And then there was the problem revealed by the experience of 1917–1918; it was difficult to keep up with rapidly advancing fields of practice. When Dr. Mayo began the surgical consultant's office, he recognized that relatively few could do all surgery and that organizing the hospitals required a systematic division of responsibility. The chief should be omnicompetent, but there should be an orthopedist, a genitourinary surgeon, and a neurologic surgeon on staff as well. Every hospital did not need eyes, ears, nose, and throat specialists, but at least some were needed. Those offering themselves as subspecialists were of extremely variable quality and experience, and the army discovered there was a dearth of omnicompetent general surgeons of sufficient experience to lead a hospital. In practice, some surgeons were good diagnosticians, but others were medically unreliable, and the sorting and medical care of patients was an arena in which there were no common standards. Nevertheless, whatever the staffing challenges, the artificial atmosphere of war and the flood of patients taught the practitioners in France, in Crile's immortal words, "to act as a unit."[84] The experience of having a laboratory and X-rays ready at hand and the opportunity to discuss a patient with another provider without social or financial risk led practitioners to wish for a more cooperative environment when they returned home. Indeed, collaborative practice was a social shock to the providers who had put on the uniform in the hour of need, but it indicates the complexity faced by patients and policy makers—what constitutes a good hospital, how should doctors work together, and how do you find the right doctor?

Yet for all the power of modern surgery as applied in the Great War, disease was hardly vanquished, and, despite the optimism of the preventive medicine community, wounds did not, at the end of the day, kill more than disease. Through the summer of 1918 it appeared that wounds would kill more than disease, and preventive medicine had made significant progress, both in the military and civil life. Recruit screening was vastly improved, and camp hygiene was dramatically better. Keen was, as a leader of American medical science, a strong proponent of immunization and led the campaign to supplement the ten-year-old typhoid fever vaccine with a newer trivalent vaccine that also protected against paratyphoid A and B organisms as well as the traditional germ.[85] Recruits' beds were separated by carefully measured spaces to limit the chances of meningococcal epidemics, and a commission was established of academics and regular officers to study pneumonia and its sequelae of empyema.[86] But study and preparation could only do so much when a new disease arrived in the summer of 1917—the influenza virus mutated in the American Midwest and spread to mobilization camps.[87] The surgeon general requested the best microbiologists and pathologists in the nation to consult, as the disease was moving with new troops, and the needs of the Allies for American troops in France as soon as possible caused military leaders to resist any suggestion of slowing the mobilization.[88] Thus, flu moved inexorably east and from the camps to the surrounding communities. In Philadelphia, health authorities suspected the housefly of transmitting the disease and so volunteer inspectors of stables were requested from the community. Major Keen was one of them, remembering the discovery in the war with Spain that flies might carry the bacteria of typhoid on their feet. But to no avail, flu struck Philadelphia and other cities with its unique "W" mortality curve, killing young adults in numbers neither expected nor understood.[89] From the East Coast, the flu boarded the troop ships with the doughboys and traveled to France and probably had as much to do with halting the 1918 German offensive as the newly arrived troops. If one stops the mortality count on November 11, 1918, wounds killed more than disease in the Great War, but if one keeps counting until the troops came home, or counts civilian deaths as the pandemic circled the globe in 1918–1919, then disease killed more than fifty million people. The disease stressed humanitarian efforts even more than the war; as a result, Red Cross recruiting became even more important and military and medical leaders assisted in every way practical. Dr. Keen, for example, provided work spaces for the new Women's Suffrage Party Auxiliary of the Southeastern Pennsylvania Red Cross in the fall of 1917.[90]

The impact of any one event on a society is a challenge for historians, since there are always many factors to consider; but the impact of war on medicine is frequently profound, and the Great War was no exception, even though the United States was engaged in it only briefly.[91] The example of the power of surgery at the hands of masters was noticeable on the medical profession in at least two ways. First, it inspired more people to study surgical therapy, and, secondly, it raised questions for further study by the research community. J. M. T. Finney, former president of the American College of Surgeons, reported to the college that in a survey of 1920 medical graduates, over 60 percent were desirous of finding a surgical hospital posting for further education and training. The need for and desire to acquire a hospital year had been growing but this was a significant jump in graduates willing to defer beginning to earn a living. Membership in surgical organizations and the growth of surgical hospitals in the 1920s clearly suggest a growing number of interventions and surgeons in the medical profession. Some of this was natural progress that was evident before the war, but much of the growth in surgical interests was tied to reports of surgical success in the period of the Great War.[92]

Beyond inspiring practitioners to pursue surgery, the war experience encouraged the growth of subspecialization in surgery. The opportunities and examples seen at General Hospital no. 2 at Fort McHenry led many to focus on reconstructive surgery. After the presentation of the experience with the management of neurological trauma at the American College of Surgeons meeting in 1919, the excitement of surgeons and particularly the endorsement of William Mayo's comment, "we have this day witnessed the birth of new specialty—neurological surgery," inspired Harvey Cushing and others to form the world's first neurosurgical organization, the Society of Neuro-logical Surgeons in 1920.[93] Such specialty organizations, by their existence, encouraged further research and sharing of new approaches to surgical problems.

After the war, the American College of Surgeons established a Committee on Fractures to examine the management of fractures in American hospitals. The questions they faced were scientific ones, like those of Orr and other war surgeons who began to work on other techniques, including closed man-agement following radical debridement (surgically removing devitalized and contaminated tissue), but successful debridement was a matter of luck as much as skill.[94] The Committee on Fractures also faced social questions: who should manage fractures: general surgeons, more readily available in hospi-tals at the time of admission, or orthopedists, increasingly more fully trained and experienced in fracture care? The committee was eventually renamed the Committee on Trauma because the questions led to discussions of emer-gency services by hospitals and the on-call and consulting responsibilities of the members of the hospital staff.[95] Similarly, the wartime experience with transfusions inspired some research on blood replacement systems, more in Europe than in the United States, where the goal was to limit blood loss by careful technique. A walking blood bank approach was used by some US hospitals to support elective surgeries when blood was needed, but, in gen-eral, civilian blood use proceeded slowly.[96]

The military medical system was also slow to adopt some lessons from the war. Despite the obvious power of specialization, in the fifteen years follow-ing the war, both the army and the navy resisted the use of specialization in regular medical corps officers. Rather, both services expected the specialized medical expertise to be found in the reserve corps and actively encouraged academic medicine's participation in the reserves.[97]

After the war, nursing anesthesia became increasingly popular across the country because of the awareness and presence of skilled providers.[98] Simi-larly there was a growth in ancillary personnel to work in laboratories, which supported the expansion of both hospital and public health-based diagnostic labs after the war. The growth of specialization and ancillary professions, all inspired to practice collaboratively, encouraged new systems and arrange-ments of practice. Crile's solution was to adopt the Mayo model of collabo-rative group practice, and many groups emerged in the years following the war, especially in the states of the Midwest and Trans-Mississippi.[99] They supported rural regions reasonably well, but 1920 is the first census in which the majority of America lived in the urban space and at least initially groups were not seen as a city solution. In the cities of America, a new building arose, the Medical Arts Building (also called the Physician and Surgeons or Doctors Building).[100] Sometimes these were adjacent to a hospital, but most often they were free standing and close to the city center, easily accessible by public transportation and, by the mid-1920s, with a multilevel parking structure adjacent. They were objects of civic pride, and it is almost impossible to find a city for which an interwar postcard image of the Medical Arts Building is not extant.[101]

The Great War, like the Civil War, saw many American medical personnel come to the colors and face social and practice challenges that were new to them. The military establishment did everything practical to ensure they provided the best care possible and encouraged new knowledge to improve care even further. The providers took this experience home to change practice in the civilian community as well. One significant difference was that in the Great War, the military medical establishment undertook to assure the American people that the soldier, sailor, airman, and marine going into harm's way would receive the best of care, unlike the Civil War when the civilian establishment worked to ensure the military provided quality care. Indices like *Reader's Guide to Periodical Literature* listed hosts of articles in popular magazines, among them *Scribner's Magazine, American Mercury,* and *Literary Digest*, which promised that care was better than in the past and would be provided when needed.[102] War Risk Insurance and the building of Veterans Hospitals were further indications of the establishment commitment to the best care.[103] But by 1918 new communications technology allowed the government to reach a larger proportion of the increasing urban population, and films like *If Your Soldier's Hit* brought the practice of modern wartime surgical care home in unprecedented visual clarity.[104] These communications certainly had some impact, so far unstudied, on American's perception of surgical therapy in their own lives.

Medicine and wars, both Civil and Great, are part of the social fabric of a nation and have diverse and powerful impacts on one another and other aspects of society. The time from the Civil War to the Great War was one practice life, albeit a long one; yet the differences are profound. The Civil War found American medicine in social and professional disarray, with little impetus or hope of transformation. And yet as Billings recalled years later,

"Looking back at the war as I remember it, it is a wonder that so many of the medical officers did as well as they did, and that the results were as good as they were." But the leadership of army medicine, using the unique social and legal situation of military life in time of war, introduced over 30 percent of the regular practitioners in Union states to the best of scientific medicine at the time, who were inspired to take that elevated commitment to science and patient care home with them to the industrial cities and towns where they practiced. This jump start was accelerated by European science in the last two decades of the nineteenth century, and American medicine came to be better positioned to assist the military with its challenges of preparedness, sickness, and wounds.

Meanwhile, the public commitment to caring for those who went in harm's way on behalf of the balance of society led to improving standards of continuing education and the prosecution of innovation in a host of areas that helped change medicine in the postwar period. Perhaps the greatest change was the recognition that the scientific impetus generated in the Civil War had reached the point by the Great War that a single practitioner could not manage it all. The brief wartime experience would not solidify changes in medical education or specialization (that would come with yet another war); but it did illustrate the challenges of a medical science that had removed all questions about the social utility of medicine and the need to make it available to Americans. The explicit question was *how*? Dr. Francis Peabody, a Harvard medical professor who spent the Great War working for the Red Cross in Eastern Europe, in his classic lecture "the Care of the Patient" a decade after the war, noted, "Good practice presupposes an understanding of the sciences which contribute to the structure of modern medicine."[105] How a doctor cared for the patient in that scientific, multispecialty, multiprofessional, team-oriented world that the Great War showed to be effective was the great question of the new medicine. It still is.

Notes

1. W. W. Keen, *Addresses and Other Papers* (Philadelphia: W. B. Saunders), 92.
2. Keen, *Addresses and Other Papers*, 93.
3. Keen, *Addresses and Other Papers*, 90.
4. Keen, *Addresses and Other Papers*, 92–93.
5. Keen, *Addresses and Other Papers*, 92–93.

6. For more on the Civil War debates surrounding the germ theory, see Shauna Devine, *Learning from the Wounded* (Chapel Hill: University of North Carolina Press, 2014), chap. 3. See also Margaret Humphrey, *Marrow of Tragedy* (Baltimore: Johns Hopkins University Press, 2013).

7. Devine, *Learning from the Wounded*, chap. 6.

8. Abraham Flexner, *Medical Education in the United States and Canada: A Report to the Carnegie Foundation for the Advancement of Teaching* (Boston: D.B. Updike, 1910); Thomas Neville Bonner, *Iconoclast: Abraham Flexner and a Life in Learning* (Baltimore: Johns Hopkins University Press, 2002). See also K. Ludmerer, *Learning to Heal: The Development of American Medical Education* (New York: Basic Books, 1985).

9. Stanley Joel Reiser, *Medicine and the Reign of Technology* (Cambridge, UK: Cambridge University Press, 1978).

10. Rosemary Stevens, *American Medicine and the Public Interest: A History of Specialization* (Berkeley: University of California Press, 1971), 27–30; George Weisz, *Divide and Conquer: A Comparative History of Medical Specialization* (New York: Oxford University Press, 2006).

11. As an example of this changing focus, Walter Reed and colleagues discovered the mosquito transmission of yellow fever in the wake of the conquest of Cuba in the Spanish-American War. Bailey K. Ashford identified hookworm disease and its causative agent in Puerto Rico during the same war. See Mary Gillett, *The Army Medical Department, 1818–1865* (Washington, DC: Government Printing Office, 1987).

12. During the summer months of 1861, the sick list routinely averaged close to 30 percent. See George Worthington Adams, *Doctors in Blue: The Medical History of the Union Army in the Civil War* (Baton Rouge: Louisiana State University Press, 1952), 14. The evacuation of troops off the field (lack of ambulance system), preventative medicine, and immediate care in the hospitals was reported as "disastrous." Many of the recruits came from rural or isolated areas and were thus vulnerable to a myriad of contagious diseases to which they had no immunity.

13. William Quentin Maxwell, *Lincoln's Fifth Wheel: The Political History of the United States Sanitary Commission* (New York: Longmans, 1956). See also Jane Schultz, *Women at the Front: Hospital Workers in Civil War America* (Chapel Hill: University of North Carolina Press, 2004) and idem., ed., *This Birth Place of Souls: The Civil War Nursing Diary of Harriet Eaton* (London: Oxford University, 2011.

14. United States Sanitary Commission, May 22, 1861, Sanitary Commission Series no. 2, Letter from the acting surgeon general (R. C. Wood) to the secretary of war, advising the institution of a commission, to be styled "A commission of inquiry and advice in respect of the sanitary interests of the United States forces" (National Library of Medicine).

15. The Thirty-Seventh Congress debated Bill no. 188 (the Wilson Bill), which proposed to "increase the efficiency of the medical department of the Army," the objective being to get "the right men wherever they may be found, whether in the Army or

the volunteer force to take these positions." The Wilson Bill was named for Free Soil Republican Henry Wilson and was signed into law on April 16, 1862. See *Congressional Globe*, 37th Congress, Second Session, 1861–1862, 995. See Bonnie Ellen Blustein, *Preserve Your Love of Science: Life of William A. Hammond, American Neurologist* (New York: Cambridge University Press, 1991), 56–57; see also idem., "To Increase the Efficiency of the Medical Department: A New Approach to Civil War Medicine," *Civil War History* 33, no. 1 (March 1987): 22–39; Frank R. Freemon, "Lincoln Finds a Surgeon General: William A. Hammond and the Transformation of the Union Army Medical Bureau," *Civil War History* 33, no. 1 (March 1987): 5–21.

16. Devine, *Learning from the Wounded*, 15.

17. Quoted in Blustein, *Preserve Your Love of Science*, 58. See also William Hammond, Biographical Directory in *The Papers of Frederick Law Olmstead: Defending the Union*, ed. Jane Turner Censor (Baltimore: Johns Hopkins University Press, 1986), 96–97.

18. The medical department under Finley and Lawson was grounded in traditionalism. They generally resisted new scientific ideas and maintained that scientific pursuits, research projects, and medical equipment were a waste of time and money. See, for example, Gillett, *Army Medical Department, 1818–1865*, chaps. 8–9.

19. However, some members of these competing sects were able to successfully pass the entrance exam and serve in a hospital or regiments. See, for example, Michael Flannery, "Another House Divided: Union Medical Service and Sectarians during the American Civil War," *Journal of the History of Medicine* 54 (October 1999): 489–490; idem., *Civil War Pharmacy: A History of Drugs, Drug Supply and Provision and Therapeutics for the Union and Confederacy* (New York: Pharmaceutical Products Press, 2004).

20. See, for example, William Rothstein, *American Medical Schools and the Practice of Medicine: A History* (New York: Oxford University Press, 1987); John Harley Warner, *Against the Spirit of the System: The French Impulse in Nineteenth-Century American Medicine* (Princeton, NJ: Princeton University Press, 1998).

21. William Hammond, ed., *Military and Medical Surgical Essays Prepared for the United States Sanitary Commission* (Philadelphia: J. B. Lippincott, 1864), iii.

22. Among numerous others, these included: Roberts Bartholow, *A Manual of Instructions for Enlisting and Discharging Soldiers* (1863); John Brinton, *Consolidated Statement of Gunshot Wounds* (1863); Henry Clark, *Inspection of Military Hospitals* (1863); Jacob M. DaCosta, *Medical Diagnosis* (1864); Charles R. Greenleaf, *A Manual for the Medical Officers of the United States Army* (1864); William A. Hammond, *A Treatise on Hygiene* (1863); DeWitt Peters, "Interesting Cases of Gunshot Wounds" (1864); Joseph Janvier Woodward, *The Hospital Steward's Manual* (1862) and *Outlines of the Chief Camp Diseases of the United States Armies as Observed during the Present War* (1863); Elisha Harris, *Hints for the Control and Prevention of Infectious Disease in Camps, Transports and Hospitals* (New York: United States Sanitary Commission, 1863).

23. Hammond to Letterman, June 19, 1862. Records of the Office of the Surgeon

General Central Office Correspondence, 1818–194, letters and endorsements sent April–October 1849, September 1, 1862, to November 25, 1862, RG 112, NARA.

24. Jonathan Letterman, *Medical Recollections of the Army of the Potomac* (New York: D. Appleton, 1866).

25. Alfred Bollet, *Civil War Medicine: Challenges and Triumphs* (Arizona: Galen Press, 2002), 99.

26. Circular no. 2, issued May 21, 1862, directed medical officers to "diligently collect and forward to the office of the Surgeon General all specimens of morbid anatomy, surgical or medical, which may be regarded as valuable; together with projectiles and foreign bodies removed; and such other matter as may prove of interest in the study of military medicine and surgery." See Devine, *Learning from the Wounded*, chap. 1.

27. In conjunction with Circular no. 2, Circular no. 5 was issued and directed that the research at the museum be published in *Medical and Surgical History of the War of the Rebellion*. See *Learning from the Wounded*, chap. 1. See also Circular no. 5, issued June 9, 1862, Washington, DC; Circulars and Circular Letters of the Surgeon General's Office, 1861–1865, entry 63, RG 112, NARA; Circular, no. 2, issued May 21, 1862, "Circulars and Circular Letters of the Surgeon General's Office," entry 63, RG 112, NARA.

28. W. W. Keen, "Surgical Reminiscences of the Civil War," in *Addresses and Other Papers*, 2–3.

29. Michael Sappol, *A Traffic of Dead Bodies: Anatomy and Embodied Social Identity in Nineteenth-Century America* (Princeton, NJ: Princeton University Press, 2002). After the war, the broad physician appreciation of practical anatomy, both normal and pathological, led to significant professional support of anatomy laws.

30. Stevens, *American Medicine and the Public Interest*; see also James G. Burrow, *AMA: Voice of American Medicine* (Baltimore: Johns Hopkins University Press, 1963).

31. Simon Flexner and James Thomas Flexner, *William Henry Welch and the Heroic Age of American Medicine* (Baltimore: Johns Hopkins University Press, 1993), 71.

32. Quoted in Robert Henry, *The Armed Forces Institute of Pathology, Its First Century* (Washington, DC: OTSG, 1964), 59.

33. Henry, *Armed Forces*, 187.

34. Fielding H. Garrison, "Medical and Surgical History of the War," *Military Surgeon* 43 (September 1918): 347–350.

35. For example, Bartholow, *A Manual of Instructions for Enlisting and Discharging Soldiers; On the Antagonism between Medicines and between Remedies and Diseases: Being the Cartwright Lectures for the Year 1880* (New York: D. Appleton, 1881); "Pathology and Treatment of Hospital Gangrene: Turpentine as a Local Application," *American Journal of the American Medical Sciences* 49 (January 1865): 274–276; *A Practical Treatise on Materia Medica and Therapeutics* (New York: D. Appleton, 1887); *The Practice and Principles of Disinfection* (Cincinnati: R. W. Carroll, 1867). See Devine, *Learning from the Wounded*, chap. 6, esp. pp. 240–246.

36. Keen, "Surgical Reminiscences of the Civil War."

37. See Humphreys, *Marrow of Tragedy*; Gert Brieger, "Sanitary Reform in New York City: Stephen Smith and the Passage of the Metropolitan Health Bill," *Bulletin of the History of Medicine* 40 (September–October 1966): 407–429; John Duffy, *The Sanitarians: A History of American Public Health* (Chicago: University of Illinois Press, 1990), 110–124; Howard Kramer, "The Effect of the War on the Public Health Movement," *Mississippi Valley Historical Review* 35 (1948): 449–462; Bobby Wintermute, *Public Health and the U.S. Military: A History of the Army Medical Department, 1818–1917* (New York: Routledge, 2011).

38. Devine, *Learning from the Wounded*, chap. 4. See also Silas Weir Mitchell, George Morehouse, and W. W. Keen, *Gunshot Wounds and Other Injuries of Nerves* (Philadelphia: J. B. Lippincott, 1864); Keen, "Surgical Reminiscences of the Civil War"; Jacob Mendes DaCosta, "On Functional Valvular Disorders of the Heart," *American Journal of the Medical Sciences*, 115 (July 1869): 17–34; idem., "On Irritable Heart: A Clinical Study of a Form of Functional Cardiac Disorder and Its Consequences," *American Journal of the Medical Sciences* 121 (January 1871): 17–52; W. W. Keen, S. Weir Mitchell, and George Morehouse, "On Malingering, Especially in Regard to Simulation of Diseases of the Nervous System," *American Journal of Medical Science* 48 (October 1864): 367–394.

39. Shephard, *A War of Nerves* (Cambridge, MA: Harvard University Press, 2001), 65.

40. L. G. Wilson, *Medical Revolution in Minnesota* (St. Paul: Midiwinin Press, 1989), 9–10. See also *Learning from the Wounded*, 260–263.

41. See E. M. Hartwell, "The Present Legal Status of the Study of Human Anatomy in the United States," *Annals of Anatomical Surgery* 4 (1881): 8–14, and idem., "The Study of Human Anatomy, Historically and Legally Considered," *Johns Hopkins Univ Stud Biol Lab* 2 (1881): 65–116. For further examples see the sources of the numerous dissection photographs in John Harley Warner and James M. Edmonson, *Dissection: Photographs of a Rite of Passage in American Medicine: 1880–1930* (New York: Blast Books, 2009) as well as discussions by Michael Sappol, *A Traffic of Dead Bodies: Anatomy and Embodied Social Identity in Nineteenth-Century America* (Princeton, NJ: Princeton University Press, 2002).

42. Edward Atwater, "Women, Surgeons, and a Worthy Enterprise: The General Hospital comes to Upper New York State," in *The American General Hospital*, ed. D. E. Long and J. Golden (Ithaca, NY: Cornell University Press, 1989). See also Charles Rosenberg, *The Care of Strangers: The Rise of America's Hospital System* (New York: Basic Books, 1987).

43. Silas Thompson Trowbridge, *Autobiography of Silas Thompson Trowbridge* (with new introduction by John S. Haller and Barbara Mason) (Carbondale: Southern Illinois Press, 2004; reprint of 1874 original), 241.

44. James C. Mohr, *Licensed to Practice: The Supreme Court Defines the American Medical Profession* (Baltimore, MD: Johns Hopkins University Press, 2013).

45. See John Burnham, *Health Care in America: A History* (Baltimore: Johns Hopkins University Press, 2015).

46. Dale C. Smith, "Appendicitis, Appendectomy and the Surgeon," *Bulletin of the History of Medicine* 70 (Fall 1996): 414–441.

47. Stephen Craig, *In the Interest of Truth: The Life and Science of Surgeon General George Miller Sternberg* (Fort Sam Houston, TX: Office of the Surgeon General, Borden Institute, US Army Medical Department Center and School, 2013).

48. Dale C. Smith, "The History of the Military Medical Officer," in *Fundamentals of Military Medicine*, ed. F. G. O'Connor, E. B. Schoomaker; and idem., *Textbook of Military Medicine* (San Antonio, TX: OTSG, Borden Institute, 2019), 3–20.

49. James Parker, "The Militia Act of 1903," *North American Review* 2 (1903): 77–287. See also Mary Gillette, *The Army Medical Department 1865–1917* (Washington, DC: Center of Military History, US Army, 1995).

50. Mary T. Sarnecky, *A History of the U.S. Army Nurse Corps* (Philadelphia: University of Pennsylvania Press, 1999).

51. John P. Finnegan, *Against the Specter of a Dragon: The Campaign for American Military Preparedness, 1914–1917* (Westport, CT: Greenwood Press, 1975); John Garry Clifford, *The Citizen Soldiers: The Plattsburg Training Camp Movement, 1913–1920* (Lexington: University Press of Kentucky, 2015).

52. See E. I. Rutkow and I. M. Rutkow, "George Crile, Harvey Cushing, and the Ambulance Americaine: Military Medical Preparedness in World War I," *Archives of Surgery* 139 (June 2004): 678–685; Grace Crile, ed., *George Crile: An Autobiography* (Philadelphia: J. B. Lippincott, 1947); Peter C. English, *Shock, Physiological Surgery, and George Washington Crile: Medical Innovation in the Progressive Era* (Westport, CT: Greenwood Press, 1980); and John Fulton, *Harvey Cushing: A Biography* (Springfield, IL: Charles Thomas, 1946).

53. Jefferson Kean, "The New Role of the American Red Cross," *Military Surgeon* (May 1916): 539.

54. "Empowers Guard to Invade: Hay Resolution in House Gives Wilson Right to Draft Militia," *New York Times*, June 23, 1916, https://timesmachine.nytimes.com/timesmachine/1916/06/23/104678405.pdf; Jerry Cooper, *The Rise of the National Guard: The Evolution of the American Militia, 1865–1920* (Lincoln: University of Nebraska Press, 1997).

55. Clark W. Nelson and John M. Kutch Jr., "The Doctors Mayo and Military Medicine," *Military Medicine* 155, no. 7 (July 1990): 293–298.

56. Mary Gillette, *Army Medical Department 1917–1941* (Washington, DC: Center for Military History, 2009). On the development of the AEF, see David R. Woodward, *The American Army and the First World War*, Armies of the Great War (Cambridge, UK: Cambridge University Press, 2014).

57. E. L. Munson, "The Needs of Medical Education as Revealed by the War," *Journal of the American Medical Association* 72, no. 15 (1919): 1050–1055.

58. Helen Clapesattle, *The Doctors Mayo* (Minneapolis: University of Minnesota Press, 1954).

59. Frederick M. Dearborn, *American Homeopathy in the World War* ([Chicago]: American Institute of Homeopathy, 1923).

60. Albert S. Bowen, *The Medical Department of the U.S. Army in the World War*, vol. 4, *Activities concerning Mobilization Camps and Ports of Embarkation* (Washington, DC: Government Printing Office, 1928) and William N. Bispham, *The Medical Department of the United States Army in the World War*, vol. 7, *Training* (Washington, DC: Government Printing Office, 1927).

61. Jonathan H. Jaffin, "Medical Support for the American Expeditionary Forces in France during the First World War" (MA thesis, US Army Command and General Staff College, 1990).

62. Stephen C. Craig, "The Life of Brigadier General Theodore C. Lyster," *Aviation, Space, and Environmental Medicine* 65 (November 1994): 1047–1053.

63. R. J. T. Joy, "Historical Aspects of Medical Defense Against Chemical Warfare," in *Medical Aspects of Chemical and Biological Warfare*, ed. Frederick R. Sidell, Ernest T. Takafuji, and David R. Franz (Washington, DC: Borden Institute, 1997), 87–110.

64. "The Owen-Dyer Bill for Increased Rank," *America Medical Association Special Bulletin*, 23 (February 1918); "Legislation for Increase Rank for Medical Officers," *Journal of the American Medical Association* 70 (March 30, 1918): 926; "Gorgas Appeals Direct to Congress," *New York Times*, March 16, 1918; and "Insubordinate, but with Good Reason," *New York Times*, March 16, 1918.

65. Richard V. N. Ginn, *The History of the U.S. Army Medical Service Corps* (San Antonio, TX: OTSG, 1997).

66. Julia C. Stimson, "The Army Nurse Corps," in *The Medical Department of the United States Army in the World War* (Washington, DC: OTSG, 1927), vol. 13, part 2, 291.

67. James R. Wright Jr. and Leland B. Baskin, "Pathology and Laboratory Medicine Support for the American Expeditionary Forces by the US Army Medical Corps during World War I," *Archives of Pathology Laboratory Medicine* 139, no. 9 (September 2015): 1161–1172.

68. Susan E. Lederer, *Flesh and Blood: Organ Transplantation and Blood Transfusion in Twentieth-Century America* (New York: Oxford University Press, 2008) and Kim Pelis, "'A Band of Lunatics down Camberwell Way': Percy Lane Oliver and Voluntary Blood Donation in Interwar Britain," in *Medicine, Madness and Social History*, ed. Bivins R. and Pickstone J. V. (London: Palgrave Macmillan, 2007). See also Pelis, "Taking Credit: The Canadian Army Medical Corps and the British Conversion to Blood Transfusion in WWI," *Journal of the History of Medicine and Allied Sciences* 56 (July 2001): 238–277.

69. Tracey Loughran, "Shell Shock, Trauma, and the First World War: The Making of a Diagnosis and Its Histories," *Journal of the History of Medicine and Allied Sciences* 67, no. 1 (January 2012): 94–119.

70. Ben Shephard, *A War of Nerves: Soldiers and Psychiatrists, 1914–1994* (London: Jonathan Cape, 2000).

71. Edgar Jones and Simon Wessely, *Shell Shock to PTSD: Military Psychiatry from 1900 to the Gulf War* (London: Psychology Press, 2005).

72. Thomas Salmon, *The Care and Treatment of Mental Diseases and War Neuroses ("Shell Shock") in the British* (New York: War Work Committee of the National Committee for Mental Hygiene, 1917).

73. Office of the Surgeon General, ed., *The Medical Department of the United States Army in the World War*, 15 vols. (Washington, DC: Government Printing Office, 1921–1929); see especially vol. 15, part 2, Albert G. Love, *Medical and Casualty Statistics* (1925).

74. W. W. Keen, *Treatment of War Wounds* (Philadelphia: Saunders, 1918).

75. Allan M. Brandt, *No Magic Bullet: A Social History of Venereal Disease in the United States since 1880* (New York: Oxford University Press, 1985).

76. J. S. Davis, "Plastic Surgery in World War I and in World War II," *Annals of Surgery* 123, no. 4 (April 1946): 610–621.

77. *Philadelphia Inquirer*, April 15, 1917, 7.

78. Dale C. Smith, "Extremity Injury and War: A Historical Reflection," *Clinical Orthopedics and Related Research* 473 (September 2015): 2771–2776.

79. Beth Linker, *War's Waste: Rehabilitation in World War I America* (Chicago: University of Chicago Press, 2011).

80. Smith, "Extremity Injury and War."

81. Elliott G. Brackett, section on orthopedic surgery, in *The Medical Department of the United States Army in the World War* , vol. 9, *Surgery* (Washington, DC: Government Printing Office, 1927).

82. Leonard F. Peltier, *Fractures: A History and Iconography of Their Treatment* (San Francisco: Norman, 1990).

83. H. Winnett Orr, *Osteomyelitis and Compound Fractures and Other Infected Wounds; Treatment by the Method of Drainage, and Rest* (St. Louis: C.V. Mosby, 1929).

84. Dale C. Smith, "Group Practice," in *The Oxford Encyclopedia of the History of American Science, Medicine and Technology*, ed. Hugh R. Slotten, vol. 1 (New York: Oxford University Press, 2014), 472–474.

85. The typhoid vaccine, developed by the British Army, was dramatically improved in 1907 by Frederick Russell of the US Army Medical Museum staff. It was added to smallpox immunization as required of all soldiers and sailors in 1911. With the discovery of the paratyphoid organisms, the museum staff developed a trivalent vaccine. See Henry, *Armed Forces Institute of Pathology* (n. 32).

86. The American experience with infectious diseases is well documented in the official history. See J. F. Siler, *The Medical Department of the United States Army in the World War, vol. 9, Communicable and Other Diseases* (Washington, DC: OTSG, 1928). But it is important to realize the Americans collaborated with other countries and enjoyed the benefit of work done by European combats before they entered the war. See L. van Bergen, *Before My Helpless Sight: Suffering, Dying, and Military Medicine on the Western Front* (Burlington, VT: Ashgate, 2009). Various individual studies are also available; see, for example, M. Bresalier, "Fighting Flu: Military Pathology, Vaccines, and the Conflicted Identity of the 1918–19 Pandemic in Britain,"

Journal of the History Medicine and Allied Sciences 68, no. 1 (January 2013): 87–128; D. S. Linton, "'War Dysentery' and the Limitations of German Military Hygiene during World War I," *Bulletin of the History of Medicine* 84, no. 4 (2010): 607–639; and M. Worboys, "Almroth Wright at Netley: Modern Medicine and the Military in Britain, 1892–1902," in *Medicine and Modern Warfare*, ed. R. Cooter, M. Harrison, and S. Sturdy (Atlanta: Rodopi, 1999), 77–98. For continued interest after the war, see Martin G. Ottolini and Mark W. Burnett, "History of U.S. Military Contributions to the Study of Respiratory Infections," *Military Medicine* 170, no. 4 Suppl (April 2005): 66–70, and A. W. Artenstein, J. M. Opal, S. M. Opal, E. C. Tramont, G. Peter, and P. K. Russell, "History of US Military Contributions to the Study of Vaccines against Infectious Diseases," *Military Medicine* 170, no. 4 Suppl (April 2005): 3–11.

87. John M. Barry, *The Great Influenza: The Epic Story of the Deadliest Plague in History* (New York: Viking Books, 2004).

88. Carol R. Byerly, *Fever of War: The Influenza Epidemic in the U.S. Army during World War I* (New York: New York University Press, 2005).

89. Most respiratory diseases have a U-shaped mortality curve, killing the very young and the very old, but most healthy adults recover; the 1918–1919 pandemic of flu killed people in their late teens, twenties, and early thirties in numbers much greater than expected.

90. *Philadelphia Inquirer*, August 4, 1917.

91. D. C. Smith, "War and Medicine," in *The Oxford Encyclopedia of the History of American Science, Medicine and Technology*, ed. Hugh R. Slotten, vol. 2 (New York: Oxford University Press, 2014), 567–586.

92. D. C. Smith, "Surgery: It's Not a Random Event," *Caduceus* 12, no. 3 (1996): 19–38. See also Rosenberg, *Care of Strangers* and David Nahrwold and Peter Kernahan, *A Century of Surgeons and Surgery: The American College of Surgeons, 1913–2012* (Chicago: ACS, 2012) for more information.

93. Samuel H. Greenblatt and Dale C. Smith, "The Emergence of Cushing's Leadership: 1900–1920," in *A History of Neurosurgery in Its Scientific and Professional Contexts*, ed. Samuel H. Greenblatt (Park Ridge, IL: American Association of Neurological Surgeons, 1997), 167–190.

94. Leonard F. Peltier, *Fractures: A History and Iconography of Their Treatment* (Novato, CA: Norman Publishing, 1990).

95. Nahrwold and Kernahan, *A Century of Surgeons and Surgery*, n. 92

96. Lederer, *Flesh and Blood*, n. 62.

97. Gillette, *Army Medical Department 1917–1941*, n. 56.

98. Marianne Bankert, *Watchful Care: A History of Americas Nurse Anesthetists* (New York: Continuum, 1989).

99. D. C. Smith, "Modern Surgery and the Development of Group Practice in the Midwest," *Caduceus* 2 (1986): 1–39.

100. The Radbill Collection of Medical Post Cards at the Moody Library in Galveston illustrates many of these buildings.

101. While postcards have been used in a variety of areas of cultural history, they

have been little used in medical history; see John Crellin and William Helfand, "Learning from medical postcards," *Postcards in the Library: Invaluable Visual Resources*, ed. Norman D. Stevens (New York: Haworth, 1995), 109–120. Probably the largest single collection of medical postcards is in the University of Texas Medical Branch at Galveston, the Blocker History of Medicine Collections, and the Moody Medical Library. The collection is described by Sarita Oertling, "Postcards from the Past," *Hospitalist* 2006, no. 11 (November 2006), www.the-hospitalist.org/hospitalist /article/123235/postcards-past. A Google image search under any of the three terms (Medical Arts Building, the Physician and Surgeons, or Doctors Building) will generate a host of images.

102. C. L. Gibson, "Caring for American Wounded in France," *Scribner's Magazine* 63 (1918): 594–607; "Caring for Pershing's Wounded at the Front," *Literary Digest* 56 (1918): 48–51; M. R. Mullett, "Chances of Getting Killed or Wounded, Interview with Surgeon General Gorgas," *American Mercury*, 85 (1918): 41–43.

103. Beth Linker, *War's Waste: Rehabilitation in World War I America* (Chicago: University of Chicago Press, 2011); Jessica L. Adler, *Burdens of War: Creating the United States Veterans Health System* (Baltimore: Johns Hopkins University Press, 2017).

104. George Creel, *How We Advertised America* (New York: Harper's 1920), 129; on the Committee for Public Information and Creel, see John Brown, "Janus Faced Public Diplomacy: Creel and Lippmann during the Great War," in *Nontraditional US Public Diplomacy: Past, Present, and Future*, ed. Deborah L. Trent (Washington, DC: Public Diplomacy Council, 2016), 43–72.

105. Francis Peabody, "The Care of the Patient," *Journal of the American Medical Association* 88, no. 12 (1927): 877–882.

6

Healing the Unseen Wounds of War

Treating Mental Trauma in the Civil War and the Great War

Kathleen Logothetis Thompson

Writing in 1920 in *The Problem of Nervous Breakdown*, Ash Edwin Lancelot noted that in the early period of the Great War, neurologists expected that "the terrible engines of destruction and the high explosives which would figure prominently in a modern conflict would place an overwhelming strain on many combatants" and that these expectations quickly became reality. Lancelot believed that the environment of the Great War placed an extraordinary strain on its combatants, creating a category of mental casualties that forced the military organizations of the Allies to create new treatments and policies. "In the actual arena of hostilities stresses and strains— both physical and mental—crowded on the combatants more and more furiously," Lancelot explained. "The fatigue of service, the long watching in the trenches by day and by night, the cunning and remorseless cruelty of the enemy, the stress of actual engagement, piled up a burden so great that the individual had not always been able to bear it."[1]

While many historians begin their studies of mental trauma with the Great War and its definition of "shell shock," trauma is also evident in earlier conflicts such as the American Civil War. For example, in the spring of 1864, George Bolsinger of the Eighty-Fifth Pennsylvania did not report to duty for a gunboat expedition and his sergeant, John G. Stephens, went to his tent to find him. Stephens testified in support of Bolsinger's pension application that he "found him all undressed except his shirt, he was hunting mice, I thought he was playing off. I had some of the men to dress him and put him on the gun boat. I was bound that he should not play off on me—consequently I would not send any men in his place." As a result, "when he returned he was crazy and was that way as long as he was in the co. He never was fit for duty." George was sent to the Government Hospital for the Insane (GHI) where he was discharged and was later admitted to the Kansas State Insane Asylum in the 1880s. George was a lifetime resident of asylums, dying at the GHI in 1921.[2] Soldiers like Bolsinger were treated as cases of insanity, but not specifically as mental casualties of war, something that would change with the Great War decades later.

In both the Civil War and the Great War, soldiers broke down under the pressure of warfare. Both conflicts were seen as particularly destructive— one for a nation and the other for the world—and the armies involved had to adapt to these psychological casualties. As seen in the case of Bolsinger, Americans in the nineteenth century did not have a definition for the break- down of men in war and they diagnosed and treated it under the umbrella of insanity in the country's new system of asylums. When it comes to the treatment of traumatized soldiers, the legacy of the Civil War included meth- ods to treat soldiers who went insane during the conflict but also a focus on hereditary and moral causation and physical treatments. There was lit- tle understanding of the connection between the traumatic events of war and the symptoms exhibited by soldiers entering the insane asylums of the nineteenth century, although there were early studies of "soldier's heart" that paved the way for future studies of cardiac and neurological ailments. The generation that fought the Great War utilized the Civil War's ideas of moral treatment and "rest cure," faced the same pressures to keep men in the ranks, and held similar cultural ideas about masculinity, breakdown, and the proper behavior of a soldier. The definition and treatment of soldiers in both wars experienced a similar cycle in the profession of psychiatry, which was initially optimistic about the curability of mental trauma but shifted during the conflict to a more pessimistic outlook that focused on hereditary predisposition, fraud or malingering, and masculine weakness. In addition, the need for military discipline and manpower overshadowed advances in diagnosis and treatment in both conflicts.

Despite these similarities, however, the treatment of traumatized soldiers in the American Civil War and by the Allied and American military in the

Great War differed in one very significant way. In contrast to the Civil War, the military and medical community of the later conflict acknowledged the legitimacy of mental wounds of war, even if only partially. Seeking to avoid the breakdown of men as military resources and creating a generation of men dependent on the government for support, as seen with the system of Civil War pensions, the Great War generation created new treatments and rehabilitation programs to bring men back to fighting strength and reintegrate them into society after their return. (For more on concerns about postwar dependency, see Kanisorn Wongsrichanalai's chapter on returning veterans in this volume.)

Care of the insane during the Civil War was based on a significant medical shift in the United States. By the early nineteenth century, mental illness was considered a treatable medical disorder instead of an economic and social issue where families had to care for the insane or lock them away to prevent them from being a burden on the community. American medicine became more scientific and the treatment of the insane moved from jails and familial homes to insane asylums. No longer were the mentally ill locked away to keep them from their community; instead, they were institutionalized in the hopes that new theory and treatment might cure them and restore them to productive members of society.[3] In these new institutions, emerging professionals developed "moral treatment" as a regime to treat and cure the insane. There was great optimism about treatment in these early asylums, indeed, a "cult of curability" emerged among psychiatrists. The prevalent notion of "environmental determinism"—the idea that the environment affected behavior—led nineteenth-century doctors to believe that mental illness was curable with a correctly managed environment and that institutionalization was crucial in order to take a person away from a "bad" environment and place them in a "good" one.[4] Thoughtfully structured environments within mental institutions provided the basis for moral treatment, attention even extending to the architecture and landscaping of insane asylums.[5] The first hospitals were small establishments housing at most 250 patients at a time, constructed to provide the ideal environment for successful treatment. Under "moral treatment," staff members showed kindness and patience toward the patients, using occupational therapy, religion, and amusements to create a positive environment in which to reeducate the patient to achieve a proper behavior and mental state.[6]

Despite the optimism surrounding "moral treatment," large numbers of

chronic or incurable patients challenged curability and forced asylum physicians to reconsider their understandings of insanity. Because the same environment or "exciting factors" could affect many individuals but cause only
a few to go insane, psychiatrists also developed theories that argued there
must be influences within individuals that made them susceptible to mental
illness. By the time of the Civil War, many believed that hereditary dispo-
sition might be the sole cause of insanity, placing the focus on the person's
physical or moral weakness and away from the environment in which the
insanity occurred. Thus, the Civil War armies understood the existence of
insanity and had measures in place to treat it but believed it to be a result
of moral or physical weakness that caused soldiers to break down under the
environment of war.[7]

One of the few categories of mental difficulty recognized by the Union
Army was labeled "nostalgia," defined by *The Medical and Surgical History
of the Civil War* as "a temporary feeling of depression."[8] The army blamed
homesickness, physical hardships, and inactivity during winter encampments
for the majority of the nostalgia cases, and only reported those that "developed to a morbid degree," usually due to temperament or troubles at home.
They also reported that two types of soldiers were the most susceptible to the
ailment: "young men of feeble will, highly developed imaginative faculties
and strong sexual desires" and "married men for the first time absent from
their families." Officials believed that maintaining activity of the mind and
body to occupy the soldiers was the best cure for nostalgia. Officers thought
it would be dangerous to send these men home because other men might use
the diagnosis as a way to shirk their duties or get out of the service.[9]

Military policies worked to maintain the military manpower needed in
warfare by keeping soldiers in their units. In order to reduce the chances
that nostalgia or mental illness would become an easy escape for soldiers, the
army put specific regulations in place regarding the treatment and discharge
of soldiers declared insane. In General Orders no. 98, the Adjutant General's
Office declared that insane soldiers were entitled to care and set up procedures to send soldiers to the GHI for treatment instead of receiving a discharge. While state and local governments ran most mental hospitals in the
country, the GHI was the first and only federally funded asylum. Founded
in 1855, the GHI was specifically tasked to treat members of the US armed
forces, with the ability to care for mentally ill residents of the District of Columbia if there was room available.[10]

Most soldiers facing mental stress never made it to Washington; rather, they received treatment at state and local asylums instead of the GHI, remained in the field for an extended time before treatment, or received no treatment at all. Often officials were convinced that any man seeking medical attention or discharge due to a mental or unseen physical disability was a shirker to be returned to their units. In several treatises written during and directly after the war, army surgeon Roberts Bartholow warned of the soldier who feigned his illness to get out of duty or out of the service entirely. He advised medical officers to be very cautious and suspicious of the men who came to them for treatment and arm themselves with a full knowledge of diseases and injuries to detect the feigners among the truly afflicted. According to Bartholow, surgeons had to carefully question the soldier about his ailments, look for him to make any mistakes about the symptoms and causes of his injury or illness, and inquire of other trusted men in the wards about the behavior of the particular soldier in case he broke character while the surgeon was not present. Bartholow advised, "As a rule, it is better for the military surgeon, in all cases of doubt, to suspect any soldier of feigning whose symptoms are obscure, unreasonable, or improbable."[11] Following these guidelines, any soldier whose ailment was invisible or did not fit the mold of an established injury or illness was considered a malingerer, and doctors saw it as their duty to return shirkers to their units. Those who exhibited physical signs of mental trauma received treatment for the physical symptoms; if the doctor found "nothing wrong," they treated the men like malingerers.[12]

For soldiers whose symptoms proved severe, transport to an asylum for treatment was the next step under army policy. During and after the war, many asylum superintendents did not analyze the environment of war, instead emphasizing moral or physical causation. In July 1861 the GHI superintendent wrote, "A large proportion of the land forces are men of no little moral and nervous susceptibility, quickly transferred from the quietude, comforts and sympathies of home to all the hardships and profound excitements of camp and field."[13] The reports of these early years reinforce the theory that the seeds of mental illness lay inside the individual and that the causes of wartime insanity could be found within a soldier's moral weakness. This view did not change over the period of the war, for in 1863 and 1864, the superintendent emphasized this point even more forcefully. In July 1864, after a year that saw the highest number of admissions at the GHI, the superintendent still pointed to the weakness of the soldier as the cause of the increased numbers of insane soldiers. He explained that "it is obvious that if the recruit lacks the mental vigor and endurance necessary to receive and practice the discipline and instruction of a soldier, he will involuntarily betray both his companions and his country in the hour of battle—the hour of his supreme trial—and render worse than useless a costly novitiate."[14]

Asylum superintendents and physicians often focused on the physical treatment of their insane patients, prescribing medicines or dietary regimes to improve the strength of the soldier. For example, when admitting a soldier of the Ninth Ohio Infantry who had been declared insane three weeks prior to arriving at Longview State Hospital, doctors noted his emaciated and sickly appearance for which they prescribed "tonic and strengthening regimen and remedies," writing that he was "much improved in general appearance and health" at his discharge.[15] Wartime and postwar asylums focused on a mixture of "moral" and medical treatments to cure insane patients, including the use of narcotics and anodynes, tonics and stimulants, nourishing diets, warm baths, and sleep.[16] In addition to a focus on the somatic symptoms of their cases, there was a marked emphasis on moral or hereditary causes. When a twenty-six-year-old soldier was admitted to Longview Hospital in November 1863 after deserting his regiment and being arrested by military authorities, he was described as periodically depressed and violent. His record entry notes, "He talks principally about the war. He now rests badly at night . . . He has several times tried to injure himself. The supposed exciting cause is the war. He was in the battle at Pittsburg Landing and seems to have been strongly affected by it. The disease is probably hereditary." While the admitting physician noted the excitement from battle as a possible contributor, he then located the base cause of the insanity in the soldier's inherited traits. The entry explains that an uncle on the soldier's father's side of the family was also insane, thus leading to the conclusion that the disease was hereditary. The entry continues to describe in detail the soldier's physical health and appearance, and physicians immediately placed him on a medicinal regimen to improve his physical health.[17] Family history or physical causation was more easily evident in these cases, whereas the idea of a traumatized mind was less accepted, which led to physicians looking to physical, family, or moral causation.

Medical research outside the asylum fell in line with the causes of insanity subscribed to by superintendents at the GHI and state institutions.

Motivated by the physical understandings of insanity, some wartime physicians focused on diseases of the nervous system to explain the symptoms they were seeing in their patients. One ward of Turner's Lane Hospital, a specialized institution set up to treat nervous disorders, was dedicated to the study of "exhausted hearts" by Dr. Jacob DaCosta. The men under DaCosta's care showed symptoms such as "fits of fluttering cardiac action," "cardiac irritability," shortness of breath, high pulse rates, fainting, and coughing up blood. Although many of the three hundred cases DaCosta studied suggest a psychogenic foundation, he defined "soldier's heart" as a physical, functional abnormality.[18] DaCosta's colleague at Turner's Lane, S. Wier Mitchell, defined and treated insanity as caused by physical damage to the nerves or nervous system. Mitchell's treatment strategy focused on testing patients to find the source of the nerve injury or disease, weed out malingerers, and use techniques to restore patients to stability. Like Bartholow, Mitchell was very concerned with those feigning symptoms to remove themselves from duty and used techniques such as questioning men under anesthesia or shock therapy to reveal or cure the potential malingerer. For those he deemed suffering from a nerve injury, Mitchell developed "rest cure," a treatment of controlled diet, medicines, bed rest, massage, and, later on, shock therapy. His idea was to restore the injured soldier to discipline, obedience, and masculinity in order to cure the internal wounds and return the soldier to duty. The studies produced from the research done at Turner's Lane Hospital are considered by doctors and historians as the foundation of the field of cardiology, not psychiatry, because they focused on the physical, cardiac symptoms exhibited by their patients as well as the functions of the heart.[19]

Transitioning into the postwar period, insanity in soldiers was still interpreted as caused by heredity, physical illness, or moral weakness. For the most part, the emphasis for causation, definition, and treatment in veterans remained on physical and moral causes, and there was no drastic change in the understanding of insanity due to the Civil War. Outside of the asylums, society and the government legitimated and supported soldiers with visible, physical wounds of war with programs to give prostheses to amputees, offer employment preference to veterans, award pensions to those disabled by disease or wounds during the war, and house veterans who could not support themselves.[20] Soldiers suffering from mental ailments connected to their service experienced the same limited options that they did during the war. As a result, these pensioners often highlighted the physical aspects of their mental ailments or sought pensions for unrelated physical injuries. Connecting their disability to physical causation or symptoms aided their ability to receive a pension and also made their disability more acceptable to both government and society. Furthermore, pensions under the Pension Act of 1862 were connected to either death, disability, or disabling disease contracted in the line of duty while serving the United States, and pension applications had to prove both disability and connection to military service. The pension office rated veterans with respect to "total disability" for performance of manual labor and set base rates of compensation for conditions such as the loss of an arm or an eye in the service. These policies made it difficult to claim benefits for mental trauma or other "invisible" illnesses.[21]

The Civil War transformed the United States in many ways, but the potential lessons about warfare and mental trauma went largely unnoticed. In the decades after the Civil War, most asylums gradually turned from "moral treatment" to more custodial care and lost much of their reformatory character, although some elements of that previous theory remained. Large numbers of chronic or incurable patients challenged the previous optimism regarding curability and forced asylum physicians and state governments to reconsider the role of mental institutions in society. In the five years of the Civil War, the population of the United States grew 2 percent but the insane population doubled, and it would double again every ten years for the rest of the century.[22] In reality, many patients did not recover, asylums treated only a small percentage of the mentally ill in the country, and most hospitals discharged unrecovered patients and minimized the numbers because those patients contradicted the claims of curability.[23] Moral management, while not dismissed, was no longer feasible with the large numbers of patients treated in asylums. Psychiatrists continued to use daily routines, good diets, exercise, and entertainments to help their patients, but moral management with its personal attention and space for amusements and work inside and outside the asylum building was found impractical.[24]

In the period between the Civil War and the Great War, the study of neurology and psychiatry increased, based on studies such as those of Jacob DaCosta and S. Weir Mitchell during the Civil War. This began in the 1860s when a British physician labeled unidentified trauma in victims of railway accidents "traumatic neurosis." The civilian version, called "railway spine," was thought to be a result of concussion to the spinal cord caused by railroad and industrial accidents. In addition, the "irritable heart" of the Civil War was rediagnosed in the 1910s as "disordered action of the heart," and studies of functional heart disease focused on issues concerning overwork, overexertion, and how a soldier's equipment lay on their backs. In all these disorders, there was a focus on somatic causation and symptoms, questions about the legitimacy of claims to these ailments, and suspicion of fraud.[25]

By the late nineteenth century and early twentieth century, the idea of "shock" became associated with modern society, newly mechanized warfare, and conditions of the nervous system. Speed, noise, and technology was the new order of the world that placed tension and strain on the human mind. In 1903 German sociologist Georg Simmel argued that humans needed to withdraw from society to maintain their mental balance, and that this sometimes manifested in the physical symptoms of hysteria—fits, fainting, paralysis—that would cause a person to seek rest and recovery. Typically, hysteria was defined as a female disorder and the "hysterical female" was the embodiment of this new trauma.[26] Because hysteria was typically "feminine," soldiers who exhibited similar symptoms threatened social understandings of gender norms.

The awareness of the Great War as an industrialized conflict was far greater than during the Civil War, although the last years of that earlier conflict foreshadowed the brutal trench warfare that would become infamous in the later one. The carnage of the Great War shocked the world with millions of soldiers and civilians dead, compared to the estimated seven hundred thousand casualties of the American Civil War. Civilians and officials alike saw the impersonal, man-made, and mechanized nature of death on the battlefields as the greatest cause of anxiety and trauma. "The dominance of long-ranged artillery, the machinegun, and barbed wire had immobilized combat," writes Eric J. Leed, "and immobility necessitated a passive stance of the soldier before the forces of mechanized slaughter." These factors then led to the neurosis seen among Great War soldiers.[27] In short, due to the larger number of combatants and the heightened awareness about mental trauma, there was more attention paid to traumatized soldiers during the Great War.

Psychiatric casualties presented themselves very quickly. At the Battle of the Marne in September 1914, soldiers found men standing dead in the trenches of the front line, positioned as if alive and ready for action. By November 1914, the chairman of the London Hospital House Committee, Lord Knutsford, published in the *Daily Mail* that a number of their "gallant soldiers" were "suffering from very severe mental and nervous shock, due to exposure, excessive strain, and tension."[28] Rumors of these casualties circulated and strengthened the understanding that new artillery technology could cause undetectable brain damage, leading to a new term used first by soldiers and then adopted by doctors. This term, "shell shock," was initially published in 1915 by Charles S. Myers, a captain in the Royal Army Medical Corps. In "A Contribution to the Study of Shell Shock," published in the *Lancet*, Myers exhibited three cases of soldiers affected by close explosions of shells with a focus on the impact on the soldier's five senses, bowel and urine movement, decision making, and memory. The cases he treated in the British Army had a variety of symptoms, including memory loss, blindness, paralysis, hearing and speech disorders, exhaustion, irritation, hallucinations, nightmares, and headaches. At first, Myers and his colleagues believed that soldiers developed symptoms after a close explosion of an artillery shell somehow damaged the brain or nerves. Another early theory, espoused by Frederick Mott, was that carbon monoxide from these blasts led to cerebral poisoning.[29] In the conclusion of his 1915 article, Myers pondered that with the loud explosions it was "difficult to understand why hearing should be (practically) unaffected, and the dissociated 'complex' be confined to the senses of sight, smell, and taste (and to memory)." He then closed by saying that the "close relation of these cases to those of 'hysteria' appears fairly certain," connecting the cases to civilian concepts of shock.[30]

Social and cultural ideas about mental illness and masculinity strongly shaped the reactions to traumatized soldiers in the Great War. On the one hand, society was familiar with "railway spine" and the idea of "weak nerves," or that all men and women might be susceptible to mental breakdown in modern society. On the other hand, like during the Civil War, society stressed self-control, willpower, masculinity, and personal responsibility for both mental and physical health, which meant breakdown was seen as shameful and emasculating. As Ash Edwin Lancelot writes, "It is, of course, clear that many manifestations of acute or chronic nervous breakdown depend on loss of mental control . . . many of the digestive and other physical disturbances are based on this failure of control."[31] Military strength and moral strength were considered to be the same and a decline in a soldier's ability to fight (i.e., mental breakdown) was connected to a decline in his morality. Despite the acknowledgment that the Great War was a mechanized slaughter, breakdown in this environment was still painted with the stigma of cowardice and the soldier was encouraged to return to the front. As military psychiatrists and officers struggled to deal with this new category of causalities within the need for military manpower, the definitions and treatments returned to the emphasis on physical causation, heredity, or moral weakness seen in the Civil War.[32]

Myers's initial conception of shell shock was quickly overturned as doctors treated patients with the same symptoms who were not near an artillery explosion, or even near the front lines. It quickly became clear that shell shock had an explanation beyond the physical effects of an explosion. Doctors argued whether shell shock was the result of physical causation—a physical injury or hereditary predisposition—or psychological causation—the result of traumatic experiences or unresolved psychic conflicts in the soldier. While both arguments remained prominent through the war, officers, physicians, and psychiatrists assessing soldiers on the front lines advanced the psychological definition as they worked with more and more traumatized soldiers. Charles Meyers changed his understanding of shell shock to a belief that functional symptoms were caused by expressions of repressed trauma that were unconscious and uncontrolled by the soldier. Similarly, W. H. R. Rivers, a specialist at Craiglockhart Military Hospital, believed that volunteer soldiers had no time to build up coping mechanisms and that when facing the emotional strain of war, they failed to adapt, particularly in regard to the conflict soldiers face between duty to comrades and the desire to protect their own lives.[33] While officials struggled to fully define shell shock, officers and psychiatrists working first hand with patients understood the connection between the war and their patients' symptoms. Captain Harold Wiltshire, responsible for diagnosing functional psychiatric cases at General Hospital no. 12, wrote in 1916 that "in the vast majority of cases of shell shock, the exciting cause is some special psychic shock. Horrible sights are the most frequent and potent factor in the production of this shock. Losses and the fright of being buried are also important in this respect."[34] At some level, mental trauma received legitimacy in the Great War that it did not gain in the Civil War.

In the same statement, however, Wiltshire also added that "gradual psychic exhaustion from continued fear is an important disposing cause of shell shock, particularly in men of neuropathic predisposition. In such subjects it may suffice to cause shell shock per se."[35] The idea of predisposition, common in the Civil War, was also prevalent in the Great War and directed military policies during the war. Arguments for predisposition claimed that cases of shell shock in fact affected soldiers with preexisting problems that happened to be discovered by receiving treatment under the military medical system. Some psychiatrists and physicians acknowledged the influence of both physical and psychic wounds; however, they also believed that "in many instances the soil was prepared by previous defect, disease, or injury . . . 'weak spots' were present before martial causes became operative."[36] Supporters of these theories upheld the idea that these men had naturally weak constitutions before they entered army service. This was particularly highlighted in the case of conscripted soldiers, who were seen as cowardly or more susceptible to weakness because they had not volunteered or enlisted sooner. Research in the Royal Army Medical Corps argued that Home Forces could not have collapsed due to combat conditions, reinforced predisposition as the more important factor when assessing cases of shell shock, and called for stricter recruiting selectiveness.[37]

The focus on predisposition or illegitimacy in cases of shell shock reflected the conflict between medical and military interpretation of the disorder. The Allies' armies viewed psychological casualties as dangerous to military discipline and manpower, while psychiatrists and soldiers understood the condition on a more personal level. Military medicine and private medicine had two different objectives; while civilian doctors treated patients to help them recover to full health for the sake of their well-being, military doctors had to nurse martial resources back to enough health for them to return to the fight. With the diagnosis of shell shock so recent and this manpower need in mind, the military viewed shell shock in the early years of the war as a threat to military discipline and took a disciplinary approach to the disorder. Early cases were misdiagnosed and treated as concussions, head or brain injuries, or insanity, leading to wrongful commitment in an asylum. Even after numerous casualties forced the development of treatment options for psychological casualties, the needs of the army institutionalized skepticism and suspicion. The relationship between soldiers and doctors was primarily military, physicians made diagnosis and treatment decisions based on the needs of the army, and within this martial atmosphere soldiers understood that mental breakdown was shameful and connected with cowardice, dereliction of duty, and moral weakness. In the end, because of inadequacies in the system of dealing with these soldiers and difficulties determining which cases were real or fraudulent, shell shock was often tied to insanity and malingering.[38]

Within these constraints, the Allies quickly developed tactics for treating shell-shocked soldiers and returning them to the front lines. In the French system, hysteria among soldiers was interpreted as insubordination, and the military refused to legitimize psychiatric war injuries, classifying all cases as malingerers. The British system was less centralized and more positive in terms of recovery and legitimating the shell shock diagnosis; however, trauma was seen as a mental and moral failure. For the most part, these European Allies adopted various "disciplinary" therapies meant to persuade or convince the soldiers to get better and return to their units. One infamous treatment was the use of electroshock therapy, either at low settings to treat physical symptoms of shell shock or at higher settings to persuade soldiers to return to normal. Other treatments used during the war included hydrotherapy, drug therapy, hypnosis and group therapy, massage, isolation, and intimidation or persuasion tactics. In many cases, physicians looked to S. Weir Mitchell's "rest cure," believing that rest, good food, and exercise was enough to cure patients for them to return to duty.[39] J. M. Binneveld states, "One of the surprising observations that can be made . . . is that the First World War presents a kind of rebirth of the early nineteenth-century moral treatment—understood in its most 'heroic' form."[40] These treatments were done in a quasi-military setting, and rewards or punishments were given depending on a soldier's progress toward recovery, or his lack thereof. The patient was largely seen as an unruly child that required an authoritarian figure to convince him to behave normally. Further, he was considered responsible for his recovery; thus, if he did not recover, it was considered a sign of constitutional weakness or a willful act of insubordination against the authority of the doctor and military that deserved punishment.[41]

Because the main objective was to maintain the manpower needed on the front lines, medical officers aimed to treat shell-shocked soldiers in a manner that would return them to duty as quickly as possible. Early casualties were transferred back to England for treatment, and it quickly became clear that the farther away from the front a soldier was treated, the less likely they would return to their units. In the first years of the war, the European Allies developed a military psychiatry response based on three main principles: "proximity," or treatment near the scene of a soldier's exposure; "positive expectancy," treating soldiers with the expectancy of a cure and with a return to the front in mind; and "immediacy"—an approach that allowed soldiers to be treated and returned to duty within a couple of weeks. This "forward psychiatry" occurred within miles of the trenches to maintain the patient's soldier status, get him treatment quickly, and maintain a focus on returning him to the front.[42]

Because shell shock was interpreted in the military as a threat to army morale, discipline, and manpower, officials also used punishment to enforce military needs. Soldiers who failed to display the expected behavior of a soldier often faced discipline, including court-martial, to enforce the obedience of soldiers and maintain the discipline needed to successfully fight the war. As Ben Shephard states, "Men were either sick, well, wounded or mad; anyone neither sick, wounded, nor mad but nonetheless unwilling or incapable of fighting was necessarily a coward, to be shot if necessary."[43] While doctors might understand shell shock as a medical diagnosis based on mental breakdown in the face of war and stress, in the eyes of the military shell shock was grounds for prosecution and conviction. In a postwar inquiry about shell shock in the United Kingdom, the line between cowardice and shell shock was demonstrated to be incredibly thin: "Fear is the chief factor in both cowardice and emotional 'shell-shock,'" the section reads, and the dividing line between a military crime punishable by death and a medical condition was the subjective idea of self-control. As one Dr. Mapother stated in his testimony for the inquiry, "Frankly I am not prepared to make a decision between cowardice and shell-shock. Cowardice I take to mean action under the influence of fear and the ordinary type of shellshock was, to my mind, persistent and chronic fear."[44] Court-martial officials often called in military doctors to testify in defenses based upon a diagnosis of shell shock, and records show that many trials and executions presented evidence of shell shock, desertion, or self-mutilation.[45] One such case was that of Second Lieutenant E. S. Poole of the Eleventh West Yorkshire Regiment. When his regiment was operating around Becourt Chateau during the Battle of the Somme, Poole disappeared from his unit overnight from July 7 to July 8, 1916. As a result he was admitted to a hospital with shell shock and did not return to his regiment until September. When his unit was again engaged heavily at the Somme in October, Poole again left his regiment, this time leading to a charge of desertion and a court-martial. Despite testimony supporting that he was not mentally stable when he wandered away from his unit, Poole was sentenced to death and executed by firing squad December 9, 1916.[46] In total, during the war the British executed 306 soldiers, the Germans 48 soldiers, and the French 700 men. Unsurprisingly in these circumstances, the definition of shell shock offered to the public stressed medical definitions and policies that emphasized discipline rather medical opinions, presenting it as a loss of confidence or low morale in soldiers produced by rumors.[47]

As the United States came closer to entering the conflict in Europe, US officials watched the Allies develop these policies to define and treat psychological casualties with great interest. The Americans had the benefit of viewing the problem from afar before their own troops were engaged and believed that they could improve the tactics used by the Europeans. Influenced by Progressivism, American psychiatry returned to the view that mental illness was curable, and military psychiatrists combined this understanding with the lessons learned from Europe to create their own policies. Tellingly, the United States sent Major Thomas Salmon, director of the National Committee for Mental Hygiene, to Europe in May 1917 to study the disorder and its treatment by the Allies and develop policies based on this advanced analysis. Based on his trip, Salmon and his colleagues suggested three main recommendations: positive and individual treatment of patients as opposed to Britain's negative and disciplinary plan, treatment centers close to the front lines, and strict screening procedures for recruits. As a result, the American Expeditionary Force (AEF) adopted a revised version of Britain's "forward psychiatry." Cases that regimental officers could not treat were referred to advanced field hospitals or casualty-clearing centers located two to nine miles from the front. Any cases too severe to recover at these forward centers were sent to an AEF specialist unit at Base Hospital no. 117. Treatment of cases began with a check of the patient for any physical or hereditary causes, then environmental causes for the trauma. Salmon's plan recommended "re-education" of the soldier through analysis, discipline, and persuasion to convince the man that his condition was not real and encourage him to regain control over his body. The American system utilized more psychological treatments than its British counterpart—including occupational therapy and art therapy—but the focus remained on treating men quickly and returning them to the front.[48]

A large focus of the AEF's plan was the screening of recruits to weed out those deemed mentally deficient or incurable to ensure that mental breakdown in soldiers was curable or did not occur at all. During recruitment, Britain only briefly evaluated a recruit's mental fitness for war; American officials believed this to be one of the biggest flaws of the European system. The American military screened recruits for any indication of disease or damage to the brain and nervous system, evaluated genetics and past family history for mental illness, studied the recruit's behavior and demeanor, and also excluded men who did not meet the sexual and gender characteristics of a heteronormative male (i.e., exhibited small genitalia, a high-pitched voice, and/or emotional tendencies associated with femininity). Ultimately, the American military of the Great War period viewed mental breakdown as a legitimate and curable disease; however, recruitment policies focused on hereditary and physical causation of mental breakdown and treatments prioritized rehabilitating soldiers back to behavior consistent with idealized, militarized manhood.[49]

Over the course of the war, this initial American optimism about curability shifted due to large numbers of patients, the need for military manpower, and resistance from military officials. Despite the efforts of psychiatrists such as Salmon, frontline physicians continued to prioritize physical wounds and believed that men who broke down in battle did so due to hereditary weakness or fraudulent motives. The realities of war frustrated the optimism of American psychiatrists and their policies shifted closer to those of the British army, with greater use of punishments instead of positive curative treatments. When soldiers did not recover from their mental disorders, Salmon discontinued the use of the term "shell shock" and reclassified patients with terms such as "sick," "nervous," or "Not Yet Diagnosed (nervous)" to prevent them from believing their ailment was permanent and encourage them to get better and return to the front. As Annessa Stagner writes, "making shell shock a question of will rather than health placed blame on the soldier for his own condition and invalidated his condition as a heroic war wound."[50] Despite their initial optimism, by the end of the war American policies largely conformed to those of the European Allies.

At the conclusion of the Great War, the Allies transitioned the conversation from wartime treatments to the burden of neuropsychiatric cases on government resources. For the British, the government preferred that issues of shell shock fade away after the war concluded; in the postwar period, they assured civilians that the ailment had been properly handled, replacing the shell shock diagnosis by "neurasthenia," "neurosis," and "psychosis" in order to downgrade the connection to wartime trauma. Ending this association would lessen the postwar burden on the government to support these wartime casualties. True, there was a government inquiry into the treatment of shell-shock cases between 1920 and 1922, but the purpose was largely to quell debates about the role of the disorder in disciplinary action and executions and determine the best ways to prevent it in future conflicts.[51] The findings of the inquiry stated that the Great War "produced no new nervous disorders" and only aggravated previous condition in soldiers, concluding that "no case of psycho-neurosis or of mental breakdown, even when attributed to a shell explosion of the effects thereof, should be classified as a battle casualty any more than sickness or disease is so regarded."[52] The rest of the inquiry report presents an analysis of argument between physical and mental ailments, whether shell-shocked soldiers were predisposed to breakdown, and how to avoid further breakdown through training, treatment, and screening soldiers. Despite the social idea that all men could break down in battle, there was still a connection in popular thought between shell shock and lunacy, insanity, and constitutional weakness.[53]

In America, postwar reformers advocated for a rehabilitation program for veterans, returning again to policies that emphasized curability in the hopes that soldiers would return to their normal lives. These programs offered medical care and vocational training to injured veterans that would "rehabilitate" them back to fully functioning men, particularly amputees and those physically wounded. The purpose behind this care was to transition veterans back to being productive members of society and the workforce and encourage them to earn wages instead of relying on the government for support. The Civil War pension system had cost the government millions of dollars, an outcome rehabilitation advocates sought to avoid.[54] If returning psychological casualties were deemed still "curable," they were sent to four months of specialized rehabilitation similar to programs for amputees and the physically wounded. The four-month rehabilitation for mentally ill veterans focused on rebuilding the soldiers' masculinity and identity as patriarch of their families. If veterans were labeled "incurable" or did not recover under rehabilitation, they were sent to St. Elizabeth's (formerly the GHI) or another insane asylum for long-term care. Despite the hopes of psychiatrists that mentally ill soldiers would return to health at the end of the war, there was a rise in mental illness among veterans that questioned the curative narrative.[55]

Similar to what happened after the Civil War, the post–Great War period saw an increase in demand for government support, not a decline as rehabilitation advocates had hoped for. Through the 1920s, 80 percent of disability benefits were awarded to neuropsychiatric claims, and suicide remained the most common cause of veteran death. By 1940 over half of hospitalized Great War veterans were neuropsychiatric cases. Some psychiatrists, like Thomas Salmon, continued to believe in the legitimacy and curability of mental trauma; Salmon in particular had some success in gaining benefits and care for affected veterans. However, the wider medical community returned to more popular explanations of mental breakdown, including hereditary weakness, insufficient screening allowing deficient soldiers on the front lines, gendered arguments including lack of heteronormative behaviors or over-bearing wives, or accusations that veterans were faking symptoms to gain government support and avoid working. As Gregory M. Thomas argues, "this history of psychiatry throughout this period reveals more continuity than change." Instead of breaking from nineteenth-century medicine, "the idea that inherited or acquired weaknesses might predispose individuals to illness did not lose ground during or after the First World War. In fact, just the opposite happened."[56] Together with the shift from legitimacy and cur-ability toward heredity and fraud, a new mental hygiene movement argued that Americans had to build the mental character of children in order to strengthen their minds against future mental injury or maladjustment.[57]

In the aftermath of the Great War, the image of the traumatized soldier remained culturally significant, but it would not be until Vietnam that true medical and military recognition of wartime trauma occurred. The mod-ern diagnosis of post-traumatic stress disorder (PTSD) has shed new light on previous conflicts and in some cases rewritten the memory of trauma-tized or executed soldiers. In June 2001 Gertrude Harris unveiled the Shot at Dawn Memorial at the National Memorial Arboretum in Staffordshire, United Kingdom. Featuring a statue of a young soldier blindfolded and tied to a stake for execution, the monument remembers British soldiers executed for desertion and other capital offenses during the Great War. Harris is the daughter of Private Harry Farr, one of the 306 British soldiers executed during the war and memorialized by a stake in the memorial. Five years af-ter the unveiling of the monument, all 306 executed soldiers were granted posthumous pardons. Both the monument and the pardons were the result of the Shot at Dawn campaign that sought justice for these men, arguing that they were killed unjustly and were most likely suffering from psychological trauma.[58]

There is a cycle with war neurosis or trauma clearly evidenced in the American Civil War and the Great War in which the presence of trauma was noted, but not understood, and optimism regarding curability turned to pessimism in the face of challenges in treating traumatized soldiers and the need for military manpower. There was also a similar pattern in both wars that interpreted mental breakdown as the result of heredity, moral weakness, or physical causes that made soldiers more vulnerable to collapse within the environment of war. In both conflicts, military expectations and manpower requirements stilted any possible growth in the medical knowledge of shell shock. Army and medical policies reflected the needs of the army, not those of the soldiers. There was opportunity for widespread observation of mental cases; however, there was little innovative research done because physicians had to work within the military system.

Despite these limitations, the Great War marks the starting point for studying war neurosis. It is the first conflict in which the disorder was recognized and a system put into place to diagnose and treat it. While the term shell shock is unique to the Great War because the military and psychiatrists quickly moved away from the appellation, it provided a point of reference for future studies of wartime trauma in soldiers.[59] The Great War also significantly advanced the social awareness of psychological casualties of war in a way that the Civil War did not. In the 1920s, the image of the shell-shocked soldier became iconic to society's understanding of that conflict, a symbol of the modern and technological warfare associated with the twentieth century. In Britain, there was a campaign to ensure that shell-shocked veterans were recognized in the memory of the war, and the Ex-Services' Welfare Society was created specifically to care for veterans with psychological injury, particularly to separate these veterans from the stigma of lunacy.[60] Unfortunately, many of the lessons about treating traumatized soldiers had to be learned again during World War II, and it would not be until the Vietnam War that a medical diagnosis was recognized to fully legitimize and treat these cases.[61]

Notes

1. Edwin Lancelot Ash, *The Problem of Nervous Breakdown* (New York: MacMillan, 1920), 6–7.

2. George W. Bolsinger pension application 594088 and certificate 586593, National Archives, Washington, DC.

3. Gerald N. Grob, *Mental Institutions in America: Social Policy to 1875* (New York: Free Press, 1973), 1–39, 84–85.

4. Carla Yanni, *The Architecture of Madness: Insane Asylums in the United States* (Minneapolis: University of Minnesota Press, 2007), 8; Grob, *Mental Institutions in America*, 42–51, 152–156, 166; J. M. Binneveld, *From Shell Shock to Combat Stress: A Comparative History of Military Psychiatry* (Amsterdam: Amsterdam University Press, 1997), 61–65.

5. For more on the use of architecture and landscaping in the development of nineteenth-century asylums, see Yanni, *Architecture of Madness*, and Francis McMillen, "Ministering to a Mind Diseased: Landscape, Architecture and Moral Treatment at St. Elizabeth's Hospital, 1852–1905" (MA thesis, University of Virginia, 2008).

6. Grob, *Mental Institutions in America*, 165–170; Yanni, *Architecture of Madness*, 1–24, 68–71.

7. Gerald N. Grob, *The Mad Among Us: A History of the Care of America's Mentally Ill* (New York: Free Press, 1994), 105–128; Norman Dain, *Concepts of Insanity in the United States, 1789–1865* (New Brunswick, NJ: Rutgers University Press, 1964), 84–112; David J. Rothman, *The Discovery of the Asylum: Social Order and Disorder in the New Republic* (Boston: Little, Brown, 1971), 237–238.

8. *The Medical and Surgical History of the Civil War*, vol. 6 [Formerly entitled *The Medical and Surgical History of the War of the Rebellion*] (Wilmington, NC: Broadfoot, 1991), 884.

9. *Medical and Surgical History of the Civil War*, 884–886.

10. *By-Laws of the Government Hospital for the Insane, etc. September 1855* (Washington, DC: G. S. Gideon, Printer, 1855), 21–23, National Archives, *Reports of the Government Hospital for the Insane, Vol. 1, 1855–1874*, Office of the Chief Clerk, Department of the Interior, Record Group 48, entry 298, box 6; William Grace, *The Army Surgeon's Manual: For the Use of Medical Officers, Cadets, Chaplains, and Hospital Stewards* [reprinted with a bibliographical introduction by Ira M. Rutkow] (San Francisco: Norman, 1992), 35–36; George Patten, *Patten's Army Manual: Containing Instruction for Officers in the Preparation of Rolls, Returns and Accounts Required of Regimental and Company Commanders, and Pertaining to the Subsistence and Quartermasters' Departments* (New York: J. W. Fortune, 1862), 213–214. The GHI was later renamed St. Elizabeth's Hospital.

11. Roberts Bartholow, *A Manual of Instructions for Enlisting and Discharging Soldiers; With Special Reference to the Medical Examination of Recruits and the Detection of Disqualifying and Feigned Diseases* [reprinted with a biographical introduction by Ira M. Rutkow] (San Francisco: Norman, 1991), 86–91, 99, 101–102.

12. Eric T. Dean Jr., *Shook Over Hell: Post-Traumatic Stress, Vietnam, and the Civil War* (Cambridge, MA: Harvard University Press, 1997), 118–120, 133–134.

13. *Reports of the Board of Visitors and the Superintendent of Construction of the Government Hospital for the Insane, for the year 1860–1861* (Washington, DC: Gideon and Pearson Printers, 1864), 17–20, National Archives, *Reports of the Government Hospital for the Insane*, vol. 1, *1855–1874*, Office of the Chief Clerk, Department of the Interior, Record Group 48, entry 298, box 6.

14. *Ninth Annual Report of the Board of Visitors, and the Twelfth Annual Reports*

of the Superintendent of Construction, Government Hospital for the Insane, for the year 1863–1864, 721–722, National Archives, *Reports of the Government Hospital for the Insane*, vol. 1, *1855–1874*, Office of the Chief Clerk, Department of the Interior, Record Group 48, entry 298, box 6.

15. Ohio Historical Society, Longview State Hospital, Case History of Male and Female Patients, 1863–1918, State Archives Series 541, p. 33.

16. Many annual superintendent reports discuss the treatments used with insane patients, including: *First Biennial Report of the Trustees, Superintendent and Treasurer, of the Iowa Hospital for the Insane, at Mount Pleasant. December 1861* (Des Moines: F. W. Palmer, State Printer, 1862), Falk Library, University of Pittsburg Health Sciences Library, Collection Ms 9, Insane Hospital Reports, vol. 1, 29–30; *Annual Report of the Resident Physician of the New York City Lunatic Asylum, January 1, 1867*, Falk Library, University of Pittsburg Health Sciences Library, Collection Ms 9, Insane Hospital Reports, vol. 2, 20–25; *Report of the State of the New York Hospital and Bloomingdale Asylum, for the Year 1866* (New York: D. Van Nostrand, 1867), Falk Library, University of Pittsburg Health Sciences Library, Collection Ms 9, Insane Hospital Reports, vol. 2, 15–18; *Twenty-Third Annual Report of the Board of Trustees and Officers of the Central Ohio Lunatic Asylum to the Governor of the State of Ohio: For the Year 1861* (Columbus: Richard Nevins, State Printer, 1862), Falk Library, University of Pittsburg Health Sciences Library, Collection Ms 9, Insane Hospital Reports, vol. 1, 29–30.

17. Ohio Historical Society, Longview State Hospital, Case History of Male and Female Patients, 1863–1918, State Archives Series 541, 56.

18. Alfred Jay Bollet, *Civil War Medicine: Challenges and Triumphs* (Tucson, AZ: Galen Press, LTD, 2002), 321–322; Charles F. Wooley, *The Irritable Heart of Soldiers and the Origins of Anglo-American Cardiology: The US Civil War (1861) to World War I (1918)* (Burlington, VT: Ashgate, 2002), 12–35; Ira M. Rutkow, *Bleeding Blue and Gray: Civil War Surgery and the Evolution of American Medicine* (New York: Random House, 2005), 253–254.

19. Mitchell becomes notorious for his use of the same techniques in the postwar period to cure "hysterical" women by using "rest cure" and other therapies to return his patients to proper forms of femininity. S. Weir Mitchell is most known for developing the idea of the "phantom limb" from his work with amputees and injuries to the nervous system. Rutkow, *Bleeding Blue and Gray*, 253–254; Lisa A. Long, *Rehabilitating Bodies: Health, History, and the American Civil War* (Philadelphia: University of Pennsylvania Press, 2004), 29–49; Nancy Cervetti, *S. Weir Mitchell, 1829–1914: Philadelphia's Literary Physician* (University Park: Pennsylvania State University Press, 2012), 75–81; S. Weir Mitchell, George R. Morehouse, and W. W. Keen Jr., *Reflex Paralysis: Circular no. 9, Surgeon General's Office, March 10, 1864. A Reprint: With Introduction* (New Haven: Yale University School of Medicine, 1941); Charles F. Wooley, "Jacob Mendez DaCosta: Medical Teacher, Clinician, and Clinical Investigator," *American Journal of Cardiology* 50 (November 1982): 1147; Wooley, *Irritable Heart of Soldiers*, 5; Elmer E. Southard, *Shell-Shock and Other Neuropsychiatric*

Problems Presented in Five Hundred and Eighty-Nine Case Histories from the War Literature, 1914–1918 (New York: Arno, 1919; 1973), vi–vii.

20. Patrick J. Kelly, *Creating a National Home: Building the Veterans' Welfare State, 1860–1900* (Cambridge, MA: Harvard University Press, 1997), 2–5, 56–57, 133–140.

21. Steven G. Livingston, *Student's Guide to Landmark Congressional Laws on Social Security and Welfare* (Westport, CT: Greenwood Press, 2002), 19–22; Thirty-Seventh Congress, Sess. II. Ch. 165, 166. 162—July 14, 1862, CHPA, CLXVI, "An Act to Grant Pensions," found at www.loc.gov/law/help/statutes-at-large/37th-congress/session-2/c37s2ch166.pdf; Theda Skocpol, *Protecting Soldiers and Mothers: The Political Origins of Social Policy in the United States* (Cambridge, MA: Belknap Press of Harvard University Press, 1992), 106–130; Peter Blanck, "Civil War Pensions and Disability," in "Symposium: Facing the Challenges of the ADA: The First Ten Years and Beyond," *Ohio State Law Journal* 62, no. 1 (2001): 117–126.

22. R. Gregory Lande, *Madness, Malingering, and Malfeasance: The Transformation of Psychiatry and the Law in the Civil War Era* (Washington, DC: Brassey's, 2003), 195.

23. Grob, *The Mad among Us*, 105–106; Benjamin Reiss, *Theaters of Madness: Insane Asylums and Nineteenth-Century American Culture* (Chicago: University of Chicago Press, 2008), 169–172, 191.

24. Yanni, *Architecture of Madness*, 105–106; Grob, *The Mad among Us*, 105–128; Dain, *Concepts of Insanity in the United States*, 84–112; Rothman, *The Discovery of the Asylum*, 237–238.

25. Edgar Jones, *Shell Shock to PTSD: Military Psychiatry from 1900 to the Gulf War* (Hove, UK: Psychology Press, 2005), 1–15; Ruth Leys, *Trauma: A Genealogy* (Chicago: University of Chicago, 2000), 3–4; Peter Leese, *Shell Shock: Traumatic Neurosis and the British Soldiers of the First World War* (New York: Palgrave Macmillan, 2002), 1.

26. Leese, *Shell Shock*, 2; Leys, *Trauma*, 4.

27. Eric J. Leed, *No Man's Land: Combat and Identity in World War I* (New York: Cambridge University Press, 1979), 165.

28. Lord Knutsford, "To the Editor at *The Daily Mail*," attached to the meeting minutes of the National Hospital for the Paralysed and Epileptic, November 10, 1914, referenced in Stefanie Carolina Linden and Edgar Jones, "'Shell Shock' Revisited: An Examination of the Case Records of the National Hospital of London," *Medical History* 58, 4 (October 2014): 519–545.

29. Binneveld, *From Shell Shock to Combat Stress*, 84–86; Jones, *Shell Shock to PTSD*, 21–23; Leese, *Shell Shock*, 1, 3; Charles S. Myers, "A Contribution to the Study of Shell Shock: Being an Account of Three Cases of Loss of Memory, Vision, Smell, and Taste, Admitted into the Duchess of Westminster's War Hospital, Le Touquet," *Lancet* 185, no. 4772 (February 1915): 316–330; Keith W. A. Horsley, "Myers—The Dawn of a New Era," *Journal of Military and Veterans' Health* 16, no. 1 (October 2007): 8.

30. Myers, "Contribution to the Study of Shell Shock," 320.

31. Ash, *Problem of Nervous Breakdown*, 14.

32. Celia Malone Kingsbury, *The Peculiar Sanity of War: Hysteria in the Literature*

of World War I (Lubbock: Texas Tech University Press, 2002), 3, 8–9; Ash, *Problem of Nervous Breakdown*, 3–5.

33. Binneveld, *From Shell Shock to Combat Stress*, 87–90; Jones, *Shell Shock to PTSD*, 23–24, 34; Leed, *No Man's Land* 166–177; Gregory M. Thomas, *Treating the Trauma of the Great War: Soldiers, Civilians, and Psychiatry in France 1914–1940* (Baton Rouge: Louisiana State University Press, 2009), 10–12.

34. Jones, *Shell Shock to PTSD*, 24.

35. Jones, *Shell Shock to PTSD*, 24.

36. Southard, *Shell-Shock*, vi.

37. Fiona Reid, *Broken Men: Shell Shock, Treatment, and Recovery in Britain, 1914–1930* (London: Continuum, 2010), 22–23; Thomas, *Treating the Trauma of the Great War*, 61–66.

38. Leese, *Shell Shock*, 32–34, 53; Reid, *Broken Men*, 16; Leed, *No Man's Land*, 166–180; Thomas, *Treating the Trauma of the Great War*, 67; Kingsbury, *Peculiar Sanity*, 118–121.

39. Binneveld, *From Shell Shock to Combat Stress*, 107–116; Leese, *Shell Shock*, 34–35, 73–87; Jones, *Shell Shock to PTSD*, 26–31; Marc Roudebush, "A Battle of Nerves: Hysteria and Its Treatment in France during World War I," in *Traumatic Pasts: History, Psychiatry, and Trauma in the Modern Age, 1870–1930*, ed. Mark S. Micale and Paul Lerner (New York: Cambridge University Press, 2001), 253–255; Kingsbury, *Peculiar Sanity*, 117–121; Peter Leese, "'Why Are They Not Cured?': British Shellshock Treatment during the Great War," in Micale and Lerner, *Traumatic Pasts*, 208–219.

40. Binneveld, *From Shell Shock to Combat Stress*, 114.

41. Binneveld, *From Shell Shock to Combat Stress*, 107–116; Leese, *Shell Shock*, 34–35, 73–87; Jones, *Shell Shock to PTSD*, 26–31; Reid, *Broken Men*, 64; Kingsbury, *Peculiar Sanity*, 118; Thomas, *Treating the Trauma of the Great War*, 20–22, 38–42, 48.

42. Binneveld, *From Shell Shock to Combat Stress*, 137; Jones, *Shell Shock to PTSD*, 21, 24–31.

43. Ben Shephard, *A War of Nerves: Soldiers and Psychiatrists in the Twentieth Century* (Cambridge, MA: Harvard University Press, 2001), 25.

44. *Report of the War Office Committee of Enquiry Into "Shell-Shock." Presented to Parliament by Command of His Majesty* (London: His Majesty's Stationery Office, 1922), 138–139.

45. Leese, *Shell Shock*, 40–45, 65–66; Reid, *Broken Men*, 58–60.

46. "Shot for desertion," National Archives (UK), accessed November 21, 2021, www.nationalarchives.gov.uk/education/resources/medicine-on-the-western-front -part-two/shot-for-desertion/; "Eric Skeffington Poole: General Court Martial," the First World War, National Archives (UK), accessed November 21, 2021, www.nation alarchives.gov.uk/pathways/firstworldwar/people/p_poole2.htm.

47. Leese, *Shell Shock*, 40–45, 65–66; Reid, *Broken Men*, 58–60.

48. Jones, *Shell Shock to PTSD*, 31–32; Annessa C. Stagner, "Defining the Soldier's Wounds: U.S. Shell Shock in International Perspective," (PhD diss., University of California, Irvine, 2014), 1, 42–48.

49. Leese, *Shell Shock*, 55; Stagner, "Defining the Soldier's Wounds," 60–79; Pearce Bailey et al., *The Medical Department of the United States Army in the World War*, vol. 10, *Neuropsychiatry. Prepared under the direction of Maj. Gen. M. W. Ireland, The Surgeon General* (Washington, DC: US Government Printing Office, 1929), 6–7, 13–14; Southard, *Shell-Shock*, viii.

50. Stagner, "Defining the Soldier's Wounds," 84–90.

51. Leese, *Shell Shock*, 123; Reid, *Broken Men*, 71–85.

52. *Report of the War Office Committee of Enquiry into "Shell-Shock,"* 92, 190.

53. Reid, *Broken Men*, 99; *Report of the War Office Committee of Enquiry into "Shell-Shock."*

54. In 1880 Civil War pensions made up 21 percent of the federal budget and this grew to almost 42 percent by 1893. At the beginning of the Great War, the government was still paying 362,000 pensioners an average of $285–$374 per year, plus widow and dependent pensions. According to a study by the Social Security Board, the US government had spent $8,077,072 for Civil War pensions by 1942. See Bernard Rostker, *Providing for the Casualties of War: The American Experience through World War II* (Santa Monica, CA: RAND, 2013), 104–105; Theda Skocpol, "America's First Social Security System: The Expansion of Benefits for Civil War Veterans," *Political Science Quarterly* 108, 1 (Spring 1993): 85–86; Franklin M. Aaronson, "Pensions and Compensation to Veterans and Their Dependents," *Social Security Bulletin* (November 1942): 18.

55. Beth Linker, *War's Waste: Rehabilitation in World War I America* (Chicago: University of Chicago Press, 2011), 2–7; Stagner, "Defining the Soldier's Wounds," 165–175.

56. Thomas, *Treating the Trauma of the Great War*, 13, 18.

57. Stagner, "Defining the Soldier's Wounds," 180–200.

58. "Soldiers Shot at Dawn Honoured after 90 Years," *Guardian*, February 19, 2007, https://www.theguardian.com/uk/2007/feb/19/military.uknews4; Christopher Bellamy, "Major Refused Pardons for Executed Soldiers," *Independent*, February 19, 1993, http://www.independent.co.uk/news/uk/major-refuses-pardons-for-execut ed-soldiers-1474227.html; "Tribute to WWI 'Cowards,'" *BBC News*, June 21, 2001, http://news.bbc.co.uk/2/hi/uk_news/1399983.stm; John Sweeny, "Lest We Forget: The 306 'Cowards' We Executed in the First World War," *Guardian*, November 13, 1999, www.theguardian.com/world/1999/nov/14/firstworldwar.uk; Ben Fenton, "Pardoned: The 306 Soldiers Shot at Dawn for 'Cowardice,'" *Telegraph*, August 16, 2006, www.telegraph.co.uk/news/1526437/Pardoned-the-306-soldiers-shot-at-dawn -for-cowardice.html.

59. Reid, *Broken Men*, 9, 45–46.

60. Reid, *Broken Men*, 1, 8–9, 100–110.

61. Shephard, *War of Nerves*, xxii; Leese, *Shell Shock*, 45; Reid, *Broken Men*, 35.

7

Blood and Soil

Americans and Environment in the Trenches of Petersburg and the Western Front

Brian Allen Drake

There is a joke among Civil War environmental historians that our biggest "discovery" has been that the war was fought outside. Humor aside, it is an observation that was not always fully appreciated by the conflict's scholars until recently. Environmental history is the study of human interactions with nature over time, and in that vein we now see the Civil War not only as a struggle between human enemies but also as an intense engagement with the natural world on multiple levels. At the macro scale, natural resources from wheat to wood to wool had to be extracted, processed, and delivered to voracious armies on both sides. Closer to the battlefield, troops trained, marched, fought, and bivouacked amid the elements. Although rain and drought, wind, heat, and cold (and the diseases associated with them) already figure into many a Civil War narrative, they have tended to serve mostly as decoration for the main events: the battles. A good case might be made, however, that Civil War soldiers' encounters with nature were not mere skirmishes but critical campaigns in their own right, even to the point of helping to determine the conflict's outcome, or at least the outcome of many of its clashes. But even if they were not always decisive, such encounters were certainly ubiquitous.[1]

The environmental context of the Great War is perhaps more familiar, at least to lay audiences. This is probably because of the famous "mud and blood" images from the worst areas of the Western Front. Like the Civil War, the Great War required massive, even global, mobilization of natural resources and Herculean movements of troops and equipment It also subjected combatants across Europe—as well as the Middle East, Africa, and the oceans—to the vagaries of weather, climate, and disease. But the "active sectors" of the Western Front in particular delivered powerful pictures of humans and nature locked in an often-literal death grip. Few descriptions of the Ypres salient, Passchendaele, Verdun, and the Somme fail to mention the all-embracing mud of the trenches of Belgium and northwestern France; British "trench poetry" positively brims with it. Add lice, rats, a blasted landscape, and the rot and reek of garbage, feces, and flesh, and the images become iconic, sometimes to the point of stereotype.

A broad comparative environmental history of the Civil and Great Wars could go in any number of directions. We might, for instance, compare the environmental impacts of mobilization and "total war" or, conversely, the impact of nature, in the form of disease or climate, on that mobilization. We might investigate the influence of geography on strategy, as the American geographer Douglas Wilson Johnson did as early as 1917. ("The violation of Belgian neutrality," he wrote in the opening line of a book on the subject, "was predetermined by events which took place in Western Europe several million years ago. Nature was fashioning the scenery which was not only to serve as a setting for the European drama, but was, in fact, to guide the current of the play into blackest tragedy.") But this chapter aims for a more rank-and-file experience. It investigates the environmental history of Civil War soldiers as both a potential prologue to and a point of comparison for the environmental experience of American soldiers in the Great War.[2]

But even this can be an impossibly broad topic. How to narrow it? It is a well-worn observation that both wars involved trench warfare on a significant scale. Here, too, we run the risk of stereotypes as well as comparing apples and oranges. Trenches in warfare were hardly new or unique to either conflict, of course. And though they bore a close physical resemblance on quick inspection, the trenches in the two conflicts differed considerably in size, organization, duration, and tactical and strategic intent. Further, the relatively brief American involvement in Great War combat, combined with an emphasis on small-unit offensive operations—an approach influenced strongly by the Civil War—meant that the trench experience did not dominate the American soldier's time in combat in the way it did his French and

British counterparts'. But conventional wisdom still links those trenches to the Civil War, and in particular to the Petersburg campaign of 1864–1865.

This chapter reconsiders those links. It will head first to Petersburg and then to the Western Front in an effort to tease out some deeper common-alities—and significant divergences—in the ways that nature and American soldiers interacted in wartime. By the Civil War's third year, its combatants had begun to entrench in ways that resembled, at least superficially, parts of the Western Front, most famously in the area east and south of Petersburg in late 1864. How did the environmental experiences of Ulysses S. Grant's and Robert E. Lee's respective armies at Petersburg foreshadow? If they did at all, what was to come for the doughboys a half century later? How were they similar? How were they different? What do we learn from laying them side by side? It is impossible to generalize, of course, about either soldiers' expe-riences or the environments in which they experienced them. But a com-parison still has its place, and what we will discover in the following one is that, while they do offer an interesting point of comparison, the trenches of Petersburg are not quite as useful in the way of a prologue. On the Western Front, nonhuman nature, technology, and human biology could combine in ways they did not at Petersburg to create a unique, and sometimes uniquely terrible, environmental context for battle.

Between the summer of 1864 and the spring of 1865, large numbers of Union and Confederate troops burrowed into the Virginia countryside in what is commonly referred to as the siege of Petersburg. Along with Sherman's March and the Shenandoah Valley campaign of late 1864, Petersburg was part of the Civil War's endgame. Earlier in 1864, Grant had assumed control of the en-tire Union army and embarked on an aggressive, no-rest, no-retreat strategy against the Confederates in the famously bloody Overland campaign, count-ing on superior Federal numbers to overcome his own high casualty rates and overwhelm rebel armies in great clashes at places like the Wilderness and Cold Harbor. Capturing the Confederate capitol of Richmond remained a Union goal. To facilitate that, Grant aimed in the wake of the Overland campaign to maintain constant pressure on the enemy and capture strategically valuable and fortified Petersburg, where multiple railroads came together to serve as a vital supply link to Richmond itself. But initial Union attempts to take the city failed, and so the Federals dug in, playing the long game, emerging occa-sionally for raids and larger assaults. Over many months, Grant stretched the

Union trenches in an effort to flank Lee's army while simultaneously weakening its defenses to allow for a frontal breakthrough.[3]

Although life in its trenches would never be pleasant, there were certainly far worse places to dig into than Petersburg, Virginia. The town and its surroundings sat on the "fall line" separating the piedmont and coastal plain regions, where the soils were largely light, fertile, and well-drained sandy loams ("Appling-Cecil" and "Emporia-Mattaponi-Slagle" soils dominate the area, according to modern scientific work). The surface landscape was primarily agricultural, with fields of tobacco, wheat, and corn accented by forested areas dominated by longleaf pine and mixed deciduous trees. Summers were hot and muggy, and winters could be cold and wet—rain was usually reliable and evenly distributed throughout a given year, with annual totals around forty-five inches. One of the biggest contrasts with the Western Front, though, was Petersburg's elevation above sea level, which would spare it some of the severe drainage problems characteristic of the former.[4]

The Petersburg trenches on both sides were essentially meandering networks of zigzagging channels, divided roughly into a main line with supporting areas in the rear. They were usually deep enough for a man to stand upright without—it was hoped, often in vain—receiving a sharpshooter's Minié ball in the head and topped by a parapet of earth and wood on the side facing the enemy; one stood on a "banquette" or "firestep" and aimed through a "loophole" to shoot at them. Short trenches called "saps" also extended outward to rifle pits, in which pickets stood as advanced guards. Punctuating the forward trenches were artillery strong points called forts, and sprinkled throughout the network were shelters for troops and officers, "bombproofs" (reinforced dugouts for artillery and mortar attacks), breastworks, embrasures, redans, gabions, and fascines. Connecting forward trenches with forts and other works, support and reserve trenches, and staging and supply areas in the rear were additional trenches called "covered ways." In front of the trenches, laid out to deter attacks, were abatis—logs or trees with sharpened ends and branches angled toward the enemy—and *chevaux de fries*, frames made of sharpened wooden pikes. Indeed, the trenches required so much wood—not only for abatis and *chevaux* but also for revetting the bottoms and sides, as well as for bombproofs, shelters, and cooking fires—that the surrounding area was practically devoid of timber by the end, a foreshadowing of the treeless wastes of the Western Front.[5]

Serving in the trenches was tough duty, far different from the Civil War's usual long marches punctuated by Napoleonic-style battles and skirmishes in more or less open terrain. When they were not on the attack or in reserve, troops were still in constant and exhausting contact with the enemy—another prologue to the Western Front—and without any obvious indications of progress. Fighting was usually limited to sniping, mortar and artillery exchanges, and the occasional spontaneous firefight or small assault. "There is nothing desirable about this place," wrote Wilbur Fisk of the Second Vermont Regiment. "It is all fighting and no fun. We neither whip nor get whipped here. It is regular cold-blooded dueling, day after day, with no decisive result on either side." The stalemate would last ten months, finally ending with the Federals' breakthrough in April 1865, after numerous failed attempts, and Lee's surrender at Appomattox.[6]

If the grinding nature of trench warfare itself was not bad enough, daily life in the trenches was a study in intimate, unpleasant, and sustained contact with elemental nature. Civil War troops were, of course, no strangers to rain, mud, sun, heat, and cold, but the Petersburg trenches could amplify their effects, especially heat. "Heat—dry, oppressive, stifling heat—was one of the defining elements of life in the trenches . . . in the summer of 1864," writes J. Tracy Power of Lee's Army of Virginia. It was "so Dry & hot I cant [sic] hardly live," one rebel declared, an observation many Union soldiers would have seconded. Union officer Stephen Weld described "broiling heat," noting that several of his men died of "sun-stroke" in June, when it was so "fearfully hot" that it was "almost dangerous" to simply "put one's head in the sun." In desperation, men of both sides erected brush arbors and stretched tent halves across the tops of the trenches for relief. Wind offered little reprieve, as it often carried so much dirt that it drove men half-mad. "Dust, dust, dust dust—dust everywhere- everything dust," as one Union artilleryman wrote. "No dust returning to dust here, where every body [sic] and everything is already dust." Rain and cooler weather, when they came, only reduced the dusty trenches to muddy ditches ("nasty, sloppy, mortar-mud," Fisk called it, which "cannot be flanked or dodged") and chilled troops to the bone. "It always rained at Petersburg," recalled Elisha Hunt Rhodes, and the relentless moisture turned hardtack, noted another Union soldier, into "sodden dough. . . . Our coffee is diluted, our sugar and salt dissolved, and our pork flabby from the drenching." For Confederates, such miseries were made all the worse for insufficient clothing, rations, and rest periods in the rear, a result of dwindling manpower.[7]

In such an environment, personal hygiene and disposal of garbage and human waste could be difficult at best, and the smell of the Petersburg trenches and environs must have rivaled its other discomforts. Bell Irvin Wiley noted how Confederate soldiers were "prone to litter the works with beef bones, melon rinds, fruit peelings, and other scraps." Union soldiers fouled the areas behind the trenches to the point that Confederates sharpshooters could concentrate their fire on the few paths left open amid the filth. The exploding populations of rats and flies, which fed on garbage, excrement, and incompletely buried corpses, spread diseases that were always a problem for soldiers but were intensified by the trench environment. Diarrhea and dysentery ravaged Union troops as it did their Southern opponents (who also suffered, the *Charleston Mercury* reported, from "swelled feet, in consequence of standing and sitting so much in the water of the trenches.") Bereft of the Union's impressive if not always palatable commissary supplies, Confederates scurried desperately to secure additional nourishment from local vendors (rumors of a New Year's Day feast courtesy of Richmond's civilians brought great disappointment when the meal failed to materialize due to shortages). And, as always during the war, there were the ubiquitous lice. Troops preened each other like primates, searching beards and scalps, and boiled their uniforms in desperate assaults against the tiny beasts.[8]

Other physical encounters with nature were perhaps less crude but no less intimate. The Civil War has not been fully appreciated as a sensory experience,[9] a swirl of noise and odor and flavor as well as the more familiar visual spectacle captured in wartime photography. The war's destruction often took on elements of the sublime, a feeling more closely associated with human views of nature. This was certainly true of duty in the Petersburg trenches, where sound and vision could play a surprising role in the experience, alongside the expected olfactory and tactile sensations. Union veteran John Billings offered some striking examples. In ceaseless contact with the enemy and constantly on the lookout for assault, he observed, troops on both sides became hypersensitive to unusual sounds, their jumpiness triggering innumerable flare-ups along the line. Meanwhile, mortar attacks (mortars were short, squat cannons that lobbed balls in a high arc in order to drop them inside the trenches) were occasions for keen attention to sight as well as sound. Some nights, the sky over the trenches would be "brilliant with the fiery arches of those lofty-soaring and . . . dignified projectiles." Soldiers could "hear the creaking whistle of the fuse" as the incoming round rose and, watching it closely, they could calculate whether it was a danger to them or not. Private John Bassett described how "they would spin like a top, and sing like a good fellow." Rebels, too, noticed the beauty in the deadly things. "The heaviest mortar shelling of the siege occurred on Tuesday night last [October 11, 1864], and the sight is described as having been sublime," wrote the *Richmond Enquirer*. "For the space of several hours the eastern Heavens seemed ablaze with brilliant meteors—ascending, descending and shooting athwart the horizon in almost countless numbers and unsurpassed beauty. . . . As shell after shell descended from the dizzy height to which it had risen into the very trenches of the enemy, our men would give vent to cheers which strangely enlivened the scene." In the Great War, soldiers in the trenches would raise such sensitivity to a deeply ironic high art.[10]

Soldiers often needed to put an ear to the ground as well as an eye to the sky. The Petersburg campaign was notorious for efforts to break through the trenches from underneath; if aboveground assaults could not breach the lines, Union strategists reasoned, it might be possible to literally undermine them from below. In this scenario, troops would dig a long "gallery" from their own trenches, terminating underneath some weak point in the enemy's line. The end of the gallery could then be packed with explosives, and the resulting blast would rip open a gap in the rebel line, into which Federal troops would pour and, it has hoped, allow for the much-desired "breakthrough." This was not a strategy new to Petersburg, and as Pennsylvania troops with mining experience dug a gallery beneath a bulge in the rebel lines known as Pegram's salient, Confederates suspected enough to begin probing with their own countermines, trying in vain to detect the sound of Federal picks and shovels. Despite the problems raised by ventilation, different soil types, and groundwater (at one point, the miners found a mastodon skull, which made its way to a museum after the war), the Federals completed their work undetected, and the Battle of the Crater commenced on July 30, 1864, quickly becoming a Union debacle of legendary proportions. With mining, too, the Great War would offer a lesson in death from below as well as from above.[11]

By the time it was over, the "mole-like existence" in Petersburg trenches had worn down many men on both sides. One Confederate artilleryman, spared duty in the trenches, saw the costs of trench life written on the faces and bodies of those who were not so fortunate. "We thought we had seen men with the marks of hard service upon them," he wrote. But "we were shocked at the condition, the complexion, the expression of the men and the officers, too. . . . Indeed, we could scarcely realize that the unwashed, un-combed, unfed and almost unclad creatures we saw were officers of rank and reputation in the army." Fifty years later, such a description could seem be-nign compared to the trenches of France. Yet it was not necessarily a true one for their Civil War ancestors in Federal blue. Historian Steven Sodergren, in the most thorough modern study of Northern soldiers at Petersburg, has written extensively on their trench experience and how it compared to the Great War. He concludes that the move to the trenches was, in many ways, a reprieve. With stable supply lines, significant (if not always reliable) pro-tection from enemy shot and shell, and the time to fortify and improve their living quarters, many Federals found in trench life a welcome change from the titanic slaughters of the Overland campaign. With time, they recovered their energy and commitment to the cause, "empowering the Army of the Potomac to survive and ultimately to attain victory" in the spring of 1865.[12]

The Western Front trenches of the Great War were a European creation, not an American one, and so to understand the eventual American "environ-mental experience," there we need to begin with the British and French one. One of the first things to note is that trench warfare was not the typical expe-rience for many Allied soldiers, such as rear-area clerks, medical personnel, artillery, aviators, drivers, muleskinners, and so on. Even infantrymen could spend a great deal of time in more traditional overland movements. Nor were all areas of the trenches equal in terms of either their natural or their combat environment. "Quiet sectors" contrasted with "active sectors;" these could exchange places as divisions with different missions and varying levels of fighting spirit and martial commitment shifted positions along the lines. Smaller units were in constant motion as well, moving between forward, re-serve, and support trenches, and rest periods in the rear. Individual soldiers also varied widely in their responses to the ebb and flow of trench life. In other words, there was no single defining experience of trench warfare on the Western Front. It was, in Tony Ashworth's words, "an infinity of profound experience," a world of "essential diversity." Indeed, even active sectors were not always as unremittingly horrible as conventional wisdom would have it. Hew Strachan warns us not to "substitute hyperbole for common sense" in our understanding of trench warfare, arguing that, in the bigger picture, the trenches saved countless lives that would have been lost in more conven-tional battles. Still, life in an active sector was hardly light duty.[13]

Digging in began early in the war. After plunging into Belgium and France and defeating their enemies to the west, German military leaders in 1914 intended to swing to the east and finish off the Russians as well. They never achieved that goal; as Germans, French, and British troops swirled madly in attempts to turn each other's flanks, they ran up against the English Channel in northwest and the Alps in the southeast. By late 1914 the Germans assumed a defensive position, digging in on high ground. The British and French responded in kind, and the result was the snaking stretch of trenches that would extend for over four hundred miles, from the coast to the Swiss border, with the majority of the fighting concentrated in the western end. And in that stretch of trenches, the war in the West would stay, with relatively minor shifts in position, for four unrelenting years. Unlike the Germans, the British and French often did not do much to make their trenches comfortable or even very habitable in the long term, the assumption being that traditional mobile warfare would resume after German trenches had been breached by powerful, concentrated offenses. Such miscalculations led to the launch of frontal assaults whose names have become synonymous with futile slaughter on a massive scale: Verdun, Ypres, Passchendaele, the Somme.[14]

Western Front trenches could be generally quite similar to those at Petersburg, but they were more complicated and far more extensive. Like those in Virginia, they zigged and zagged below high parapets, with the frontline trenches linked by communication trenches to support and reserve trenches in the rear, and saps extending outward into the infamous "No Man's Land." Trench floors were usually lined with duckboards and trench sides were revetted, depending on the style favored by each nationality, with sticks, boards, sandbags, corrugated metal sheets, and sometimes masonry (although bricks and the like were dangerous when hit, their chunks flying like shrapnel). The air above famously active sectors like the Ypres salient cracked with bullets; the area bristled with snipers in hidden positions, their work made more deadly by advances in technology. It was suicide to pop one's head above the parapet, so soldiers employed handheld periscopes instead. Meanwhile, trench mortars and howitzers dropped shells into the trenches in vast numbers and with massive explosive power, dwarfing anything at Petersburg. Consequently, the Western Front trenches abounded in reinforced underground shelters and living spaces called "dugouts," which offered limited protection from such barrages. Being buried alive in one of them was among the keenest of soldiers' fears, and with good reason, for death by artillery was one of the most common ways to perish. Starting in 1915 poisonous gases—chlorine, phosgene, mustard—joined the fray. The consequences of gas attacks could be gruesome and terrifying and offered an ideal metaphor for war critics of a literary bent, as Winfield Owen's legendary poem "Dulce et Decorum Est" makes famously clear (a victim "flound'ring like a man in fire or lime" dies as Owen watches: "In all my dreams before my helpless sight / He plunges at me, guttering, choking, drowning"). Yet soldiers learned to cope through training and experience.[15]

Occasionally, orders came to assault the enemy's trenches directly in pursuit of the coveted "breakthrough." Soldiers clambered "over the top" or emerged from saps to encounter machine guns chattering and shells roaring overhead as their own artillery attempted to clear a way through the thickets of barbed wire that had replaced Petersburg's abatis and *chevaux* in No Man's Land (a "rolling barrage"). Simultaneously, the enemy's shells and machine gunners sought to destroy them. When or if they closed with their enemies, they added hand grenades, bayonets, and small arms to the deadly mix. Most large attacks either failed or made limited progress at the cost of thousands of lives. Much of the action on active sectors, then, came instead via static artillery barrages, snipers, hit-and-run raids, contact between patrols and work parties in No Man's Land, and other lower-level encounters.

Daily life in the Western Front trenches could be an exhausting encounter with nature in some of its rawest forms. Heat was rarely an issue; what usually tormented soldiers in Flanders and northern France was the cold and wet. The region's plentiful rainfall was, in the words of one historian, an "implacable enemy" that could make routine trench duty a waterlogged misery and the trenches themselves physically unstable. British soldier Henry Gregory described how winter rains made trenches "give way and [fall] in. What a state they were in; they were two and three feet deep in water and mud. In some places it came above our thighs." Coal-burning "braziers" and specialized clothing offered little real warmth and no dryness. Even in summer the trenches were damp and chilly, but in winter they could freeze "as hard as a brick," in Gregory's words, and men perished from exposure. Another of Wilfred Owen's poems bears that single word as its title—in "Exposure," he writes of men slowly dying of the cold in the midst of hallucinatory reveries of sunshine and flowers: "Tonight, this frost will fasten on this mud and us / Shriveling many hands, and puckering foreheads crisp. The burying-party, picks and shovels in shaking grasp / Pause over half-known faces. All their eyes are ice / But nothing happens."[16]

More than any other medium, it was mud that defined the iconic environmental context of the Western Front's worst sectors. It was difficult, in Belgium and northern France, to dig a trench in low-lying areas without hitting waterlogged soil, a result of the region's proximity to the sea—unlike Petersburg's position well above sea level, parts of the Western Front were at or even below it. Combined with regular rains, this made mud often ubiquitous and at times all-consuming. It found its way into everything from boots to rations to weapons, which had to be cleaned constantly. It could make simple movement incredibly difficult. Routine life in the trenches involved a tremendous amount of physical labor to maintain them (work details were known, tellingly, as "fatigues"), and there was a constant stream of men carrying things to and from the rear areas: ammunition and rations, additional revetments, wounded soldiers, written orders, and so on. At night, troops snuck into No Man's Land to occupy listening posts, repair barbed wire, cut the enemy's wire, and launch raids. Doing all these things while battling mud that could, at times, rise to a man's waist was no easy task. Indeed, it was often impossible. Men literally stuck fast in it, even drowned in it, especially the wounded. Fighting the enemy in such an environment could be a horror. One British soldier at Passchendaele wrote later, in a telling natural metaphor, that during the assault, "we fell into the mud and writhed out like wasps crawling from rotten plums." French solider Henri Desagneaux saw some of the worst fighting of the war, and his diary details, with increasing bitterness as the war dragged on, the costs of eating, sleeping, and fighting in what he called "a shapeless chaos of slime" and "one almighty quagmire." At times, it was almost more than he could stand. "Life," he wrote in October 1917, "is becoming unbearable."[17]

The mud even inspired some of the Great War's most haunting poetic verses. Poetry is not history, of course, and the line between Western Front poetic and historical reality has been particularly blurry. Literary traditions of nature-as-metaphor prevents us from reading Great War poetry as truth and thus substituting, as Strachan warned, hyperbole for common sense. But the horrors of mud were common enough in verse to suggest that they were also common in real life. Mary Borden, an American nurse working for the British army, put pen to paper after the Battle of the Somme in 1916. So horrified was she by its infamous mud that she dedicated long stanzas to it, each packed with desperate adjectives—"frothing, squirting, spurting, liquid mud . . . the impertinent, the intrusive, the ubiquitous, the unwelcome / The slimy inveterate nuisance / That fills the trenches"—which strive mightily but nevertheless fail, one imagines, to describe it adequately. In the end, the mud consumes the soldiers themselves. "This is the hymn of mud," Borden wrote:

> the obscene, the filthy, the putrid,
> The vast liquid grave of our armies. It has drowned our men.
> Its monstrous distended belly reeks with the undigested dead . . .
> Our men have gone into it, sinking slowly, and struggling and slowly
>   disappearing . . .
> There is not a trace of them.

Another famously shocking image comes in Siegfried Sassoon's "Glory of Women," from 1918: "While you are knitting socks to send your son," he writes to the blindly patriotic mother of a dead German soldier, "his face is trodden deeper in the mud" by fleeing British troops. Painters, too, cast a horrified eye on the mud. In Paul Nash's *We Are Making a New World* (1918), for example, the rising—or perhaps setting—sun casts ironic beams on endless waves of slime and blackened, shattered trees. In such a "troglo-dyte world," as Paul Fussell called it in his classic *The Great War and Modern Memory*, humans could lose their grip on their own humanity, their sense of separation from nature, and even their very physical reality. Santanu Das has termed the trenches a "slimescape," where mud-bound soldiers confronted "both physical and psychic . . . *dissolution into formless matter* [emphasis his] at a time when modern industrial weaponry was eviscerating human form." In memoirs like French soldier Henri Barbusse's *Under Fire*, Das argues, it was mud and not battle that was the trenches' ultimate horror, the scene of "the regression of man" not only into animals but beyond, "into primordial slime."[18]

Indeed, one of the most interesting aspects of the mud itself is that it, too, was a literal mix of the human and the natural. For nearly four years, soldiers in the Western trenches evacuated their bowels, emptied their blad-ders, expectorated, sweated, and bled into the earth around them. They tossed garbage and scraps of food into it. They died and decomposed in it, trampled down by the living or hastily buried in any place that could be found for them—construction in or expansion of the trenches regularly turned up corpses. Bodies littered the water-filled shell craters of No Man's land, and rotted limbs protruded from the sides of trenches. Rats and enormous clouds of flies grew fat on the dead and added their own organic contributions to the stew, as did legions of dead trees and vegetation. Poison gas attacks tainted the soil further, along with untold pieces of lost and discarded equipment, clothing, bullets, shell casings, and on and on (recent scientific work suggests that, even today, high levels of copper in the soil around Ypres derive from millions of corroded brass shell casings). Artillery fire and the ceaseless movement of troops churned the whole mix into an unholy amalgam of "the remnants of men and of murdered Nature," notes anthropologist Matt Leonard. Nothing quite like it had ever existed. "The very term 'landscape' is misleading" when applied to the trenches, Fabio Gygi argues, "for there [was] nothing to perceive, no land, no hills, no vegetation," only endless mud and wreckage.[19]

As could be expected, disease and vermin thrived in such an environment. Constant immersion in mud turned Petersburg's "swelled feet" into the infamous trench foot, with its blackened, ulcerated necrosis of toes and heels. Like rats and flies, lice also swarmed in apocalyptic numbers, and in addition to being a general nuisance, they also served as vectors for "trench fever," which wracked its victims with malaria-like fever and chills. The infamous "Spanish flu" epidemic of 1918 hit the trenches as it did the larger civilian world, forging a profound biological link between the two and possibly hastening the end of the war itself. Recent scientific research has found evidence of numerous intestinal parasites among German troops. Thousands of men in the British army would die of disease on the Western Front.[20]

Yet, amid it all, more uplifting elements of the natural world remained. In *The Great War and Modern Memory*, Fussell notes at length how British troops, raised in a Victorian era saturated in Arcadian and pastoral traditions in verse and painting, drew heavily on those traditions in their letters, memoirs, and poems. Much of that use was intensely ironic, of course—Fussell details the widespread ironic usage of sunrise and sunset in wartime writing, for example—but also ambivalent, for even in the slimescape, men still responded to natural beauty. Strange as it appears, some wildlife could still be found in the trenches, seemingly oblivious to the destruction around them. Willoughby Weaving wrote of "Ye fearless birds that live and fly where men

> Can venture not and live, that even build
> Your nests where oft the searching shrapnel shrilled . . .
> Sweet disregarders of man's miseries
> And his most murderous methods, winging slow
> About your perilous nests—we thank you, so
> Unconscious of sweet domesticities

Even the awful trench rats reminded Isaac Rosenberg of life beyond war and conflict: "Droll rat, they would shoot you if they knew / Your cosmopolitan sympathies. Now you have touched this English hand / You will do the same to a German / Soon, no doubt, if it be your pleasure / To cross the sleeping green between." The poppy that Rosenberg places behind his ear at the poem's end, so famous as a symbol of remembrance and which grew in profuse numbers amid the trenches, might also be seen as an example of nature's regenerative powers even in the midst of hell.[21]

Finally, the Western Front trenches fostered an intense sensitivity to smell, sight, and sound both above and below ground. The aroma of the trenches was a mix of lime and creosol, feces, gunpowder, smoke, sweat, blood, and, above all, a pervasive rottenness, so strong that armies would sometimes issue double rations of tobacco to mask it. Fearful of gas attacks, soldiers became adept at distinguishing different gases by smell and taste. Meanwhile, mining efforts à la the Petersburg Crater were common occurrences now, requiring a constant ear to the ground. But when death came, it usually came from the sky in the form of artillery. Technological advances since the Civil War had revolutionized the latter. The "trench mortar" was a portable version of the mortars used at (and before) Petersburg, carried by a crew to firing positions along the trenches. Joining it now was a fearsome array of other large-caliber heavy weapons. The terror these produced was almost unbearable because troops were helpless to do much to protect themselves, besides hunkering down in a dugout and hoping for the best. Survival instinct made the noise of an approaching shell a matter of some interest, and many soldiers developed an intuition that enabled them to anticipate when and when it would hit. The noises that shells themselves made varied wildly, depending on size, velocity, and local conditions: "the pop of a champagne cork . . . [or] an approaching express train . . . [Some] echoed strangely. . . . Some shells whistled, others shrieked, others wobbled through space gurgling like water poured from a decanter." When the war finally ended, one British soldier was struck powerfully by the silence. "The everlasting din to which we had grown accustomed," he wrote, "had suddenly ceased . . . To-morrow [*sic*] the sun rises over a new world."[22]

Such was the state of the trench environment in 1918, when the majority of American combat troops joined the combat. Most of them had been born decades after the end of the Civil War, but the cultural memory of that conflict certainly shaped their reasons for joining the military and their expectations of what lay in store. Many doughboys had come of age in a culture, both northern and southern, that lionized its Civil War veterans and allegedly unquestioned dedication to duty, honor, and cause. They consumed books like Stephen Crane's 1895 Civil War novel *The Red Badge of Courage* and histories of the war that were filled with martial glorification. They sat enraptured by the war stories of veterans in the family. They watched as Southerners and Northerners, some of them Civil War veterans, united in imperialistic fervor to invade Cuba in 1898. Furthermore, future doughboys grew up in a Victorian culture that emphasized the broad role of violence in masculinity, especially for white men. The result was "a strong connection," as Edward Gutiérrez writes, "with Billy Yank and Johnny Reb."[23]

Meanwhile, the Civil War's legacy hung over the American military in a more direct way. That conflict as well as the Spanish-American War and the hunt for Pancho Villa had convinced American military leaders—foremost among them General John Pershing—of the superiority of "open warfare." The trench warfare of 1918 was a "horrific aberration," they believed, and the key to victory there was to drive the enemy out of them and into the open, where infantry units (woefully lacking in firepower, according to critics) could close with and destroy them, a "battle script more akin to a Civil War meeting engagement," writes Mark Ethan Grotelueschen, "than to the massive battles of attrition on the Western Front." Some in the ranks agreed; one soldier anticipated that the American presence in Europe would bring "the warfare of our own West and South, when sabers flashed to the beats of galloping horses, and men went miles over the top rather than yards."[24]

Nevertheless, American troops usually engaged in at least some training for trench warfare both at home and overseas (where they were often overseen by British and French officers) before moving into the lines. The misery of trench life quickly became apparent, even before combat. One marine, training with the French in a quiet sector near Verdun, summed his impressions up succinctly. "Life in the trenches is real hell," wrote Private Martin Gulberg. "Once can never fully realize the hardship . . . unless he has been there. . . . The trenches were in the worst condition, the mud ankle deep all over and in some spots knee deep. The dugouts were small and they leaked, to say nothing of the vermin. . . . The rats played over us as we slept. They even got at our reserve rations, sometimes gnawing through our packs." It was not an auspicious beginning for young men weaned on the sanitized glories of Civil War memory.[25]

Petersburg veterans would have sympathized, though, especially when it came to things like the ever-present trench lice. The "cooties" infested everything, and no amount of washing, disinfection, insecticide, or flame could deter them for long. "We kill them by the thousands, and an hour later we are full of them again," lamented one doughboy. "A mother cootie must lay a million eggs at a time." "I don't mind being under shell fire, or in the front line," said another, "but these damn cooties are driving me nutty." Others were even moved to poetry, albeit without the literary skill of a Winfred Owen: "If I were a cootie / I'd deem it my duty / To thus treat the Kaiser / Ah oui!" So too might the combatants at Petersburg sympathized with the agonies of weather, as autumn approached in 1918. France was damp and miserable and the doughboys' gear inadequate, especially boots, with the resulting trench foot reminiscent of the swelled feet of Petersburg. And then there was the mud, which was as ubiquitous as the lice and just as hard to eliminate. "Simply put," observes Richard Faulkner,

mud compounded the miseries of every one of the soldiers' other miseries. It further weighed down already heavy uniforms and equipment; it clung to boots, dogging each footfall, and hindered efforts to dry out shoes; it clogged equipment, and mud made it harder for units to do routine things such as run resupply operations. The mess undermined the Americans' combat capabilities and operations.

"The way I feel now," one doughboy wrote his family, "I don't think I will ever get or feel clean again." Unsurprisingly, disease soon ran rampant.[26]

Indeed, the experience in the trenches gave the doughboys a deep draught of what their European allies had been experiencing for four grueling years. Faulkner sums it up:

[During] their time in the trenches, the doughboys were at much at war with nature (if not more so) than they were with the Germans. Depending on the seasons and the geography, the trenches could be cold, wet, uncomfortable places to live. The dugout shelters were poorly ventilated. The odor of unwashed bodies and rotting food and the haze from cigarette smoke and wood- or coal-burning stoves left the occupants half-asphyxiated. Rain or melting snow led to rivers of mud and posed the danger of sodden trench walls collapsing in on the occupants. . . . Mud to the doughboy was a Jobian curse . . . , a thing to be endured rather than overcome.

It was an environment far removed from the idealized one of Civil War memory. To be sure, many doughboys latched onto the Union General William T. Sherman's famous "war is hell" comment to describe their own experiences (although one noted that Sherman "didn't have so much mud & such large rats to contend with"). One doughboy seemed to find trench warfare almost un-American. Near the end of the war, as the American Second Division advanced up Blanc Mont, PFC Elton Mackin likened the combat to hunting at home. The doughboys left their trenches and assaulted the German trenches in classic "open warfare" style, where they "shot the gunners down and chased the survivors into the cover of a patch of wood beyond." They were finally "in their element," he declared tellingly—the "Yankee style of fighting amid the trees."[27]

A century after the Armistice, Petersburg and the Great War are often linked in casual conversation and in nonacademic forums on the internet. The website history.net notes, for example, that "the Siege of Petersburg continues to be known as an early example of trench warfare, which would be used extensively in World War I." In 2011 a blogger at coyoteblog.com called Petersburg "the first battle of World War I." Academics, too, have drawn links between them. The legendary Civil War historian Earl Hess writes in *The Union Soldier in Battle* that trench warfare at places like Petersburg was "eerily prescient of World War I," and at least one master's thesis has taken the Petersburg/Western Front comparison as its focus.[28]

But is the comparison valid beyond basics? Some historians have said no. Gerald Linderman notes that conditions at Petersburg, "it should be recorded, seldom [touched] on either side that order of severity that would come to characterize conditions on the Western Front during World War I."

This is certainly true in the larger picture. To begin, the Western Front's environmental experience could be significantly more miserable for its human participants than that at Petersburg, largely because of its duration and volume. The Great War trenches lasted for four years in total, while the Petersburg trenches lasted only ten months, and the doughboys' own tenure in the trenches was shorter than that. Similarly, millions of men were eventually wounded or killed on the Western Front, a number larger than the entire casualty list in the Civil War as a whole, let alone Petersburg, which served to swell the collective level and length of the misery.[29]

But the particular awfulness of the Great War's trenches also emerged from the intersection of its geographic and environmental characteristics with modern military technologies. It was in mud where that awfulness resided most clearly. Rain, combined with low-lying, badly drained soil, set the stage for it, and industrial technology joined in to complete it. As noted previously, the landscape created by the interaction of advanced weaponry with soil, garbage, feces, and flesh had never been seen before, inside or outside warfare. It was a literal amalgamation of humanity and nature at the most basic level, a slimy, stinking, sucking, soul-scarring, and ultimately dehumanizing brew. Like the European societies from which most of them emerged, soldiers of the Great War had inherited a conception of nature as subordinate to, and rightfully managed by, humans. But as so many environmental historians have argued, the natural world has a stubbornly reliable tendency not to do what people want to do. It has, if not "agency," then certainly the *appearance* of agency as it responds to human actions on its own terms, as it were. To the horror of trench residents, this was on full display on the Western Front. Petersburg had its moments, to be sure, but without that specific combination of blood and soil, they simply could not compare.[30]

Perhaps that helps explain why Petersburg, for all its own muddy moments, seems to have produced no Siegfried Sassoons or Mary Bordens, or any of its own hymns to the mud. Similarly, it is telling that American soldiers in the trenches seem to have seldom, if ever, linked the Petersburg experience with their own, even as broader Civil War memory shaped their expectations and reactions. Like their European counterparts, in their diaries they recorded the horrors of mud and filth, rats and lice, and the sights and smells of mass death. Some were certainly alive to the costs that warfare imposed on nature in general, as well. Texan José de la Luz Sáenz lamented in 1918, for example, that "even the poor and defenseless trees that adorn

Mother Nature suffer man's barbarity! This is civilization in the twentieth century and these are our scientific advancements, man's most arrogant source of pride!" Nels Andersen complained bitterly about the "slop and mud," agonized over the fate of mules and horses, and mused on the scene of a rainbow over No Man's Land as an ironic metaphor. "What a beautiful land to be torn by war," wrote Elmer Sherwood. "And here we are mere men mutilating, scarring, hurting you but for what [?]" But they did not mention Petersburg among their extensive reflections, and neither, it appears, did other doughboys.

Here, it seems, we run up against the limits of Civil War memory as an influence on American soldiers' understandings of the Western front. The Civil War as a whole certainly did shape the Americans' expectations and experiences of the Great War, as the Introduction to this volume notes. But their vision of the Civil War was a very specific one, namely one of glory and honor, of Napoleonic charges and great "open" battles like Gettysburg and Chattanooga—"fighting amid the trees," as it were. This vision of motion and action was certainly more romantic than one that focused on the dreariness of the Petersburg trenches. John J. Pershing himself had idealized the mobile nature of the Civil War and envisioned the American Expeditionary Force somehow breaking the trench stalemate and bringing movement back to the Allied offensive. In memory and imaginings, obstacles created by nature seem easily overcome, and warfare can take place on an even field devoid of natural conditions and impediments. But the realities of the Petersburg campaign, with its static miseries of heat, cold, water, and vermin, did not mesh well with such idealization. Perhaps that explains Petersburg's absence from doughboys' reflections, even as they lived a version of it in the trenches of France.[31]

Interestingly, it tended to be civilians—those physically distant from both conflicts—who drew connections between the two wars. "There is much similarity" between the Great War and the Civil War, noted the Athens, Georgia, *Banner* in December 1915, speculating that Germany would, like the Confederacy at Petersburg, be exhausted into surrender by trench warfare. In July 1916, amid the first Battle of the Somme, the *New York Times* noted (in a piece on the First Earl of Cromer's time observing Federal troops at Petersburg) that Grant's assaults on Lee's trenches were "another reminder of what we hear concerning the present war." The next year, a South Carolina paper argued that Grant and Lee's Petersburg campaign "was the first real example" of the trench warfare then raging in France. But even these comparisons went no further than brief observations; here, too, one sees limits of Civil War memory *vis* à *vis* Great War reality.[32]

Upon the United States' entrance into the Great War in April 1917, construction work soon began on Camp Lee, located just outside of Petersburg and named for the Confederacy's most lionized and mythologized military leader. Here the US Army's Eightieth Infantry Division would train for action in Europe, and part of that training included the creation of a two-mile-long stretch of trenches modeled closely on those in the Western Front. French and British military advisers arrived to assist the Americans in learning the intricacies of daily trench life as well as a simulated attack, which found the recruits "miserable and unprepared for the experience." Perhaps some of them ruminated on the experiences of their Petersburg forebearers, although no evidence suggests that the Eightieth Division went on to see serious combat in France, where no doubt its troops found the miseries even more acute than those of the trenches of Camp Lee. There is potential symbolism in the idea of training at Petersburg for the war it allegedly foreshadowed. But the distance between the idea and the reality was ultimately a bit wider than the doughboys' descendants have often believed.[33]

Notes

1. See Judkin Browning and Timothy Silver, *An Environmental History of the Civil War* (Chapel Hill: University of North Carolina Press, 2020); Kenneth W. Noe, *The Howling Storm: Weather, Climate, and the American Civil War* (Baton Rouge: Louisiana State University Press, 2020); idem., "Fateful Lightning: The Significance of Weather and Climate to Civil War History," in *The Blue, the Gray, and the Green: Toward an Environmental History of the Civil War*, ed. Brian Allen Drake (Athens: University of Georgia Press, 2015), 16; idem., "Heat of Battle: Climate, Weather, and the First Battle of Manassas," *Civil War Monitor* 5 (Fall 2015): 54–76.

2. Douglas Wilson Johnson, *Topography and Strategy in the War* (New York: Henry Holt, 1917), 1.

3. As for most other Civil War battles, there are many general histories of the Petersburg campaign. The most thorough are Edwin C. Bearss and Bryce Suderow, *The Petersburg Campaign*, vol. 1, *The Eastern Front Battles, June–August 1864* (El Dorado, CA: Savas Beatie, 2012), and *The Petersburg Campaign*, vol. 2, *The Western Front Battles, September 1864–April 1865* (El Dorado, CA: Savas Beatie, 2014).

4. On Petersburg's soil and landscape, see James A. Clausen,. Daniel J. Crowner, Joanne B. Dixon, and Jerry S. Quisenberry, *Soil Survey of Dinwiddie Area, Virginia* (Washington, DC: US Department of Agriculture, 1996); T. R. Lookingbill, B. M. Miller, J. M. Madron, J. C. Finn, and A. T. Valenski, "Petersburg National Battlefield Natural Resource Condition Assessment," *Natural Resource Report NPS/PETE/NRR—2013/704* (Washington, DC: National Park Service, 2013), available at https://irma.nps.gov/DataStore/DownloadFile/481812, and John Auwaerter and George W. Curry, "Cultural Landscape Report for Poplar Grove National Cemetery. Petersburg National Battlefield" (Washington, DC: National Park Service, 2009), available at https://permanent.access.gpo.gov/gpo3039/popular_grove_clr.pdf.

5. Some of the best descriptions of the Petersburg trenches are in Earl J. Hess, *In the Trenches At Petersburg: Field Fortifications and Confederate Defeat* (Chapel Hill: University of North Carolina Press, 2009), 50–77. On the destruction of trees, see page 65.

6. Gerald F. Linderman, *Embattled Courage: The Experience of Combat in the American Civil War* (New York: Free Press, 1987), 147; Emil and Ruth Rosenblatt, eds., *Hard Marching Every Day: The Civil War Letters of Private Wilbur Fisk, 1861–1865* (Lawrence: University Press of Kansas, 1983), 285.

7. J. Tracy Power, *Lee's Miserables: Life in the Army of Northern Virginia from the Wilderness to Appomattox* (Chapel Hill: University of North Carolina Press, 1998), 121–122; Stephen M. Weld, *War Diaries and Letters of Stephen M. Weld* (Riverside Press: privately printed, 1912), 320, 322, 325, available at https://archive.org/details/wardiarylettersoooweld; A. Wilson Greene, *The Final Battles of the Petersburg Campaign: Breaking the Backbone of the Rebellion*, 2nd ed., (Knoxville: University of Tennessee Press, 2008), 45; Fisk quoted in Rosenblatt and Rosenblatt, *Hard Marching Every Day*, 310; Elisha Hunt Rhodes, "The Second Rhode Island Volunteers at the Siege of Petersburg," in *Personal Narratives of the Events in the War of the Rebellion, Being Papers Read before the Rhode Island Soldiers and Sailors Historical Society, Seventh Series, no. 10* (Providence, RI: Soldiers and Sailors Historical Society, 1915), 18; Steven E. Sodergren, *The Army of the Potomac in the Overland & Petersburg Campaigns: Union Soldiers and Trench Warfare, 1864–1865* (Baton Rouge: Louisiana State University Press, 2017), 109; Power, *Lee's Miserables*, 223–225. Excellent contemporary images of Union soldiers protecting themselves from the Petersburg sun may be found in *Harper's Weekly* vol. 8, no. 397 (August 1864): 504–505.

8. Bell Irvin Wiley, *The Life of Johnny Reb: The Common Soldier of the Confederacy* (Baton Rouge: Louisiana State University Press, 1943), 248; Hess, *In the Trenches at Petersburg*, 68; Power, *Lee's Miserables*, 229–234; Warren Wilkinson, *Mother, May You Never See the Sights I Have Seen: The Fifty-Seventh Massachusetts Veteran Volunteers in the Army of the Potomac, 1864–1865* (New York: Harper and Row, 1990), 203–209; "Letter from Richmond," *Charleston Mercury*, August 29, 1864; John D. Billings, *Hard Tack and Coffee, or, the Unwritten Story of Army Life* (Boston: Berwick and Smith, 1887), 79–82.

9. This is a point usefully made by Mark M. Smith, in *The Smell of Battle, The*

Taste of Siege: A Sensory History of the Civil War (New York: Oxford University Press, 2015).

10. On the sublime, see Megan Kate Nelson, *Ruin Nation: Destruction and the American Civil War* (Athens: University of Georgia Press, 2012); Billings, *Hard Tack and Coffee*, 58–60; Bassett quoted in Sodergren, *Army of the Potomac*, 99; "From Petersburg," *Richmond Enquirer*, October 18, 1864.

11. Earl J. Hess, *Into the Crater: The Mine Attack at Petersburg* (Columbia: University of South Carolina Press, 2010), 1–86. For the mastodon skull, see p. 14.

12. Linderman, *Embattled Courage*, 155; Sodergren, *Army of the Potomac*, xx, 87, 88–145.

13. Tony Ashworth, *Trench Warfare 1914–1918: The Live and Let Live System* (New York: Holmes and Meier, 1980) 22; Hew Strachan, *The First World War* (New York: Viking, 2003), 164.

14. For a broad history of the war, with some limited environmental analyses, see William Kelleher Storey, *The First World War: A Concise Global History* (Lanham, MD: Rowman and Littlefield, 2009).

15. There are many books on life in the Western Front trenches. Some classic examples are Ashworth, *Trench Warfare*; Alan Lloyd, *The War in the Trenches* (London: Hart-Davis, MacGibbon, 1976); John Ellis, *Eye-Deep in Hell: The Western Front, 1914–1918* (London: Penguin, 1976); Andy Simpson, ed., *Hot Blood and Cold Steel: Life and Death in the Trenches of the First World War* (Staplehurst, UK: Spellmount, 2002); Wilfred Owen, "Dulce et Decorum Est," accessed February 20, 2017, www.warpoetry.co.uk/owen1.html. On gas, see Rolf-Dieter Müller, "Total War as a Result of New Weapons? The Use of Chemical Agents in World War I," in *Great War, Total War: Combat and Mobilization on the Western Front, 1914–1918*, ed. Roger Chickering and Stig Förster (New York: Cambridge University Press, 2000): 95–112; Ellis, *Eye-Deep in Hell*, 44; Tim Cook, *No Place to Run: The Canadian Corps and Gas Warfare in the First World War* (Vancouver: University of British Columbia Press, 1999).

16. Gregory quoted in Simpson, *Hot Blood and Cold Steel*, 4; Wilfred Owen, "Exposure," accessed February 11, 2017, www.poetryfoundation.org/poems-and-poets/poems/detail/57261.

17. Lloyd, *War in the Trenches*, 163; Henri Desegneaux, *A French Soldier's Wartime Diary, 1914–1918*, ed. Jean Dasegneaux (Barnsley, Yorkshire, UK: Pen and Sword, 2014), 54, 61.

18. Mary Borden, "At the Somme—The Hymn of the Mud," available at www.poetryfoundation.org/poems-and-poets/poems/detail/57329, accessed February 20, 2017; Paul Fussell, *The Great War and Modern Memory* (London: Oxford University Press, 1975), 36–74; Santanu Das, *Touch and Intimacy in First World War Literature* (New York: Cambridge University Press, 2005), 37, 54.

19. Matt Leonard, "Mud," *Military History Monthly* (May 2012): 58; M. Van Miervenne, T. Meklit, S. Verstraete, M. De Boever, and F. Tack, "Could Shelling from the First World War Have Increased Copper Concentrations in the Soil around Ypres?" *European Journal of Soil Science* 59 (April 2009): 372–379; Matt Leonard, "Muddy

Hell: The Realities of the Western Front Conflict Landscape during the Great War," https://modernconflictarchaeology.com/muddy-hell-the-realities-of-the-western -front-conflict-landscape-during-the-great-war/; Fabio Gygi, "Shattered Experiences—Recycled Relics: Strategies of Representation and the Legacy of the Great War," in *Matters of Conflict: Material Culture, Memory, and the First World War*, ed. Nicholas J. Saunders (New York: Routledge, 2004), 76.

20. Simpson, *Hot Blood and Cold Steel*, 38–42; M. Le Bailly, M. Landolt, and F. Bouchet, "First World War German Intestinal Worms: An Original Study of a Trench Latrine in France," *Journal of Parasitology* 98 (December 2012): 1273–1275.

21. Fussell, *The Great War and Modern Memory*, 51–63, 231–269; Willougby Weaving, "Birds in the Trenches," available at www.firstworldwar.com/poetsandprose /mia_birdstrenches.htm, accessed February 20, 2017; Isaac Rosenberg, "Break of Day in the Trenches," available at www.poetryfoundation.org/poetrymagazine/poems /detail/13535, accessed February 20, 2017.

22. Cook, *No Place to Run*, 68; Ellis, *Eye-Deep in Hell*, 59; Simpson, *Hot Blood and Cold Steel*, 80, 199–200.

23. Edward A. Gutiérrez, *Doughboys on the Great War: How American Soldiers Viewed Their Military Experience* (Lawrence: University Press of Kansas, 2014), 18.

24. Mark Evan Grotelueschen, *The AEF Way of War: The American Army and Combat in World War I* (New York: Cambridge University Press, 2007), 12, 16; the "one soldier" talking of flashing sabres and horses is quoted in Richard S. Faulkner, *Pershing's Crusaders: The American Soldier in World War I* (Lawrence: University Press of Kansas, 2017), 440.

25. George B. Clark, ed., *Devil Dog Chronicles: Voices of the 4th Marine Brigade in World War I* (Lawrence: University Press of Kansas, 2013), 116.

26. James H. Hallas, ed., *Doughboy War: The American Expeditionary Force in World War I* (London: Lynne Rienner, 2000), 185; the "cooties driving me nutty" comment comes from Faulkner, *Pershing's Crusaders*, 488; the cootie poem comes from Gutiérrez, *Doughboys on the Great War*, 85; the last sentence from the "one doughboy" is quoted in *Pershing's Crusaders*, 486.

27. Faulkner, *Pershing's Crusaders*, 345; Guitiérrez, *Doughboys on the Great War*, 106–108; "Yankee style of fighting is quoted in Clark, *Devil Dog Chronicles*, 311.

28. "Battle of St. Petersburg," www.historynet.com/battle-of-petersburg, accessed 20 February 2017; "Petersburg: First Battle of World War I," www.coyoteblog.com /coyote_blog/2011/11/petersberg-first-battle-of-wwi.html?doing_wp_cron=14873423 30.7209830284118652343750, accessed February 20, 2017; Earl J. Hess, *The Union Soldier in Battle: Enduring the Ordeal of Combat* (Lawrence: University Press of Kansas, 1997), 68; Richard H. Hephner, "'Where Youth and Laughter Go': The Experience of Trench Warfare from Petersburg to the Western Front" (MA thesis, Virginia Polytechnic Institute and State University, 1997), available at https://vtechworks.lib .vt.edu/bitstream/handle/10919/36824/THESIS.PDF?sequence=1&isAllowed=y.

29. Linderman, *Embattled Courage*, 154.

30. The literature touching on "nature's agency" is immense. For an in-depth

discussion of relatively recent examples, see Paul Sutter, "The World With Us: The State of Environmental History," *Journal of American History* 100 (June 2013): 94–119. For the Civil War, see Browning and Silver, *Environmental History of the Civil War*, xx, and Lisa Brady, *War Upon the Land: Military Strategy and the Transformation of Southern Landscapes during the American Civil War* (Athens: University of Georgia Press, 2012), 26, 29–32.

31. Emilio Zamora, ed., *The World War I Diary of José de la Luz Sáenz* (College Station: Texas A&M University Press, 2014), 228; Allan Kent Powell, ed., *Nels Andersons' World War I Diary* (Salt Lake City: University of Utah Press, 2013), 128, 104, 98; Robert H. Ferrell, ed., *A Soldier in World War I: The Diary of Elmer W. Sherwood* (Indianapolis: Indianapolis Historical Society Press, 2004), 58–59.

32. "There Is Much Similarity," *Athens Banner*, December 17, 1915; "Lord Cromer Tells His Civil War Adventures," *New York Times*, July 16, 1916; "Germans and Others," *State* (Columbia, SC), August 12, 1917.

33. A detailed history of Camp Lee's role in World War I may be found at the Petersburg National Battlefield website, www.nps.gov/articles/training-for-trench-warfare.htm, accessed June 27, 2020, and Kenneth Finlayson, "The Three Lives of Fort Lee, Virginia: World War I," *Army Sustainment* 49 (July–August 2017): 65–69, www.army.mil/article/189328/the_three_lives_of_fort_lee_virginia_world_war_i.

"We Owe Everything to Their Valor and Sacrifice"

The Experiences of Civil War and Great War Veterans

Kanisorn Wongsrichanalai

On September 29, 1915, around thirty thousand Union Civil War veterans—with an average age of seventy-two—retraced the route of their triumphal parade down Pennsylvania Avenue in 1865. A crowd of one hundred thousand lined the streets to watch a reenactment of the Grand Review that marked the end of America's deadliest conflict. Instead of President Andrew Johnson presiding over the veterans, however, this time, President Woodrow Wilson awaited them in front of the White House. The first Southerner since Johnson to become president, Wilson's memories must have returned to the Civil War Era even as he considered the ramifications of the raging conflict then engulfing Europe. With growing tension between the United States and the Central Powers, the president must have pondered his and the nation's options in this uncertain time. Should he commit the nation to entering a world war that had nearly bled Europe dry? As he watched the aged Union veterans parade by his stand, perhaps he thought also of his predecessor, Abraham Lincoln, who had led the nation through its greatest crisis a half-century earlier.[1]

Two years later, as Wilson and his officials contemplated raising an army with which to intervene in the Great War, they considered the lessons of the Civil War Era, the last time that the nation had mobilized on such a massive scale. Both Wilson and his war planners knew what they wished to avoid at the conflict's end: they did not wish for veterans to become dependent upon government aid and cause huge postwar expenditures. Such beliefs came from their understanding of what the Civil War veterans had cost the nation.

To win the War of the Rebellion, the Lincoln government had to summon an enormous number of men. In the wake of the war's carnage, all levels of government sought to help the brave saviors of the Union return to their civilian lives if possible. That included everything from training for new vocations (if the returning veterans had suffered lingering injuries that prohibited them from picking up their former professions) to government pensions. By the turn of the twentieth century, these pensions represented the largest expenditure for the federal government and became a sore subject. Critics viewed those who received pensions as dependent on the government and a drain on public funds. The war of 1861–1865 had emerged out of a clash between two systems of labor: free and enslaved. Free labor meant, in essence, self-sufficiency, and, during the Reconstruction era, Northerners believed that they needed to teach the newly freed people the importance of self-sufficiency and independence. Hence, the quick criticism of aid agencies such as the Freedmen's Bureau for cultivating dependence. Such concerns existed for whites as well. In time, critics viewed pension-gaining Civil War veterans as, essentially, dependents of the state. By the time of the Great War, government leaders wanted to make sure that the doughboys would not gain the same benefits that they believed the Civil War veterans had mistakenly received.

Ultimately, Wilson's government did succeed in quickly cutting the doughboys loose once they returned to the United States, but the soldiers themselves would not forget about the financial support their Civil War predecessors had received. The American economy during the Great War had benefitted the civilian population but disadvantaged the returning soldier. Monetary remuneration would even the score, some veterans argued, emphasizing that they merely wanted what the nation owed: unlike the Civil War veterans, they were not asking for additional aid. Despite opposition from successive presidents, congressional representatives in the 1920s, pressured by veterans' organizations, passed a bill to provide a bonus to veterans, due in 1945. When the Great Depression struck, suffering veterans demanded their payment early, setting the stage for the infamous Bonus March on Washington, DC. But even in 1932, the doughboys made clear the distinction between themselves and the Civil War veterans. "There is much talk about the so-called bonus being a gift," Great War veteran Halford Williams wrote in April 1932. "I want to emphasize the fact that it was not a gift in any sense, but an adjustment in pay to make up the difference between high civilian rates and service rates, and even then they were highly unequal."[2]

The fiasco that marred President Herbert Hoover's reputation beyond repair taught his successor President Franklin D. Roosevelt and his officials that they could not ignore veteran compensation during World War II. The monumental Servicemen's Readjustment Act (better known as the "G. I. Bill") of 1944 came out of the lessons of the Great War. Of course, Wilson and his officials considered their actions as simply rectifying what they viewed as a failure from the Civil War generation. In terms of lasting legacies then, national leaders in both the Civil War and Great War Eras helped establish the commitment that the nation-state offered to those it sent into war.

Civil War Veterans

Postwar adjustment to civilian life challenged veterans of both conflicts, especially those who had to contend with war wounds, both physical and psychological. The prospect of unemployment also haunted the soldiers who made it home. Those with missing limbs faced additional difficulties.[3] Approximately twenty-two thousand Union soldiers and sailors came back from the war with an amputated limb and many Northerners attempted to help them assimilate back into peacetime society. Some businesses started hiring amputees while Sanitary Commission officials attempted to match veterans with jobs. Rather than turning their backs on the Union's protectors, Northerners tried to help veterans who could not help themselves.[4] This represented somewhat of a shift. Nineteenth-century Americans were used to blaming the impoverished for their own misfortune but in this case, they distinguished between common vagrants and wounded veterans. Homes for veterans cropped up in various communities, while programs at these sites taught new skills like bookkeeping, classroom instruction, and telegraph operations. Veterans also attempted to obtain civil service jobs; generally, because of their willingness to work, they stood apart from those considered a drain on society.[5]

The federal government certainly understood the necessity of caring for the wartime wounded. Near the end of the war in 1865, Congress passed and

President Lincoln signed the National Asylum for Disabled Volunteer Soldiers Act. The law established the National Asylum for Disabled Volunteer Soldiers (which later became the National Home for Disabled Volunteer Soldiers), with four regional locations (in Maine, Virginia, Wisconsin, and Ohio) that initially only helped honorably discharged veterans who suffered from war-related wounds or illnesses. Later on, the system welcomed nearly every veteran who needed help and served tens of thousands of Union veterans. The law itself represented a major leap in how the government expanded its role in caring for veterans. "In an era that championed laissez-faire government and heroic individualism," one historian writes, "the act signaled a dramatic expansion of the social contract between disabled veterans and the American state." The lawmakers signaled that "it was no longer enough to reward disabled veterans with pensions or other forms of monetary assistance; now the federal government had to provide them with food, shelter, and a chance to live out their lives in dignity." The facilities provided shelter as well as job training, allowing veterans to learn new skills like shoemaking in order to earn income on top of their pensions. Such activities gave them a small level of independence. The residents of the veterans' homes performed routine tasks and thus helped maintain the facilities, demonstrating some level of masculine control over their circumstances.[6] The fact that men who had served the nation and still contributed to society by helping with the upkeep of their homes occupied these new facilities allowed civilians to better tolerate their existence. One historian explained the difference between the unacceptable *asylums* and the acceptable *homes* by noting that the former "housed the desperately poor, the insane, and other adults unable to care for themselves," while the latter "housed orphans, redeemable delinquents, and other more sympathetic persons who deserved government assistance." Soldiers' homes "were meant to be safe, comfortable, respectable environments for the men who had fought but were now unable to survive without help."[7]

In time, the veterans' homes became model communities and demonstrated just how disabled veterans could still contribute to society by independently maintaining these facilities. Some of the homes boasted grand designs and lush surroundings, so much so that they became tourist attractions. They remained, however, isolated from urban areas to keep the veterans secluded but "also [to] prevent sick, disfigured, and otherwise disturbing men from violating the public sphere with their presence." The lives of those in the homes remained under strict control and regulation. In the late nineteenth and early twentieth centuries, these facilities expanded to take in Spanish-American and Great War veterans as well.[8] The isolation of the homes protected the veterans' privacy but also kept battle scars and disfigured bodies out of constant public view. As much as northern civilians honored the sacrifices of these soldiers, many did not want to see the manifest cost of war in their day-to-day lives.

Not all war wounds, however, manifested themselves for all to see. Some veterans returned home with intestinal or respiratory illnesses and suffered in private. Psychological scars, meanwhile, debilitated others who feared that a society with no understanding of mental wounds would shun them. "Mental illness or chronic diarrhea," one historian explains, "were harder to translate into a heroic badge of honor than the visible display of courage shown by an empty sleeve."[9] Civilians who did not understand the full scale of veterans' pain viewed their suffering through the frame of dependency, questioning the manhood of these individuals. Lacking a clear understanding of psychological scars inflicted by war, civilians had a difficult time feeling sympathy for veterans whose wounds they could not see.[10] Unable to understand the problems that plagued them and unwilling to face the judgment of society, tormented veterans sought remedies in the form of opiates or alcohol.[11]

Despite the availability of aid societies and homes, not all veterans took advantage of the opportunities offered to them. As products of a culture that idealized individual labor and independence, returning veterans may not have viewed themselves as victims and preferred to confront their challenges personally. Others might have taken their grief out on their family members or, feeling unable to return to civilian life, set out on their own, abandoning the domestic life they could no longer tolerate. Some veterans with no place to go ended up on city streets where residents called them "bummers," a term used by wartime rebels to refer to stragglers and foragers from William Tecumseh Sherman's western armies.[12] Meanwhile, African American veterans faced the extra burden of having to convince skeptical pension officers that they deserved treatment due to psychological wounds sustained during their service. Failure to receive support and treatment sometimes led veterans of both races to commit suicide.[13]

Northern civilians honored and supported the veterans who returned home but, as the years passed, also felt the desire to move on from the conflict. They hoped that the veterans would readjust to civilian life and also participate in the process of reconciliation. Veterans who could not leave the war behind, whether mentally or physically, reminded others that the shadow of war still cast a pall over all of postwar society. Some veterans, particularly those who had languished in rebel prisons, could not easily forgive and forget the actions of former foes. They sought to tell their stories to both demonstrate their contribution to the war effort and to remind the public of how they had suffered at rebel hands. The issue of burying and commemorating the war dead also hindered forgiveness and reconciliation among veterans. Some civilians began criticizing veterans for hanging onto sectional animosities. Meanwhile, the wounds of war also affected those who did not have to live with the handicap but still encountered the walking wounded on a daily basis. Missing limbs served as a constant reminder of the war and dampened reconciliationist impulses among civilians. "Throbbing stumps weeping a foul brew of pus and blood," one historian has argued, "were hardly an advertisement for the kind of glorious, sanitized war the public wanted to remember." Not many Union veterans wore or chose to wear their artificial limbs—some deliberately and others because they felt uncomfortable with the prosthetics.[14] Even United States veterans who had not suffered physical disabilities upset some Northerners. As James Marten has argued, "veterans in the North were seen through multiple lenses" and those down and out "were often seen as agents of their own decline, almost purposefully swimming against the stream of progress, economic growth, and opportunity." Many Northerners expected them to "get over their experiences and move on." Veterans' adjustment issues as well as pensions "led to a clash between the nations' natural gratitude and deep-seated notions about independence, charity, and the role of government."[15] In time, the presence of veterans in northern society began to bother a growing number of citizens.

Finding that they could not rely on civilians to stand firm and understand how they suffered, veterans banded together to establish organizations of like-minded former soldiers. Veterans from the State of Maine, for example, reunited at cottages along the coast. In these isolated locations and surrounded by their former comrades in arms, these veterans could talk about their experiences in a more relaxed manner. These smaller veterans' organizations served the needs of those who felt that the Grand Army of the Republic (GAR), the nation's foremost veterans' organization, promoted too broad of an experience. In unit-level spaces, veterans had greater control over how they wished to craft their wartime memories as they began piecing together regimental histories. Furthermore, exclusive unit gatherings allowed veterans to voice their unfiltered opinions about their former foes in the midst of a reconciliationist fervor that swept the nation in the final decades of the nineteenth century. While some veterans paid public lip service to the idea of reconciling with their former foes, in private, they clung to bitter feelings that they could only express with men who had shared similar experiences.[16]

After the Civil War, the GAR emerged as the nation's most prominent veterans' group, with hundreds of thousands of members nationwide. It served as a "fraternal lodge, charitable society, special-interest lobby, patriotic group, [and] political club." The organization wanted Americans to support pensions, respect the national flag, and tell the "correct" story of the war by publishing "loyal" textbooks. Specifically, these men who had fought to preserve the Union worried that northern textbooks in the 1880s and 1890s did not clearly state the justness of their cause against the traitorous rebels.[17] These groups thus also took on the role of policing the memory of the war. In galvanizing public support for veterans, GAR posts made the case for the uniqueness of the war they had fought in. The soldiers of that titanic struggle had saved the nation and thus deserved the admiration and support of the nation in the postwar years. The GAR's success came from its lofty political power. With a combined membership that dwarfed all other veterans' organizations and representing former soldiers in nearly every town, the GAR became what one historian has referred to as "the single most powerful political lobby of the age."[18]

Perhaps some veterans felt more comfortable in smaller, more local reunion groups but, when it came to national politics, they needed the GAR's power and political influence in pushing for and ultimately obtaining benefits and pensions. In 1862 Congress passed legislation providing pensions for veterans and widows. Qualified candidates received a monthly stipend depending on their rank and their level of disability. Physicians verified physical wounds but had a more difficult time diagnosing psychological trauma. Few soldiers took advantage of the legislation early on.[19] After all, not all Americans, even during the war, liked the idea of pensions, fearing the burden on the federal government. Caring for the war's wounded cost the government nearly $9 million annually by early 1865. Pensions also became controversial because they kept the fraught issues of the war in the foreground as the northern impulse for reconciliation grew. For many civilians, the demand for veterans' pensions kept the uncomfortable issues of the war at the forefront of the public mind. The fact that US veterans could obtain pensions while Confederate veterans could not, meanwhile, kept reminding people of the treason of the secessionists, reawakening bitter memories.[20]

The pension issue became a tricky political matter in the Gilded Age as reformers pressed the issue of civil service reform and championed anti-corruption campaigns. While some Americans agreed that veterans deserved preferential treatment in obtaining federal jobs and care, others feared that a larger government bureaucracy would lead to greater corruption. Reformers argued that a whole new pension system would threaten their goals and also feared waste if veterans who did not need pensions received them anyway. But Union soldiers liked the idea of expanding access to pensions and, since they made up an important voting bloc, Republicans in Congress acquiesced to their demands. Democrats, with their southern voting bloc of rebel veterans ineligible for pensions, opposed these payments. The GAR, however, successfully championed the Arrears Act of 1879, which allowed for retroactive pension payments. In 1887 they succeeded in lobbying Congress to pass a "dependent" pension, which paid $12 per month to fully disabled veterans, reasoning that such individuals relied on others for help. President Grover Cleveland vetoed the bill. That action, coupled with the president's lack of wartime service and his return of Confederate battle flags to the South in 1887, led to a full mobilization of veterans to unseat him. In the election of 1888, veteran Benjamin Harrison won the Electoral College (but lost the popular vote) to defeat Cleveland. Harrison mentioned veterans in his inaugural address—the title of this essay comes from that speech—and supported expanded pensions, which now allowed the widows of veterans to receive payments as well. In 1890 the federal government made any disabled veteran—even if they had not been disabled during their service—who had been honorably discharged after having served at least ninety days eligible for a pension. Not long after that, the rules for pension even expanded to include age as a disability.[21]

In the end, payments to Civil War veterans cost the nation more than anticipated. By the fiftieth anniversary of Appomattox, the pension system had cost over $3 billion, greater than the cost of the war itself. The federal government paid more than $200 million annually, with costs increasing at the dawn of the twentieth century. Reformers who fought to curtail corruption in government viewed these expenditures as wasteful given that the veterans did nothing *more* in service of their nation. Some critics of the pension system blamed "pension agents" who "prowl through the country endeavoring to get old soldiers to become claimants for pensions who otherwise would never have dreamed themselves pensionable," thus absolving the veterans themselves from blame but still indicting the corrupt system. One editorial from 1901 declared the "pension problem . . . one of the most serious . . . which now confront this country" and argued it "robbed" the American people of "millions every year." "The Pension Bureau," the author claimed, "is steeped in fraud," elaborating, "It is conducted solely in the interest of the Republican party. It has become a part of the Republican political machine—a part of the unholy conspiracy for the perpetuation of the Republican party in power." In 1911, for example, Secretary of the Treasury Franklin MacVeigh criticized the Civil War pension list, which he described as "not a credit to us." Although he conceded that "a worthy motive gave it origin," MacVeigh reasoned that the pension "never had a scientific or a just basis" and condemned it for having "lost its patriotic aspects," becoming "a political list," and "costing the government about $160,000,000 per year." Beliefs that the pension system only opened the door to waste and dependency had important ramifications for the doughboys when they returned from their war.[22]

Great War Veterans

Woodrow Wilson's officials used the opportunity of the Great War to reform the Civil War pension system that they often criticized. Some supporters argued that the Civil War veterans themselves could help advise lawmakers in drafting new legislation and "render valuable assistance." After all, the Civil War veterans, "know the weaknesses of the pension legislation of the past" and "have reached a time in life when their own personal interests cannot be affected. They can approach the subject with intelligent appreciation of the needs of the veteran and his dependents and yet without undue prejudice in favor of liberal provisions for those who suffer the misfortunes of war." In July 1917 one newspaper touted the "most revolutionary proposal in war legislation yet considered," a plan to provide for servicemembers and undo the system leftover from the post–Civil War Era. One month later, another newspaper reported that the new legislation "does away with the old Civil war [sic] pension system altogether." This system included life insurance paid for through an allotment from the doughboys' salaries, payment to the families of those who were disabled as a result of or died in combat, and "a system for reeducation of injured men to fit them as far as possible for lives of usefulness either in their former or in other vocations." Such legislation, one reporter pointed out, supposedly relieved soldiers and their families: "The men should know in advance that if they come back armless, legless and sightless they are not going to be left to uncertainties of future legislation or the scandals of the old pension system." In support of passing legislation to clarify such matters in 1917, he argued, "The compensation should not be offered as a gratuity, nor deferred until the end of the war." Reformers thus presented their own plan as a chance to reform the pension system, provide assurance, and set up returning veterans to succeed in post-war lives.[23]

In planning for rehabilitation, Wilson's officials certainly understood the dangers of this new age of warfare. Modern weaponry produced unprecedented numbers of wounded soldiers, straining medical facilities both during and after the Great War. The Wilson administration had prepared for the returning wounded, offering some compensation to those in need while the Federal Board for Vocational Education aided veterans by training them for various jobs. To a certain extent, such actions mirrored the Civil War generation's response to wounded veterans. Those unable to work received small allowances while military hospitals tended to their medical care and tried to make them whole again. In 1921 the federal government under President Warren Harding's administration also established the Veterans' Bureau, which worked with the Bureau of Pensions and the National Home for Disabled Volunteer Soldiers to care for the over two hundred thousand wounded veterans.[24]

The increase in services for veterans grew in response to the call for monetary payments to even out the scales of economic imbalance. Congressional representatives proposed over fifty pieces of legislation in 1919 to increase soldier pay to what they would have made on the home front. Postwar vocational training and hospital access presented a cheaper solution and also had the benefit of assuaging the concerns of reformers worried about repeating the excesses of the post–Civil War era.[25]

By the Great War period, many critics had condemned the old NHDV system of nationally funded soldiers' homes as an enormous waste that also promoted idleness and laziness among veterans. Although the homes made sure that the residents helped with caring for the facilities, the cost of maintaining them remained high in an age of limited government expenditures. More importantly perhaps, to a generation that continued to view economic independence as the true marker of the masculine ideal, the residents of these homes seemed all too comfortable and unable to fulfill their obligations to society. Great War–era policymakers shifted to rehabilitation as a more "modern" approach to aiding wounded veterans, in the belief that this would ultimately allow them to return to society as productive members.[26]

Wilson's government also understood the need to quickly return idle doughboys to full employment. Some civilians already worried about returning troops milling about urban areas rather than returning home and thus made sure to provide the veterans with discounted tickets to send them back to civilian life.[27] Observers feared that idle veterans could become susceptible to Bolshevik ideology, radicalize, and threaten social order. General Leonard Wood, a renowned prewar military leader, referred to returning veterans as "potential reds" and urged the federal government to step in and make sure to reemploy these individuals lest they go down the road of radicalism.[28] One group distributed booklets urging returning soldiers to take the first job they could get so as not to remain unemployed for a long time. It also provided a list of groups that could help secure employment.[29]

The return of millions of soldiers combined with the economic downturn, labor strikes, and rising unemployment limited the Department of Labor's ability to respond to the multiple crises. Concerned that restless and unemployed soldiers would turn to radical groups and embrace revolutionary ideology, the Emergency Employment Committee for Soldiers, Sailors, and Marines of the Council of National Defense under the War Department helped put these returning veterans to work and provided training to make them ready for new job opportunities. The Emergency Employment Committee largely succeeded in its mission, finding jobs for nearly 950,000 of the 1.3 million veterans who sought help.[30]

Not all veterans could easily return to civilian life, however. Some, as a result of war-related disabilities, needed ongoing care. When the war ended, the army quickly shuttered its hospitals, believing that the end of the conflict also meant it did not need so many facilities. Unfortunately, veterans still suffered from lingering wounds and continued to require medical services. With reduced numbers of beds and a growing number of veterans who could not receive aid, complaints made their way through the American Legion as well as to members of Congress.[31] The Harding administration established

the Veterans Bureau (later the Department of Veterans Affairs) to help deal
with the long waits and bureaucratic logjams that kept veterans from receiving help. Infighting, poor management, and a political scandal marred
the early years of the department. Supplies designated for veterans ended up
for sale instead. Whether through malpractice or corruption, the scandal led
to the first bureau director, Charles R. Forbes, resigning and later going to
prison.[32]

American civilians of the Great War period placed a good deal of faith in
modern prostheses to mask the effects of warfare. Although they generally
wished to rectify the postwar mistakes of the Civil War generation, they understood that vocational training had served a useful purpose. The generation that fought the Great War sought to expand on this good example. The
Vocational Rehabilitation Act of 1918 provided a two-step approach to helping wounded soldiers. First, physicians sought to heal wounds and make the
soldier as whole as possible, both physically and cosmetically. Second, the
veterans received vocational training from government and public sources.[33]
The process, lawmakers hoped, would teach veterans how to care for themselves and live productive lives with their disabilities. This, in turn, would
allow the nation to avoid what they considered the negative example of the
post–Civil War generation.[34] Rehabilitation, historian Beth Linker notes,
"was . . . a way to restore social order after the chaos of war by (re)making
men into producers of capital." Because being able to maintain one's independence through labor remained a vital trait of masculinity, she continues,
"rehabilitation was, in essence, a process of making a man manly." Early
twentieth-century Americans, wishing to turn the page on the Civil War–era
pension system that had defined disability as missing a limb, suggested that
a wounded veteran's unwillingness to work represented an even greater disability.[35] Proponents of rehabilitation viewed it as a cost-saving measure as
well. The government, they argued, ought to provide rehabilitative services
rather than pensions since fixing human bodies would cost less in the long
run than paying stipends. Rehabilitation facilities for veterans arose as a result. Once they were rehabilitated and properly prepared for a return to the
world of work, the government would neither have to worry about these
veterans nor arrange for any financial support.[36]

The progressive reformers who championed rehabilitation hoped that
veterans would return to productive and fruitful lives without relying on
pensions.[37] Opponents of soldier pensions claimed that such payments

threatened the character and manhood of the nation. The depiction of pension recipients as emasculating "was particularly troublesome," writes Linker, "since the very group who received pensions were supposed to be the pinnacle of masculinity, soldiers of war who were revered for their courage, honor, and duty to the country." "If the most manly of men became dependent on the state," pension opponents wondered, "what was to keep the rest of the country—the 'unmanly' men and women—from expecting the same?"[38] Nor did progressive reformers stand alone. Orthopedic surgeons also wished to discard the pension system, making the case that surgery and rehabilitation had helped so much that disabled veterans did not need monetary support. Ongoing pension payments challenged that image of restorative surgery.[39] Despite the best efforts of many leading physicians, they could neither heal nor help all the war wounded to live healthy and independent lives. Some veterans had to live in homes, following the model set up after the Civil War when the federal government established the national system of homes for disabled volunteer soldiers with the goal of "institutional domestication," permanently setting veterans apart from the rest of society. In the 1920s, farm colonies in the rural Midwest once again sought to isolate veterans in their own communities and away from the American public.[40] Doing so certainly provided veterans with privacy but it also served the purpose of keeping the war's ongoing suffering and cost beyond the everyday gaze of civilians.

Similar to the post–Civil War period, many civilians sought to turn the page after the Great War ended. Yet, lingering wounds, both physical and psychological ("shell shock" entered the vernacular), kept the war on people's minds. Over a decade after the war ended, its terminology remained in use. Some referred to the effects of the Great Depression as "economic shell shock." The nation's suffering reminded some people of the struggling veterans who still lived with the mental wounds caused by the war in the midst of financial catastrophe.[41] Psychological issues, less well understood during both the Civil War (when physicians diagnosed solders with "irritable heart" or "nostalgia") and Great War ("shell shock") eras also affected many veterans, as Kathleen Thompson explains in her essay in this volume.

Despite the faith placed in the miracles of medical care and rehabilitation, success for physically disabled veterans did not silence the chorus of those who still pushed for some form of monetary compensation. The consequences of the GAR's success on pensions had long-lasting consequences for the doughboys. Whether because it continued to view pensions as a source of corruption or because former Confederate soldiers had no claim to such payments, the administration of the first southern president since the Civil War sought to prevent history from repeating itself on the pension matter. When healthy veterans of the Great War returned to the United States, they received discharge pay of sixty dollars and some life insurance options. Many political leaders—Democratic and Republican—believed that the government owed the doughboys nothing beyond that and some veterans themselves agreed. "Raised in a culture that told men to stand up for themselves," one scholar notes, "the men of the First World War generation took pride in their willingness to do without government aid." Those who came home whole already took substantial pride in their service. Additionally, many Great War soldiers grew up with the belief that Civil War veterans had gamed the system and thus did not wish to emulate that behavior. The Wilson administration based its post-conflict actions on lessons learned from the Civil War, hoping to quickly demobilize the troops and "dissuade them from thinking, as Union veterans . . . that they deserved any further monetary or medical benefits." Thus neither returning veterans nor government leaders envisioned an ongoing relationship between the doughboys and the state. Postwar circumstances, however, led veterans to reassess their initial stance.[42]

Initial acceptance of conventional belief did not last long as Great War veterans looked at the American society they had returned to and saw enormous disparity between themselves and those who had remained on the home front. Even though American men registered for the draft, the federal government determined whom to send overseas and who ought to continue with their civilian duties. While the doughboys labored in Europe for a soldier's pay (about a dollar a day), civilians saw their wages dramatically increase during wartime. One congressional champion of a bonus payment for veterans, Rep. John W. W. Patman of Texas, made the case that the doughboys had received "twenty-one dollars a month" but "had to pay their own laundry bills. If they made an allotment to a wife or child they had nothing left." Meanwhile, shipyard workers received twenty dollars a day for their work on the home front. Companies benefited even more from huge wartime contracts and profits. Many returning veterans soon came to the conclusion that the government needed to do more to compensate them for their service. Perhaps even more so than Civil War veterans, the Great War generation saw enormous disparity in their economic circumstances and those of civilians who, unlike during the Civil War, did not face the risk of invasion and reaped the rewards of a wartime economy in a peaceful setting. The former doughboys wanted help in balancing the scales of economic justice. Why, they wondered, should they see their financial prospects set back simply because they did their duty in a time of national emergency?[43]

Supportive civilians and legislators attempted to help the veterans. State and federal lawmakers introduced bills that provided additional pay for wartime service.[44] Many opponents, however, leaned on racist views in their criticism, since Black veterans would also benefit from any proposed bonus. In 1920 the US Chamber of Commerce warned that providing a monetary payout to returning veterans would lead to Blacks quitting their jobs to spend the amount provided by the government. Most importantly, however, opponents declared that a bonus would simply cost too much money when the nation still needed to climb out of the postwar recession and pay down the war debt.[45]

When Great War veterans failed to obtain additional financial compensation from the government, they felt that federal lawmakers had failed to honor the social contract binding the two parties. Perhaps learning the lesson of strength in organization and numbers from the GAR, the doughboys sought help from veterans' organizations, with mixed success. For example, the American Legion did not initially involve itself in the compensation issue. Indeed, its message of unquestioning loyalty to the government stood in stark contrast to the veterans' position and demands. When the legion seemed unwilling to advocate for veterans' demands, many former doughboys turned to alternative organizations. The Veterans of Foreign Wars (VFW) benefited from an influx of new members as they advocated for immediate payment for wartime service. The desire to placate working-class members and fear of declining membership ultimately pushed the American Legion to take on the issue of compensation. Soon thereafter, pro-compensation doughboys co-opted the legion's primarily nationalistic intents and mobilized its organization and power on behalf of their cause. The veterans continued to make the case that additional payment for services would merely make up for what the veterans would have earned if they had not gone to war, therefore the money did not count as some sort of reward.[46]

Congress passed a bonus bill in 1922 but President Harding vetoed the legislation. When supporters mustered enough strength to try again a few years later, they succeeded in passing the bill over President Coolidge's veto. Coolidge had reasoned, "Patriotism which is bought and paid for is not patriotism" and argued that "to attempt to make a money payment out of the earnings of the people to those who are physically well and financially able is to abandon one of our most cherished American ideals."[47] The law Coolidge had attempted but failed to halt granted certificates for a "bonus" to veterans payable in 1945.

Despite this victory, some veterans grumbled about the date of their payments, referring to the compromise as the "Tombstone Bonus" or "Grave Yard Bonus." Although they initially agreed with deferring the compensation, the VFW soon called for immediate payment for severely or completely disabled veterans. These calls went unheeded. During the boom times of the 1920s, few worried about the delayed compensation but, when the Great Depression struck, more veterans requested their advance payments. Suffering veterans made the case that they lacked the financial advantage that civilians who had not gone to Europe benefited from. Furthermore, they pointed to the fact that, by voting for the bonuses in 1924, the government already acknowledged that veterans deserved some form of compensation. Veteran John Morris quoted President Wilson, who told the men of the First Division, "The American people and the government of the United States owe you, men, a debt they never can repay." Now, Morris noted, "when the ex-serviceman asks for what is due him, he is told that it will bankrupt the country if the balance of the money is paid." He pointed to the hypocrisy of loaning "a few billion dollars . . . to foreign countries, with no chance ever of getting the interest, let alone the principal, but let the ex-service man ask for his just dues and some of these supposed-to-be patriotic people . . . are ready to condemn him" "We don't want charity or anything that we haven't earned," he declared, "All we want is what belongs to us. Why wait until 1945 for the money when we need it now, and not when we are dead?"[48]

Despite pleas from various quarters, President Hoover refused to budge, claiming that if they received their bonuses early, the veterans would spend it on "wasteful expenditures." The president again brought up the issue of dependence, noting that an immediate payment would "break the barriers of self-reliance and self-support in our people." In order to demonstrate their plight and urge the president and Congress to reconsider their decision, around twenty-five thousand veterans, the so-called Bonus Army, marched on and sheltered in abandoned federal buildings in Washington, DC, in the summer of 1932. When negotiations to clear the capital failed, army units under the command of Gen. Douglas MacArthur used bayonets and tear gas to clear out the veterans from their positions. According to one historian, the clearing out of the Bonus Army "marked the final betrayal by a country ungrateful for their sacrifices."[49] The incident (perhaps unjustly) also gave contemporary Americans the impression that President Hoover did not care about their plight and "remains historical shorthand for the failure of the Hoover presidency."[50]

The Bonus March fiasco did teach national leaders some key lessons. Franklin D. Roosevelt, who had benefited from Hoover's mismanagement of the affair to become his successor, faced the Bonus Marchers in the summer of 1933 when they returned to the nation's capital. Having just signed the Civilian Conservation Corps (CCC) legislation into law, Roosevelt issued an executive order that created a separate division of the CCC for veterans who had received honorable discharges. For their toil in the nation's forests, they would receive food, shelter, and $30 per month. But jobs for some veterans did not make up for FDR's slashing of veterans' benefits. Great War veterans became a key bloc that kept pressuring the government for additional help during the early 1930s.[51]

FDR's attempts to help veterans by putting them back to work rather than paying out their bonuses early led to disaster for some unlucky doughboys as a horrific natural disaster compounded their suffering. The Federal Emergency Relief Administration (FERA), which recruited veterans for its various projects, sent some of them to construct roads in the Florida Keys. On September 2, 1935, a powerful and devastating hurricane hit the keys. Hundreds, including many veterans, died in the tragedy. In the aftermath of the storm, veterans and their allies continued to pressure lawmakers who, in early 1936, finally succeeded in pushing through an early payout bill. Congress passed the bill over FDR's veto and paid the veterans well before 1945.[52] The advance bonuses gave veterans a much-needed income boost and they quickly injected that money into the local economies.[53]

Doughboys' demands on the federal government, something they initially did not wish to push for as since it seemed to emulate the Civil War generation, ultimately set an important precedent and taught the government a valuable lesson. Historian Jennifer Keene concludes that the Great War veterans, by seeking "to clarify the government's responsibility to ensure their well-being," left a "truly revolutionary" legacy. "The GI Bill [of 1944]," she writes, "is rarely remembered as the final legacy of World War to the nation." The doughboys had helped "establish the principle that total war gave soldiers and the state a mutual obligation to ensure each other a safe and prosperous future" by forcing "the government to accept responsibility for redistributing profits and opportunities from advantaged civilians to disadvantaged veterans in the aftermath of total war." The GI Bill helped veterans of that second global conflict gain access to unemployment benefits, low-interest loans, college classes, and health care.[54] Looking at how the Great War generation took their cue from a nineteenth-century precedent, one might ask, if the doughboys helped make the GI Bill possible, did the Civil War veterans not also contribute in their own way?

Conclusions

The emphasis on self-sufficiency and independence remained a dominant and idealized theme in American life between the Civil War and the Great War eras. Many Americans looked down on those who failed to live up to these lofty ideals. The Great Depression's widespread economic devastation would finally challenge this long-standing belief. But even if they accepted the plight of veterans, civilians still felt uncomfortable with the ongoing costs of military engagement. Veterans who carried lingering physical scars and had lost limbs in the war received great sympathy but also became the subjects of conversations themselves. The *bodies* of veterans represented ideological battlegrounds between veterans, civilians, and policymakers. Some veterans bore their wounds as "honorable scars" and demonstrated self-discipline by mastering their circumstances. By learning to use their remaining limbs to get by in peacetime, they demonstrated themselves to be "the ideal citizen soldier." Some veterans viewed their missing limbs as a badge of honor that demonstrated how they had sacrificed for the nation's cause.[55] Civilians, however, did not always agree with this view. Some saw limbless veterans as a negative reminder of war. In essence, such concerns reveal civilian discomfort at the sight of war's human cost. In the 1920s the wounded veteran became a prop for both pacifists and internationalists. While some saw rehabilitation as an adequate solution to healing soldiers, others presented the wounded as evidence of the cost of war and international engagement.[56]

Ultimately, as John M. Kinder argues, "much of the appeal of soldiers' reha-bilitation . . . stems from its promise of trauma-free warfare."[57]

Eventually, veterans groups transitioned into organizations that chan-neled and amplified the needs of their fellow veterans. They interacted with government officials and attempted to shape the public's view of veterans' needs as well as influence how civilians viewed their service. They kept vet-erans' demands at the forefront of public issues and government business. Veterans' organizations thus stood at the intersection of advocating veter-ans' needs and proselytizing a positive image of the conflict that had made them all veterans in the first place. The Civil War generation set a precedent by advocating for benefits, something that the federal government had never provided before and something that the Great War generation viewed as a serious mistake.[58] In both eras, therefore, returning soldiers clashed with ci-vilians about what the society owed those who served.

The Civil War generation established the precedent for how the issue of compensation would be dealt with in the future. Veterans in both periods made a similar case for monetary aid from the federal government. In es-sence, returning soldiers of both generations claimed that their service had held them back financially when compared to civilians. Seemingly all but the nation's soldiers had benefited from the booming wartime economy. Veterans' organizations in both postwar periods exercised their consider-able political power to influence government policy. Although initially crit-icizing their Civil War predecessors, the doughboys came to the belief that they too deserved compensation beyond their regular pay for service that had set them economically behind civilians in terms of financial prospects and stability.

What did the Great War generation learn from their Civil War ances-tors? Instead of holding a position of reverence in American society, Union veterans found themselves fending off criticisms about how their pensions drained the national budget. The lessons that Woodrow Wilson's contem-poraries took from the conflict between North and South hint at a more complex and less heroic view of the Civil War generation. Examining the Civil War from the vantage point of the Great War era also allows scholars to chart changing beliefs about the nature and role of the federal government. Because of its unprecedented nature, the Civil War required Lincoln and his officials to adopt radical measures. The Union government levied an income tax and conscripted men for the first time in American history. The war to save the republic required a massive expansion in the power and role of the federal government. These measures lapsed and went away after the conflict as the federal government reduced its wartime authority and role. However, it continued to maintain a more active function in various ways: suppressing labor strikes, policing morality, tracking counterfeiters, and pursuing fugitives in foreign countries, for example. The Great War generation grew up in a time when Progressives criticized the corruption and waste of the government but ultimately harnessed and embraced the authority of the state to rectify what they considered an injustice against men who had loyally served their country overseas in a time of war. From the Civil War on, therefore, the American tolerance for federal power grew, although not without some grumbling and criticism along the way. Most citizens, however, came around to the idea that the state had a duty to help those in need. The neediest, in the eyes of some, happened to have worn the nation's uniform and answered the country's summons when it sounded the call to arms.

Notes

1. In his inaugural address, President Benjamin Harrison, himself a veteran and a man whose election may have been the result of veteran mobilization against Grover Cleveland's opposition to increasing pension benefits, spoke of providing "more adequate and discriminating relief to the Union soldiers and sailors and to their widows and orphans." He also reminded the audience, "Such occasions as this should remind us that we owe everything to their valor and sacrifice." Benjamin Harrison, "Inaugural Address, March 4, 1889," in Benjamin Harrison, *Public Papers and Addresses of Benjamin Harrison, Twenty-Third President of the United States, March 4, 1889 to March 4, 1893* (1893; New York: Kraus Reprint, 1969), 33. On Bob Wilson, Beth Linker, *War's Waste: Rehabilitation in World War I America* (Chicago: University of Chicago Press, 2014), 10–11.

2. Halford Williams, letter to the editor, *Indianapolis Times*, April 15, 1932.

3. Brian Matthew Jordan, *Marching Home: Union Veterans and Their Unending Civil War* (New York: Liveright, 2014), 3–4.

4. Frances Clarke, "'Honorable Scars': Northern Amputees and the Meanings of Civil War Injuries," in *Union Soldiers and the Northern Home Front: Wartime Experiences, Postwar Adjustments*, ed. Paul A. Cimbala and Randall M. Miller (New York: Fordham University Press, 2002), 368–369. Northern governments and communities had many more resources to help the wounded soldiers who returned home as compared to what the defeated and devastated southern towns could offer. For the

Southern experience, see Brian Craig Miller, *Empty Sleeves: Amputation in the Civil War South* (Athens: University of Georgia Press, 2015), chaps. 4–5.

5. Adrienne Phelps Coco, "Diseased, Maimed, Mutilated: Categorizations of Disability and an Ugly Law in Late Nineteenth-Century Chicago," *Journal of Social History* 44, no. 1 (Fall 2010): 29.

6. John M. Kinder, "Architecture of Injury: Disabled Veterans, Federal Policy, and the Built Environment in the Early Twentieth Century," in *Veterans' Policies, Veterans' Politics: New Perspectives on Veterans in the Modern United States,* ed. Stephen R. Ortiz (Gainesville: University Press of Florida, 2012), 70–74.

7. James Marten, *Sing Not War: The Lives of Union and Confederate Veterans in Gilded Age America* (Chapel Hill: University of North Carolina Press, 2011), 13–14, 159.

8. Kinder, "Architecture of Injury," 74–75.

9. Paul A. Cimbala, *Soldiers North and South: The Everyday Experiences of the Men Who Fought America's Civil War* (New York: Fordham University Press, 2010), 215.

10. Marten, *Sing Not War,* 77.

11. Cimbala, *Soldiers North and South,* 215.

12. Cimbala, *Soldiers North and South,* 216.

13. Marten, *Sing Not War,* 87; Richard Reid, "USCT Veterans in Post-Civil War North Carolina" in *Black Soldiers in Blue: African American Troops in the Civil War Era,* ed. John David Smith (Chapel Hill: University of North Carolina Press, 2002), 409; Jordan, *Marching Home,* 189. See also Eric Dean, *Shook over Hell: Post-Traumatic Stress, Vietnam, and the Civil War* (Cambridge, MA: Harvard University Press, 1999). Wayne Wei-Siang Hsieh has offered a corrective to the trend of treating soldiers as victims. Although historians "can find in many individual Civil War veterans unredeemed suffering," he writes, "a larger transnational perspective also finds resilience among veterans and meaningful reintegration into society." Nineteenth-century Americans, he reminds readers, "did not look at human suffering through the lens of our conception of trauma, while looking askance at pensions and Decoration Day ceremonies with the arched eyebrow of modernist irony." Hsieh urges scholars to acknowledge how, in comparison to other veterans in other nations, the returning Civil War soldiers "found a comparatively generous set of circumstances to facilitate demobilization" and recognize "that they were not just passive victims" of their circumstances. Wayne Wei-Siang Hsieh, "'Go to Your Gawd Like a Soldier': Transnational Reflections on Veteranhood," *Journal of the Civil War Era* 5, no. 4 (December 2015): 553, 569.

14. Jordan, *Marching Home,* 108–109, at 145; M. Keith Harris, *Across the Bloody Chasm: The Culture of Commemoration among Civil War Veterans* (Baton Rouge: Louisiana State University Press, 2014), 16; Lesley J. Gordon, "'Surely They Remember Me': The 16th Connecticut in War, Captivity, and Public Memory," in *Union Soldiers and the Northern Home Front: Wartime Experiences, Postwar Adjustments,* ed. Paul A. Cimbala and Randall M. Miller (New York: Fordham University Press, 2002), 327–328; John R. Neff, *Honoring the Civil War Dead: Commemoration and the Problem of Reconciliation* (Lawrence: University Press of Kansas, 2005), 1–6.

15. Marten, *Sing Not War*, 19–20, 200. Many civilians, Marten explains, "believed that veterans were not expressing enough gratitude for the unprecedented programs already created by the federal government. Veterans never seemed to say thank you for the homes and pensions at least some men received; the public never quite understood the ways in which veterans, even those who seemed to have emerged from the war sound in body and spirit, could demand so much of their fellow countrymen."

16. C. Ian Stevenson, "Vacationing with the Civil War: Maine's Regimental Summer Cottages," *Civil War History* 63, no. 1 (March 2017): 153–154, 172, and 178; Harris, *Across the Bloody Chasm*, 10–11.

17. Stuart McConnell, *Glorious Contentment: The Grand Army of the Republic, 1865-1900* (Chapel Hill: University of North Carolina Press, 1992), xiv, 15, 208; Marten, *Sing Not War*, 277–278; Barbara A. Gannon, *The Won Cause: Black and White Comradeship in the Grand Army of the Republic* (Chapel Hill: University of North Carolina Press, 2011), 186. The author of one textbook's "evenhandedness incensed GAR members," writes Marten, who notes that veterans also "protested the book's straightforward chronology" because it "seemed to make the Confederates victors in battles that were really draws, including Cold Harbor, the Wilderness, and Spotsylvania. The sectional conflict was presented as a chronicle of political debates rather than a struggle between right and wrong" (277–278). Former Confederates, according to Marten, meanwhile, also felt the same way, with some complaining "that most books about the war, even those written by southern men from a southern point of view, constituted defensive apologies rather than aggressive justifications for southern principles" (278). In her study of the GAR, Barbara Gannon observes that the organization's members "consistently characterized the failed Confederate national experience as treason" even as early twentieth century Americans tried to present both sides as equally patriotic, smoothing over the former rebels' crimes. For a book-length discussion of how Americans of and after the Civil War Era remembered and shaped the memory of the conflict, see Caroline E. Janney, *Remembering the Civil War: Reunion and the Limits of Reconciliation* (Chapel Hill: University of North Carolina Press, 2013).

18. McConnell, *Glorious Contentment*, 108, 142–143, 167; James Marten, "Not a Veteran in the Poorhouse: Civil War Pensions and Soldiers' Homes," in Joan Waugh and Gary W. Gallagher, eds., *Wars within a War: Controversy and Conflict Over the American Civil War* (Chapel Hill: University of North Carolina Press, 2009), 205; Larry M. Logue, *To Appomattox and Beyond: The Civil War Soldier in War and Peace* (Chicago: Ivan R. Dee, 1996), 91–92. See also Patrick J. Kelly, *Creating a National Home: Building the Veterans' Welfare State, 1860–1900* (Cambridge, MA: Harvard University Press, 1997). Donald R. Shaffer has noted that Black veterans "were underrepresented throughout the network" of veterans homes. Where Black soldiers made up around 9 percent of the Union armed forces during the Civil War, "they constituted only around 1 percent of the residents of NHDVS [National Home for Disabled Volunteer Soldiers] between 1876 and 1905." Shaffer notes, however, that this may be due to the fact that Blacks had a shorter life expectancy than whites (by

about a decade). African Americans made up "only about 2 percent of the Union veterans still alive" in 1890. See Donald R. Shaffer, *After the Glory: The Struggles of Black Civil War Veterans* (Lawrence: University Press of Kansas, 2004), 137–138.

19. Logue, *To Appomattox and Beyond*, 89.

20. Jordan, *Marching Home*, 154, 160. James Marten notes that most civilians "urged the nation not to fall into the trap of providing excessive aid to disabled veterans out of a misplaced sense of gratitude or pity" (*Sing Not War*, 95).

21. Marten, "Not a Veteran in the Poorhouse," 207–208; Marten, *Sing Not War*, 15–16, 21, 201–219. See also Theda Skocpol, *Protecting Soldiers and Mothers: The Political Origins of Social Policy in the United States* (Cambridge, MA: Belknap Press of Harvard University Press, 1992); Logue, *To Appomattox and Beyond*, 90, 97–100. "It is impossible to know for certain how individuals voted," Larry M. Logue concludes, "but we can estimate their behavior with reasonable accuracy." "Such an estimate for the crucial state of Indiana," he explains, "can be made from its distribution of veterans, GAR members, and vote totals. At the time of the 1888 election, Indiana had sixty-three thousand veterans, twenty-four thousand of whom were GAR members. As we would expect, an estimate of GAR members' voting shows a considerable Republican majority—virtually all members turned out to vote, and they voted more than two-to-one for Harrison. Indiana veterans who did not belong to the GAR, however, voted quite differently: like noncombatants, non-GAR veterans were divided evenly between Cleveland and Harrison. The political activism and soldier-first attitude of the GAR applied primarily to those who joined the order; in their voting behavior, the large number of veterans who did not join were scarcely distinguishable from the nonveteran population." "Veterans' dominance of politics reached its peak under Harrison," Logue concludes. Congress increased the pension funds available to the veteran depending on the level of their disability. Veterans, as a result of this modification, "could now earn a pension if they were disabled for almost any reason (except from 'their own vicious habits'), and widows could qualify if their husband had died from any cause." Over 650,000 claim applications swamped the pension officials within the first year of the new law. "By the end of Harrison's term," Logue notes, "more than 70 percent of veterans were on the pension rolls, compared with approximately 20 percent in 1885."

22. "Pension Commissioner," *Conservative*, August 10, 1899; "Some Pension Figures," *Silver State*, February 13, 1901; MacVeigh quoted in "Attacks the Pension List," *Durham Recorder*, April 11, 1911; Linker, *War's Waste*, 12–13, 27, 33–34; Gannon, *Won Cause*, 131–132. Linker lists the ways that reformers and other northern civilians viewed veterans in a negative light. In the eyes of critics, pension-seeking Union veterans "threatened the moral fabric of the country," "stood in the way of putting the War of the Rebellion in the past," "encouraged a political system based on favoritism and patronage rather than neutrality and fairness," "made money by filing claims with the Pension Bureau, rather than by the sweat of his own brow," "lived in a federally funded soldier's home," and "greedily took" rather than giving "anything back in return" (33–34). Gannon notes that the pension issue has "affected

how scholars view organization," with criticisms aimed at both the GAR and federal pension officials. Many Civil War veterans, however, pointed to the ongoing toll of war that continued to cause suffering decades after Appomattox as justification for the pension program.

23. The position of the Republican Publicity Association quoted in "A Pension System," *Arizona Republican*, August 4, 1917; "Insurance Planned in Lieu of Pensions," *Sun*, July 9, 1917; George Martin, "Pensions Sent to the Scrap Pile," *Daily Star-Mirror*, August 16, 1917; idem., "Government Plan Is to Insure All Engaged in War," *Daily Capital Journal*, August 10, 1917.

24. Edward G. Lengel, *To Conquer Hell: The Meuse-Argonne, 1918* (New York: Henry Holt, 2008), 424–426.

25. Rosemary A. Stevens, "The Invention, Stumbling, and Reinvention of the Modern U.S. Veterans Health Care System, 1918–1924," in Ortiz, *Veterans' Policies, Veterans' Politics*, 48.

26. Kinder, "Architecture of Injury," 76–77.

27. Nancy Gentile Ford, "'Put Fighting Blood in Your Business': The U.S. War Department and the Reemployment of World War I Soldiers," in Ortiz, *Veterans' Policies, Veterans' Politics*, 120.

28. Ford, "'Put Fighting Blood in Your Business,'" 125.

29. Ford, "'Put Fighting Blood in Your Business,'" 127. The desires of the veterans themselves and that of the government officials sometimes conflicted since they had differing goals. The returning soldiers viewed new training and job opportunities as a way to advance themselves and catch up to civilians who had not served in the war and thus reaped the full rewards of a wartime economy. The government, meanwhile, sought to simply transition soldiers back to laborers in whatever job available as soon as possible. Jennifer Keene, "The Long Journey Home," in Ortiz, *Veterans' Policies, Veterans' Politics*, 146, 153–154.

30. Ford, "'Put Fighting Blood in Your Business,'" in 140–141; Eric Foner, *Reconstruction: America's Unfinished Revolution, 1863–1877* (New York: Perennial Classics, 2002), 17–20. The Civil War generation had a different economic landscape to contend with after the fighting ended. Whereas the American South had been devastated (physically and economically) by the war, the northern economy continued its wartime boom into the postwar era. "If economic devastation stalked the South," Eric Foner writes, "for the North the Civil War was a time of unprecedented prosperity" (18). Considering the two generations, post–Civil War Americans saw two worlds: white Southerners faced both economic and political ruin while Northerners returned to a booming economy. A united post–Great War America, however, seemingly faced greater economic challenges that encompassed the entire country.

31. Stevens, "The Invention, Stumbling, and Reinvention," 42–43.

32. Stevens argues that "a second, concurrent force" helped spur the need for reforming the Veterans Bureau alongside the desire to placate veterans who called for bonuses to level the economic playing field between civilians who had benefited

from the wartime economy and soldiers who had missed out on those gains. See "The Invention, Stumbling, and Reinvention," 38–39, 55.

33. Kinder, "Architecture of Injury," 78–79.

34. Kinder, "Architecture of Injury," 81.

35. Linker, *War's Waste*, 4.

36. Linker, *War's Waste*, 81.

37. Linker, *War's Waste*, 2.

38. Linker, *War's Waste*, 20–21.

39. Linker, *War's Waste*, 37, and Annessa C. Stagner, "Healing the Soldier, Restoring the Nation: Representations of Shell Shock in the USA during and after the First World War," *Journal of Contemporary History* 49, no. 2 (April 2014): 262.

40. Kinder, "Architecture of Injury," 65.

41. Stagner, "Healing the Soldier, Restoring the Nation," 270–271, 273.

42. Lengel, *To Conquer Hell*, 423; Jennifer D. Keene, *Doughboys, the Great War, and the Remaking of America* (Baltimore, MD: Johns Hopkins University Press, 2001), 162, 171.

43. Keene, *Doughboys*, 162–163, 173, 176; Marten, *Sing Not War*, 54, 61, 233–234; Jerome Tuccille, *The War against the Vets: The World War I Bonus Army during the Great Depression* (Lincoln, NE: Potomac Books, 2018), 14, 21–22. Keene notes that Great War veterans distinguished themselves from other historical groups asking for compensation—veterans of the Revolutionary War and Civil War, along with the mothers, the elderly, and the destitute—by claiming that all veterans, regardless of where they served in the conflict, deserved aid. "The authoritarian power that the modern state had assumed over their lives," she writes, "justified all veterans' claims to redistributive federal entitlements, and this argument would form the foundation of the more generous GI Bill in 1944" (176).

44. Tuccille, *War against the Vets*, 15.

45. Tuccille, *War against the Vets*, 6–7, 14, 17.

46. Keene, *Doughboys*, 165, 170; Steven Trout, *On the Battlefield of Memory: The First World War and American Remembrance, 1919–1941* (Tuscaloosa: University of Alabama Press, 2010), 88–89; Stephen R. Ortiz, "Rethinking the Bonus March: Federal Bonus Policy, the Veterans of Foreign Wars, and the Origins of a Protest Movement," *Journal of Policy History* 18, no. 3 (2006): 276–280, 290–91, 297–299; idem., "Rethinking the Bonus March: Federal Bonus Policy, Veteran Organizations, and the Origins of a Protest Movement," in Ortiz, *Veterans' Policies, Veterans' Politics*, 173–174. See also Stephen R. Ortiz, *Beyond the Bonus March and GI Bill: How Veteran Politics Shaped the New Deal Era* (New York: New York University Press, 2010). Keene argues that the politicization of veterans helped them challenge but, ultimately, maintain the government systems that they appealed to for aid. "The drive for adjusted compensation," she writes, "diminished the appeal of organized, politically-motivated violence." See Jennifer Keene, "A 'Brutalizing' War? The USA after the First World War," *Journal of Contemporary History* 50, no. 1 (January 2015): 78, 85, 99.

47. Tuccille, *War against the Vets*, 18–20.

48. Keene, *Doughboys*, 180; Ortiz, "Rethinking the Bonus March," in Ortiz, *Veterans' Policies, Veterans' Politics*, 175–177; John Morris, letter to the editor, *Indianapolis Times*, April 15, 1932.

49. Lengel, *To Conquer Hell*, 427; Tuccille, *War against the Vets*, 20, 33, 62–63.

50. Ortiz, "Rethinking the Bonus March," in Ortiz, *Veterans' Policies, Veterans' Politics*, 174.

51. Thomas W. Patton, "When the Veterans Came to Vermont: The Civilian Conversation Corps and the Winooski River Flood Control Project," *Vermont History* 73 (Summer/Fall 2005): 163. See also Ortiz, *Beyond the Bonus March and GI Bill*.

52. Tuccille, *War against the Vets*, 8, 144, 189, 197–198.

53. Joshua K. Hausman, "Fiscal Policy and Economic Recovery: The Case of the 1936 Veterans' Bonus," *American Economic Review* 106, no. 4 (April 2016): 1100–1102, 1139.

54. Patton, "When the Veterans Came to Vermont," 178–179; Keene, *Doughboys*, 204–205, 214; idem., *World War I: The American Soldier Experience* (Lincoln: University of Nebraska Press, 2011), 189.

55. Clarke, "'Honorable Scars," 363, 365–366. See also Frances M. Clarke, *War Stories: Suffering and Sacrifice in the Civil War North* (Chicago: University of Chicago Press, 2011).

56. John M. Kinder, *Paying with Their Bodies: American War and the Problem of the Disabled Veteran* (Chicago: University of Chicago Press, 2015).

57. Kinder, "Architecture of Injury," 88.

58. McConnell, *Glorious Contentment*, 9; Marten, *Sing Not War*, 229–230.

Afterword

Memoirs Great and Not-So-Great:
Ulysses S. Grant's and John J. Pershing's
Narratives of Command

Steven Trout

As John Keegan demonstrated, decades ago in landmark studies like *The Face of Battle* (1976) and *The Price of Admiralty* (1988), *comparison* almost always produces insight.[1] Yet historical studies of war and American society that move back and forth between various conflicts remain surprisingly uncommon. Likewise, the field of memory studies has been slow to adopt a comparative approach when considering the complex processes through which Americans assign meaning to past wars. Published near the end of the twentieth century, Edward Linenthal's *Sacred Ground: Americans and Their Battlefields* (1991) and Kurt Piehler's *Remembering War the American Way* (1995) pointed the way forward with collections of case studies that jumped from one conflict to another, spanning multiple centuries.[2] But academic authors have only rarely emulated these works, perhaps because expertise is so often divided-up into one-hundred-year blocks. As we all know, nineteenth-century scholars write about the American Civil War. For a twentieth-century scholar, to do so would be unusual—and not universally welcome either.

The eight essays collected in this volume vividly illustrate what we have been missing. In each one, we see an author extending their reach and challenging themselves to think in terms of what the editors call the "long nineteenth century." The results could not be more exciting or illuminating. Whether considering wartime leadership (political and military), race, loyalty to the state, medicine, mental trauma, trench warfare, or the status of veterans, these pieces offer insights that would never have been reached without a mandate to think outside the box, if you will, represented by standard periodization. What seems initially an eccentric pairing of wars ultimately opens a new window on the past.

Consider a few examples. In Brian Dirck's incisive comparison of two wartime presidents—Lincoln and Wilson—we realize just how quickly presidential rhetoric in 1917 came to control and define the meaning of death on the battlefield. In contrast, Lincoln had to find his way, both rhetorically and ideologically, as the North became a republic of unprecedented suffering, and he was surprisingly slow to offer a public interpretation of loss during America's most lethal conflict. Dirck's analysis also brings into relief the advantages that Wilson enjoyed over Lincoln as a wartime leader, a point that many readers may not have considered before. For instance, by the time of the Great War, the president could communicate his vision through press conferences (something that did not exist in Lincoln's day) and assisted by the new "science" of public relations, as seen in the work of the George Creel's Committee on Public Information, which served, in effect, as the Wilson administration's wartime propaganda bureau. Lincoln had none of this apparatus at his disposal, and his public messaging on the subject of wartime death, such as it was, remained remarkably informal and improvisational in comparison.

In Kathleen Logothetis Thompson's illuminating chapter on mental health treatment during the two wars, it is the similarities that perhaps matter more than the differences. Although a half-century of advancement in psychiatric understanding separated the American Civil War from the Great War, Thompson sees essentially the same "cycle" at work during both conflicts. Mental health practitioners in 1917, like those of 1861, initially expressed optimism when it came to the treatment of combat-induced trauma, but the scale of the problem, coupled with the military's insistence that psychological casualties be returned to the front as quicky as possible, ultimately hampered their efforts. Thompson also notes an unwillingness, operative at both moments in history, to accept war itself as a fundamental cause of mental illness. Many medical authorities during the Great War ultimately explained shell shock in terms of "heredity, moral weakness, or physical causes." A half-century earlier, these very same factors surfaced in diagnoses that stressed a traumatized patient's predisposition to behavior deemed unmanly. That the right combination of hellish battlefield circumstances could lead *any* soldier to suffer a breakdown remained a largely unthinkable notion during both wars and would not gain currency until much later in the twentieth century.

Finally, while Thompson's chapter forces us to consider a surprising, little-known continuity between the two conflicts, Brian Allen Drake's adroit comparison of trench warfare during the closing years of the Civil War with that of 1914–1918 does the reverse, problematizing a historical linkage long widely accepted. As we all know, battlefield conditions outside Petersburg, Virginia, in 1864 and 1865, characterized by parallel lines of earthworks that remained essentially static for months on end, anticipated the "troglodyte world" (as Paul Fussell memorably put it) of the Western Front more than a half-century later.[3] Or did they? Writing from the perspective of an environmental historian, Drake reexamines this claim, and he discovers more contrasts than connections between these two military settings. If transported to the trenches of the Great War, a Union or Confederate veteran of the Overland Campaign would have seen much that was familiar—but even more that was not. *Years* of trench warfare created an environment whose filthiness and ubiquitous reminders of death surpassed anything that could have been imagined at the close of the Civil War.

The three chapters I have noted above reflect the broad parameters of this exploratory volume, offering the viewpoints of, respectively, political, medical, and environmental history. In what follows, I will add to this eclecticism by taking a memory-studies approach (combined with some hopefully inoffensive elements of literary criticism) that considers two commemorative artifacts, one closely identified with the American Civil War, the other with the Great War—namely, *The Personal Memoirs of U.S. Grant* (1885) and John J. Pershing's *My Experiences in the World War* (1931). This afterword will bring these two texts into conversation with one another for perhaps the first time. In this way, I will seek to extend some of the points made earlier in this collection and to delineate further the similarities and differences between America's great war of 1861–1865 and the world war it entered in 1917. I will also offer some reflections on the role of rhetoric in both accounts and then consider each one as a textual site of memory, a public memorial in book form.

A Tale of Two Memoirs

John J. Pershing was no writer, and he knew it. For more than a decade, from 1919 until 1931, the General of the Armies chipped away at his wartime memoirs, and as biographer Gene Smith notes, "he enjoyed not a minute" of it.[4] To anyone who would listen, Pershing complained about the task. For example, during one of his postwar sojourns in Paris, where the Iron Commander conducted his Sisyphean literary labors in the company of his partner Micheline Resco, Pershing wrote to a cousin, "I sometimes feel like chucking the whole thing and making no attempt to record my war experiences which will probably not interest anyone." Pershing's sister Bess received discouraging updates as well. "I have done considerable work [on the memoirs]," her brother reported in one of his letters, "but like all that is previously done, it seems quite banal and stupid and I am not satisfied with any of it. Maybe I should drop it or file it away for posterity to handle as I am sick and tired of the whole thing from beginning to end." Fighting four wars, Pershing remarked to George Marshall, would be infinitely preferable to writing an account of one.[5]

The anxiety of influence perhaps contributed to Pershing's writerly woes. After all, he was, as David Silbey reminds us in his essay for this volume, a great admirer of Ulysses S. Grant, and no American in the 1920s with even a passing interest in military history would have been unfamiliar with the Union commander's celebrated two-volume account of his military service. In the judgment of Grant's most recent biographer, Ron Chernow, *The Personal Memoirs of U. S. Grant* (1885) "is probably the foremost military memoir in the English language."[6]

The notoriety of Grant's book was helped in no small measure by the extraordinary circumstances of its composition. Most readers will know the story already. Grant wrote all 336,000 words while dying of throat cancer, in a desperate effort to save his wife, Julia, from penury after having lost the couple's fortune to a fraudulent investment scheme. Grant was encouraged in his literary endeavor by none other than Mark Twain, who on behalf of his publishing house Webster and Co. offered an advance contract with exceedingly generous terms. Ordinarily inept in business matters, Twain saw a proverbial gold mine in the general's account, and for once he was right. The only question was whether the memoirist would last long enough to finish the memoir. For most of the final year of his life, Grant did nothing but write and suffer, enduring searing pain with each swallow and the sensation of choking whenever he tried to sleep. By the time his agony finally ended on July 23, 1885, the tumor in his throat had grown to the size of "two fists put together,'" as a journalist put it, and the once-robust general had shed sixty pounds.[7] But Grant's characteristic determination paid off. He completed the story of his military career just a week before his death, and *The Personal Memoirs of U. S. Grant* went on to become one of the biggest American literary sensations of the nineteenth century, perhaps second in sales only to Harriet Beecher Stowe's *Uncle Tom's Cabin* (1852). Julia Grant received more than $400,000 in royalties.[8]

All of this background—or at least much of it—Pershing would have known, and it must have added to his frustration as his own memoirs, which would invariably be compared with Grant's, stubbornly refused to come together. Despite his pain and the effects of medical opiates, of which the dying man took as little as possible, Grant wrote with exceptional fluency, usually for several hours a day, and he relished the work, his only distraction from illness. Twain marveled at the general's unassuming but polished style, which required little in the way of editing.[9] In contrast, Pershing's prose seemed to get worse the more he revised it. His manuscript pages, preserved in the Library of Congress, are a sea of tortured emendations that, in biographer Donald Smythe's words, show "how much he fretted over the text."[10]

Ultimately, Pershing produced a narrative that unlike Grant's has rarely, if ever, been thought of as a work of literature. And for good reason. Loaded with information, and often little else, *My Experiences in the World War* is, for the ambitious reader who tackles the whole thing, a long march with a heavy pack. Part of the problem, as Smythe notes, is Pershing's use of diary entries as the basis for his organization. This means that if the AEF commander dealt with ten different unrelated issues on a given day in 1917 or 1918, then his prose account slavishly mirrors that content, scattering fragmentary treatments of various topics across multiple chapters. This approach vividly conveys how much multitasking, if you will, Pershing had to do on a daily basis, and it leaves the impression that his command situation was far more difficult and complex than Grant's, which it most certainly was.

But the cost to readability is enormous, and Pershing's tedious habit of reproducing various documents—cablegrams, memoranda, orders, etc.—in their entirety, often for pages at a time, does not help matters. *My Experiences in the World War* sometimes resembles the work of a freshman composition student who uses unnecessary block quotations to reach a required word count. Poor sales, partly a result of the Great Depression, further confirmed the inferiority of Pershing's two-volume work to Grant's: one year after the memoir's appearance, only half of the first edition of fifty thousand sets had sold; Pershing's unfortunate publisher, the Frederick A. Stokes Company, knocked the remainder down to two dollars apiece, one-fifth of the original price.[11]

In short, despite winning the Pulitzer Prize for History in 1932 (a decision that surely had more to do with the General of the Armies' wartime accomplishments than the quality of his book), *My Experiences in the World War* never enjoyed even a fraction of the acclaim showered upon *The Personal Memoirs of U.S. Grant.* Skeptical of his writing ability from the start, Pershing probably blamed himself for this failure. In fairness, however, *most* memoirs offered by the Great War's major military and political leaders left little lasting impression. High-level figures such as Ferdinand Foch, Erich Von Falkenhayn, Newton Baker, Peyton March, James Harbord, and Robert Lee Bullard (to name just a few) all wrote books that vanished from cultural memory almost as soon as they were printed. Not one is considered a "classic" in the canon of military writing, perhaps because the Great War left so many readers, European and American alike, suspicious of the motives and competence of supposedly great and powerful men. The war books that truly mattered to the reading public during the interwar period involved more modest perspectives—those of subalterns, volunteer nurses, ambulance drivers, and enlisted men. Tellingly, the highest-earning literary depiction of the Great War (translated into thirty-two languages with eight million copies sold by the mid-1970s) was Erich Maria Remarque's *All Quiet on the Western Front* (1929), a story of ordinary German soldiers so divorced from the world of political or military leadership that officers are scarcely mentioned.[12]

Nevertheless, reading Pershing's account, whatever its shortcomings (or irrelevance where cultural memory is concerned), alongside Grant's masterpiece (an influential *agent* of cultural memory) is an illuminating exercise, especially if we consider the rhetorical dimensions of each work. My analysis below considers what these memoirs say, what they leave unsaid, and why.

Autobiography, Rhetoric, and History

As historian Joan Waugh notes, *The Personal Memoirs of U.S. Grant* does a number of things at once. The work offers a detailed, precise, and generally dispassionate history of several major campaigns; chronicles the general's relationship with key historical figures like Abraham Lincoln, Edwin Stanton, and William Tecumseh Sherman; corrects misperceptions (or, rather, what Grant regarded as misperceptions) of various military events (such as the Army of the Tennessee's supposed near-defeat at Shiloh); pays tribute to the soldiers Grant commanded in the West and later in Virginia; and lays out an "exegesis of the Union Cause" intended explicitly to debunk the Lost Cause.[13] On the latter subject, Grant is emphatic: the protection of slavery, not the issue of states' rights, formed the ideological cornerstone of the Confederacy. Ironically, however, one thing that Grant's *Personal Memoirs* doesn't do is live up to the adjective featured in its title. The general's account is, by and large, anything but "personal." Ron Chernow notes the absence of any reference to Grant's struggle with alcohol, a hardly surprising omission.[14] But Grant's penchant for nondisclosure goes much further than that. For example, barely two sentences cover his courtship of Julia, his family life receives almost no mention at all, and when his eldest son joins him for the Overland Campaign in 1864, we learn next to nothing about how this thirteen-year-old reacted to the bloodiest military operation ever conducted on American soil.

Grant records his own responses to wartime death and injury in a handful of scenes where he alludes briefly to the unpleasant sights and sounds of field hospitals, but does not describe them. Battlefield gore appears just once, in a matter-of-fact passage from Grant's account of his service in the Mexican-American War: "One cannon ball passed through our ranks, not far from me. It took off the head of an enlisted man, and the under jaw of Captain Paige of my regiment, while the splinters from the musket of the killed soldier, and his brains and bones, knocked down two or three others."[15] And so it goes. Never again in the two volumes does the perspective zoom in so tightly on the carnage of battle. Understandably, given the scale of the operations that Grant oversaw in the Civil War from the Vicksburg campaign onward, soldiers below the rank of general appear almost exclusively in the collective—as "Armies," "Corps," and "Divisions" whose complicated movements take up the bulk of the narrative (at the expense of more personal matters) and can be traced in the volumes' forty-three microscopically detailed maps. Indeed, after noting the suppression of "inner life" in the memoirs of Civil War commanders in general, literary critic Cody Marrs remarks, "It does Grant's *Personal Memoirs* only a slight disservice to say that it is less an autobiography than an annotated series of topographic charts."[16]

Grant's audience in 1885 would not necessarily have expected intimate details about his personal affairs or deepest emotions. As Joan Waugh notes, nineteenth-century readers of memoirs by celebrated figures tended to value the didactic over the confessional.[17] Nevertheless, the degree of Grant's self-effacement in a work of supposed autobiography is remarkable, and it serves, I would argue, a paradoxical rhetorical function: in this instance, deflection away from the self actually contributes to the version of the self that the text seeks to promote. In other words, Grant's reticence reinforces his humble image as the determined servant of a cause that *chose him*, as opposed to a larger-than-life hero who assertively came to the rescue of the Union. Literary critic Edmund Wilson makes a similar point in his classic *Patriotic Gore: Studies in the Literature of the American Civil War* (1962): Grant's "ideal"— put another way, his constructed persona—in the *Personal Memoirs* is that of "the powerful leader, with no glamor and no pretensions, who is equally accessible to everyone and who almost disclaims his official rank."[18] The text's frequent avoidance of the personal reinforces this persona—as if Grant's supposed ordinariness makes autobiographical details unnecessary—and so, attractively, does the absence of score-settling (something that most military memoirists find irresistible) in his characterization of fellow commanders. Even Henry Halleck, with whom Grant had an exceedingly difficult relationship, to put it mildly, receives a measured treatment.

Pershing's persona in *My Experiences in the World War* is in many respects similar. Indeed, the General of the Armies may have learned a great deal about literary self-fashioning from his Civil War precursor—starting with the avoidance of anything that would smack of vanity or ambition. Just as Grant maintains that he never wanted to go to West Point (attending the academy was supposedly his father's idea) and that he never entered a battle eagerly, Pershing makes the rather improbable claim that he expected to command a division in France, not the entire American Expeditionary Force (AEF).[19] Like Grant, he is modest throughout his narrative, silent on matters he deems private (basically *everything*, that is, not directly related to his command), dispassionate in his treatment of various antagonists (no small achievement given his combative relationship with the French and British high commands), and absolutely indifferent to the sort of theatrics (think Patton or Montgomery) that inspire a military cult of personality. Though Pershing certainly looked the part of a commander in chief with his ramrod-straight posture, broad shoulders, and granite features, he generally disliked public speaking (almost as much as Grant did) and there was nothing particularly flashy about his leadership style.

The same can be said of his narrative, which Smyth describes as "restrained, temperate, and fair," adjectives that also fit *Grant's Personal Memoirs*.[20] When AEF veterans opened Pershing's book, many hoped to discover the specific reasons why the General of the Armies had sacked various subordinates, including and especially General Clarence Edwards, the controversial commander of the Twenty-Sixth Division. Characteristically, Pershing never mentions any of the officers he relieved; like Grant's, his narrative passes on almost every opportunity to humiliate or to engage in payback.

However. Pershing's tone is not as placid as Grant's, and a note of annoyance or frustration periodically creeps into his narrative. Personality partly explains this. More likely to inspire respect than affection, the Iron Commander enjoyed a well-earned reputation as a cold taskmaster, impatient and forbidding in manner. Pershing concealed his warm and boyish side, which did exist, from nearly everyone but Micheline Resco. But rhetoric plays a role here as well. Pershing's book is sterner than Grant's because it takes the form of a cautionary tale. In his foreword, Pershing declared that he wrote his memoirs in order to provide "lessons useful to the American people," lessons that all stem from the general's conviction that the federal government had failed the nation by not maintaining a larger, truly war-ready peacetime army.[21] His foreword places this pedagogical agenda at the very heart of the narrative:

The World War found us absorbed in the pursuits of peace and quite unconscious of probable threat to our security. We would listen to no warnings of danger. We had made small preparation for defense and none for aggression. So when war actually came upon us we had to change the very habits of our lives and minds to meet its realities. The slow processes by which we achieved these changes and applied our latent power to the problems of combat in Europe, despite our will, our numbers, and our wealth, I endeavor to describe. Therein lie the lessons of which I write.[22]

In other words, *My Experiences in the World War* is a story of American triumph achieved despite massive self-imposed handicaps.[23] Pershing's rhetorical approach to his memoirs, combined with his temperament, guaranteed that the latter would receive extensive, even obsessive treatment.

As David Silbey observes, the commander of the AEF had to build his army, as well as lead it, an even more monumental task than the one faced by Grant in 1864. In his memoirs, Pershing does not exactly complain about the challenges he faced in this regard, but he never lets the reader forget that his army *should* have been built already—hence the aggrieved posture that he assumes whenever describing the inadequate tonnage delivered by American shipping, the nonexistence of American tanks (promised in the hundreds), the aircraft-production debacle, and the lethally hurried training that his doughboys received stateside. Thanks to the general's repetitive diary format, these specific failures, and many others, surfaced with such frequency that Army Chief of Staff Peyton March, a man of volatile temper (and no fan of Pershing), wrote his own book in response.[24] In March's view, Pershing failed to understand that the stateside mobilization effort had faced its own challenges, all resulting from the same lack of preparedness that the General of the Armies identified as the chief source of his woes.

Yet Pershing's "lessons" take on their keenest edge when he describes his interactions with Foch and other Allied commanders: again and again, his narrative shows that the absence of a large-scale peacetime army not only delayed the American troop build-up overseas, it also lessened the nation's standing among the other Allied powers and made Pershing's job a political nightmare. Supported by Secretary of War Newton Baker and President Woodrow Wilson, Pershing insisted from the start that American forces would fight on the Western Front as an independent army—not as units of replacements fed into French or British organizations—but he was on shaky ground. To get its soldiers across the Atlantic, the United States had to rely heavily upon British transports, an arrangement that hardly put Pershing in a strong bargaining position. And then there was the looming threat, created by Russia's withdrawal from the war, of major German offensives on the Western Front. As Allied leaders continually reminded the AEF commander during various high-pressure meetings during the winter and spring of 1918, Pershing's plans put the manpower-starved armies of France and Britain at risk. Creating an all-American organization ate up precious time—while Germany prepared to deliver its final hammer blow.

As a result of these historical circumstances (as well as the text's didactic agenda), Pershing's desperate fight to keep American soldiers together and under his command is *the* central drama in his memoirs, and it overshadows everything else, giving his narrative a flavor quite distinct from Grant's.

Even more than the technological advances (if that's the right word) that separate Pershing's era of weaponry from Grant's—machineguns, tanks, poison gas, etc.—the political stresses and strains of coalition warfare define his narrative.

Nothing could be further from the main storyline of the *Personal Memoirs of U. S. Grant*. Although Grant's account contains descriptions of static trench warfare, especially at Petersburg, that presage the deadlock on the Western Front (though far from precisely, as Brian Allen Drake's chapter in this volume notes), his focus falls primarily on the dramatic movement of armies across a vast American landscape—hence those forty-three maps. Moreover, almost all of the action in his account occurs outdoors, typically amid sparsely populated countryside, and often involves encounters with geographical obstacles, especially rivers and streams. Words like "forge," "cross," "bank," and "bridge" recur on almost every other page, and while Grant characteristically provides few details regarding his day-to-day camp life, his narrative vividly captures the peripatetic nature of Civil War generalship, as conducted under an open sky and often on horseback (Grant suffered at least two injuries while riding from battle to battle). Grant's is a war story lived in close proximity to the natural world and intimately shaped by mountains, hills, valleys, and bodies of water.

In contrast, Pershing's narrative, as much a record of tortured diplomacy as anything else, takes place primarily within interior spaces. Although war is typically an outdoor activity, as Drake reminds us, Pershing's book stays mostly—frustratingly—indoors. Gone is the campaigning on horseback. Here, it is words like "luncheon," "meeting," "headquarters," and "war council"—words that Pershing must have come to dread at the time—that appear with the greatest frequency. In other words, the Iron Commander was very much a chateau general, but not a particularly happy one, as his painful accounts of indoor meetings with Allied leaders, replete with pages of presumably transcribed dialog (much of it heated and frustration-filled), make clear. Indeed, Pershing's scuffles with French and British commanders (especially Foch, appointed Generalissimo of the Allied forces in the spring of 1918) over the creation of an independent American army occurred with so much regularity that he might have titled his memoir *My Experiences in the War against Amalgamation*. The narrative presents a pattern of recurring rising and falling action as Pershing fends off an effort to remove American troops from his command, then receives a conciliatory expression of understanding from his opponent, and then fights the same battle all over again (sometimes with the same individual), all the while knowing that Allied leaders are routinely attempting to go over his head to appeal directly to Baker or Wilson.

Ironically, the moments of highest drama come not when Pershing describes actual military operations—his diary-driven account of the Meuse-Argonne Offensive, for example, is almost impossible to follow—but when he details verbal clashes with Foch. Consider this climactic passage, for example, where Pershing, in effect, declares that he would rather see Paris fall than give up his plans for an all-American army. The setting is the meeting of the Supreme War Council at Versailles in early May 1918.

Here Foch said: "You are willing to risk our being driven back to the Loire?"

I said: "Yes, I am willing to take the risk. Moreover, there may come a time when the American Army will have to stand the brunt of this war, and it is not wise to fritter away our resources in this manner. The morale of the British, French, and Italian armies is low, while, as you know, that of the American Army is very high. It would be a grave mistake to give up the idea of building an American army in all its details as rapidly as possible."

Then Foch again said that the war might be over before we were ready.

I said that the war could not, in my opinion, be saved by feeding untrained American recruits into Allied armies, but that we must build up an American army, and concessions for the time being to meet the present emergency [the German Spring Offensives] were all I would approve.[25]

While this kind of extended dialogue runs throughout *My Experiences in the World War*, it is almost entirely absent in Grant's account. Different circumstances and different rhetorical objectives explain why. Pershing's construction of his memoirs as a cautionary tale demanded that he emphasize in often excruciating detail and through dialogue the diplomatic consequences—both for him and for the AEF as a whole—of America's failure to prepare for entry into a European war. At the same time, his largely chateau-bound narrative, a cyclical record of tense exchanges and verbal siege-warfare, shows how unprecedented historical circumstances (America's first taste of modern war by coalition) both complicated and defined his leadership.

Grant was, of course, mercifully spared having to deal with allied powers, and different goals drive his narrative. His general avoidance of dialogue fits with the bluff, unassuming persona he constructs, as if the position of supreme command simply *came his way* without any exercise of verbal agency on his part. Tellingly, the few instances of dialogue or paraphrased speech that he does present occur at moments of rapport, not conflict, as when he warmly recalls Sherman's praise of his leadership on the eve of the Vicksburg siege and his first private interview with Lincoln after receiving the rank of Lieutenant General.[26] Grant's rendition of the latter conversation contains a particularly priceless example of his rhetoric of humility and deflection. When obliquely referring to previous generals who had failed him (such as the hypercautious and dithering McClellan), Lincoln stresses that "all he wanted or had ever wanted was [a commander] who would take the responsibility and act."[27] The narrator's deadpan response is pure Grant: I "assur[ed] him that I would do the best I could with the means at hand, and avoid as far as possible annoying him or the War Department."[28]

So even in tone and so free from complaining, Grant's memoirs make it easy to forget that he too was in a politically fraught situation throughout his command, one even more perilous than Pershing's. After all, a McClellan victory in the 1864 presidential election would have instantly ended Grant's career. Lincoln's fighting general also had his share of run-ins with Secretary of War Stanton, who tried to wedge his own plans between those of the president and the field commander. And then there were the inevitable attempts, on the part of officers whom Grant had relieved or otherwise somehow alienated, to undermine Lincoln's confidence in him.

As my discussion has hopefully made clear by this point, a comparison of Grant's memoirs with Pershing's brings a number of historical points into focus. We see, for example, that generalship at the level of supreme command meant something profoundly different for Pershing as opposed to Grant. When the latter assumed control of all federal forces in 1864, he inherited a fully functioning army—an army that, as David Silbey observes, his critics would soon accuse him of squandering through mass "butchery." In contrast, Pershing became free of the constant worry associated with logistical matters—when would he *ever* get enough men or materiel?—and the nagging threat of amalgamation only very late in the war. As massive as Grant's responsibilities were, Pershing's surpassed them, even after he achieved his goal of an independent American army. It is no coincidence that the doughboys' climactic performance at the Meuse-Argonne, where they fought under one flag in the largest and deadliest battle in American history, significantly improved after the Iron Commander handed leadership of the First Army over to Hunter Liggett.[29] Up to that point in the battle, Pershing had tried to manage operational details while also running the entire AEF. That kind of combined responsibility was still possible in Grant's day, if just barely; by 1918, the scale and complexity of modern warfare had made it dangerously unmanageable. If nothing else, *My Experiences in the World War* forces the reader to feel the weight of Pershing's multifaceted administrative duties, an element of command rarely mentioned in Grant's memoirs, where the focus falls squarely on the positioning of forces and engagement with the enemy.

Setting these two accounts of generalship side-by-side also reveals an important commonality: Grant and Pershing both faced enormous political pressures (though from different directions and amid very different circumstances) and could not have led their forces to victory without unwavering presidential support. Despite their best efforts, the Allied leaders who attempted unsuccessfully to bully Pershing into handing over American manpower never found a way to outflank him. Although there were moments of vacillation when the pressure to amalgamate nearly became too much, Wilson ultimately backed his commander. As did Lincoln, even when the death toll and sluggishness of the 1864 Overland Campaign threatened to turn Grant into a political liability. For an example of the reverse, of what could happen when a civilian head of state and a supreme military commander were not on the same page, one need look no further than the acrimonious relationship between David Lloyd-George and Douglas Haig, as outlined earlier in this volume.

However, perhaps the most interesting conclusion to arise so far from this comparative treatment has to do with rhetoric and the extent to which it determines the content of military memoirs (just as it does in the case of any written document). Grant's invariably placid tone, omission of almost anything truly worthy of the label "personal," ubiquitous modesty, general avoidance of dialogue, and bird's-eye view of troop movements and battles (supported by those forty-three maps) all make for a memoir in which the "I" of the first-person narrator is metaphorically lower-case—and thereby all the more attractive and admirable. Pershing's book adopts a similar strategy. Here too the recounting of historic events, as laboriously supported in this instance by numerous official documents, matters more than individual experience, even though Pershing's speech, displayed in his skirmishes with Foch and others, is far more prominent than Grant's and his day-to-day activities easier to imagine, thanks to the memoir's basis in diary entries.

It is telling in this regard that *My Experiences in the World War* won the 1932 Pulitzer Prize in history, not biography, a genre that in the language of the Pulitzer Board explicitly includes "autobiography and memoir."[30] Over the past several decades, a number of nominated biographies have slipped into the history category, but Pershing's memoir remains the only work of autobiographical writing to receive the history prize in the Pulitzer's 104-year history. The General of the Armies' status as a national hero helps explain this; however, the way that his narrative *reads* perhaps also played a role. As we have seen, Pershing not only subordinates the autobiographical to the historical, those personal details that he *does* include generally serve a cautionary message of national importance. His restraint when it comes to personal disclosures is in some ways even more remarkable than Grant's: no one reading *My Experiences in the World War* would guess, for example, that Pershing had lost his wife and three daughters in a fire at the Presidio in 1915, or that he came close to having a breakdown at the height of Meuse-Argonne Offense, or that on the heels of a passionate romance with Ann Wilson Patton (George Patton's sister), he fell in love with the French-Romanian painter Micheline Resco, his partner from 1917 until his death. Always the center of female attention, the ruggedly handsome Pershing included just one insider detail that hinted at the current state of his robust love life: the portrait of the general in uniform that serves as the frontispiece for volume two was drawn by none other than Resco.

Memoirs and Memorials

My copy of Pershing's memoirs (not exactly a regular on the nightstand) contains a page that was obviously added after the two-volume set was bound. Facing the copyright information in the first volume, a sheet decorated with an American eagle and the shield of Columbia bears the name of one Jesse C. Tarr (obviously a veteran of the AEF) printed above a message of tribute offered by none other than the Iron Commander: "As an individual, your part in the world war has been an important one in the sum total of our achievements. Whether keeping lonely vigil in the trenches, or gallantly storming the enemy's stronghold; whether enduring monotonous drudgery at the rear or sustaining the fighting line at the front, each has bravely and efficiently played his part."[31] A facsimile of Pershing's signature follows.

The disastrous sales performance of *My Experiences in the World War* presumably explains this quasi-personalized address, which appears (ironically enough) just before the book's actual dedication to the Unknown Soldier. With stacks of unsold books on its hands—recall that the first printing of Pershing's memoirs was much too optimistically set at fifty-thousand copies—the Frederick A. Stokes Company probably turned to the gimmick of faux presentation copies in desperation. Pershing's dedication to the Unknown Soldier was all well and good, but a *known* soldier might just purchase the memoir if it bore his name. It is not difficult to imagine the advertising pitch: Don't miss this chance to own a *personalized* copy of the great general's epic story, a stirring reminder of service and patriotism you will treasure for a lifetime. In the case of Jesse C. Tarr, the sales strategy apparently worked.

But something more significant is going on here as well. By packaging the supreme commander's account as a souvenir, each set specifically named for an individual veteran (not unlike an award certificate, diploma, or sports trophy), Pershing's publisher transformed the text into a portable *lieu de mémoire*, a location, in other words, where the individual feels the pull of an enshrined version of past events. Although completely bogus on one level (there is no real connection between the veteran's printed name and Pershing's phony signature or his generic praise of the common soldier), this individualized dedication page established the two volumes as more than mere books. Now they became keepsakes—handheld memorials, in effect—that linked the reader's individual wartime experience to the general's rendition of collective action. Mr. Tarr's copy of *My Experiences in the World War* (now mine) encourages us to think of the text as a commemorative object with connections to Pershing's other remembrance endeavors.

The theme of memorialization was, of course, very much on Pershing's mind as he composed his memoirs, and it would be surprising, given his immersion in matters of public memory, if he did not regard his text as both a work of history (offered by a highly placed insider) and a monument for posterity. Few commanders in history have played such a central role in memorializing their army's achievements, as well as establishing the official meaning of its dead. In 1923 Pershing became chairman of the newly

created American Battle Monuments Commission (ABMC), the organization charged by Congress to design and maintain permanent American war
cemeteries and memorials overseas. To some, the general's role in the commission seemed largely titular. However, as historian Thomas H. Conner
asserts in his recent history of the ABMC, the Iron Commander's devotion
to the organization and to its solemn mission of remembrance went much
deeper than many in Washington, DC, were aware. Much deeper indeed. No
mere figurehead, Pershing "chaired thirty-four of the forty-one commission
meetings prior to the outbreak of World War II. For the last quarter of [his]
life, in fact, the bulk of his official energies and efforts went into the work of
the new agency."[32]

As it turns out, Pershing, more than anyone, shaped the ABMC's distinctive approach to battlefield commemoration. For example, he rejected the
cluttered style of remembrance that had become the norm at Civil War sites
such as Gettysburg and Antietam, where legions of state- and unit-specific
monuments vied for attention, and embraced a more streamlined aesthetic
that emphasized national unity and federal power. Just one memorial, no
more than that, would stand at each American battlefield on the Western
Front.[33] In addition, Pershing stressed the sanctity of wartime sacrifice, as
seen in his directive that a memorial chapel be erected next to each of the
ABMC's eight European cemeteries. The commission's anything-but-secular
grave markers—white marble crucifixes and Stars of David—also reflected
the Iron Commander's preference for remembrance infused with religiosity.

But while Pershing left his mark on the ABMC's commemorative practices,
the memorials and cemeteries he helped to create ultimately failed to make
much of an impression on the American public. And in this way, they paralleled *My Experiences in the World War*, a monument in prose that attracted
few literary pilgrims and never significantly influenced collective memory.
Despite a brief uptick in media attention during the early 1930s, inspired by
the federal program that sent Gold Star Mothers on expense-paid junkets to
the former Western Front, the ABMC's various shrines to the fallen (most of
them completed more than a decade after the Armistice) never took hold in
the public's imagination as sites of living memory. There are many explanations for this. For one thing, once the Depression hit, few Americans could
afford an expedition to European battlefields. In addition, many veterans
found the ABMC's commemorative agenda off-putting. There was a reason
why sites of Civil War memory became so encrusted with competing statues

and markers: former soldiers generally preferred forms of remembrance that focused on *their* specific unit and its achievements in combat. The scheme adopted by Pershing's commission left little room for such expression. The enormous ABMC monuments constructed at Château-Thierry, Montsec, and Montfaucon (commemorating, respectively, the fighting in the Aisne-Marne, St. Mihiel, and Meuse-Argonne regions) acknowledged the divisions that participated in each campaign but, by necessity, ignored the smaller, more-cohesive organizations—the regiments, battalions, and companies—that meant the most to veterans. And, finally, widely held doubts about the value and necessity of American intervention in the Great War, a supposed crusade that clearly had not made the world any safer for democracy, contributed to a lack of interest in battlefield commemoration.

However, perhaps the most ironic and telling of the various setbacks associated with Pershing and public memory came after his death in 1948, when a plan to memorialize the General of the Armies in Washington, DC, quickly emerged. Undertaken by the ABMC as its very first domestic project, the effort dragged on until 1981, when Pershing Park on Pennsylvania Avenue finally opened. Two years later, a nine-foot-tall bronze statue of the once-celebrated commander (depicted standing, not on horseback) was installed at the site and greeted, as historian Andrew S. Walgren notes, "without fanfare."[34] Lack of funding (for the first time, the ABMC had to solicit resources from the private sector), competing commercial interests, and red-tape created by various urban renewal schemes in the nation's capital all contributed to the more than three-decade delay, and once the memorial became a reality, it quickly fell into disrepair and neglect.[35] Today, Pershing Park is the chosen site for the capital's new National World War I Memorial. But what we might call the memory malaise associated with Pershing and the park that bears his name still stubbornly refuses to dissipate. The United States World War One Centennial Commission, which received no tax dollars, had hoped to finish the new memorial in time for the one-hundredth anniversary of the Armistice on November 11, 2018. But funding shortfalls, combined with the COVID-19 pandemic and other vicissitudes, have now pushed the anticipated completion into 2024. This ironic situation becomes more ironic still when one considers that a National World War I Memorial already exists—namely, the Liberty Memorial, a vast commemorative complex in Kansas City, Missouri, that received its federal designation as the National Memorial in 2014.

The parallels between the reception of Pershing's memoirs and the almost instant irrelevance of the various public memorials associated with him suggest that *My Experiences in the World War* flopped for reasons that went well beyond Pershing's sometimes chilly personality or his performance as a writer ("horrible" in the succinct judgment of historian Kimberly Lamay Licursi).[36] Like the commemorative scheme that he oversaw in Europe, Pershing's narrative of command did little to clear up the historical ambiguities that caused so many Americans in the 1930s to question whether their nation should ever have entered the so-called War to End All Wars; instead, his overpriced memoirs ($177 per set in today's currency![37]) buried its reader in historical details while advancing an ill-timed argument for military preparedness unlikely to appeal to anyone but a handful of like-minded regular officers.[38] In retrospect, it is hard to imagine why anyone thought the Iron Commander's even-handed but at times unintelligible (and, worse, *dull*) account would go big.

In contrast, Grant's wildly successful memoirs drew much of their power from their perceived sanctity, precisely the effect that Pershing had hoped the ABMC's cemeteries and memorials would achieve. To read or even simply to own the general's (and two-term president's) farewell text was to connect with a hallowed story of suffering and perseverance in the face of death. Indeed, Grant's book functioned as a funerary object, akin to the black crepe and framed locks of hair that signified Victorian mourning. Though the price of each two-volume set was actually higher (once we account for inflation) than the amount originally asked by Pershing's publisher, *The Personal Memoirs of U. S. Grant* became a fixture in more than three hundred thousand (mostly northern) American households during the Gilded Age[39]; reverently showcased on a mantle or bookshelf, the volumes signaled their owner's solidarity with Grant's Unionist version of history, linked the domestic space in which they were displayed to the sphere of public action and public memory-formation, and served as a mournful reminder of a lost American hero, almost like a pair of headstones brought indoors. And while Grant's reputation waxed and waned over the coming decades, reaching its nadir in the 1920s and 1930s, the status of his personal account as an important work of American literature remained largely intact. Never out of print, the general's narrative would, in the words of Joan Waugh, prove "his most powerful memorial, self-made."[40]

His actual resting place, the largest mausoleum in America, fared less well—though decidedly better than ill-fated Pershing Park. More than a decade of fundraising was required before Grant's Tomb, built to house his remains alongside Julia's, was completed on the north end of Manhattan's Riverside Park. Attended by thousands, the elaborate dedication ceremony in 1897 evoked memories of Grant's state funeral in 1885, an unprecedented spectacle (far grander than Lincoln's memorial service) suffused with Reconciliation rhetoric and imagery, and for a time, Grant's Tomb drew more visitors than any other attraction in New York City.[41] But after the Great War, as Lost Cause ideology became increasingly influential *north* of the Mason-Dixon line, the site lost much of its traction in public memory—and became visually diminished to boot. Completed in 1930 and built with near cathedral-like dimensions, the nearby Riverside Church towers over the tomb, which, as a result, no longer serves as the focal point for the area. Deterioration set in as well, and by the 1970s, graffiti covered a commemorative edifice now frequented by drug dealers and vagrants.

Triggered in part by Ken Burns's enormously successful PBS documentary *The Civil War* (1990), a restoration effort at the end of the twentieth century brought Grant's Tomb back from the brink, and today this once-imperiled shrine is a well-maintained, if marginal, place of public remembrance.[42] Overseen by the National Park Service and now known as the General Grant National Memorial ("General," rather than "President," is perhaps telling), the Tomb at last features an interpretive visitors center that addresses Grant's complicated reputation and legacy. However, few tourists venture to Highland Park to see the memorial. For the moment at least, the site remains overshadowed by the various presidential libraries that memorialize later national leaders such as Harry S. Truman, Dwight D. Eisenhower, Jimmy Carter, and Bill Clinton.

As Waugh remarks, Grant, unlike Lincoln, never evolved into a "mythological figure" in the national imagination, arguably the primary reason for his monument's neglect.[43] His presidency, in particular, remains a clouded and unsettled topic. Grant's defense of civil rights for emancipated African Americans during Reconstruction has won him admirers, but the memory of rampant corruption and cronyism in his administration persists. Thus, perhaps part of the reason why Grant's memoirs have fared so well since the Gilded Age (in contrast with Grant's Tomb) is because they focus exclusively on the story of his generalship. As a military leader, Grant has, of course, had his share of detractors, especially between the world wars, when his attrition campaign against Lee in 1864 was widely interpreted as a harbinger of sense-less slaughters like the Somme or Passchendaele. Nevertheless, the narrative that he offers in his memoirs has a coherence and a satisfying plotline that would have been difficult to achieve in an account of messy presidential politics. And, again, the story of how Grant raced against death to complete his two-volume work remains an integral part of the memoirs' appeal, as well as a vital component in Grant's public image. This part of Grant's life truly is *mythic*. Not surprisingly, Ron Chernow's massive biography of Grant, which became a *New York Times* bestseller in 2017 (a sign of Grant's continued relevance despite his commemorative ups and downs), uses the general's heroic struggle to compose his memoirs as a framing device.

But what of Pershing's gravesite? Where does it fit in this consideration of memoirs and memorials? A pilgrim in search of the Iron Commander's final resting place will find it at Arlington National Cemetery amid a section reserved for Americans who served in the Great War. A standard white head-stone, identical to every other soldier's, marks the location of his remains, and except for the wide clearing that surrounds the grave (an enviable distinction at such a closely packed burial ground), nothing elevates the general above his men. Years before his final illness, Pershing personally selected this specific location and supposedly remarked, "Here let me rest among the World War veterans. When the last bugle call is sounded, I want to stand up with my soldiers."[44] Ironically, of all the places associated with Pershing's memory—or his memory-work as the head of the ABMC—his modest gravesite is the most powerful. His simple stone marker stands in contrast to the gigantism of the commission's imposing Great War monuments in Europe, which never caught on with the American public, and the turgid didacticism of his memoirs, a literary and commercial failure. Thus, it is at Arlington, perhaps, and not after all in the pages of his book, that Pershing comes closest to the approachable, down-to-earth commander described in *The Personal Memoirs of U.S. Grant.*

As I have attempted to demonstrate through this discussion of narratives by Grant and Pershing, comparing the written texts of the American Civil War with those of the Great War offers insights both literary and historical, especially in connection with the history of public war commemoration. After all, people understand war—any war—through story, and it is the desire for coherent narrative, more than anything, that animates cultural war remembrance. Thus, as other scholars contemplate the two central conflicts of America's "long nineteenth century," an exciting new paradigm, and build on the work offered in this volume, they may find it useful to bring history into direct conversation with literary study and to consider works of war writing—the great *and* the not-so-great—as influential agents of collective memory or signposts of collective forgetting.

Notes

1. See John Keegan, *The Face of Battle: A Study of Agincourt, Waterloo, and the Somme* (New York: Viking, 1976) and *The Price of Admiralty: The Evolution of Naval Warfare* (New York: Viking, 1988).

2. See Edward Linenthal, *Sacred Ground: Americans and Their Battlefields* (Urbana: University of Illinois Press, 1991) and Kurt Piehler, *Remembering War the American Way* (Washington, DC: Smithsonian Institution Press, 1995).

3. Paul Fussell, *The Great War and Modern Memory* (New York: Oxford University Press, 1975), 36.

4. Gene Smith, *Until the Last Trumpet Sounds: The Life of General of the Armies John J. Pershing* (New York: John Wiley, 1998), 250.

5. Smith, *Until the Last Trumpet Sounds*, 250.

6. Ron Chernow, *Grant* (New York: Penguin, 2017), 952.

7. Quoted in Chernow, *Grant*, 948.

8. Chernow, *Grant*, 953.

9. Chernow, *Grant*, 939.

10. Donald Smythe, *Pershing: General of the Armies* (Bloomington: Indiana University Press, 1986), 291.

11. Smythe, *Pershing*, 291.

12. Brian A. Rowley, "Journalism into Fiction: *Im Westen nichts Neues*," in *The First World War in Fiction*, ed. Holger Klein (London: Macmillan, 1978), 101.

13. Joan Waugh, *U.S. Grant: American Hero, American Myth* (Chapel Hill: University of North Carolina Press, 2009), 201.

14. Chernow, *Grant*, 953.

15. Ulysses S. Grant, *Personal Memoirs of U.S. Grant* (New York: Charles L. Webster, 1885), 96.

16. Cody Marrs, *Not Even Past: The Stories We Keep Telling about the Civil War* (Baltimore: Johns Hopkins University Press, 2020), 68, 70.

17. Waugh, *U.S. Grant*, 205.

18. Edmund Wilson, *Patriotic Gore: Studies in the Literature of the American Civil War* (London: Hogarth Press, 1987), 148. One does not need to be a literary theorist to see that the "Grant" who speaks in *The Personal Memoirs* is a construction of

language that exists apart from its flesh-and-blood creator, hence my use of the term "persona."

19. Donald Smythe notes that this was "simply not true." Smythe, *Pershing*, 4.

20. Smythe, *Pershing*, 289.

21. John J. Pershing, *My Experiences in the World War* (New York: Frederick A. Stokes, 1931), xv.

22. Pershing, *My Experiences*, xv.

23. Pershing's charge that the United States was ill-prepared for a war that it should have regarded as inevitable is difficult to refute. In terms of numbers, the US Army in April 1917 ranked seventeenth in the world, "alongside Chile, Denmark, and the Netherlands." Mark Whalan, *World War One, American Literature, and the Federal State* (Cambridge, UK: Cambridge University Press, 2018), 4. However, as Brian Dirck observes in his chapter for this volume, Woodrow Wilson was far from oblivious to the likelihood of war, and he worked "quietly behind the scenes" in 1915 and 1916 to expand and improve the American military.

24. Smythe, *Pershing*, 294. See Payton C. March, *The Nation at War* (Garden City, NY: Doubleday, Doran, 1932).

25. Pershing, *My Experiences in the World War*, 28–29.

26. Here, it is worth noting that Grant's bromance with Sherman is one of the very few personal relationships actually developed in his memoirs.

27. Grant, *Personal Memoirs*, 122.

28. Grant, *Personal*, 122.

29. For more on Hunter Liggett's contribution to victory in the Meuse-Argonne, see Mitchell Yockelson, *Forty-Seven Days: How Pershing's Warriors Came of Age to Defeat the German Army in World War I* (New York: Dutton, 2016).

30. "The Pulitzer Prizes," accessed March 4, 2021, https://www.pulitzer.org/prize-winners-by-category/222.

31. Pershing, *My Experiences in the World War*, n. p.

32. Thomas H. Conner, *War and Remembrance: The Story of the American Battle Monuments Commission* (Lexington: University Press of Kentucky, 2018), 49.

33. What to do with battlefield monuments that were already installed by various divisional or regimental societies proved a thorny issue for the ABMC. The commission convinced some organizations to remove their memorials; in other cases, the memorials remained, but without any obligation on the part of the ABMC to maintain them. For more, see Lisa Budreau, *Bodies of War: World War I and the Politics of Commemoration in America, 1919–1933* (New York: New York University Press, 2010).

34. Andrew S. Walgren, "The 'Forgotten Man' of Washington: The Pershing Memorial and the Battle over Military Memorialization" (MA thesis, University of South Carolina, 2016), 68. https://scholarcommons.sc.edu/etd/3543.

35. Walgren, "Forgotten Man," 72.

36. Kimberly J. Lamay Licursi, *Remembering World War I in America* (Lincoln: University of Nebraska Press, 2018), 73.

37. Licursi, *Remembering World War I*, 73. My inflation calculation comes from

"Inflation Calculator," https://www.in2013dollars.com/us/inflation, accessed on June 24, 2021.

38. With the economy in freefall, 1931 was hardly the best time to make an argument for an expanded peacetime military and increased defense spending. Ironically, Pershing's memoirs appeared one year before thousands of ragged American Great War veterans, members of the famous Bonus Army, poured into Washington, DC, to demand immediate payment of their bonuses (compensation for lost wartime wages). Federal troops under the command of Douglas MacArthur (aided by a reluctant Dwight D. Eisenhower) drove them from the capital.

39. Waugh, *U.S. Grant*, 209. A cloth-bound set of Grant's memoirs cost $9.00 in 1885; the deluxe leather-bound set retailed for $25.00. These prices are equivalent to $250.00 and $693.00 today. See "Inflation Calculator," https://www.in2013dollars.com/us/inflation, accessed July 11, 2021.

40. Waugh, *U.S. Grant*, 168.

41. Waugh, *U.S. Grant*, 262.

42. Waugh, *U.S. Grant*, 263.

43. Waugh, *U.S. Grant*, 264.

44. Quoted in Smythe, *Pershing*, 309.

Shauna Devine has a PhD in medical history and currently holds a joint appointment as an assistant professor at the Schulich School of Medicine and as an associate research professor in the Department of History at Western University. Her first book entitled, *Learning from the Wounded: The Civil War and the Rise of American Medical Science* (University of North Carolina Press, 2014), received a number of awards, including the Tom Watson Brown Book Award from the Society of Civil War Historians and the Watson-Brown Foundation and the Wiley-Silver Prize from the Center for Civil War Research at the University of Mississippi.

Brian Dirck is a professor of history at Anderson University. His first book, *Lincoln and Davis: Imagining America, 1809–1865* offered a comparative analysis of the two Civil War presidents. He has since published *Lincoln the Lawyer*, a study of Lincoln's legal career, as well as *Lincoln and the Constitution, Abraham Lincoln and White America, Lincoln in Indiana*, and *The Black Heavens: Abraham Lincoln and Death*. He has also written numerous articles, and spoken at Harvard University, the National Archives in Washington, DC, the Lincoln Forum and the Lincoln Colloquium in Springfield, Illinois, and Gettysburg's Civil War Institute.

Brian Allen Drake specializes in environmental history, a discipline that explores the ways in which nature has affected human history and vice versa. He is the author of *Loving Nature, Fearing the State: Environmentalism and Antigovernment Politics Before Reagan* (University of Washington Press, 2013) and the editor of *The Blue, the Gray, and the Green: Toward an Environmental History of the Civil War* (University of Georgia Press, 2015). Drake has published articles in *Great Plains Quarterly*, the *Georgia Historical Quarterly*, and *Environmental History* as well as chapters in several edited volumes. He earned his PhD at the University of Kansas.

Debra Sheffer is a professor of history at Park University in Parkville, Missouri. She holds a PhD in Military History from the University of Kansas. She was a 2007 fellow at the West Point Summer Seminar in Military History. Her published works include *The Buffalo Soldiers*, "Lincoln's Wartime Diplomacy and the Emancipation Proclamation" in *The Routledge Handbook of Military and Diplomatic History: The Colonial Period to 1877*, and "The Convergence" in *A Companion to Custer and the Little Big Horn Campaign*.

David J. Silbey is a military historian at Cornell University. He specializes in the industrialized total wars of the twentieth century and the asymmetric responses (guerrilla warfare, insurgency, and terrorism) that evolved to those wars. He has written books on the British Army in the Great War, the Philippine-American War, the Boxer Rebellion, and American military encounters with non-Western nations. He is the series editor for Cornell University Press's military history series and is a trustee for the Society for Military History. Silbey earned his PhD from Duke University and his BA from Cornell University.

Dale Smith is a professor emeritus of military medicine and history in the Department of Military and Emergency Medicine, Uniformed Services University of the Health Sciences, Bethesda, Maryland. His most recent book is *Glimpsing Modernity: Military Medicine in World War One* (2015), edited with Dr. Stephen Craig. He is also one of the senior editors of the textbook *Fundamentals of Military Medicine*, published by the Borden Institute in 2019. His professional interests include the history of medical education, the history of infectious diseases, the history of surgery, and the problems of patient evacuation in military operations.

Kathleen Logothetis Thompson earned her PhD in nineteenth-century/ Civil War America from West Virginia University. Her research is on mental trauma and coping among Union soldiers and she is currently working on her first book, tentatively titled *War on the Mind*. She currently teaches history at several colleges and universities and is serving as a Preserve West Virginia AmeriCorps member. Kathleen was a seasonal interpreter at Fredericksburg and Spotsylvania National Military Park for several years, led tours of Frank Lloyd Wright's Fallingwater, and is the co-editor of *Civil Discourse*, a blog on the long Civil War.

Steven Trout is a professor of English at the University of Alabama. He is the author of *The Vietnam Veterans Memorial at Angel Fire: War, Remembrance, and an American Tragedy* (University Press of Kansas, 2020), *On the Battlefield of Memory: The First World War and American Remembrance, 1919–1941* (University of Alabama Press, 2010), and *Memorial Fictions: Willa Cather and the First World War* (University of Nebraska Press, 2002). In addition, he has edited or co-edited many volumes, including *Portraits of Remembrance: Painting, Memory, and the First World War* (University of Alabama Press, 2020). Trout edits the series "War, Memory, and Culture" for the University of Alabama Press.

Kanisorn Wongsrichanalai is the director of research at the Massachusetts Historical Society. He was an associate professor of history at Angelo State University where he co-directed (with Prof. Christine Lamberson) the National Endowment for the Humanities-sponsored project "West Texans and the Experience of War: World War I to the Present." He is the author of *Northern Character: College-Educated New Englanders, Honor, Nationalism, and Leadership in the Civil War Era* (Fordham University Press, 2016) and co-editor (with Prof. Lorien Foote) of *So Conceived and So Dedicated: Northern Intellectuals in the Civil War Era* (Fordham University Press, 2015).

INDEX

Note: page numbers followed by n refer to notes, with note number.

greater awareness of, 179–180
and mental illness as large portion of
postwar debilities, 187–188
and military's goal of returning soldiers to
front, 182–184, 186
number of soldiers executed for dereliction
of duty, 184
and shell shock, identification and
treatment of, 154, 180–181, 186, 189, 231
similarities with Civil War, 172
theories on causes of, 180–182
treatment, differences among allies in,
183–184
treatment of, as similar in Civil War,
188–189, 246–247
US policies on prevention and treatment of,
185–186, 187
mental trauma in Vietnam War, 188
Merritt, Wesley, 25–26
Mexico
hostilities in Wilson administration, 57, 60
Punitive Expedition into, 82–83
Militia Act of 1792, 74, 75, 149
Mitchell, Silas Weir, 139, 146, 177, 178, 183,
191n19
Monash, John, 24
Morehouse, George, 146
Mormons
Civil War loyalty as issue, 102–103
post–Civil War suspicions about, 126–127n2
Mott, Frederick, 180
Myers, Charles S., 180–181
My Experiences in the World War (Pershing),
252–255
avoidance of personal disclosure, 259
and complexity of Pershing's command,
257–258
as data-heavy, difficult read, 249–250
faux-personalized dedications used to sell,
259–260
focus on negotiations with allies, 255–256
Grant's *Memoirs* as model for, 248, 249,
252–253
vs. Grant's *Personal Memoirs*, 255–259
and importance of presidential support,
258
as *lieu de mémoire*, 260
necessity of military readiness as central
theme of, 253–254, 256, 267n23, 268n38
Pershing's avoidance of personal attacks,
253

Pershing's persona in, 252–253, 258–259
Pershing's struggle to write, 248
poor sales of, 250, 263
and preservation of memory of war, 37
as Pulitzer Prize winner, 250, 259
on struggle to maintain unified US
command, 254–255

NAACP, 83–84, 90, 91, 121
Nash, Paul, 206
National Asylums [Homes] for Disabled
Volunteer Soldiers, 222–223, 228
Nicolay, John, 56, 64
nineteenth century, long, 2–3

Officers' Reserve Corps, 151
Orr, Hiram, 156, 159
Orth, John C., 118
Owen, Winfield, 204–205
Owsley, Frank, 129n25

Panic of 1873, and African American rights, 6
Peabody, Francis, 161
Pershing, John J.
and American Battle Monuments
Commission, 260–262
and building of American Expeditionary
Forces, 16
and casualties, gains as justification for,
23–24
and demands of working in coalition, 37
extraordinary responsibility of, 17
funeral of, 34
gravesite of, 265
and Great Man approach to history, 37–38
on Great War success as product of his
maneuver tactics, 26, 28
as icon of nation's war effort, 15, 36, 37–38
and idealized view of Civil War, 213
influence of Grant's maneuver tactics on, 4,
26, 28, 213
memorial to, in Washington, DC, 34, 262
memories of Civil War, 4
military education on lessons of Civil War,
25–26
personality of, 253
pivotal role in Great War, 16
as political threat to Wilson, 28–29, 30–31
remembrance of, centered on Great War
role, 14, 38n2
retirement of, 33–34